Barn door to balance sheet Derbyshire boy – what happened next

John G. Smith

Copyright, reproduction and sale conditions.

John G Smith has asserted his rights under the Copyright, Design and Patents Act 1988 to be identified as the author of this work.
All rights reserved. No part of this publication may be reproduced, stored in or introduced into a retrieval system, or transmitted in any form or by any means (electronic, mechanical, photocopying, recording or otherwise) without the prior written permission of the publisher.

Anyperson who does any unauthorized act in relation to this publicationmay be liable to criminal publication and civil claims for damages.

This book is sold subject to the condition that it shall not, by way of trade or otherwise, be lent, re-sold, hired out, or otherwise circulated without the publisher's prior consent in any form of binding or cover other than that in which it is published and without a similar condition including this condition being imposed on the subsequent purchaser.

Disclaimer

All persons and organisations mentioned in this book are real. If I have caused offence to any party, this was unintentional and not wilful. All events described in this work reflect my honest recollection and interpretation.

ISBN: 9798792511224

Copyright © 2021 John G. Smith
All rights reserved

This book is dedicated to Julia
Life saver, lover, best friend.

I want to thank

The same Julia for giving me time and space to think and write and for boring proof-reading.

My mum and dad for setting a value standard never surpassed.

David Robinson for his technical skill and advice and for persisting with me timelessly.

- and finally, all the characters referred to for giving me the story.

CONTENTS

Chapter 1 - Down on a Derbyshire Farm......................1

Chapter 2 - Secondary Modern...................................25

Chapter 3 - Steam trains and office gossip.................43

Chapter 4 - Colonel Redmond and campanology.......58

Chapter 5 - Work and study: work and study.............84

Chapter 6 - Finding the girl: finding the path...........101

Chapter 7 - Organisation and Methods....................117

Chapter 8 - Consultancy, here we come...................138

Chapter 9 - Singapore...181

Chapter 10 - PW : an Indian odyssey........................229

Chapter 11 - Bell-Fruit..284

Chapter 12 - Life shock...396

Chapter 13 - A new beginning..................................434

Chapter14 - Philosophy of a retiring mind................ 476

CHAPTER ONE
Down on a Derbyshire farm

1942 – 1953. Born to the land. Of fields, animals and farming jobs. A drowned baby. Working horses to a first Ferguson 35 tractor. The child characters, dreaded school cane. Church versus Chapel.

The violets were there. The timing was right although I can't remember the season exactly but it must have been early spring. Anyway they were spread out beneath the hedge almost hidden by a mass of broad thick leaves and in tight clumps on the ditch side. For some unknown reason it was the only place on the whole farm they could be found and so very tiny. You had to know exactly where to look.

Looking back now I suppose they should not have been picked. Left as one of nature's treasures from probably centuries past. A place left as rough pasture, not even worth fertilizing for early eating grass since this fringe of the pit-hills was unworkable. So were the pit-hills themselves, or so I was later to be told and would come to appreciate. Of-course not now. This was the most magical adventure land. That little bunch of violets were in a small hand and taken with much pride back to the bottom gate over the stile which was never crossed without an expectant look at the small indentation on the huge stone foot-slab that had once, and only once, held a cuckoo's egg, to start the long steep climb through the little field. Then passed the gate to the rough pieces field that lay parallel to the fresh-water spring, and on up the field below the stack yard to approach the top knob until the first chimney pot of the farmhouse came into view. Now came the measure of the climb and the gradual reward for the effort as successively more of the chimneys came into view. Now the red tip of the roof, now the blue, now the gable-end of the eastern eave and finally the pigsty's galvanised roof as simultaneously the farm-yard gate and stackyard were on the last one hundred yards or so of level if undulating grass-field.

That hard little journey would be taken so many times as to be so etched into a small mind as to be as clear now some fifty-five years later as it was wearisome then. In winter it would be slogged in mud churned by tractor and trailer tyres, in summer hindered by deep hard ruts baked from the same rough transport and in the seasons between sloshed in Wellington boots wet from heavy dew or drizzle or downpour. Once, it was done in fog so thick that the certain straight line from the rough pieces gate to the top knob went bewilderingly wrong. A first push into unknown territory with no familiar pointers. Disorientation, disbelief at setting out when a path with clear markers was so much a better bet and deep self-doubt were quickly all enveloping. Did the fact that eventually a hedge was reached, that an enforced decision of left or right had to be taken and that by tracking this natural barrier the stackyard was found, influence the future? Did it cause the future?

There was more than violets of-course. It's just that they always seem the genesis. My mum teaching "there is a flower that shall be mine, it is the little celandine". We never knew the proper names. Cowslip, may-blop, ladysmock, egg and bacon plant, peckeye, scarlet pimpernel, red campion. It seemed so natural to know them, pick them and bring them back to the kitchen. Just like in early Spring the catkins and pussy-willows.

In the earliest days, before the grey Ferguson 35 appeared, there were two working horses. I can only just remember this. Strangely, because the connection had not stuck before, one was called Violet and the other was Daisy. Small delicate names for big awkward things. Always seemed the most awkward to me when made to back into the shafts, that is, pulled backwards onto the bridle and bit into the cart. Two very different carts stick in my mind. One synonymous with lightness and one with heavy work. In the first category, or so it seems to me now, was the summer Sunday after tea and very rare trip out in the horse and tub. This two large-wheeled cart with its hinged back door would be taken up Woodlane, over Wildhill to Teversal, touching Pleasley and back via the tight narrow lanes leading to and from Hardwick Hall. Obviously there must have been other routes but only this remains. The other use was daily. It was really work but did not seem to be. Two churns of milk, ten to twelve gallons on a good day, had to be taken each morning to the wooden stand at the end of Goodalls drive in the village in time to catch the Co-op lorry. This brought in my dad's sole regular income of any note from Red Barn Farm. The second cart was a truly multi-purpose monster. It carried muck for spreading, brought in hay and corn-sheaves - wheat and oats, hulked turnips and mangolds and kale and carried all the tools for fencing and ditching.

In those first days of memory, Violet and Daisy were first and foremost not recognised for their use but simply as huge, warm, hairy and plodding friends. Hairy because of the flowing mane that had to be hung onto for grim death once lifted aloft onto that enormous and high back. Hairy too, now I think about it, because of the slip in the mud and the being galloped over without a scratch.

So, here we are then. Wild flowers, trees, hedgerows, up-hill walks home, horses and milk and spreading out and bringing in and the first Fergie 35 and no thought of incarceration at school. But it had to come and it did come as certain as a fifth birthday with angel cake and jelly. A reluctant drag across the back field, over the stile and up the lane to cobblers path leading directly to the school playing field and two wooden huts known as infants but which were actually open prisons that were not open. Hatred wasn't in it. Of the abrupt end to freedom, of the mindless paper exercises, of the noisy others in the way, of the place itself but most of all of the adults in it and of the very institutional effrontery. This wanton disregard for what I wanted and needed was never to go away. Here's John Smith from the Red Barn. He'll help you read and now you are behind, he'll help you catch up and, somewhat later, of-course I'll do your sums but you have to be in my gang. I do have this big advantage. A paradise to play in after school and Saturdays. It sets me apart. There is one other big asset. It seems that I can sing. In a few years this will send me to an important Cathedral out of the rut school to be tested. Of-course, I will not know music theory and so will fail.

A motley collection may seem a hackneyed expression for those friends that were regular visitors to the farm and on my side. Nevertheless, it is apt. For a start there was Terry Haydon. He must have come from a strange family albeit, as far as I ever knew, a stable one. I never once got invited to his home, which was unique amongst the others, and he had a propensity to brag in an extraordinary exaggerated way about the feats of his dad. He told my mum whilst eating biscuits in the kitchen that his dad had jumped clean over a double-decker bus. This was acquiesced with great seriousness. The reason for his clear favouritism with my mum was his ability, willingly demonstrated on any occasion, to play the mouth-organ. I think he must have had a lot of natural raw talent because years later as a teenager he led a music band of local lads complete with a manager who, as the Newtones, actually made a record or so rumour had it. Whither a pre-Beetles beetle or a pre-skittle Lonnie? Anyway, his other two attributes were first that whilst the rest of us home-made our adventure toys, Terry could always produce a super proper shop-bought job courtesy of his fabulous dad. A fantastic bow and arrow set and later a box-kite certainly fell into this category. Secondly, and at an incredibly early age, he was the first to smoke. Eventually, he was to get me started although I had reached fifteen - just.

Then there was Dougie and he was reckoned to be just slightly better than the rest partly because his home was as much a cottage as it got in the village and just past the war memorial but mainly because his parents were both school teachers. It became recognised that he was being pushed and so not surprisingly he was the only one in our year who would eventually pass the 11 plus examination. This of-course really bestowed elitist status since the grammar school was some miles away and demanded a special bus and he got robed in special uniform. Inevitably he would leave our humble circle. Not that that mattered when we were fighting on the hay-stacks, having pitch battles in the back field with vicious home-made wooden swords and guarded with dustbin lid shields or playing hide and seek on the pit-hills. Indeed, Dougie was if anything disadvantaged since uniquely amongst an exceedingly skinny lot he was a bit on the chubby side.

Brian Sheriff was somewhat from the wrong side of the track. A miner's son, he lived in the bottom end and the only one of the regulars to do so apart from Ossie Rhodes. Brian was always very cheerful and good looking in a happy sort of way and had flaming red hair. He was destined to follow the family pattern and start his working life in the coal-mine although as an apprentice electrician which, whilst paying much less, was recognised as a considerable step up from working on the coal-face. He was destined to die young. My closest friend in those infant and junior school days was Kenny Milward. He was a top ender and lived with a very respectable mum and dad in Sherwood Street in a linked terrace house next to a genell (alleyway). I do not recall ever falling out with Kenny and we became pretty much inseparable. Interestingly and looking back now he like Terry would not find work in either a manual or technical job but in retail. Terry went into the sports shop Redmayne and Todd in Nottingham and Kenny an electrical goods and radio shop in Huthwaite.

Ossie was a different kettle of fish altogether. He was much older than ourselves and had been kept back at the junior school over the leaving age of eleven years because he could not read. He was a bottom-ender and generally regarded as rough. I had been earmarked to help him read and because this seemed to be going well he made occasional visits to the farm. Normally, he would not have come close to this play circle. The big pay-off for me was protection. From the minute I started to help Ossie, it was understood that it would not be a good idea to pick a fight with me. The brains for brawn trade-off. What with new-found friends, bearing in mind the pre-five years had been absolutely isolated, and with the farm as a playground and given the protection of Ossie, slowly the prison of school became more tolerable. Even so, I was always amongst the last to arrive in a morning and ran home as fast as my legs would carry me in the afternoon. I could never get home soon enough.

More tolerable or not, still there were three enduring nightmares about these early school years. First was the mid-day dinner time. To most of the others it was obviously the best time. To me it was hell. The pre-cooked main meal arrived at the school in a large van and from where I never knew and in metal trays. Almost always it consisted of some form of encrusted pie. This would be cut into squares by the dinner ladies and heaved onto the plate. If one was lucky or unlucky, depending on how one viewed the pastry mound, the received item might be a corner piece to be added to by successive ladies ladling mashed potato, cabbage and most revolting of all, thick gravy. Always having had a poor digestive system, these dinners were either cause or effect. It's hard to say but, whatever, the smell alone made me heave. There was a boy called Alan Dillinger who was not a farm-playing friend and very much a bottom-ender and who almost always received my pie dinner. As I recall he also regularly went back for seconds. Years later I saw him in a pub and marvelled with secret delight at his huge frame. The puddings got me through. Once again this would invariably consist of a pastry pie but with some jammy type filling which with custard could be ingested. On extremely rare occasions, I even remember getting seconds. But the real savour was being old enough to run fast enough to make it back home for dinner. Then it was always delicious hot-pot. This of-course was hot and since time was short the practice was to pick out the potato pieces and lay them along the edges of the bowl out of the stew liquid to cool. This worked because by the time the stew proper has been eaten with bread dropped in, the stranded potato pieces had cooled down. There must have been other home dinners but only this is etched on a hungry brain.

The demarcation between bottom-enders and top-enders was very marked and understood in the late 1940s. The war had made little difference. This was not a proper village. Rather, it was a thrown together community. The reason was initially the coal-mines. Later the railways. The housing was cheap. In the bottom-end, the terrace houses were cheaper and more closely packed than in the top-end. The dividing line was the war memorial and the church hall. The latter was something of a travesty since there actually was no church. The church was a mile away down Cragg Lane to Old Blackwell. This was a tiny but genuine old village with small stone cottages and whose only concession to the current times was a red-brick Victorian pub the Robin Hood or Thack built to serve the Irish navvies who cut the deep channels needed to take the new Great Central Railway line en-route to Edinburgh and most importantly in its day the crack train the Master Cutler.

What Newton did have was a Methodist Chapel. This was planted decisively in the bottom-end and was looked down upon in the most un-Christian way by those in authority in the Church and most particularly by those who ran the church hall. This might have been not so much generic as specific to my Great Aunt Pem (her proper name was Emily though I never heard anyone call her that). She was a most formidable woman. A spinster school teacher all her working life, now well into retirement she exerted her authority over the young, poor and innocent Sunday School attendees. These, despite a good deal of pressure and cajoling, did not include me. Other than day school, which itself was barely acceptable as compulsory, the abject refusal to join any group activity extended to the youth club, boy scouts, boys brigade and most probably others long forgotten. I wandered the pit-hills as a loner, picked wild flowers for mum as a loner, started to help dad with the cows as a loner and a loner I would stay. Being sure that those attending Sunday school were learning good things - such children included my sister - was soon tempered by a growing belief that in equal measure they were poisoned against chapel. According to Great Aunt Pem, nothing good ever came of going to chapel. Yet, some of the friends made at day school went to chapel instead of Sunday school and actually liked it. Most of the songs were jolly and the games loads of fun. It was hard to see what was wrong with chapel or why those attending were banned absolutely from riding on the carts, lorries and other assorted floats which made up the Whitsuntide procession.

It became accepted that I had regular jobs to do for

Great Aunt Pem. These included filling up the coal bucket from the coal-house, sweeping up the paths and driveway and posting letters. This latter activity never failed to fill me with amazement because at the instant of being asked, the letter or letters had not even been written. There I stood mesmerised by the rapid scribbling which no doubt told the distant cousin in the Isle of Wight that a young nervous great-nephew was still performing the chores. A further regular job introduced a few years later was fetching five-shillings-worth of best steak from Browns the Butchers down the road. The good thing about this my first employment was that it was paid for. Great Aunt Pem was my sole source of pocket-money.

In the earliest days, Uncle Jack lived there too. He was a cripple. Both of his legs were withered and he could only move with the aid of crutches. It was rumoured that he had been dropped by an aunt soon after birth. The full story never quite emerged and the aunt in question was never revealed. He was a very kind man and kept biscuits in a red tin in the cupboard to his left-hand side. I never called but that he gave me a biscuit. Much later I was told by an elderly lady who lived with another aunt of mine in one of the very few original cottages that as a young man Uncle Jack had gone drinking with his pals "just as if he was normal" and could propel himself from pub to pub as fast as any of them and that if a fight broke out he could brandish his crutches to great effect. I never knew if this was true but I was very sad when he died. Many years later I would sit with Great Aunt Pem on Saturday evenings and play Canasta and sometimes on Sunday afternoons listen with her to the radio programmes by Flotsam and Jetsam and George Cole. By then she was mellowing and I was more confident. She outlived the nephew who looked after her in later years. She lived to be 94.

A proper village would have been in a proper county. Even that didn't apply. Although strictly in Derbyshire, it was not a Derbyshire village. Derbyshire villages are pretty, always on steep hillsides so that walkers can do the Peak District and the houses are made of stone. In fact it was right on the Nottinghamshire border where again the mining villages serviced the coal-face. Not until one goes South, North and especially East do the attractive Nottinghamshire villages set in. In such a setting, the differences between bottom-enders and top-enders could never be cosmetic. The rough, and it had to be said for particular families unclean, bottom-enders were actually at war with the more refined top-enders. This was from time to time a real war fought out in pitch battles on Tommy Newners rough ground just this side the woodyard that formed a natural barrier with the residents of the next village of Tibshelf. These were scary does that I was careful to avoid and the scars of battle, as appearing on the kids in the schoolyard, always seemed justification enough especially as my own territory was protected. As to schooling itself, reading came quickly and easily. More surprising to me was how simple arithmetic was. I could not understand the problems most of the others had and just how slow they were.

After the awful dinners, the second really hateful aspect of early schooling aside from the boring monotony of repetition was the headmaster's obsession with football. He must have been obsessed because it was the only game for boys that was played and occupied just about every afternoon. I was hopeless. The sheer time absorbed must have gone some way to explaining why only those who were coached by school-teacher parents ever passed the 11+ and so via grammar school ever stood a realistic chance of an education. As an act of rebellious defiance, I never possessed a pair of proper football boots in my entire school life. My farming boots always sufficed. Caning was the third big dread. It never happened to me but the Sword of Damocles was ever present. Certain troublemakers were perpetual recipients and one in particular learned to be so supple with his wrist that a hand angle from an extended arm almost reached the vertical. This clearly saved some pain from the form teacher that used a rounded ruler as the weapon. It did not however help much with the head teacher who cleverly used a bamboo cane with such a fast whip action as to defeat any small boy's antics. This particular child took a massive revenge when aged ten. He set fire to the school.

One specific incident has always stayed with me. Our class of eight-to-nine year olds was taken by Miss Pollard and this was for the whole year irrespective of subject matter with the single exception of football for boys and netball for girls. She was a very severe spinster and had been there so long that most of our parents had also been through her mill. She was, however, the one that decided that I had singing talents and had me sent for testing to the dioceses cathedral school at Southwell in neighbouring Nottinghamshire. Had I passed, then undoubtedly the future would have been much changed and for the better.

The memory-lodged incident occurred when a girl in the class reported to Miss Pollard that her Mars Bar had disappeared from her desk. On being asked to own up on three separate occasions during the last lesson of the day, the thief remained a mystery at going home time. As a result the redoubtable Miss Pollard was not going to let matters rest. We were all to stay behind "all night if necessary, and bringing in every child's parents if necessary" until the culprit came forward and handed back the Mars Bar or agreed to replace it. This overtime kangaroo court was particularly distressful for me because by this time my job was to run home and fetch the cows up the fields for milking and tie them up in the stalls. I was one of the first to start agitating for whoever did the deed to own up and let us go home. As child by child Miss Pollard required each of us to stand up and relate in minute detail exactly what we had done at the afternoon playtime, one boy started to cry quietly and visibly tremble at his desk. Miss Pollard went over to him, raised the lid of his desk and, of-course, inside was the missing chocolate bar. This ranked amongst the most talked about events ever. Though not before this incident, this particular boy was to become a very good friend of mine and eventually an academic rival. Ironic that he was to break free from the secondary schooling dead-end and become very senior in a poacher turned gamekeeper way. So, skeletons in the cupboard from skeletons in the desk and soon to be skeletons in the fields.

Because my sister was only sixteen months older than me and because she also had friends to play, there was at certain times some inquisitive horseplay between particular boys and particular girls. This would reach a head at haymaking time when the weather was warm, the new-mown grass soft and aromatic and there was a general air of high-spiritedness. It also seemed to coincide with my inability to get involved due to my job of loading the hay cart. Loading meant placing the hay, and in later years the hay bales, in an orderly manner on the cart from the disorderly way it was thrown up by pitch-forks from the hay-cocks that had been made to help the grass dry out and have some protection from the weather. As I grew stronger, my job developed into driving the tractor and pitching up the hay. Whatever, the work was a complete deterrent from larking about with the girls and one boy in particular had a reputation for falling on top of a girl and staying there. Rather than this being deprecated, most of the girls were drawn to him. This was a subject of wonderment to me since in other respects he appeared quite ordinary. In later life it occurred to me that a natural biological clock might run faster for certain individuals if they were destined for a short lifecycle. This advanced boy was to die young of multiple sclerosis. Short of things physical, experiments of a look-see type were commonplace and appeared quite natural. Since after junior school and certainly for the next six years or so I must have been too shy and/or introvert to have anything to do with girls, any thought of whether these little experiments came to be regarded as skeletons in the fields escaped me. Not that such thoughts haven't occurred since.

As time passed, the question of where babies came from started to arise and on this subject I was clear leader of the pack. My experiences allowed for an authoritative explanation of the reproductive process although this was never really believed. These experiences were based upon occasional trips with my dad to walk one of our two big white sows to a neighbouring farm that kept a boar for the specific purpose of breeding. Three things stuck in my mind about these quite long journeys across the fields. First, the sheer speed and willingness with which the sow made the outward journey, almost as if the purpose was both known and to be greatly enjoyed. Secondly, the length of time it took the boar to perform and the massive physical effort required of its owner to separate him from our animal. Thirdly, and most amazing of all, the vast amount of spunk that oozed from the sow during her long and slow and reluctant walk back home. It was incredulous to me that there would be any left to make the babies that were, after all, the only reason for the trip. This word for what the boar put into the sow was part of farming parlance and, because I was getting very interested in words at school, I had looked it up in our battered Chambers dictionary. Its prime definition of courage worked quite well with some of my compositions and so I used it, much to the acute embarrassment of two of my form teachers. One of these was the aforesaid Miss Pollard.

A further and similar experience of the worldly kind was undertaken much more frequently when one of our milking cows being in season was taken to a nearer neighbour's bull. What struck me here was the difference from the pig in terms of speed and lasting interest. The bull required one jump, as it was referred to, and the owner always knew when this momentous event had occurred. Immediately the bull was led away seemingly now disinterested. This was in stark contrast to the boar and I immediately related the difference to the number of off-spring in that in the cow's case there would be just one, or on rare occasions two, but in the pig's case many. Whether this observation has any basis in fact, I never knew but I relayed it to my audience all the same. They still disbelieved.

The other experience I could relate was an everyday occurrence in that my first job each morning was to let out the fowls. These fowls had been locked up each night in a big shed once they had roosted and to prevent foxes from getting at them. The instant that they emerged once the stone slab had been knocked away from the shed aperture, the cocks would engage in a veritable orgy of servicing the hens. It was the first priority above even eating. I knew that if this did not occur, the eggs would be infertile should we want to get a broody hen to sit and hatch them. But again, I did not convince my friends who saw no connection with the matter of making babies. But I knew for sure and this made me superior. This blessing from being brought up on a farm and my dad having a business was to stay with me as setting me apart and being somewhat *above them*. The fact that we had very little in material terms did not enter into it.

Apart from the established job of fetching in the cows after school, there developed a host of tasks undertaken as a matter of course. Increasingly as time passed these jobs kept me distant from other children. This seemed to be a natural consequence of living down a long winding lane away from any other houses. My life was entirely with mum and dad and the farmyard and buildings and dog and cats and cows and pigs and fowls and ducks and the fields and the weather. I neither knew nor wanted anything else. School was a time-using nuisance and more and more the goings on of the other children outside school was of no interest.

During the course of a week, the hens' eggs were collected from nesting boxes located in various places around the farm. Most were in the large fowl-shed in the orchard and I still itch now recalling the visits inside their flee-infested domain although not on the wholesale scale occurring at the annual clean out. This full-day job would leave me covered in bites. My dad alongside was never touched. Strange. Other nesting boxes were in the stables, cow shed and chamber. Some hens however would choose to lay where they wanted to and so a search of the stackyard and under the elderberry trees had to be undertaken. The big give-away of their hiding places was the cackling which accompanies the laying of an egg. A mental note of where this was taking place would be made for the collection job later. This was not to say that a hen might not be successful in hiding her clutch of eggs. In such cases the evidence came to light later either in the form of a very happy hen appearing with her brand new family of chicks and for whom she would scratch around furiously or on the discovery of an abandoned batch of eggs. In the latter case the trick was to put one egg in a bucket of water. If it floated, the egg would be bad and my job was then to throw it at the pig-sty wall as an act of enjoyable failure. It was interesting that the free-range hens and cockerels had no problem with consuming the stinking remnants. If the egg did not float then the batch would be taken indoors but put aside from the rest for home consumption, just in case. This exercise was of-course how I knew for sure about the consequences of the cockerels early morning activity.

All the eggs that had accumulated during the week had to be washed and crated on a Friday night. These eggs would be taken along with the milk churns to the village on the Saturday morning. My job working in partnership with my dad was to deliver these cleaned eggs by half-dozen or full dozen in a straw basket to the regular customers and collect the money. Sometimes, the regular customer had to be told that "this week there aren't any" because the quantity of supply was never consistent due to the weather, season or simply because less than normal had been laid. Also, sometimes the price would be lower since the eggs were from pullets and smaller than normal. When I first started delivering on my own, the customers were all relatives. This was easy and very welcoming although there was always the surprise that whilst I had been up and about for hours, these aunts and uncles were only just having breakfast and indeed sometimes actually waiting for me so they could add the eggs to their frying pan. At this time, we all had a cooked breakfast every morning.

As time passed, my customers grew to include non-family. With these I was much less happy. One house kept a bull-dog of which I was terrified, one family had a boy with a heavily skin grafted face that I hated to see and another customer was stone deaf and I had great difficulty getting my money out of him.

Another regular job was fencing. This meant repairing or replacing the fences of the fields to stop the cows from breaking out into fields of growing crops or into neighbours' fields. Occasionally there would be an emergency. A cow or cows had broken through a fence and a gap had to be plugged. Routinely this was a Saturday afternoon job. The heavy cart was loaded with stakes, barbed wire, nails and staples and together with spades and heavy hammers the trip around the perimeter fencing would begin. This was tough and often quite treacherous work and one of the few times that gloves would be worn. Another and strong-man activity was muck-spreading. My role was to drive the tractor and due to the work being largely winter based and slow in execution, it was usually a cold experience not least because the Fergie 35 had no protection at all from the elements. All the filling of the cart and the spreading on the fields was manual, done by my dad with a fork and was very heavy and laborious work. My fondest memory was the cue command to return to base on the cart being empty "home James and don't spare the horses". My name was not James and we were not using horses!

A much more pleasant job was spudding. This had nothing to do with potatoes which were colloquially known as spuds and I never knew where the term came from but the tool was a narrow-bladed spade with a cut-out v-shape on the top edge. The job was to dig out thistles from the meadow grass and because the intent was to do so before they seeded and thus spread, the job was deputed to me in the early Spring to early Summer season. The fact that the weather would normally be fairly kind and that the result was immediate destruction of the thistle, added to my liking for the task. However, the real treat was the isolation of the job. I loved being alone and attacking thistle after thistle. Gotcha, gotcha, great.

The meadow where most of the biggest thistles grew abutted the pit hills and the soil was poor because it had never been ploughed and fertilized. This in turn was due to the presence just below and above the surface of foundation remains of the pit buildings. Beneath one stone slab was a deep well and jumping up and down on that stone was irresistible. The pit had ceased working about 1890. This meadow was known as Deadwater and the stream running alongside was Deadwater Brook. I was told from an early age that it acquired this name due to a tragedy in the mid 1800's when a young girl was seen walking down our lane and continuing towards the pit carrying a baby. Because later she was seen returning but alone, a search revealed a drowned baby in the pit pond located in that meadow fed by that brook. A sad pedigree for a beautiful peaceful place.

The next field along was known as the Wharf. This was

because along its straight narrow length was a raised edge that had once carried railway truck rails. Horses pulled coal trucks from the pit some five miles to Pinxton Wharf from where the canal system eventually fed the river Trent. Industry comes and industry goes. Today those fields remain the same although light industrial buildings creep closer and closer and traffic from the M1 is just audible. But it was very quiet when I spudded and picked violets to take home.

A dual activity as heavy and physical as muck spreading was hedging and ditching. It shared the late autumn and early winter season and I was little more than an observer. Ditching in particular was incredibly tough and slow work and the main tool was a spade with an elongated head with turned in sides. Its purpose was to get depth in heavy clay-based soil but it needed a strong man to use it. That same man would wield a long-handled hedge knife to pare down the season's growth of chiefly hawthorn and with new hedges cut through young stems about half-way to layer at about a 45 degree angle. This process that we called pleaching produced a strong thick hedge from the next year. Even today whenever I see it I never fail to stop and admire this age-old practice with nostalgic pangs. Smallholding farmers such as my dad had to be strong and skilful and multi-tasked, though I never knew it at the time.

Because it didn't start until well into December and went on throughout the winter and was prevented only by the tractor and trailer being bogged down in the mud, turnip-pulling and gathering-in was the consistently coldest occupation. Gloves were never worn. Instead, the swinging of both arms across the chest to bash against the rib-cage like some demented scarecrow was the practised method of getting some feeling back into the figures. Then would follow hot-aches and a re-start to work.

The process was simple enough in that a turnip, actually a swede, pulled from the soil and held in the left hand was separated from its green top by a swipe of the evil looking curved turnip knife. The root part was allowed to drop to the left and the greenery thrown to the right. Since the next row was pulled whilst walking in the opposite direction, it followed that two rows of produce and tops were available for collecting later. These turnips were hand thrown into a cart and taken to the farmyard for pitting, that is, put into one big pile on which straw and then soil was thrown as a protection from frost. A never-ending chore from this point until the cows were turned out in mid- April was the collection of turnips from the pit to be thrown into a turnip grinder. At first turned by hand and later by a small machine, the grinder reduced the vegetable to slivers for shovelling into the cow troughs as winter feed. When I was aged three, it also reduced the large finger of my left hand by about an inch as internal inquisitiveness went unnoticed by a small helper.

A rushed trip by horse and cart and then bus to Chesterfield Royal Hospital restored the figure end but the resultant shape at the tip of this big finger and scar are testimony to the excitement. There seemed to be lots of lurking dangers for a growing boy at that time although I had to wait until aged ten before falling off the top of the hay cart and sustaining what I was proud to repeat as a greenstick fracture. My pot arm lasted for six weeks.

Haymaking was the most magical time. This was probably because it signalled the start of summer and a new farming season although always tempered in my mind by the worry of whether, once we got started, there would be enough dry days strung together to allow the hay to form without damage from rain and then the constant knocking about as the outdoor drying processes took place. Another knock-back for me was the frustration from knowing that things would not be ready.

Even though a late June to early July start was a virtual certainty, it would always come to light that some essential part was needed for the mowing machine and that the only way out was to get the blacksmith in the next village of Tibshelf to make it. Since this was not his proper job and since he had had no notice, there was no certainty when it might be ready and if it would work. Even up to the very day selected to start mowing the first field, the mowing knife would not be sharpened and my dad would instigate a search for the one used at the end last year and the back-up spare. Even when located -probably in its wooden box tied round with binder twine and hanging from a rafter in the Chamber - there was always the chance that it would need repairing and maybe welding and at a minimum some of the blades would need replacing or re-riveting. Once all this was sorted out and invariably having lost three or four good sunny days, the sharpening process was neither easy nor quick.

Each knife consisted of many triangular blades riveted to a metal arm that had to fit into the mowing machine bed. The two edges of each triangle had to be sharpened and so with twenty or so blades, this was a major job. Also, and depending upon the condition and type of grass being mown, the knife as a whole needed re-sharpening periodically. This is where the spare came into play if mowing was to carry on. From my perspective all this got in the way of doing the best job there was. It was also the most essential job because without hay to feed the cows during the winter and as turnips and kale and cabbage were only supplements there would be no or little milk and with no milk my dad had no income. Perhaps my business brain was forming. My dad saw no such need for urgency, pre-planning and preparation. He continued to scratch a living for 35 years from 35 acres of undulating poor coal-infested soil until the day he died, having just collected the eggs.

Enforced farmer: enslaved wife

In truth, my dad had too good a brain to be a small farmer. He had, however, no choice. Born the next to youngest of seven children in a terraced house on Littlemoor Lane and therefore a top-ender, he had been moved to Red Barn Farm at the age of twelve to live with his paternal grandmother following the death through cancer of his mother aged 50. Eight year later, his father was killed in a fall of clay at the nearby clay pits where he worked aged 59. In that same year, 1935, his grandmother died aged 94 "and never having a day's illness in her life". "She often drank the milk after it had gone sour and I've seen her pick maggots out with a kitchen knife from the meat hanging in the dairy before eating the meat, didn't seem to do her any harm". Dad also told me that an hour before she died she asked to see him whilst lying in bed in the front room and said "George I'm going now, look after the farm and be a good boy". So, at the age of twenty-one, he was left alone to run the tenanted farm just as he had been told. The farmhouse and a few surrounding acres called the back field had actually been purchased years before by his grandfather and the rest of the land was taken on later as a tenancy from Chatsworth Estate, the seat of the Duke of Devonshire. His grandfather had clearly been a man of some ability having risen from being a miner to a mining contracts manager who ran contracts for the pit owner, employed the men directly and participated in profits. He had died a man of substance owning not only the farmhouse and adjacent land but also a row of houses in the bottom end of the village as well as two or three in the top end. He was born in 1843 and sired 10 children the youngest of which was my Great Aunt Pem. His name was John Smith.

Having left the village school aged fourteen, I feel sure my dad harboured a secret ambition to get a proper if late education. In his teens he had cycled during several winters to night-school in the village of Heanor which was at least ten hilly miles away. He must have studied mathematics because I still have his textbooks on geometry and trigonometry. Why this led to nowhere I never knew. Perhaps it was as compensation that he took to reading. In those early days I would meet him once a fortnight after school at the mobile library where he would hand in a shopping bag full of books and replenish them. I cannot remember what type of material he went for but a book would go up the stairs to bed with him at night and in the morning it was read. There were perhaps two pointers. He quoted Shakespeare often and when the trips to the mobile library finished a large book in the cabinet in the front-room H E Bates – Short Stories was taken out over and over again. Certainly he was intellectually frustrated and spent this anger in deliberately picking an argument on some emotionally charged subject. Usually this peaked with his elder sister and her family at a traditionally Boxing Day tea. The perfect trigger would be an inevitable reference at some stage in the proceedings to the Royal Family. My dad's stock response that always precipitated our departure, to my mother's disgrace, was "Line 'em all up against a wall and shoot the buggers". At age 50 when my younger brother left school and the farm income had reduced to a pittance, he left the work with the animals to Alan and got a job in the cable-shop at the pit "my first pay packet". This was on days but also on night-shift and lasted until he was 65. To my eyes this was a very sad comedown but he did enjoy the company of the other men and they seemed to take to him judging from the greetings in the local pub on occasional Sunday lunchtimes. Farmer George he was called.

When I was seven years old and looking with my dad at some young beast kept in a building 100 yards or so remote from the farmyard and known as the hovel, he suddenly turned to me for a serious talk. He explained that some time before, the seventh Duke of Devonshire had died leaving substantial death duties to be paid. To meet these liabilities, the succeeding duke had decided to sell off much of the tenanted farm acreage. Our place was included. There were two options. Either we leave and he got an employed job somewhere which he explained my mum would prefer or he attempted to raise a mortgage from the National Westminster Bank to purchase the land at a preferential price as offered to the sitting tenant. I may have been only seven but the thought of leaving hit me like a kick from one of our horses, as he would have known in advance. I immediately said he should try to buy the land. I think he needed the confidence of the two-to-one vote that he had been certain to get.

That little chat condemned my mother, who was about to give birth to a third child and had miscarried two years earlier, to a life of some considerable isolation and for many years not much comfort. But how was I to know and what would the alternative have been? I didn't even know she had come from a successful family of butchers with a large spacious house and most of the amenities the times had to offer. I didn't know she married at 21 to a tenant farmer of poor soil and a house lacking electricity, proper mains water, water closets (toilets) and which would be so damp over enough years to bring on the rheumatics. Still, it was the start of the strongest possible bond with my dad and it did cause me to help him as much as I could so the mortgage could be paid and we could keep our farm.

That my mum spent all day Mondays in the washhouse with no machinery at all and the rest of the days cleaning, cooking, caring and slaving was just one of those things. That she got jobs like dashing down the yard from the dairy with a bowl of warm fresh pig's blood stirring rapidly to avoid it clotting before adding pearl barley and whatever else produced black pudding, was all part of the contract. That she was saddled with nursing me as the sickly child with the constant trips to the doctors and the seemingly endless waits for our turn for him to once again stick some horrible needle type instrument into the unfathomable problem of my near constant ear-ache. That she sat through my nightmare rants of seeing strange objects threaded to the edge of the blankets and then to face another day when I hadn't, again, gone to the toilet but had had bad indigestion and felt very sick. And why should this be when my dad could eat a raw Spanish onion with a stick of celery and freshly pulled radishes on the side, just before going to bed?

These were the days when ignorance was bliss on the need for roughage food, and the non-need for fatty food such as the suet dumplings as a staple item of both main course dinner and pudding and when temperature control for fevers was ill-understood. All this and more was part of my mum's contract.

She would have liked to have gone in the winter months to the church hall dances and sometimes did go with her sister but my dad didn't do that sort of thing. He didn't buy her birthday presents either. Nor did he agree with the request made personally on a special visit to the farm by the headmaster during my first year at secondary school, for me to be transferred to William Rhodes School at Chesterfield. It seems I came top in a maths exam set for all years from age eleven to fifteen. The Mars Bar boy went instead.

CHAPTER TWO
Seconday Modern

1953-1957. A first real school, the librarian
teacher, an eccentric bird breeder and bantams.
The rare parental row. Village children mixed and
streamed. A girl to excite.

It is a truism that whether one endures a distasteful phase with acquiescence or by kicking and knocking over the traces, it passes. If you have reached eleven years of age and have failed the 11 plus exam then a shift to the big Secondary Modern school is enforced. It might only be three miles or so away but its huge size and mixture of children from six villages the size of mine and numerous tiny hamlets, made it a fabulously new world. The one thing that started to boost my confidence was that we learned from day one that each new intake had been pre-graded. Our first Form Class was to be 1A, 1B, or 1C. How this decision had been arrived at I never knew nor cared because I was in 1A and furthermore after a series of tests on different subjects it appeared I was either top of the class or number two. Also, although my aptitude was reckoned to be with figures, the English teacher had, after one of these initial tests, made me stand at the front of the class and explain to the others what the word mortgage meant. This I proceeded to do with great assuredness. Of-course no-one including Mr Finney, who knew how I had acquired this advanced knowledge.

To me, the big difference in the learning stakes from the junior school was that at the end of each lesson we moved physically to another classroom for the next subject. This was a rock-solid guarantee that in the, let's say, History Room, would be a teacher who knew everything there was to know about history and the classroom would be bedecked with history charts and related material and the books would be solely dedicated to history. I thought that this was magical and it started to occur to me that there existed many areas of knowledge that were just not related to each other and that any one could be explored in depth.

The time blocked off in the schedule of lessons for Geography had a particular thrill. I loved hearing about foreign places and memorising their locations and was soon badgering my favourite uncle for one of his old world atlases. He became a very special person in my early thirst for knowledge. Having married one of my dad's elder sisters, in fact the sister my dad used to taunt on Boxing Day and any other day he got the chance, he worked in a library at a very early age and eventually would become chief librarian of three local centres. He had a quiet cultured disposition and at this stage of my early growth, would come to the farm every Wednesday and Saturday afternoon. These were his two half days off and he came specifically to help my dad on the farm. He travelled always by bus and walked the last mile or so across the fields. He was a boundless source of knowledge. He named wild flowers that had not been known to us and when it got dark early under a clear sky and we went back down the fields to burn thorns from the hedge cutting of earlier in the day, he would look up and point out to me the main star constellations. Whilst I have recognised the main ones ever since "and look along the line of the last two stars of the bucket of the Plough – keep going and there is the bright North Star – you will never lose your direction if you can find the North Star", the cluster he pointed out that I have never heard mentioned since was the Red Indian Eye Test. He said there were 24 stars in the tightly bunched pack. The number that could be counted determined the quality of eyesight. I could never see more than about 12 and so concluded that I would have made a poor Indian Brave.

When my sister and I were very young, he always brought the Dandy and Beano comics "last weeks issue from the library". Later on he brought me the Hotspur, Wizard and the Eagle because they contained proper stories. Later still he brought library books. White Fang by Jack London, Tom Sawyer, Huckleberry Finn, Biggles and this was why at Tibshelf Secondary Modern I was an avid listener above the desk lid and an avid reader below. Agatha Christie, J B Priestly, the adventures of Captain Hornblower it went on and on. Uncle Harold told me about his holidays walking in the Highlands of Scotland and on Arran and in the Shetlands and Orkneys. I positively ached to do the same someday. By the year of his death 1967, he had spent 42 years in the library service. At the funeral service at Teversal church, the vicar described him as "well-read, filled with erudition, filled with kindliness and firm but companionable". I could have added that he was my best grown-up friend and teacher and brought bones for our dog every Saturday, except that I couldn't because although 25 by then, I was too choked to speak. From letters written to the local paper along with the funeral report it turned out that he had been the founder member and first president of Sutton and District Rambling Club. There was a reminder too that he introduced the winter lectures and I recall vividly the one given by Percy Edwards the bird whistler. And that's another lesson now so easy to forget, how to recognise the whistles and calls of the many different birds in the fields and stackyard and do not forget also that a member of the finch family can always be recognised because it flies in bursts not continuously.

If geography became a favourite by interest, so English did by effort. At first my spelling was abysmal but gradually and probably through reading it started to improve. It was when the zenith of 16 out of 20 was reached that a realisation dawned that there must somehow be rules, must be something useful in grammar that hitherto had been unbelievably dry and abstract. As I started to unravel the structure of sentences, detect the adjective, noun, pronoun and verb, so the rules of spelling started to make sense and if just exceptions accounted for the 4 out of 20 I got wrong then it felt an achievement.

Looking back, there must have been much self-deception about this but still it propelled me forward and English grew closer to Maths in the ability stakes. Added to this, there was something gloriously unstructured about the English lessons. Mr Finney was thought to have been ticked-off by the headmaster for having been spotted reading to us when we should have been working. Yet, his passion for Robert Louis Stevenson's Travels with a Donkey stay with me to this day as it is spotted on special offer in a shop in Barcelona and was this, even if subconsciously, the linkage of the very separate subjects of English, Geography and History? Special offer though says it all.

Whatever the merits of how English was taught, my confidence grew perceptively and when in the fourth year he asked me to be the assistant editor of the school magazine and awarded a special prize for the effort, Doctor in the House and Doctor at Sea, the seeds of a lifelong interest in words were well and truly sown. It's strange to look back on this hater of institutionalised junior school, the one who got there last and who couldn't wait to get back home, the lonesome always introvert non-joiner of any team thing, actually being presented on the annual prize-giving day with The Cruel Sea credit prize 2nd boy in second year and Atomic Energy first prize 1st boy in 3rd year. The date of the ceremony for the fourth and final year was never reached and there would be no call back. I left school on my fifteenth birthday and started work the following day.

It's one thing to find an interest and to want to work at it, quite another to have to do things for which one has no aptitude, zero interest and can see no sense in spending time at. Woodwork and metalwork were not only compulsory but took up the whole of one afternoon a week when things should have been and needed to be learnt. Here I was firmly in the "C" category and never graduated from soft to hard wood and was only let loose on metalwork at all because it appeared that some time had to be devoted to this harder discipline irrespective of the progress or lack of it at woodwork. The abject failures still haunt me. A wooden toy boat, the first and most basic article, that sank instantly. The coffee table that was proudly presented to my great Aunt Pem, many lessons after the rest of the class had moved onto more advanced things, and the legs of which broke as soon as she put some magazines on it. It nevertheless stayed in her parlour semi-propped up. The metal fish-slice complete with holes that my mum kept in her cutlery drawer to the very end even though the rivets were obviously out of line and it was branded with the number 15, my role number in the ill-fated class, that I assume should never have been there in the first place. Whilst the rest turned out innumerable multi-grained fruit bowls, my single product looked like something dropped from outer space. Even my Mum never really took to it. The same teacher who supervised these two vital crafts also took Practical Science and consequently was completely unmoved on the afternoon that a bunsen burner conspired to singe the hair on the front of my head.

Sports absorbed about as big a proportion of the

timetable as it had unfortunately done at junior school. All activities were highly competitive and came to a public head at the annual sports day held at a municipal facility some distance from the school that had no field of its own. The competitive spirit was generated by the clever trick of dividing us up into four houses. At the great annual event, each house collected points in each year according to the positioning of the child in a race. The allocation to a house was permanent and so lasted for the whole four years. It was supposed to be somehow fair and equal although the selection method was never clear and if it was why did the winning points tally always seem to follow the known importance of the Derbyshire house in question such that Chatsworth (blue) invariably came first, Hardwick (red) second, Haddon (green) third and Wingfield Ruin (yellow) last. I was in Wingfield. Whilst I did have some minor success in two areas, both were attributable to my upbringing and in no way any coaching on offer.

The first was cricket. On some Saturday evenings in the summer and going back as far as could be remembered, a game of cricket was organised. In took place in the field below the stackyard using hay pegs for wickets and bails and a home-made bat until uncle Harold's son Philip appeared one glorious day with a proper bat that had three springs. I was allowed to use this provided the ball was hit properly in the middle of the bat and not too hard. There was no team but whoever made the most runs was the winner. There were only three players normally, uncle Harold, Philip and myself. Very occasionally and when he was not too busy after milking the cows, my dad would be persuaded to take part. He had a most strange way of bowling and this baffled me such that I rarely managed a proper hit. My superior knowledge now suggests that he was a form of leg spinner. The one advantage that was derived from these enjoyable evenings was the absolute necessity on my part to bowl like a veritable demon if Philip with his new proper bat was ever to be dislodged. Ofcourse, the bumpy surface of the meadow helped as did the occasional cowpat. This grounding could well have produced the next in a long line of Derbyshire fast bowlers for county and England. Instead it produced an opening bowler for Wingfield and the rarely held school-year team match with a local rival. I cannot recall a single victory but only taking a blinding catch once at cover-point. It must have been so because it got a special mention by the headmaster at school assembly the following morning.

The second claim to fame arose undoubtedly from the routine run down the fields to fetch up the cows for milking or the emergency run to recapture a cow that had broken out into a neighbour's field. It so happened that Tibshelf Secondary Modern had a similar obsession as Newton Junior with football or perhaps a sports master that wanted or knew no other winter sport. Whatever the cause, my anti campaign was to continue. Still no boots and still a disposition to shoulder-charge or deliberately trip any opposing forward heading in my direction. As a result, those who would never make any of the football teams were no longer required to turn up. Instead and on each football afternoon we would go on a long-distance run. This was fine in its way except that first there was no sports master to supervise, guide or otherwise instruct and secondly there was no actual course to run. This was solved by someone suggesting that we take one of two alternate routes each week. The first was from the school to a nearby village of Morton and return. This was all on the road. The second and much longer run was to Hardwick Hall and back a distance of about five miles partly on the road and partly across fields by footpath. It is strange to think that all we abandoned football drop-outs could easily have got out of sight of school and just rested and generally messed about. Yet, a kind of unvoiced competitiveness set in. Most actually did try to do the course as fast as possible and an elite few proved to have more stamina than the others. These budding marathon athletes, that included me, were all wiry and skinny whilst the ones who trailed behind were mostly fat.

After a while, my superior stamina for the longer distance was being challenged by just one boy. He was from Newton and a bottom-ender and not someone with whom I had previously been friends. However our solitary running battles started a friendship that would last to this day and his ability to smoke a surreptitious fag amazes me as much now as then. Whether under the stone bridge that carried the railway line over Morton or resting on the fallen oak tree up the hill into Hardwick Hall park, he would produce from heaven knows where secreted on his skinny running top and shorts-dressed person a single Park Drive cigarette and from somewhere else a single match which when struck on a stone created the contented smoker. I knew of no one else this young who had started to smoke and I was to hold off this manly habit until I was well over sixteen years of age.

An eccentric couple

It was around this time that my second source of income arose. My aunt Gladys had arrived at the farm one day carrying a large box containing several bantam chicks that we called banties. She had been instructed to bring them by her husband uncle Leslie for me because they were a very special breed that I was to look after. She explained that they were a variety called Polish Tufted that uncle Leslie had acquired from Nottingham University's experimental department. Obtained as eggs, he had used one of his own broody hens to hatch them. Although uncle Leslie worked for British Railways as a painter of signal boxes and the like, he had a part-time job in the evenings and some nights as a caretaker and watchman for the University, the grounds of which abutted their garden.

Quite what went on in this experimental department it never occurred to me to ask and even if I had the probability is that he either wouldn't have known or told. Still, these most unusual chicks arrived complete with little tufts on their heads and the first tiny evidence of spikes on the rear of the legs of those destined to be cocks. Seeing these miniature fowls gave me an idea. I approached my dad with a proposition. If they were to become my sole responsibility as regards building special coups to segregate them from the main flock and keep them clean and manage the breeding, would he supply the feed. Could I then keep any money that was forthcoming from the sale of the eggs?

To my relief this deal was agreed. It followed that in due course there were banty eggs collected, washed, crated and ready to sell. At first this was not as easy as I had thought since the regular customers were accustomed to getting proper full-sized eggs, sometimes the bonus of a double-yoked one, and were even prone to complain if they believed too many white eggs had been mixed with the preferred brown ones. However, my selling was achieved on three counts. First, the audience was largely a captive one consisting in the main of my aunts, secondly the price was less at four shillings a dozen as distinct from six shillings for the hen eggs and the coup-de-grace was my heart-felt knowledge imparted to them with great sincerity that once cracked into the frying pan, the size was hardly any less than a hen's egg.

Once the banty eggs started to get larger as I augmented my small flock of Polish Tufted with other strains, the sideline proved a winner. Now I had my second income stream to add to aunt Pem's weekly pocket money for the chores. Also, and although it wasn't obvious to me in a technical sense at the time, the distinction between revenue and capital cash spend became important. The only means available to buy more birds and in pursuit of which I avidly scoured advertisements in the Derbyshire Times, was to save some of the egg money. And so a good business lesson was learned. Capital is an investment for the future and short of borrowing, current income must be set aside. Also to have to borrow like my dad's mortgage would mean paying interest and no one else was going to have a slice of my profit.

My dad got his own back from providing the feed in that about 50% of new chicks would turn out to be cock birds and because a ratio of only about one to ten was needed to keep the eggs fertile, fully grown males were killed for eating. I was assured that they were too small to sell and so they entered the farm food chain and usually for a Sunday lunch. A few years later and again by pure chance I was to start bell-ringing and it was only after a good deal of proficiency had been attained that the invitations started to arrive to ring for the wedding on a Saturday. Now here was a real money-spinner because the fee per bell was substantial and there were no costs at all just a modest amount of personal time. A sure omen for a slice of the future in consultancy.

Aunt Gladys was my favourite aunt. She was the third eldest on my dad's side of the family and like most girls at that time had gone into service on leaving school. That was a polite expression for becoming a servant of a wealthy family. She had started a somewhat unusual and thereafter fairly eccentric life after her early working years by marrying uncle Leslie who already had a daughter by a first wife who had died very young. She had inherited money on her father's death before she was thirty and had bought a house on the west side of Nottingham and invested and hung on to the rest. The couple had a highly charged but close relationship that became familiar to my sister and I from an early age because of the custom that developed over a few years of fetching us to stay with them for two weeks in the summer to give my mum and dad a break on their own.

The world of this aunt and uncle was vastly different

from the farm. They lived on a street with semi-detached neighbours in a densely built-up area on the fringe of the city. Consequently, people and noise bamboozled me. Aside from the environmental aspect, my mum and dad were quiet and apart from on just two occasions lived at peace with each other. This was not the case during our Nottingham holiday. Aunt Gladys was a large lady abounding with household energy. As she charged around and most obviously when she rushed to the front door, the whole house seemed to shake and certainly the floorboards did.

Uncle Lesley was also dynamic in a less noisy way but the really frighteningly new experience was their arguments. It was as if anything could trigger one and once on a bus coming back from Nottingham Slab Square it happened over which was the nearest bus stop to alight for their house. Apart from the fact that they had lived there long enough to have measured it out to the inch if it was important, it was to my sister and I completely baffling in that either of the two options were very close and no distance at all compared with the walks to and from school that we did quite thoughtlessly each day. This particular and public bust-up so upset my sister that she refused to go on holiday to their place ever again. And didn't.

Having a childhood punctuated by no more than two parental arguments must be a rarity and maybe for this very reason are remembered for their devastating effect as utter surprises. One arose when after an afternoon's milking session, my dad could not find any filter papers. These papers were placed between two metal discs themselves filled with tiny holes and literally filtered the milk as it was poured from the milking bucket before being cooled and entering the churn. Without being filtered, the milk could not therefore be made ready for collection by the dairy lorry. For some inexplicable reason the misunderstanding about whether my dad or mum should have fetched a new supply of these filters developed into a full-scale argument. And, for the first and only time, it became clear to me and my sister that mum not only knew how to swear but could deliver a certain word to great and loud impact. We were shocked and frightened and it was obviously my dad who was backing off. When things quietened down my mum in a low and sweet voice started to sing over and over again and to herself a rhyme that I had never heard before or indeed since and have no inkling of its origin:-

> We're miserable, so miserable, down on misery farm
> The hens won't lay
> We can't make hay
> We work all day and get no pay
> We're miserable, so miserable, down on misery farm

The second altercation must have occurred in the early hours of one new year's day because being woken by a huge noise downstairs and creeping halfway down the winding staircase to explore, it appeared that my dad's attempt to let in the new year had gone badly wrong and mum was shouting at him and he was falling all over the kitchen and bumping into chairs and the table. Only years later did realisation dawn that he had been the worse for drink and on being pressed my uncle Ernie admitted that he and his son Edwin and a few others may have "spiked your dad's beer to send him on his way".

Years later still, a photograph emerged of my dad with a pint in one hand and a cigarette in the other and taken in the upstairs room at the George and Dragon pub in the village. For a virtual non-drinker and only an occasional pipe smoker, it must have been quite a night and not one my mum was likely to let him forget. The only other thing I can actually recall of the incident at the time, was his great difficulty in milking the following morning on account of "my bad head" and my mum "having to do a lot of cleaning up".

What made uncle Leslie so different was that he kept cage birds for a hobby. Perhaps hobby is the wrong perspective since he traded these birds and had many stories of his financial success in this regard. Such successes were invariably challenged by my aunt Gladys on the basis of "and who bought them and fed them". Whilst this was usually voiced with a laugh for my benefit, it could lead to a major argument that to me was very upsetting.

The birds themselves were kept in the garden in huge wire cages attached to sheds and all of which he had built himself. These constructions went around all three fences of the back garden with more down the middle. There were also many small cages in the kitchen and in a conservatory. He also kept tropical fish in innumerable tanks and had several ponds in the garden where special forms of flies were bred for their eggs to feed the fish. In his later years when the house was sold for a retirement place with his daughter and although the birds were all disposed of, some fish tanks remained and were re-installed in the new abode. As I grew older it became apparent that this hobby stemmed from a deep-seated interest and considerable knowledge.

As well as the more common birds such as canaries, budgerigars and Java sparrows others that stick in my mind with great affection were love birds, cockateels, and the small game-like birds that scurried around in the bottom of the cages, Chinese painted quail. He had some sort of relationship with a pet-shop not far away and to which we made frequent visits and much later when I had a car he would get me to take him to fellow hobbyists for swaps and deliveries. He also introduced me to a rudimentary form of fishing on a nearby canal. All these activities were a million miles away from how I had been brought up as was the electricity supply, flush toilets and the occasional presence of an Irish lodger who worked in the railway workshops and who brought in some useful income. My vocabulary was broadened by certain of his words that I later realised were an inheritance from his roots in Cumbria. The most memorable was twerp which it seems I frequently was.

In his prime, uncle Lesley had been a main-line train driver with the London Midland Region (LMR) based in Nottingham and on one occasion when being taken to London for a day out, he related not only the gradients and likely speed restrictions along the entire stretch of line but also explained how to calculate the speed of the train by counting the seconds between the quarter-mile posts that he pointed out ran beside the track. 60 seconds times 60 minutes divided by four (for the quarter mile) = 900 divided by the number of seconds that has passed between the two markers. The arithmetic of this appealed to me enormously. He had for some reason fallen from grace and it was hinted that this may have been due somehow to my blood uncle, my dad's eldest brother who by this time was getting quite senior with LMR. I would never know the truth even though this brother-in-law my uncle Edmund was to play a big part in my post school early life. Certainly there was some needle between the two men. After some intermediary jobs, uncle Leslie had been re-employed in the industry but at a very different and lower level. First as a blacksmith and then as a painter.

It was during this phase that aunt Gladys and uncle Leslie arrived at the farm one day asking my dad to store some paint though if he wanted to use any for the gates and building doors or the house window frames he was welcome to do so. Since however the paint turned out to be all one colour and a bit "on the bright side" according to my dad, it wasn't ever used and nor was it ever fetched back. Some time later I remember a most indignant aunt Gladys telling my dad that they had had a visit from the railway police about some missing stock after an anonymous tip-off. It seems uncle Lesley had turned his hand to some spare-time external house painting in the neighbourhood. The whistle-blower had apparently noticed that just about all of the houses in one street had been painted the same colour. This was a pure coincidence in relation to their storage of the paint as was proved by the accusation not coming to anything.

Aunt Gladys was a great moral supporter of my dad in his difficult early years at the farm and had promised to help financially if needed and to come and live there with uncle Leslie to help run the place. This offer was never taken up. In any case since she couldn't abide her elder sister who was married to uncle Harold and he was already helping by his visits twice a week, the potential for a major family feud did not escape my Dad. Interestingly, he did a few years later accept financial help from his youngest sister and who out of the father's will had been privately educated and was a successful school teacher. I had been asked in an off-hand manner to ride over to pick up a small package that had equally casually been put under the pannier spring of my cycle. On handing it over at the farm my dad opened it up to reveal what to me looked like a vast quantity of money notes. I was further involved in several repayment trips over years to come.

Mixed and streamed

Because of the A, B, & C streaming, Tibshelf school threw me up against a number of child characters that even my experiences at Newton Junior school with its bottom-enders and top-enders had not prepared me for. The very fact that the villages were now all mixed up dictated a hybrid of social backgrounds and it soon became clear to me educational standards. Those from the two junior schools in Tibshelf itself were way ahead of the rest of us and conversely those from Hilcote, known as B-Winning because this was the name of the coal-mine there, were behind. I decided that those from Blackwell (A-Winning), and Westhouses were about on a par with our lot from Newton. As a result of this, it took the first year for me to catch up with the Tibshelf children. As regards home backgrounds, Tibshelf was a much bigger village and had a spattering of big houses and some professional and business people. By contrast, Hilcote was predominantly a mining community and the children even spoke differently. The pronouns thee and thou were still in use and yet just two miles away in Newton this was not so. Westhouses was a railway village dominated by the main line to Nottingham down the Erewash valley and the station and marshalling yards. Blackwell was a mixture of the two.

Colin Churn from Tibshelf came to my attention first. There wasn't much choice in this. At one of the very first morning assembly lessons when standing right next to me he, without any warning, fell flat on his face with a frightening bang of his head on the wooden floor. I was dumbfounded and the whole proceedings came to a sudden end. Once an alarmed chatter had gone round the hall, a teacher rushed in and carried him off. It transpired that he had fainted and periodically from then on continued to do so during assembly and without any apparent harm. Eventually he was excused. He was a quiet and quite brainy boy who after leaving school would become an apprentice electrician. He had a best friend and they were as different as chalk and cheese. In fact he was a stooge to Alan Stapleton the plump joker of huge noise and energy. Alan was very bright and knew it. He had natural repartee and a vast collection of jokes for all occasions. By the third and fourth years, he alone was making advances to girls and one in particular from Hilcote who was not only intelligent but had certain attributes ahead of the others and flirted with Alan quite openly in order to display them. In due course he was to claim success but whether this really was so or just bravado I never could tell. He was an early smoker and also a surprisingly good runner but his main characteristic that sticks in my mind was his defence of Colin come what may.

Another boy whose father had taught him to be an expert coarse fisherman at a very early age struck a sort of mutually beneficial pact with me. His main talent was artwork and his drawings of coarse fish were extremely good. Through his lectures to me on each fish and how and when it was caught, an idea was born that he would do my drawing and paintwork - with some variations from his own - and I would do his maths. This liaison lasted quite some time and appeared successful. A rudimentary and early form of networking.

Oddly, I developed a friendship with two very different girls. After Mars Bar boy left for a better school, my classwork competitor was another Smith, Jennifer. She was from Tibshelf and a very good family. We often did some studying together and discussed forthcoming tests. She was quiet, well dressed and very pleasant. It's strange but I haven't the faintest idea what happened to her after school. With Pam Cobb I had very much wanted to keep in touch, metaphorically and literally. She appeared on the scene late having been moved to Tibshelf by her parents after living in Kenya. Her father was something to do with the Armed Forces or Government apparently but whatever she took the elder boys by storm because of her exceptionally good looks and figure. It was the avowed aim to catch a glimpse of her during the brief period of change-over from girls to boys at the swimming baths.

The school had no swimming facilities of its own but we were taken by bus to Clay Cross to the public baths. Segregation was severe, no mix as in the classrooms but if the timing was a bit awry it might happen that the girls were just leaving the pool as we arrived. After Pam appeared on the scene there was only ever one objective on swimming days. She would have remained a distant image of loveliness and excitement had it not been for Mr Finney asking her to assist me in discharging my heavy responsibility as assistant editor of the school magazine. To say that I couldn't believe my luck would be a massive understatement and not least because at times nearing publication, we absolutely needed to stay late at school to get everything in. This meant that aside from working in close proximity, I started as a natural consequence to walk her home down the village nonchalantly pushing my bike. As time passed I desperately wanted to ask her out for a date but never actually plucked up enough courage. She was way out of my league and anyway I would not have known what to do. This should not have prevented me trying later however, but it did.

CHAPTER THREE
Steam trains and office gossip

1957 – 1960 Brotherly conflict. Holiday Fellowship walking and the powerful uncle pulling strings. LMR Motive Power Department. The Great Central line to Marylebone. Train commuters playing nap. A railway office, a ladies lav.

After a second attempt to keep me at school had failed, this time via a personal letter from the headmaster to my dad suggesting that I sit an entrance exam for the Chesterfield College of Further Education, talk started on what work might be suitable for when I left Tibshelf Secondary Modern. Furthermore, since my dad needed some money brought into the house as soon as possible, it became apparent that these expectations centred on my fifteenth birthday and not even staying in the fourth form until the end of the summer term. Apparently I was not likely to learn much more after that anyway.

The point about moving on to Chesterfield College was that they were authorised to set "O" levels whereas Tibshelf school was not. A careers' advisor arrived with a bundle of pamphlets that were to be taken home to discuss and "Look carefully at the one called How to Become a Pharmacist". Since I had no idea what a pharmacist did having never even heard the word before, I called is as usual on the way home to do the jobs for great aunt Pem and as it happened her nephew my uncle Edmund was there too. They both pored over the pamphlets and when I highlighted the one on becoming a pharmacist great aunt Pem expressed vociferously the immediate view that I was certainly not suited to that.

They were both taken aback with the imminent prospect of my leaving school. This bright lad who they knew had been given by my aunt Madge at age ten The Childrens'Guide to Knowledge because I wouldn't stop asking questions and by my favourite uncle Harold Thorndykes Junior English Dictionary which had pictures as well as definitions. So it was that uncle Edmund must have got to work on my behalf.

Following the family tradition of christening the eldest son John Smith, he had chosen to adopt his rather more posh middle name of Edmund. He started work aged fourteen as a cleaner at the British Rail London Midland Region engine sheds at Westhouses. This is not the same job as the name infers today. A cleaner, meaning cleaning engines, was the lowest grade in a career that would if successful ultimately lead to being an engine driver. Such a job carried great status at that time. The career path was actually, cleaner to past cleaner, meaning past out to undertake under supervision the next higher grade of work, to fireman to past fireman to driver.

As I was soon to learn drivers themselves went up, and in their later career often back down, through a grading structure that determined pay and the ability to earn substantial bonuses. The lowest grade driver would be shunting freight carriages in sidings, the highest would be driving the main line expresses. Normally, the pinnacle of a career would be attained by joining the elite link 1 express drivers. In the case of uncle Edmund however, he had progressed further by becoming first an Inspector and finally Chief Inspector of LMR based at Leicester station.

His responsibilities included passing out the grades and the general operating efficiency of the trains and their crew. It was a very senior position and externally represented by wearing a company issue bowler hat.

Sometime after the leaving school discussion, uncle Edmund appeared at the farm. This was a rare event. There was little mutual respect between him and my dad. At our solitary working sessions down the fields, dad had often said "your uncle Edmund will never marry, he's too mean for any woman to have him". But the deep reason was that despite his career success and obvious spare funds, uncle Edmund had flatly refused to get involved when my dad had really struggled financially and "he'd sooner me have the farm go under than lift a finger to help" and it is certainly true that only aunt Gladys and aunt Ruth offered practical support at crucial times. One of my dad's often told stories was that whilst the whole family were still at home his mother at Sunday tea might say "there is only one egg, that's for Edmund." Early life resentment runs deep.

For his part, uncle Edmund once told me on one of our many future train journeys that "your dad is no business man and never will be". Also, I think he was piqued that the farm and subsequently the tenanted land had fallen to my dad. In his last years it must have been patently obvious to him that his own cash had far less value than my dad's capital. The twelve years age gap wouldn't have helped and the head of the family was supposed at that time to command automatic respect irrespective of actions and situations. However, this would have cut no mustard with my dad.

There was much more to uncle Edmund than his railway career as I was to learn as the years passed. He was self-educated, and read widely and given a different start in life ought probably to have been in academia. He was an acknowledged expert on Mediaeval England and the Reformation and had given lectures on these subjects in the

Leicester area. In his very last years, he was still reading huge tomes on English history in between looking after great aunt Pem with whom he then lived.

Although he worked right through to his 65th birthday, and duly collected his gold watch on retirement, he was to contract sugar diabetes and to neglect himself badly. He died aged 72 a somewhat sad and lonely figure having had a gangrene-infected foot removed at Chesterfield Royal Hospital. He didn't even have time to formalise a gift of £500 he promised to my mother who had taken over the most unpleasant role of looking after Great Aunt Pem. Through his reading and being an organist, he was also very knowledgeable about church and cathedral architecture. A good proportion of his holiday time was spent visiting these places. I never knew from where the music side came but he was the resident organist at Leicester Cathedral for many years and after retirement at Old Blackwell and then Tibshelf church. He also gave piano lessons conducted from Great Aunt Pem's parlour. The great legacy he left me was a love of walking and generally for the great outdoors and the freedom of remote places.

When I was fourteen, he invited me to join him on holiday. This was to be two weeks at the Holiday Fellowship centre at Scarborough. These centres were Methodist based and therefore alcohol free and devoted to walking the local area. This was a most marvellous experience because everyone joined the A, B, or C groups according to their ability and desire for distance and difficulty. We, of-course, were "A" material because uncle Edmund as it soon became apparent was an accomplished rambler and had been on these holidays many times before and indeed to this centre. I had no walking boots and so the farming boots had to make do, just as they had for football.

The procedure was to be taken to the start of a walk by coach and then to follow a leader for a prescribed route. As the week passed, so the walks became gradually longer and tougher. Group B followed the same format with easier walks and Group C basically stuck to the coach. The second big concept was self entertainment. In the evenings at the HF centres, lectures and film slide shows and dances were held. I soon learned the basics of Scottish dancing and such favourites as the Military Two-Step, Gay Gordons and the Valeta. Quite a change from school and farm life. All these activities built up to the grand concert on Friday night. At this, absolutely everyone with no excuses had to do a turn. Because I had no such turn, it was apparently accepted that I would be part of the play. There seemed to be a selection of well-tried little playlets with well know parts. The lines had to be learned during the week and rehearsed with the other unfortunates that did not have their own slot. I went through the motions with little enthusiasm. The life of a thespian would never be for me.

On the other hand, uncle Edmund was a revelation. He specialised in monologues. These were lengthy, amusing, known off by heart and always a great hit particularly I noticed to a jolly lady who was here on her own. She started to sit next to him on the coach journeys to and from the walks and they struck up an affable association. The curious thing was that he booked into the centre and insisted on being called John not Edmund. I heard her ask for his address when we left. On relating this experience to mum and dad on returning home, they believed that he had had some friendships with ladies met on holidays before and indeed "nearly got engaged once".

My dad repeated his staunchly held view that "he was too mean to commit himself to any woman". He was never mean to me. This holiday and those of the following two years in Torquay and Hythe were paid for entirely by him. I had no idea what the cost was and had no money of my own. We always travelled by train because of his work and therefore his free pass but also the pleasantness of it and novelty for me. This was the time of steam and style. On the outward journey he would sit opposite me puffing his pipe and take out his wallet bulging with paper money. Diligently counting it out, he would proceed to divide the total exactly into two equal amounts. One half went back on one side of the wallet, the other on the other side. "This is for week one and this is for week two". Looking back, what an excellent lesson in budgetary control.

At the end of each daily walk and as we arrived back by coach to the centre, it was my job to jump off the coach first, dash indoors and upstairs and to the largest bathroom, turn on the taps fully and drape our towels on the side of the bath, so reserving the room. Resourceful too. Each Christmas I gave him a two-ounce tin of St Bruno Flake but not until the very end did I make proper if meagre payback for his generosity of three wonderful holidays that opened up a world of walking moors, high fells and cliff tops and for explaining the structure and history of Canterbury Cathedral and for the thrill of riding the Romney, Hythe and Dymchurch steam railway. On his death he left me a specific legacy of £500. All his savings went into a trust fund to pay for the upkeep of a younger sister who for all her life had been somewhat inadequate.

The purpose of uncle Edmund's rare visit to the farm was to let us know that there was a vacancy for a junior clerk in the Motive Power Department office of British Railways LMR based at Middle Furlong Road in Nottingham. He could get me an interview because he knew the chief clerk Mr Jennings very well. If I got the job it would open up a career in offices instead of what otherwise would most probably happen which was following his footsteps as a cleaner at Westhouses. He felt sure that I was much more cut out for an office-based job. My dad agreed and so the die was cast.

The date for the interview was duly set and the programme was to have a medical in the morning at a centre adjacent to the main line Midland Station in

Nottingham, go to aunt Gladys's house for lunch and then to the Motive Power Department for the interview in the afternoon. What surprised me about the medical was the inclusion and indeed heavy concentration on an eyesight test. This was no simple "can you read the letters on the third row from the bottom" type check that had been conducted periodically at school. It was all to do with recognising numbers and shapes arrayed in dots of varying colours. Even my acute shyness could not prevent a little query as to why. Apparently I was taking the standard colour blindness test that was compulsory for engine drivers periodically and indeed the passing of which was mandatory to remain in this elite job due to the absolute dependency on colour signalling. I didn't think there would be a lot of call for signals in the Motive Power office but it seems that "if you want a job on the railways then you take and pass the standard test". So that was that.

What actually happened in the interview proper is totally lost on me due entirely to the drama of being sick half way through. That in turn was due to aunt Gladys insisting on me eating rice pudding for lunch, or dinner as it was called then, "to build you up for the afternoon". I never could digest milk in its raw state and had been excused it at school since infant days. Whether this resulted from a physiological defect or the sight in my earliest memories of dad milking cows by hand twice a day, I never really knew. The outcome on this crucial occasion was perhaps psychosomatic, perhaps not. At any rate either through dint of sympathy, achievement or the pulling of strings by Chief Inspector Edmund Smith, I got the job. The start date was fixed at April 9th 1957 when I was fifteen years and one day old.

The journey to work involved cycle, train and foot. The archetypal commuter. I had to be out of the door by ten minutes to seven to bike up the lane, down the village bottom end, under the two railway bridges leading to Tibshelf up the gravely Station Road, along the Chicken

Run to Tibshelf Station a total distance of about three miles. It was great on fine mornings in the summer but horrible in rain and during most of the winter because apart from the bit in the village itself, the route was not made up and the lane in particular was full of potholes and its due share of mud. Cycle clobber including galoshes was essential much of the time. The train left at 7.20 and arrived at 8.00. I never once missed it but only through murderous dashes into the station compound at times.

The official designation as slow did not relate so much to the actual speed of the train as the fact that it was scheduled to stop at all the stations on the fifteen-mile route. Being steam powered, acceleration from a standing start was sedate and given that stops were made at Kirkby Bentinck, Annesley Central, Hucknall, Bulwell and New Basford before actually passing through a station called Carrington, the journey after the initial novelty was somewhat tortuous. Eventually of course this wonderful little commuter line providing an excellent and economically productive service to the local Nottinghamshire and Derbyshire villages would be scrapped under the Einsteinly-brilliant Beeching Plan.

After this act of lawful vandalism the travellers who all worked in Nottingham City would buy cars and make their separate way and after which under an equally brilliant plan a new commuter line would be opened many years later in a failed attempt to reduce city congestion from cars and to further the economic prosperity of the East Midlands towns. This new service took a slightly different route that cut out the Derbyshire villages since the original line that was part of the Great Central Line into London Marylebone had been dug up.

Of course this destruction had its compensations in that the great gaping hole left by the closure of Nottingham Victoria Station, that had been blasted out of solid rock by the Victorians, was to be filled by the monolithic Victoria

Shopping Centre specifically intended to bring hoards of unproductive shoppers into the City as opposed to economic creators. There might have been some sense in leaving the shops in the villages and then taking the brain-workers into town by developing the well-conceived Victorian-created service routes. To compound this fantastical testament to integrated transport and town planning, Nottingham City Centre has now been dug up at heaven knows what cost and consequential damage to productivity in order to lay tracks for trams. Less than fifty years ago, there was a good working system throughout the city of virtually silent and electrically driven trolley buses. It is, however, all progress don't you know. Well, if not exactly progress, it all makes work.

It probably took about a year before my intense shyness and lack of contact with real-world adults loosened sufficiently to allow for any sort of conversation with the, by then, regular group of men travelling from Tibshelf to Nottingham every morning. A group of card-players started to shepherd me into their regular compartment. I, the solitary young man traveller with his wooden carry-case for his lunch and nothing else. A case made especially for the purpose by uncle Ernie in his joinery workshop in Sherwood Street. Years before he made a scooter each for me and my sister, the best Christmas present I could ever remember. What was a man with those skills doing working on a road-sweeping gang?

Uncle Ernie was the husband of my mum's eldest sister and one of my egg delivery customers. A survivor of the Middle East Campaign in Egypt and then the push from Sicily up Italy to finally rest in Greece, he often told me of his admiration through his war experiences of the Aussies and his hatred of the Greeks. I never knew why on either count but it seemed particularly cruel that a man who had been through so much ended up with so little leisure: the joinery workshop, the horse betting, the walk down the road to the working men's club for a pint on Saturday night. Once aunt Annie died he lost heart and ended up falling onto his own oven top. Poor old aunt Annie and uncle Ernie, the only couple to go out with us in the pony and trap when he would catch the horse droppings in a little bucket for his vegetable patch. A lost world.

Napping on a train

The train carriages had no corridors. Each was a private little world and the peace of which was disturbed only by the arrival at a station and the prospect, much detested, of someone having the effrontery to open the door and enter. These doors were the slam type that still exist today in certain financially frozen backwaters of the Southern Region of British Rail (where did the "Ways" go, perhaps the new name was always intended to focus attention on the stationary hardware and away from the actual moving parts?). The overhead luggage holders were of the string-net type and pictures were real scenes or sea-side town destination advertisements Visit Torquay for the English Riviera and hung in proper frames.

The card game was nap and the four played for money. I was incredibly impressed with the system of scoring. The stakes were 1d for 3 tricks, 2d for 4 tricks and 3d for 5 tricks or nap. The keeping tabs was always done by Brian and consisted of pluses and minuses against each named player and on a pad brought for the purpose. It followed that reading across any line of numbers produced zero pence, that is to say it balanced. This was to be a foretaste of dreads to come. It worked such that if for example a winning call was "4 without" thus beating "4 with" when no "5" was called, a win would net the caller 6d and each of the three losers would be reduced by 2d from their cumulative score to date. Whilst it is often said that in life over many issues and over time things even themselves out, this was certainly not so with this little group of gamblers. At a settlement at the end of the Friday evening journey back from Nottingham, it always seemed that Brian was a recipient, that Joe might be if he had had a lucky week but the other two were payers. I often marvelled at this and wondered if there was some deep lesson to be learned since the cards were meticulously shuffled after each hand and, in the course of a week, many such hands were played. It would be great to believe that some blinding insight so detected the cause of these consistent wins by Brian as to ensure for myself a financially successful future *by chance*. However, this was not to be the case.

I developed a sneaking admiration for Brian due to his laid-back and nonchalant if belligerent air. When not scoring, playing and winning at nap, he compiled the Daily Telegraph cryptic crossword with apparently no more effort than it took to read the clues. The only thing I ever knew about him was that he lived on the High Street in Tibshelf was a civil servant and worked at the Department of Labour situated on the junction of Castle Boulevard and Wilford Road. I knew this because it was on my walking route to Middle Furlong Road and we often walked together.

Joe was older than the others and was a manager at a motor dealership also on Castle Boulevard. He was extremely kind to me and after about two years would pick me up on Saturday mornings in his Morris Minor and bring me back in the early afternoon. This saved a lot of time because there was no suitably timed train on Saturday and my only option had been to use the Erewash line to Westhouses and this meant not getting home until after three pm.

Working Saturday mornings was a standard part of the week and I so envied Brian and Tom who didn't have to in their jobs. Tom was always very smartly dressed and it was through him that I started to wear a top-pocket handkerchief, a habit to last a lifetime. He worked for Old's Discount on High Pavement in a position I vaguely thought to be a financial city one although I never understood what he did. He cycled from Morton each morning which was much further to the station than anyone else. During my third year of commuting, he took a holiday in Norway. On his return he talked longingly of the beauty of the Fiords and of the freedom from the rat race. A little later he packed everything in to travel the world and I never saw him again. The fourth member of the card school was a chirpy gum-chewing chap whose name escapes me and I never knew what his job was. Strange how some people leave an indelible impression and others do not.

The office that I was about to start work in was attached to the engine sheds of the London Midland Region. They were about one mile down line to London from the main Midland Station and across the centre of Nottingham City from Victoria Station. As such it was a long walk and passing en-route the third Nottingham station known as London Road that served the East to West traffic. Leaving the office at five-thirty to catch the six ten to arrive back at Tibshelf at seven and home by seven-thirty, made for long days and coupled with the Saturday mornings, made for a long week. Hearing my dad rolling the milk churns up the yard outside my bedroom window early on a Sunday morning gave a first taste of all days merging into one.

The office itself would not be recognised as one today. It consisted of what might be thought of as a church hall with fixed desks attached to all four walls. These desks had steeply sloping lids with a ridge along the top for pens and an inkwell still in use. They were high off the ground so the seating consisted of high padded stools. The only floor mounted conventional desk was located at one end of the room, was huge and accommodated three people, the chief clerk, the assistant chief clerk and a female secretary. The only private office was located off this main room close to where the chief clerk sat. This housed the superintendent. He was the boss of the whole Motive Power Department and was very important. Though rarely seen, he wore a railway issue suit and overcoat and like my uncle Edmund had a bowler hat. The chief clerk, Mr Jennings, who had interviewed me spent much of each day dashing back and forth into this private office of the superintendent. I never knew why and indeed never knew what either of them actually did.

From the earliest days the role of the assistant chief clerk was obvious. He supervised all of us with a close intensity. He had a specific job of paying the staff each fortnight in cash in a brown paper envelope. My initial fortnightly pay before tax and National Insurance was £7-2s-8d. His peculiar sense of humour came into its own on the payday immediately following my successful passing of six months probation. This event, it seems, triggered my compulsory entry into the Railway Superannuation Scheme and as such, six months back contributions. Instead of giving out my pay packet as normal, he felt in his back pocket and handed me three coins. Later he substituted these for a packet containing three shillings.

He was a particularly bright man and very good with figures. He had a habit of jerking his head back when walking across the office under time pressure and when thinking hard. His name was Claude Driver and it was rumoured that he had a niece named Betty who was on the stage. This lady is still acting and is known to the nation as Betty Turpin in Coronation Street.

The goings on at or around the top desk was my introduction to office gossip. The secretary to the chief clerk was a fine energetic woman in her prime. She wore loose frocks, had flowing hair and wore the highest of high heels to noisily show everything off to its full potential whilst tripping between the desk, the chief clerk himself and the superintendent's office. She rarely ventured into the vastness of the open office itself. It was said amongst the staff that she enjoyed special privileges from her exalted position and that there must be many secret goings on because of the intense whispering that went on in this distant corner. Furthermore, it seems she was having a relationship with a certain member of the general staff, that one that sits down there close to them. As a result, he also enjoyed special privileges by being part of the elite group. Apparently they slipped away at lunchtime together. This outsider was never part of any group staff discussion and his actions had to be viewed with great suspicion. Actually he seemed a pleasant chap and always treated me with great kindness, which just shows that one never can tell.

A new experience for me was the female sounds in a lavatory. Back home, going to the lav was a solitary affair and even at this time consisted of an earth closet in a separate brick building across the stackyard. Here however and although still housed in a separate building across a yard, it was at least a modern-type water flush closet. There was just one lavatory for all the male staff and this was kept permanently locked in order to keep the non-office employees out. The key hung next to the outside door on a string attached to a large wooden block. It followed that if the block was present, the lavatory was free. Otherwise there was no option but to wait and if the occupier happened to be a particular person, this could be a long wait because on certain mornings that person was known to be engaged in the serious business of picking winners ahead of slipping out later to the bookies.

When I first arrived I could have been forgiven for thinking that having plucked up the courage to grasp the elusive key, the lavatory would be as solitary and therefore as private as had been the case at home. It was therefore a massive shock when on about day three, the unmistakable sound of the high heels came clip-clopping ever closer to my little room. With a sound like bedlam a key turned in a lock and a door opened and slammed shut. It was so close it might well have been exactly where I sat. But then the sound as if our farm horse daisy had peed directly onto a concrete floor came as fast as it was noisy. In an instant it was over and the door re-slammed and was locked and the clip-clopping gave away the hasty departure. I was mortified. Only later was I to learn that this event was a standing joke amongst my colleagues. She had a reputation for the most and the fastest in the West. It could be avoided only by the convergence of finding not merely that the male key was available but also that the female had gone into the superintendent's room or else was in deep whispering confabulation with the chief clerk. A tricky business.

CHAPTER FOUR
Colonel Redmond and campanology

Fire Raisers and Fire Droppers, wage calculations and pay day. Sunday rosters, rest days, privilege tickets plus free passes. Of selling fags and mileage bonuses, 8 & 9 freights. Spliced bell-ringing – methods and peals. The gathering storm of Hollerith punch cards and the man with the bulging eyes.

The reason for a vacancy was the promotion of the previous junior clerk to the Grade 4 designated post of mileage clerk. Patel, a very polite and well spoken young man whose parents were Indian, had two weeks to teach me the ropes. The main aspect of the junior position was checking in and out the manual work force. This consisted of being handed literally a metal check or disc through my office window flap as men come on and went off duty. Each check had a number and it was important to put a face and therefore name to that number so that the time attendance records were accurate and there were no fiddles going on. The times, counted back to the last minute from the huge clock on the office wall, were entered onto a large weekly sheet against the name of the correct person. This included the mid-day break but not the tea breaks. At first the recognition part was difficult not only because there were hundreds of men involved but also some came to the window almost pitch black from their work. A few were pitch black because they were black, the first I had even seen and I formed a view that their race was a far happier one than ours. To a man they always laughed and joked and one in particular always had a banter with me. This was in stark contrast to certain of the others who obviously lived in permanent purgatory. There was also the smart Alec flashing past the window and throwing in a disk with a speed to match any magician. Eventually though and by compartmentalising the groups by their job titles, it became second nature to recognise the men and to know who had deposited more than one disc in a further attempted slight of hand. Some of the job titles were fascinating. There were, amongst others, Fire Raisers (who built the fires to get the engines into steam), Fire Droppers (who put the fires out and got the boilers ready to be worked upon), Plate Layers, Boilermakers and Shunters.

Each day the sheets of the previous working day were extended to produce for each worker the total clock hours taking into account the rules for lateness and leaving early. These figures were transferred to a time card and the sheets and cards passed to a more senior person for checking. By the Tuesday of a week every person in the office had a responsibility for totalling and pricing a batch of time cards. It worked by seniority so that as the sole junior clerk, I would have relatively few cards and only for those workers who tended to have a set week on fairly low rates of pay. The easy pick. On the other hand, the four most senior Grade 3 men each had a large batch that included the most complicated employment terms. These complications arose because for the senior footplate men, that is the drivers and firemen whose time details came not from my checking in but from the foremen working next door, the rate for a standard week was pretty much academic. It took a while for me to realise that this work was the real rationale for the existence of the whole office. Footplate men worked around the clock and seven days a week. There was time and a quarter, time and a half, double time and in the most extreme case of working on a rostered rest day that happened to fall on a Bank Holiday three-fold time.

In addition to the calculations to produce total clock hours for pay purposes, drivers were paid mileage bonuses. In the case of daily excursion to a seaside town there was a condition known as short rest under which if the driver spent no more than a given number of hours at the destination, his time was counted as right through from clocking on to clocking off at the depot. Because there were time allowances for the act of clocking itself and for getting from the depot to the mainline station to start work, all this made for a very long clock day. It could for example be from six am to ten pm and since most of these special excursions were on a Sunday, then this was all double time. These factors made the basic rate of £11-2s-6d a week for a top driver meaningless in terms of actual earnings and as a result put much pressure on the seniors in the office. (This basic rate made me realise how high were the aspirations of my aunt Madge when presenting the Children's Guide to Knowledge when I was aged 10 "one day you will be on £10 per week, mark my words.")

So complex were the calculations for the top drivers and firemen and so large the resultant pay that the procedure demanded that every time card once extended into monetary value had to be checked and initialled by a colleague of equal or senior rank. That is why on days building up to payday the assistant chief clerk could often be seen dashing around like a headless chicken grabbing cards fully extended for checking and urging greater speed of extension. When all the cards were complete and priced to gross pay per employee, they were rushed to the pay-office in Derby to be put into gross to net pay terms by machine. The master net pay sheet with individual packets and deduction details per employee were returned on the Friday morning for actual cash payment and with the actual money pre-calculated into the correct denominations of £5, £1,10s notes and coinage. Then the fun really started.

Each Friday morning, pay day, three teams of two men each had to be installed in the pay-office that was located in a separate brick building within the main engine sheds. At nine o'clock the security van arrived with the cash together with the assistant chief clerk who signed for each of the three bags of cash pre-prepared from the three-way split payroll sheets. Each batch of money with the accompanying sheet was handed to the senior in each team for counter-signing. This done, the assistant chief clerk and the security men left, locking we six in the room. Then the race was on. The structure was that two of the teams consisting of senior staff from the office and who were very experienced in the job, took two large payrolls whilst the third team took a smaller payroll. This was deliberate as a form of training for the junior in team three. After two weeks of observation and some practice, I was the junior in team three. It was fortunate that the boss of this team was the recognised fastest and most accurate of everyone and in my case he needed to be. The ability to count out notes and coins was vital but a skill soon learned. The determining quality however was dexterity and here I was found wanting. All fingers and thumbs was an expression that springs to mind.

The procedure was that member one of each team found the name of the employee on the pay sheet and noted the total net pay. Then to the nearest £5 grabbed such a note from his team's pile of money, next the nearest £1's and so on until the pay was counted out. He then passed the pay packet, that was already embossed with this net pay and name and payroll number of the recipient, to the senior of the team. His job was to duplicate the procedure and if satisfied stuff the pay packet making sure the flap was not sealed down. Since there were many hundred employees and a decided air of competition in the room, this Friday morning job had a good deal of stress attached to it and heightened by two factors. First, there was a twelve noon deadline when the pay-office officially opened for the collection of wages and secondly if the money did not work out there was no second chance saloon.

Money failed to work out if either some was left over at the end or there was not enough to make up the last pay figure. Either was equally serious. The two senior teams were very slick and always appeared to balance first time and the job would be over by about eleven o'clock. Because the idea was to get finished just as the pay-office opened for business, these four would disappear once completed. I sometimes suspected a bit of trickery, it all seemed too good to be true. This may have been borne out by the occasional excitement directed anytime after noon at Herbert Dale. Herbert was a bit older and more senior than the other staff, aside from the top desk. He did higher grade work the purpose of which always eluded me except it was something to do with traffic and freight statistics. Not however on a Friday afternoon because he was the official cashier and therefore payer-out of earnings.

Either instantly on ripping open a packet or very soon afterwards there would sometimes be a rumpus in the works. The person involved and the details very soon penetrated the office "old Sid is down a quid" or similar expression would ring out. Herbert had to sort this out but without recourse to those involved in the morning's work since by definition they had not been allowed to leave the pay office until the balance had been struck and therefore everything had been left as perfect. How Herbert did the sorting out was a constant puzzle to me. He was such a quiet cultured man and the outrage of certain workers had to be seen to be believed. I think he must have had some high-level latitude to settle and it was not unknown for "that bloody machine in Derby" to be blamed.

I was never slick. My fingers could not quite build up the speed needed to finish an hour early. The best Roy and I could hope for was to finish about thirty minutes early and, halleluiah, to balance first time. Often though there would be a 10s note left over or short and we would have to re-check every packet - which was why they were all left unsealed until the end. I can honestly say that we always found the error eventually and never once did he dig into his personal money or pocket anything. On several occasions we got perilously close to the noon deadline and might still be sealing packets with the British Railways wet sponge as Herbert approached with his slow steady walk across the yard. Once when we had had a stupendously successful morning and actually finished just after eleven o'clock, Roy said "as a reward I'll let you into a little secret". Instead of going back to the office he led me through one of the main engine sheds and up the side of the line onto Wilford Road. Having crossed the road we entered a building opposite went up the stairs and into a huge smoke-filled room. At one of the snooker tables were our four pay-packet-filling colleagues. From that day on, I was accepted as "one of us lads".

Just as the terms and conditions attached to the footplate men were structured such that the top few could earn substantially more than the union negotiated basic pay, so the threesome of Ted, Dennis and Phil had managed to work the system to the same end. It took me a long time to discover this and even then only due to the kinship that was to develop between myself and Herbert. It transpired that these three received a higher rate for their work than the official Grade 3 due to recognition, albeit on a temporary basis, of increased responsibility. In addition, they were collectively doing the work of four members of the office establishment and to achieve this meant coming in one hour earlier than the official start time each morning and staying one hour later. Also, they worked through their lunch hour break. This constituted higher-grade overtime. Also, when one of the three was on holiday, rather than draft someone else in, they had agreed to cover this work too and claim the extra hours. This was an exclusive arrangement and did not extend to Roy, or the friend of the secretary or indeed anyone else. How it had started and was allowed to continue, I never knew.

Aside from the common work of time sheet compilation and pay packet filling, each member of the office had a very specific job. Ted, for instance, did Sunday rostering. This was an extremely important subject for the more senior footplate men since it was the source of high earnings. To boost the earnings from long days and from high mileage bonuses it was of the essence to work a Sunday because at a minimum it meant double time and should this particular Sunday fall on a rest day then triple time came into play. Permutations of choice of driver and fireman for Sunday rostering were endless as Ted explained to me one day. There were two main determinants. One was whether the driver was passed to take a particular route and the second was the system of links. One might think as an ignorant outsider that once the skill of actually driving a steam train had been mastered and especially having undergone the learning curve from being a fireman and then a passed fireman, such trains could be taken anywhere on the rail system. This was not so.

A driver had to learn a route and this involved doubling up with an already passed driver and on several occasions building up to being tested on the particular route for real by the likes of my uncle Edmund, the inspection officer. Only on being passed could that driver take charge of a train on a route. Thus this was the first qualifying factor for selection for a lucrative Sunday job.

Learning a route involved knowing where all the signals were located, where the gradients and bends were and their magnitude, understanding the station and platform features and most importantly the prevailing speed restrictions. Every driver once passed had, before every journey, to sign on with a depot foreman and receive that day's printed instructions for the route. These gave all the latest speed restrictions as dictated by engineering works or by any number of special factors. One such factor that always caused mayhem in the foremen's office - that room linked to ours that buzzed with highly charged male activity and choice words - was the passing through the rail network of a royal train since clear passage for the privileged meant disruption for the masses. Information on engineering and other works such as the seismological train or the snow plough train emanated from the central traffic department located in Derby. The dissemination of such routine information and its interpretation into operational instructions was a key job of the more senior staff in the office.

The second qualifier for Sunday working, as with all work allocations, was the link into which a driver was placed. Links were the ultimate arbiter of driver selection because they reflected seniority. Only the most senior men were in link 1. Such drivers would have been in post the longest time, would be passed for the most routes and certainly the main line to London and most vitally would not have failed the crucial and mandatory periodical medical including as it did the colour vision test. Link 1 drivers were the elite and made the most money. At the other end of the scale were link 4 drivers who were reduced to shunting engines around in the marshalling yards or taking freight trains on slow local journeys.

It followed from these two criteria that Ted was often the fulcrum of angry scenes from a driver stamping through the office to his stool demanding restitution for not being allocated a forthcoming juicy Sunday job. Certain drivers got extremely excited and because Ted's desk was towards the centre of the long wall of the office, it was impossible to work whilst explanations were offered. Perhaps it was due to Ted's tall, rather stern and ex-RAF moustached appearance but I never once witnessed a decision being changed or intervention from the top desk. Either he was exceptionally good at his job or else the ultimate authority of his office was always going to prevail. I never knew.

Rest days were another high-earning minefield. A colleague of Ted and sitting next to him was Dennis and one of his jobs was to work out and publish weekly the rest-day roster. He too had his confrontational moments with certain members of the footplate staff. This was because a driver or fireman asked to work his rest day was in for double money and if that day happened to fall at the weekend or on a bank holiday, then triple time was due. Whilst rest days were quite normal and as such scheduled into the routine matching of men to work, the limitations were severe due to sickness, holidays, absence without leave and the required qualification of being passed for the route and being in the right link. Consequently, and as with Sunday working, a fair deal of judgement went into the choice of crews asked to work on their rest day.

It occurred to me that Dennis was not quite in Ted's league in handling a large and powerfully irate engine driver who had "just been done out of working my rest day". Several times there were red-faced emotional explosions centred on Dennis's area and a small group might gather round to calm things down. Such events presented a baptism of fire for someone as young and innocent as me who had never even heard my parents swear or argue or get particularly emotional about anything to do with work. And here we had two fully-grown men threatening to beat the living daylights out of each other. Of course, much later in my working life there would be confrontations infinitely more deadly if more subtle.

There was a third area of malcontent between the

outside workers and a member of the office. We lads were blessed with a second lady member. Lillian was small, a bit on the plump side and, I started to think, not best suited to her specialisation. Lillian was queen of free passes and privilege tickets (P T's). Every employee was entitled to concessionary travel on the railways. The allowance was five free tickets per year and of these three could be, but did not have to be, foreign. Foreign meant outside the region of employment. Working for the London Midland Region therefore entitled the employee, for example, to go to London five times a year should they choose, absolutely free. Or, say, three times and perhaps to the South coast twice - being partly on the network of a region other than the home region.

Once the free passes had run out, any number of P T's could be obtained and these facilitated much reduced train fares. One would have thought that this valuable fringe benefit would have been a constant source of joy and happiness to all especially since for married employees, it covered the whole family. However, this did not prove to be universally the case. A seemingly endless procession of workers of all types from the most elite driver to the humblest yard labourer sought out Lillian's desk to challenge her records.

Herbert with his pay-packets and Ted and Dennis with their Sundays and rest days had their bad confrontational times but at least they were fully fledged men of some senior stature. Poor little Lillian had no such natural armour. Time and again she must have entered the wrong date or the wrong destination because there should always have been one free pass left. But Lillian's box-card system never lied and there before their very eyes was the evidence in bright blue ink of the passes issued previously. But then, what about the cancellation, what about the late decision to change the destination, what about her errors?

Poor Lillian. And when she cried her nearest colleague

Arnold would climb down from his high stool and walk over and put his arms round her plump shoulders and tell the offending employee with all the gruffness he could muster to "bugger off". Barbara the important secretary would take her out to the ladies to get over it. I began to wonder if, from the employer perspective, these benefits were really achieving anything. If there was any gratitude from the employee, then I never saw it and if everyone gets the same, can there only be disgruntlement by sort of definition? After all, where is the exceptional advantage? Can there only be the chance of losing out? The chance of being diddled? I resolved to tuck this thought away. It might come in useful later.

During all my three-and-a-half-years in that office, I never discovered what Arnold actually did. What I do remember with great affection was his nickname, which was disparagingly derived from a combination of his squatty frame and his surname of Sidebotham. I also remember his sideline. In this age of smoke and smoking, Arnold was a champion of the briar pipe but the little package that it became my custom to pick up from the specialist smokers' shop on Wheeler Gate did not consist solely of pipe tobacco. Almost everyone in the office smoked cigarettes and it was common to run out, especially in the afternoon and especially on urgent need of the key. The closest desk to the key belonged to Arnold. The little brown paper package contained an assortment of the most popular brands of fags. Arnold didn't lend out fags or provide a charitable service. He sold them individually and at a considerable mark-up. Everyone knew he was on to a nice little earner but when one needs a fag, one needs a fag and if nothing else his supply never faulted. Arnold was hated but happy. My first encounter with a true entrepreneur.

After about six months I was promoted. It owed nothing to my being the world's or London Midland Region's finest junior clerk. It appeared that Patel was leaving to pursue his career in the retail sector or more specifically as he explained to me to work in a shop in the middle of the city that sold wall-paper. As I was to deduce later, this decidedly downward move was caused partly by the mass of statistical data that had to be memorised to make a reasonable fist of the mileage clerk job but mainly by the trauma of playing second fiddle to the head of the two-man section. My first real clerical position placed me at the bottom of the Grade 4 salary scale and represented quite an increase in pay. I was over the moon with the letter from the chief clerk announcing my new status and terms but it did not seem to impress my dad greatly. Still, mum increased my pocket money.

The mileage section turned out to be all to do with the determination of bonuses earned by the footplate staff. Mileage bonus was staged according to the total mileage covered in each week. Not that my new position involved the actual calculation of money but just the mileages. As with the hours aspect of pay, details per man were fed to the offices in Derby for conversion into money and the subsequent payroll. The routine was quaint. In the adjoining forman's office was a sliding window through which was pushed the daily journey sheet of each driver and fireman after it had been approved with the initials of the foreman on duty at the end of each shift. On our side of the wall was a large wooden box into which these sheets dropped. As a result, this box was about half full each morning and positively packed on a Monday morning. The task was to convert the journeys into mileages and tot up each stage to give the shift total.

There was no difference between the work of the junior and senior positions aside from the quantity of sheets that could be processed. This in turn depended upon knowledge and memory and the ability to graft. In essence it was no different from a factory production line with the speed of the belt self-determined by these factors. The fact was though that a new hand had no knowledge. Mileages from one point to another had to be looked up on a series of cards that had been written out over the years by previous incumbents of the position. The longer this research took, the slower the processing and the larger the pile of uncleared sheets.

The same deadline as applied to time for payroll input applied to mileages. Missed input to Derby would inevitably lead to held-over bonuses and when this had occurred in the past, angry drivers had stormed in seeking the blood of the mileage section. Whilst it would take time for me to learn the journey mileages, there was a limit to how long I could be carried on the section. As far as Patel was concerned, the limit had been passed and Colonel John Redmond had been forced to recommend a change. The colonel was a fairly fearsome and self-contained character. Short, bald and with heavy rimmed spectacles, he did not mix with the others and chose to keep himself to himself. He had no truck with the office gossip and did his job diligently and efficiently. His good army pension added to his independence. Also, he was the only one in the entire office who came to work by car.

Being terrified of failing and not having met anyone remotely like my new boss before, there was no way the colonel would be displeased with my work effort. My head was down over those sheets and the mileage cards from the minute I got there until I left. The effect of this was probably exaggerated by the fact that the colonel was doing no overtime or covering other positions or higher-grade work and so did the bare minimum hours. In fact rather less. He walked in just a little late and usually left just a little early.

My endeavour coupled to a good memory for numbers paid off. Less and less was there a need to refer to him for route details from a start to a finish journey and more and more I learned the routes common to each link. Soon, only the complicated Sunday specials presented any problem and I soon discovered that they did for the colonel too. So it was that we started to get on well together and to the point that sometimes by mid-afternoon we engaged in a little game. Once we were straight up meaning there were no sheets waiting to be done we would open our side of the box and take turns to surprise the next unsuspecting pusher-through of his sheet by whipping it out of his hand from the tip first exposed to us. We would then revel or groan depending on the simplicity or complexity of the sheet thus obtained.

I must have pleased the colonel really because he started to take me in his car across Nottingham to my station after work and on his way home. It was on these journeys in his Ford Popular that I learned just how awful every other single driver was and how proficient he was. It must have come from his army training but the anger and invective from inside that little car had to be seen and heard to be believed.

Actually, the mileages and routes were interesting in themselves. I began to like my job. The crack train in the week from Nottingham to London St Pancras left on time every morning at precisely 8.04 am and took two hours and four minutes. This was the prestigious route and taken by only a link 1 crew. It ran via Leicester round the trent loop - where the Derby trains joined the track - and had a total mileage of 127. This consisted of 28 to Leicester, and in 28 minutes, and 99 forward to London. Unlike today however, this was not the sole route to London. Trains were scheduled via Melton Mowbray also on track long since abandoned except in places for local journey specials on cute steam trains. This route was shorter at 123 miles.

At the other end of the spectrum were the many freight trains and especially carrying coal. The places themselves were unknown to me except as specific mileages between each and in total. There is a touch of irony in that many of these places becoming known to me intimately years later whilst the mining industry being served would be wholly eradicated. Go North East to Calverton, Farnsfield and Bilsthorpe or North West to Hucknall, Linby and Papplewick. These coal pits fuelled the power stations on the Trent and Soar that in turn fed the East Midlands with electricity and served the National Grid, though it would take a job move to appreciate this.

I started to appreciate the steam engines that hauled these great loads and sometimes when the colonel and I were straight up I wandered through the massive motive power sheds to get close to these fantastic examples of British engineering. I loved the little 0-4-2 and 4-2-2's and started to identify for myself the engine that pulled the trains along the track just one field away from our top field on the farm. This was the little branch line taking coal from the pits at Teversal and Pleasley down to the main Erewash line at its junction at Westhouses and onto who knows where.

Down was the operative word because rail track is supposed to be as near flat as possible and hence the steep embankments and tunnels and viaducts. The constructors of this branch line either forgot this or more likely decided its worth was so little as not to justify the spend. Consequently, when the full load reached a point opposite our field, the crew had to stop the train, alight and walk from wagon to wagon applying a brake to each by hand. There was still a driver, a fireman and a guardsman but their leisurely stroll along the length of the train and the overall journey time schedule was a million miles removed from the 8.04. It taught me a powerful lesson for the future. Never reckon that people with the same job title or professional label, even having an identical start to their career, are the same. The top of link 1 and the bottom of link 4 exist everywhere.

If the little engines were lovable, the giant 8 and 9

freights were positively awesome. Their magnificence was not dented by the quietness and stillness of being at rest in the great engine sheds. Nor was their dignity impugned by the ant-like men in boiler suits with strange sounding trade names who crawled over and inside them. Years later when the last working beasts in the UK had long since taken a dead-end journey to the breakers yard, I was literally reduced to tears when my taxi entering Cochin in Southern India came to a shuddering stop to allow an 8 freight to pass over the level crossing hauling its gargantuan load of coal. What the British introduced, the ex-colonials had had the sense to retain.

Of all the staff in the office, two stick in my memory most. Ted because of the lunch time horseplay when he was to demonstrate to the others and on me some of his RAF close-combat fighting skills. He had some technique, was much taller than me and had secured a strange sort of grip but he was a chain-smoker and perhaps unaware that I had mucked-out the cows for years and was used to heaving sacks of corn and potatoes. Anyway, I only hit him once in the lower lumbar region. He sank slowly to the floor and rested. Ted did not do his overtime that day and in fact left slightly early. He was off for six weeks.

The other was Herbert because he reminded me of uncle Harold with his quiet authoritative manner and because in the afternoons, not Fridays, he had the ability to go soundly to sleep whilst sitting bolt upright at his desk over the statistical returns that I never understood. But more importantly because one afternoon overlaying his vital returns I spotted a diary. Not the main body holding the days but the rear section containing complex grids with zigzag lines in blue ink. To most they would remain a mystery and in the office were no doubt thought of as useful references for his scientific work. To me however they were recognised instantly as diagrammatical representations of bell-ringing methods.

Some months before and having cycled to Matlock on a Sunday afternoon with my best friend John Smithson there was panic stations to get back fast. It seems he had to be at Old Blackwell church by a quarter to six to ring the bells. This was news to me but apparently for the past few weeks he had been receiving lessons from his dad and was in the team ringing the treble.

We walked not into the main entrance of St Werburgh's church but in the side to the vestry, turned sharp left and having opened a small wooden door climbed the circular stone steps until opposite was a door with a handle at its foot. The technique was to step onto the opposite stone ledge and pull up the door and whilst holding it aloft, step inside. The room inside was a revelation to me and I entered a new world. There were five men with coats off and sleeves rolled up and six ropes with thick brightly coloured middles sections draped round pegs in a circle but climbing up through their own little hole cut neatly in the ceiling. This was the holy grail, the bell-ringing chamber, and we were late.

John took off his coat, rolled up his sleeves and walked sheepishly to the bell rope on the far side of the chamber. The rope was untied from its peg and its end held in the left hand along with a few loops of loose rope. The right hand held the woollen middle section. Slowly the chatter stopped and five men did the same with their appointed bell rope. I cowered in the background and watched. John tugged the centre section of his rope downwards and the others followed in rotation in a clockwise direction. Immediately the bells started to clang, 1,2,3,4,5,6 from the highest to the lowest note and repeat and repeat. After each round the middle section moved higher and higher until almost touching the ceiling with all the spare rope taken up. After a few rounds of this extreme length, John's dad shouted "stand next sally" and from 1 to 6 the middle section or sally was slowly eased to rest were it had started.

Awestruck was not in it. Mesmerised would be a better description of how I felt. That Sunday evening's session was not the best advertisement for the art of change-bell ringing. John had not yet got full control of the bell or the striking art of the treble and there were numerous clashes of bells and consequential yells from Arthur, John's dad and bell-ringing captain, attempting to get others back into the correct sequence. Rather than putting me off, this cauldron of human effort somehow drew me in. It looked physically and mentally hard and when Arthur asked if I would like to see the actual bells before the next mid-week practice, the bell-ringing die was cast.

Blackwell church has six bells with the largest, the tenor, weighing 7cwts,2qrs and having a diameter of thirty-four and a half inches and tuned to note A. It is believed that originally the tower had just three bells and the second bears the mark of the Nottingham founder Henry Oldfield with the legend "Jesus be our Spede, 1587". These facts are set out in an excellent little book written and compiled by Glyn Holdgate and published in 1999 "Ting Tangs, Trebles and Tenors". It records that in 1901 two further bells were added as cast by John Taylor at the Loughborough foundry and that of the reconstituted five bells, the "Oldfield" bell became the fifth.

Although completely ignorant of this history at the time, this fifth bell was to become mine for a five-year period until 1964. The first full peal on the five bells was achieved in 1928. In that same year, two young men who would become very special to Blackwell church rang their first peal on these bells. One was the Arthur now inviting me to "take a look at the bells" and the other was Wilf Riley who quite co-incidentally was my dad's nearest neighbour. Wilf and his family lived in a bungalow in an adjoining field across from our *back field* and from where, apart from his full-time job in the mine, he ran a small but flourishing market garden business. He was the proud owner of a

Javelin motor car the likes of which I had never seen before or since. These same two men also rang a peal to celebrate a lifetime as bell-ringers. It was achieved on the fiftieth anniversary of their first peal. A truly fantastic feat.

One of the very last peals to be rung at St Werburgh's, Old Blackwell on the five bells before the augmentation to a full six, took place on 15th August 1945 and was one of only a handful of peals of the full 5,040 changes in the country to take place actually on V.J.Day to celebrate victory in the Far East and the end of hostilities. Of the team that day, three were ringing in that chamber as I watched fourteen years later. Each man proved to be quite remarkable and collectively they taught me one very important lesson that would stand me in good stead throughout my later career. Never underestimate the mental capacity of a seemingly humble person. Absence of opportunity and even ambition is no guide to ability.

Arthur had been elected tower captain at the age of 21. He had lost half of his right arm in an accident towards the end of the war. He was a shunter of freight wagons in the railway sidings at Westhouses both before and after this accident. He re-mastered the art of bell-ringing using his good arm and hand and the stump of his amputated arm. He also looked after the tower including tending to the bells and repairing the stays and wound up the clock for a total period of 55 years. If ever there was a true Knight of the Realm, it was Arthur Smithson.

The second longevity medal should have gone to Albert Wheeler who rang the tenor and heaviest bell. Back in 1945 he was undertaking his first peal in that valedictory ring and was the backbone strong man. He was a train driver and in my first year of work a solid respect for this skill had been growing. He was an excellent ringer and his striking skill on the tenor was such that he was an obvious challenger to Arthur who because of his handicap could only operate on the No2 or No3 bell.

However, despite some needle between the two men, he was never a serious contender for tower captain because Arthur's rope sight was far superior. Albert was a widower and drove to church in a Baby Austin car often accompanied by a lady friend who was later to become his second wife. He was a dedicated pipe smoker and in an era when whether it was safe to fake (draw into the lungs) cigarette smoke was already being debated, Albert took deep lung draughts of pipe smoke that made his eyes almost pop from his head. Not that that did any apparent harm. He was over 90 when he died.

The third man was not Harry Lime but Billy Steele. It had not been Billy's first peal in 1945 and he remained a faithful member of what was to become a very sophisticated and technically proficient team. He came from solid farming stock was small in stature and always immaculately dressed in collar and tie. A true gentleman in the old fashioned sense and marvellous to get to know and to talk to.

Flashing down Cragg Lane on my bike the following Wednesday evening having barely had time to gulp down my meal after cycling from the train station, I passed Arthur peddling his old sit-up-and-beg model and slowed down to ride together to the lich gate. He led the way up the stone steps of the tower but passed the door to the ringing chamber until after a further revolution we stepped onto a ledge and through a door into a small room the principal feature of which was a large glass case. Arthur opened the case with his key and from a ledge pulled out a large handle and inserted it into its housing.

Without a word he started his twice-weekly job of winding up the church clock. For a one-handed man this was no mean accomplishment since the mechanism was heavy and the drop deep. I was innocently amazed. It had never occurred to me that church clocks had to be hand-wound. That this was happening as an act of casual routine by such a disabled man and had been for many years without help arose in me a sense of immediate admiration. It proved however to be small fry compared to what would follow. Having re-locked the mechanism we left the clock chamber and walked higher up the stone steps that led to the bells themselves. Their size seen at this close proximity was huge as they hung dormant each in its wooden cage lined up in two rows of three and here began my first lesson.

Arthur took me round the bells on a wooden catwalk pointing out the smallest treble and graduating to the largest, the tenor. He explained that connected to the wheel-like frame of each bell and now in an upward facing position was the stay and that when the bell was fully inverted and so upside-down, this stay could travel a few degrees off the perpendicular before hitting against a cross beam designed to stop the bell traversing completely. It was a safety devise for someone such as he hoped I would become, namely a learner. A skilled bell-ringer could hold a bell in the upside-down position just off centre and with minimum physical strength awaiting the precise split-second to pull-off and strike at exactly the right time in relation to that bell's correct position in a sequence of changes. Such a sequence of changes was known as a method. There were simple symmetrical methods and surprise non-symmetrical methods.

The true skill was the timing of the strike and a big bell would take longer from pull-off to strike than a smaller one. Thus it may be that the tenor would pull off before the treble and yet strike later. The skill of holding the bell balance whilst upside-down largely negated the need for physical strength once the bells had been rung-up. This was important because it meant that females could become expert bell-ringers and indeed some of the best ringers that Arthur had tutored had been girls. My head was swimming with facts but this one I was more careful than the others to tuck away for future reference.

This first teach-in was concluded by the classical prospective bell-ringers' dire warning. Before the necessary skill of rope handling was attained, the bell in its dangerous upside-down position might fail to be held just passed perpendicular and if so, the sheer weight of the bell could so smash the stay against its cross beam, the slide, as to break it. If this happened, the bell would do a complete revolution and the bell-rope that traversed it would rush to the ceiling of the ringing tower. If the unfortunate learner was still hanging onto the rope, it followed that a swift upward journey was enforced and it was not unknown, as was the case at Blackwell, for the ceiling to intervene. The same accident would occur if during normal ringing the sally failed to be caught in order to hold the balance. This possibility haunted me throughout the bell-ringing years and led to several sweaty nightmares.

And so it was that my bell-ringing career started. First the handling of the bell. In one-to-one little sessions before mid-week practice nights Arthur patiently taught me how to ease the bell from its resting position into gradual first movements to-and-fro by slight downward pulls on the sally and gradually increase the momentum until this brightly coloured blob of wool was almost touching the ceiling on its upward flight. The crucial bit was to catch the sally as it returned lest once in full flow the bell should rush over the top and the rope take me with it to the ceiling. It is a truly wonderful feeling when the fear goes and the bell can be held just past its balance in the inverted position. This keen learner could handle a bell.

Next came ringing up with the team on a light inside bell. The skill is to follow precisely the bell in front by facing that bell-ringer and pulling the rope just after his and if going too fast then to slow down and vice-versa. It takes time to master this task and even more to ring down at the end of a session since once the bell is in free-flow and off the balance, there is little or no control and yet the follow-my-leader must be maintained for the sound of the bells to be rhythmical and musical. Once these rudimentary operations become easy, the true skill is accurate striking. This means timing the hit of the clanger on the face of the bell such that the resultant sound is evenly spaced with the other bells. When a team of ringers are striking together well, then the sound is lyrical and melodious. Conversely, if the spacing of sound in uneven or worst of all clashing, then the noise is dreadful. A bit like getting life right or wrong.

Perfect striking calls for highly skilled rope handling and a good ear. It soon became apparent that some quite adequate ringers never made good strikers. There was more required than conscious observation. Sub-conscious timing was of the essence. Big takes longer, small takes shorter. Two valuable lessons that were to be tucked away and applied elsewhere later. After the technique comes the application.

The art of change-ringing is about methods and methods are about extracting a given number of bell combinations without duplication and without returning to the 1 to 6 (or less or more) strict sequence. In its extreme, 5,040 (6x5x4x3x2x1x7) changes are mathematically possible on six bells provided the rotations are consciously changed to set patterns. Such a feat is called a peal and would take typically two and three-quarter hours to complete. For the whole of this time concentration is intense and even with six experienced competent ringers familiar with the chosen method, mistakes are almost certain to be made. This is where the most skilful factor of all comes into play namely rope sight. A few highly gifted individuals, and Arthur Smithson was the most gifted that I even knew, could from one ringing position and whilst ringing a method themselves, correct errors made by others and sometimes by several others simultaneously.

Because a method involves exact rules of where to interchange sequence positions with another bell, known as dodging, and where to stay in a position, holding, it follows that to keep right on one's own bell for long periods is very difficult. To do so and correct others at the same time is nothing short of miraculous. It was something that I could not master. But then, a one-armed man dedicated to a church bell-ringing team and bringing on new learners for fifty-five years, winding up a heavy clock mechanism, keeping the grounds tidy, riding a bike, doing a full-time job, setting a vegetable garden and bricklaying for a local farm, is a miracle.

I was a keen student and learned so much from this marvellous man. Three things always stayed with me. Never be content to stick with what has been learned so far, there is so much more. Proof; I graduated from simple Bob Minor as a method to what was generally accepted as the most difficult of all London Surprise and developed from just ringing to conducting and achieved a number of peals with this excellent team. Next, and whether it is corny or not, there is no more powerful organism in this world for achievement than a small closely knit team of like-minded people all pulling together and lastly and most important of all, it is possible to look straight ahead and yet see what is going on to one's left and right.

The journal The Ringing World has been published weekly since 1911. In it was advertised their official diary. In this diary I had been studying the various bell-ringing methods on the increasingly tedious morning train journeys to Nottingham. The path of a bell throughout a method was drawn as a diagram across pages until the whole sequence was covered. In addition, the rules at the conductor's call of *bob* or *single* to change the routine, were shown separately.

There are simple methods such as Bob Minor, Double Bob and Grandsire and more complex surprise methods such as Oxford, Cambridge, Kent and the dreaded London. To see Herbert doing the same concentrated work in the motive power office was like finding a long-lost friend. After I had tentatively expressed my interest, it was as if we two were drawn into some secret society. I had unwittingly penetrated a part of Herbert's secret afternoon armoury. Soon we were deep in discussion about some of the more tricky sections of the surprise methods and before long I was being invited to the practice evenings at the two big city-centre churches. I was way out of my depth at both.

St Peters was dominated by undergraduates from Nottingham University and although occasionally getting a ring my time was spent mostly marvelling at eight bells rung to complex pieces and a hotbed of animated discussion. These Thursday evenings were alternated with Mondays at the absolutely huge St Marys in the Hockley district. This was a quantum leap from Blackwell having all ten bells regularly in use and seeing two men standing on a box handling the two-ton tenor. How I envied the student bonhomie and the city's night time energy. How I enjoyed the half-pint after work with Herbert and picking up his habit of a mini pork-pie from under its glass cover with mustard and a knife. The cost of this extra-work activity was increasing tiredness. No sooner had I got to bed after catching the last train back, than I seemed to be getting up again.

The feeling of great tiredness and the difficulty in getting up on Sunday morning to ring for morning service, my one day off, was not being helped by a recent decision to attend Clarendon College on two nights a week for a course on shorthand, typing and English. The mileage clerk's job was now boring and there was no prospect of moving to one of the other sections since the little deals to cover higher grade work and absences with overtime stifled any openings, or so it was beginning to appear to me. Another thing was that mysterious punch cards from the Hollerith section in Derby were starting to replace some of the manual work in the office. There were vague rumblings about computer analysis and the future being in Derby not Nottingham. There were vacancies being advertised internally for jobs at the Derby offices but to get there I would need a motorbike that I could not afford. Being turned down for an *outward bound* course sponsored by the traffic department in Derby did not bode well either.

As by now an avid reader of the evening paper on the train home, the answer was to become a journalist and for that shorthand was needed and hence the course. The English part was interesting and ought to be kept up. The touch-typing came easily and I passed a 30-words-a-minute exam at the end of the first term but the key shorthand part was not working. What was the point of learning the Pitman swish curve only for it to be replaced the following week? My ambition to become a journalist was receding. There was a man often on the later trains with thick-rimmed spectacles and bulging eyes who kept wanting to touch me and had some good suits at home that would fit me and I should visit him at the weekend and try them. It was time to move on.

John G. Smith

CHAPTER FIVE
Work and study: work and study

1960-1964. A job move and a Vespa 125. ONC Business Studies to start a long study road. The beauty of words. "Go and be an accountant." EMEB office rivalries. The faltering start to ACCA professional exams. Switching to H Foulks Lynch for a correspondence course. The accident. "Stick at it John."

And there it was in the small job ads "Junior Clerk wanted East Midlands Electricity Board, Lime Tree Place, Mansfield". The salary was quoted as £330 a year and although £20 a year less than my present pay and although surely I was two-and-a-half years on from being a junior clerk, I began to weigh things up on the journey home. No hours and hours spent on the trek to Nottingham six days a week. I could cycle to Mansfield and I reckoned that although hilly, the service bus could probably be beaten and so that meant a journey time of about 30 minutes or less. It would be cheap, I would save the whole of the rail fare and furthermore, I liked the sound of Lime Tree Place. What a fantastic sounding work location. A world away from Middle Furlong Road and its rows and rows of back-to-back cheap tired houses and the outside lavatory with its noises.

And another thing, although I loved the railways and

had great respect for the men who spent a whole lifetime working on them, it would be a relief to be rid of the ever-present stigma attached and the passionate un-escapable need I always felt to defend the system. "Look", I would say, "You cannot compare the price of rail travel with road. The railways maintain their own track and signals and have a self-contained independent network. How can that be compared in cost terms with just getting onto a ready-made road and driving away? What about maintenance, what about signs?" But I always ended up as a minority of one, overwrought and frustrated and of course the Beeching Plan would come along and prove the uneconomic case for much of the local network of railways. My own commuter line would be ripped out along with hundreds of other local service lines. The claimed financial benefit to future generations would be enormous. So it was good to turn away; the alternative was probably to explode as I still feel like doing when I think about it today.

There could surely be little to defend in the shiny new electricity industry. Overall, the attraction was overwhelming. Still, I was getting paid well now especially with the overtime through working bank holidays that I always volunteered for and the free passes - especially to London - that had become increasingly attractive. I turned the idea over in my mind until Saturday afternoon and went into the cowhouse where my dad was milking to get his seal of approval "Please yourself John, they're both nationalised industries so you won't have to work hard in either". Hardly the glowing encouragement I was craving but as usual he had a point. It seemed big and safe and I did like the idea of Lime Tree Place.

The interview at the Lime Tree Place office block, that turned out to be a large ugly utilitarian brick and concrete building next to the Gas Board offices and close to the sprawling Mansfield Brewery site, was conducted by a Don Smith who was introduced as the head of administration at this the Mansfield and North Nottinghamshire District and Harold Lucas head of the income section within which the vacancy apparently lay. Both were very pleasant men and treated me gently and kindly.

After my smooth passage for the railway job in Nottingham I began to think that I must have a natural talent for interviews especially since most time was spent with me explaining the finer points of bell-ringing. This held the senior man in obvious rapt attention. There was no doubt in my mind as the discussion wound to a leisurely close that I would be offered this most junior of jobs and not least once I had mentioned that my dad had had to pay a capital contribution towards the cost of getting an electricity supply to the farm some two years earlier. I consciously held back the information that he had refused permission for the board's wayleave officer to enter the land to inspect the overhead lines on the grounds that it was a ploy to get sightings for "more bloody poles." Of-course this was no personal affront to the unsuspecting wayleave man, he just hated all officials of any kind and in any case the wayleave payments were a pittance far outweighed by the trouble of working round the poles and their bracing supports.

Many years later, my wife's best friend Diana died a long slow death from cancer and along the way I became friendly with Diana's husband who rose to be chairman of this same electricity board. He told me a story about how as a young thrusting engineer in a rural district he had been asked to go and see a retired senior military man (second in command of the Berlin airlift at the end of the war) to persuade him not to object to plans to erect an overhead line on fields in the view of his large imposing house. After making coffee and sitting him down in a comfortable armchair, the distinguished war hero sat opposite and said very gently "look Mr Harris I came to live here for five negative reasons, no road traffic, no aircraft noise, no neighbours, no tourists and NO BLOODY ELECTRICITY POLES." The overhead line went up anyway.

As I was getting up to leave, Don Smith said he would like to set me on but there was a snag. A snag? This vacancy was expected to be a route to better things and the successful candidate would be enrolled on a day release Business Administration course at the local West Notts Technical College. The snag was that the minimum entry qualification for the course was having 5 GCE's including Maths and English and I didn't possess these did I? The blow was devastating. No Lime Tree Place. No Electricity Board. No route to the top. Don Smith said there was just one hope though. He had influence with the college because the Board provided many candidates for courses and not least from the engineering side. He would put a case forward for getting exemption on the grounds of my experience to date coupled to the fact that the school I attended did not do GCE's. With a heavy heart I caught the bus back home. He was just being nice. There must be oodles of candidates with 5 GCE's. The date was 29th August 1960. Seven years later to the day, my first son would be born.

The letter came four days later. It bore a splendiferous letterhead, embossed and coloured and of a kind I had never seen before and from Lime Tree Place. I had got the job and when could I start and I was enrolled on the Business Administration Course starting in September. Whoopee for Don Smith and whoopee for bell-ringing. I met John Smithson and bought him a pint.

It turned out that there were two financial benefits from my leaving at this time. Because my total service after the probationary period would be just under three years, I would in due course receive back my contributions from the pension superannuation scheme in full. The significance of this was apparent when six months later a cheque for £125 arrived. After sweating like a pig having beaten the bus again on my battered cycle each morning and after work, the attraction of a certain shop window on Clumber Street, Mansfield begot a yearning satisfied by the purchase outright of a brand new and green Vespa 125 motor scooter. £97 plus road tax and insurance. The bill was exactly £125. Heaven sent. Years later in a lovely small private hotel in Amsterdam whilst cogitating on our backgrounds, I was to my surprise telling my boss that this act of purchase was the determining liberating factor in my life.

The second benefit was that the Provident Mutual contributions I had been making through the payroll each fortnight could be carried on after leaving the railway. The salesman who came around the office soon after I started had been persuasive but because of my dire financial state, only to the tune of the very minimum contribution which was one shilling and six pence per week. Consequently, nineteen shillings and sixpence was forked out each quarter thereafter until it became £3 and eighteen shillings a year and later still a bit less when tax deduction at source came in. This policy premium was paid annually in sentimental memory of those first years in the Motive Power office and ran its full 30 year course. On leaving, Mr Jennings presented me with a Parker pen and propelling pencil set. The lads took me out for a drink and Lillian cried.

As it turned out, I was not going to be working at the romantically sounding Lime Tree Place after all. I was going to be this year's fast track management trainee spending six months in each of four departments, pre-billing, post-billing, credit control and possibly financial accounting - depending on my progress at college during the day release. Pre-billing was located in a satellite office above the electricity showrooms on Regent Street.

As was being discovered in the first few weeks and as

would be reinforced more and more strongly with subsequent job moves, there are four discernable interactions taking place. At the highest level is the self-appraisal of whether the anticipated advantages over the previous job are actually there. The time saving and ease of getting from home to office were indeed major plus factors. The office was modern with proper desks and the work seemed to be fairly evenly distributed using laid down routines. The language and paperwork had a modern feel. A big tick here.

But what of number two, the disadvantages? The characters in the railway office left a big gaping hole. I was homesick for the bustle, the in-fighting, the scheming, the deadline pressure on timecards, the rows over Sunday rostering and most of all railway men from yardies to link 1 drivers in their issue uniforms dirty and clean bantering their way through a working week. And I missed the engines with their hissing, fizzing steam, their sheer size and power. And I missed the train journeys and travellers I had got to know so well. And I missed Nottingham with its traffic and shops and market and Herbert and the mini pork-pies.

At a third and fourth tangent are the surprise plus and surprise minus. One thing that never occurred in forethought was a different stature of work colleague arising. In this new office were young people, some younger than myself. Most had good school leaving qualifications and all were well dressed and behaved. Not a single stand-up row or swear word in these early weeks. The ambience was businesslike and quiet. Was this what a modern office was really like? No ex RAF officer or ex army colonel or chief clerk from a Dickensian era with mature lady secretary flaunting herself in high-heels and overseen by a superintendent complete with bowler hat. Yes this surprise find was a plus. It felt a better place for me to be.

The surprise minus was the work type. Even after one

week, that which was actually done appeared so mentally simple. Accuracy was obviously of the essence but comparisons with the wage calculations and mileage statistics of the last job left me both puzzled and worried. And so I sought for myself an honest conclusion. Had I made a good or bad decision?

I had wanted to get rid of the all-pervasive and debilitating tiredness, to cut down on wasted travelling time, to find a more modern industry and to seek a way to grow a career. But, deep down, there was a nagging feeling that I could have made a very bad mistake. If all that there was to this comfort was a routine checking future then I had to move quickly and push and push to get out and on.

It did not take an Einstein brain to work out that more difficult and hopefully more interesting things could be sought out and I wanted to, and indeed had to, justify the faith Don Smith must have had in me. I discovered that last year's fast track trainee, Mike Truman and who was one year younger than me was doing well in the income section and that the trainee of two years ago, Derek Hooton, was flying and already in financial accounts as a permanent appointment. Both had joined the EMEB on leaving school aged 16 and with a clutch of GCE's. This knowledge made my being set-on even more puzzling but I had been and so my effort was going to be exceptional.

These two predecessors had to be at least caught if not passed. Furthermore, I was not going to be bogged down in some clerical morass, not after the efforts and memories of the motive power office anyway. After stints in pre-billing, post-billing, credit control on the streets with the debt collectors and cashing-up the pre-payment meter men with the chief cashier, I received a letter form Don Smith awarding me four accelerated increments on the clerical pay scale and thanking me for my "meritorious achievement". I kept the letter for years. On pay at least I had caught my two peers already. Things were looking up. Perhaps I did make the right decision after all. Pressure was building in the financial accounts section and I was to join that team immediately as a permanent position.

My lost two years were brought into even sharper focus on the ONC business studies course. Apart from two mature students, all were sixteen year old school leavers with their qualifying GCE's and sent by a local employer to get a broader business-based education. They came from the National Coal Board office, Mansfield Building Society, a car distributorship business, a crane hire company and so on. Failure in year one or year two or both, would put me further behind them in building a career as well as throwing me off the fast track management scheme back at the office.

With one or two exceptions my classmates had one thing in common, they were here to enjoy their day off work and it soon became evident that so were the lecturers. The evening classes in Nottingham had been short and intense but this was something else. Progress from week to week was slow, days were short, lecture times brief, break periods elongated and timekeeping from the lecturers was accidental. What was more, to try to accelerate by reading a chapter ahead proved fruitless. The lecturer hadn't got there yet. With so much at stake, this was all very frustrating. Gradually I learned to adapt to academic life fall in with the flow and be patient. Once this stage was reached and I made friends with a number of the students, I too began to enjoy my day of freedom. Some years later I would be best man at the wedding of one and I would stay in touch with another for many years.

There is a case for believing that specialist knowledge is best left until it has to be acquired and applied and when its by-products are needed and that all the early years should be devoted to basic structures. If only the sound principles of English usage, etymology, grammatical construction and syntax had been driven into the young brain. If only arithmetic and maths had be shown to be conceptual as well as mechanical. If only just an outline of classical studies had been forthcoming as a further part of the foundation blocks of the earliest schooling. Then, what a sheer luxury would have been these new explorations into economics, economic history, commercial law, statistics, and bookkeeping and accounts instead of the doubly hard and uncertain task of building on sand. What a waste at Newton school. Criminal. How silly-sounding would the reply from the well meaning teacher at Tibshelf school have been to my mild request for a foreign language class, "You all need to learn English first." And how much easier to compete later with the educated ones and how much sooner the joy of cryptic crossword puzzle solving would have arrived. Perhaps and paradoxically the consequence was worth the void and disappointment and these new subjects were appreciated for themselves as a result of having to work at the underlying basics. Certainly over time they were developed and never really dropped.

The absolute challenge of words in particular must have had its seed corn in this most unlikely place. The sign that has hung for years at the entrance of an always empty field alongside the Norfolk coastal path at Burnham Overy Staithe, "Sharpies Only". What no Thickies? Especially wasteful since apparently, given the empty field, there must be only thickies around here. The cautionary warning on a local re-surfaced road "Slow Tar". Yes it would be. The incredulous warning at the health club "Pool Fire Rules". Presumably applicable only if such troubled areas have been soothed with oil? The advisory arrow pointing to "Polish War Graves" – which Polish war was that then or am I being asked to buff them up a bit? The brand-new sign that has been "erected" to point into an absolutely flat area of Harlow Wood "Nomanshill Wood". Either this innocuous piece of woodland was picked out from the rest by a council committee unfathomably aware of some deep historical connection or as a masterful phonetic pun on a different sort of connection. Everyone around knows that that piece of territory has been taken over at every hour of day and night by homosexuals and those that walk their dog that way in innocence will soon be acquainted with the fact. So, is it in fact rather brilliant? Nomans? Certainly. 'ill? Well have you been to Africa lately? Wood? No thanks.

After the two years of business studies I pass with a credit rating and now ensconced in the mysterious world of financial accounting, things are starting to move at pace. On the studying front there is a decision to be taken. My predecessor by two years, Derek, is deep into the mire of the IMTA (Institute of Municipal Treasures and Accountants) whilst he of one year ago, Mike, opted for ACCA (Association of Certified and Corporate Accountants). This latter qualification was known colloquially as the poor man's chartered accountant because it did not call for articles to be served in a professional accountancy office yet still allowed the accomplisher to sign off the accounts and audit a public liability company. Also, apparently, the syllabus was more structured towards industry as distinct from the profession. All this became relevant once the English tutor at college thought the best next step and the one most likely to further my career was to move straight onto the HNC in Business Studies (higher national).

My experience of the slow pace of the past two years added to the twin pieces of information that the HNC "was as far as this college goes" and "the ONC provides exemption from the preliminary examinations of each of the three professional accounting bodies" was beginning to make the decision seem easy. Added to this, one of my new-found friends from the course had already opted for the Association of Cost and Works Accountants exams because he was moving from the local building society to the office of a local textile factory. Years later and long after

I had been best man on his marriage to a most beautiful girl and long after she had had a very serious illness and long after they had split, I met him by pure chance at Glasgow airport. He was with a group of very serious looking and sounding men. He was a senior director of the largest textile group in the UK. The same firm whose local office he had joined on gaining his ONC in Business Studies. I never knew if he qualified as an accountant but it seems he found a career.

Once more I took my dilemma to the cowhouse at the Saturday afternoon milking session. I explained to my dad that, as I saw it, the easy option was to proceed to the HNC course since the studies would almost certainly be no more than an extension of the past two years, there was no real journey involved and my scooter made it an easy day. I had got a permanent placement in financial accounting and my prospects were starting to blossom.

Studying for the exams of any one of the three professional accountancy bodies was likely to be a different proposition altogether. Although a one-day release was still available, the nearest college was Clarendon in Nottingham - where I had taken the evening classes whilst working for the railway - the work according to my two predecessors was of a different magnitude of difficulty and most of all I did not know whether I would be good enough to pass the exams. If I started to fail, it would affect my fast-tracking at EMEB and consequently I would be in a worst position than taking the easier option of the HNC.

Unlike the schooling options, unlike the change of job "please yourself", he listened carefully and stopped milking. Putting the milk bucket down and taking off his cap, he looked me straight in the eye and said "Go and be an accountant, you're good enough".

Back at the office in Lime Tree Place, financial accounting was regarded as the elite section. It soon became evident that only the best brains could do the work which as I was soon to learn entailed bringing together all the different outputs of the other sections to create a single set of figures for the returns sent monthly to head office at Foxhall Lodge in Nottingham. It was here that all the district's income was summarised by category, domestic, commercial, agricultural and industrial. All the job costings on capital and revenue account had to balance to the control accounts and all the cash receipts had to agree to the income and debtors.

Because this work was undertaken manually and written into double-entry ledgers, it truly represented a thorough grounding in accountancy. Furthermore, any entry mistakes and most posting errors resulted in the dreaded month-end "doesn't balance" admission. This is where the head of the section and qualified accountant Roy and second in command Stan came into their own. This is where deadlines ran the risk of being breached, where the intense searching for mistakes began and where the swearing started. It was not unknown for the head of all accounting to apply his cultured mind to the problem even if only to take some heat out of the situation.

Roy was tall, slim, energetic, articulate and well dressed . Stan was fat, morose, smelled none too sweet and of tramp-like appearance. It was not a recipe for harmony under pressure. I just worked and worked and hoped for the best. This section provided my second grounding in office undercurrents, rivalries and politics. Roy was younger than his contemporaries in charge of other sections. He was there due to his qualification and prospects. The others due to time in job and experience. He was going places. They were not. And so the brutish Alec on capital costing was never to be hurried in closing off a capital scheme so that it could be submitted on the return, always knew the technical categories of capital works and never, never made a mistake. This attitude rubbed off on his assistant Jim who although the same age as Roy had been on costing work since leaving school. He was not to be convinced that any of Roy's decisions on definitions of expenditure were correct.

I could never see that it overly mattered already knowing that all capital will be revenue eventually. Still it taught me to think about it. It also taught me that young whippersnappers will always be opposed, simply because they probably are. It taught me to keep my head down, to work hard and to work fast. But, the petty jealousies were mind-numbing. It nearly taught me that to set out to change the established is amongst the hardest of tasks. But that would come later.

I hated Clarendon College just as much as Newton school and the first few terms on the ONC course. It was packed with people, noisy and hugely impersonal. Having embarked on Intermediate Part 1, ACCA, having bought the prescribed official text book and having worked through a section of a chapter on the blackboard with the lecturer, it soon became evident bearing in mind the late start, the coffee and tea breaks, the long lunch break and the innumerable interruptions, that to pass these entire professional exams in the theoretically shortest time of four years would be just that. Theoretical. It took time to get into Nottingham and back and as the release-days and therefore weeks past, I could find no input from the lecturers beyond the content of the text books. The year is 1962, I am 20 and behind and late.

In the hallowed pages of Accountancy Age magazine that is now received weekly due to my ACCA student status, are the advertisements for correspondence courses for the three professional bodies. There is the Rapid Results College promising sure-fire first-time success with minimum effort and others but also a much more sombre missive from a H Foulks Lynch whose papers promise a step-by-step key point synopsis of each chapter of, for example, Ranking Spicer & Pegler's Mercantile Law incorporating Partnership Law and The Law of Arbitration and Awards – Eleventh Edition. I note that the publishers of this tome are "H.F.L." and that the text book shop on Wheeler Gate is Spicer and Pegler's. Perhaps for the first time in a quasi-business sort of sense some connections are manifest. As yet I have no idea who ultimately sets the exams but if this horse is to be led by the nose, there appears to be more sense in the puller being H Foulks Lynch than these lecturers who are most certainly no more than a half-chapter ahead.

This potential correspondence tutor was the most expensive of those advertising but if they really do know what standard is expected and which track is the most likely to lead to success, then it looks like the best bet. I send off the money for the full Part 1 Intermediate tutorial papers, pack up the college in mid-term and start work alone. The one good outcome from this false start was meeting Tony Webster on the same course and who turned out to be employed by the Derby area of EMEB. He was to become and remain a very good friend. There would be much bonhomie to come but for him also some early and life-changing pain.

The correspondence course work was not in the main intellectually hard. After tackling the first few papers, a feeling of vindication came to me strongly in that there was surely far more detailed work to be done, far more ground to cover in each subject than could possibly have been handled in the time available and using the methodology of the college approach. The sheer number of papers comprising the whole course demanded a tight calendar deadline from receipt to textbook study to cross-reference with the key-point tutorial to answering each question to return to Foulks Lynch to a study of their marking. It was clear also that all of the papers must be completed on this rigorous programme to stand any realistic chance of passing the ultimate professional exams that were rumoured to only let a predetermined number through irrespective of the marks attained.

Whether this was the actual practice of ACCA I never knew but it served to provide added motivation and to urge the need to pay, at a point just a few weeks before the exams, for model answers to past papers. From reading Accountancy Age, it became evident that few students went this far on the grounds that no question would be repeated. But I needed to know what Foulks Lynch thought the examiners were after and I had to time my effort as a guide to speed and when to move on to the next question even if the current one was not finished. Imperfect full coverage rather than perfect bits seemed common sense to meet the rules of the game as I now saw it. Right or wrong? No-one to bounce the theory off. Just have to take the risk.

But one risk did not come off. Rather I came off, the scooter that is. Making steady progress to the office in dense fog one bitterly cold winter morning; bang. Whilst vaguely aware of being inside an ambulance but thinking it could not possibly be happening to me and even more dreamily being pushed on some sort of trolley, my first conscious recollection was June staring down at me. I was in Mansfield General Hospital having hit a service bus that was stationary at a bus-stop. She was crying and the nurse had said that if I had been going any faster ……….

Although the staff's main concern was my face, I just wanted something done about my left knee that ached like mad. But instead there were x-rays and an operation on the upper left cheekbone that was broken by the impact. It took time to be able to tell a nurse about the pain in my knee and more time to get it x-rayed and the diagnosis was only severe bruising. For years and years afterwards the tell-tale sign of being over tired or under special stress would be an ache in the left upper cheek and a slight swelling of the left temple. I would stare at this in the mirror and tell myself to slow down. But, eventually, it went away. Not so the knee.

Even today there is an almost sub-conscious search for the left-hand isle seat in a cinema or theatre to enable the leg to be stretched out. The black eye lingered long enough for the girls from the office to see it on their surprise visit to the farm for my twenty-first birthday tea.

I wonder if it is always the more obvious damage that heals and disappears and the less obvious that does not.

The days leading up to the first professional exams to occupy two-and-a-half days at the Albert Hall in Nottingham were hideous. My mum's advice to ease my heavy head-cold was to place a cloth over this stuffed up head, itself suspended over a bowl of steaming water filled with a vapour producing substance, "Vic". The dilemma of getting to the hall, do I risk my scooter and another possible accident or go by bus for safety? But worst of all, the last minute trudge into the exam room alongside all the brighter people with their rimless spectacles and string of expensive pens and good suits and dresses. So these were the competitors for this backwoodian. Any confidence, any hopes I may have secretly harboured in those lonesome hours of painstaking study with my remote friend Foulks Lynch, increasingly ebbed away with each step to the allotted exam table. At least I did not leave before the three hours of each paper expired, as many did. But the big points question on costing in the most important accounting paper did not work out which meant a mistake was made early on. This was likely to spell disaster.

There is a quandary with timing with these professional exams. Sat in the first week of June, the results are not out until mid-September. If just one subject is dipped, that subject can be re-taken in December. If more than one is failed, the whole must be re-taken. If a pass is recorded and no work has been done over the summer, the time for the next correspondence course has to be squashed into a sort of academic year

. What to do for the best? No holiday was planned, I

had no spare money and I was still trying to recover from the bash in the head and knee from when my scooter ran into a service bus that foggy March morning en-route to work. I bought the books and sent off for the course for Part 2 and carried on with the study routine hoping against hope that the gamble on success would pay off. No-one was more surprised and overjoyed than I was to get a blue paper pass letter that September. As was published later, the pass rate for that examination some 19%. Now I had to believe that I could compete with these others.

Over the next year I worked doggedly at the tutorial papers and the past exam papers and never missed a mailing-off deadline. Each evening and much of the weekend was taken up and so much so that several times I had a heart-to-heart chat to dad on whether I could continue on the set timetable or whether in fact to pack it all in and have some leisure time. Each time to his eternal credit he would say "stick at it John – it will be worth it". Without this I would never have got through the work. He and mum helped enormously by giving me time and space to quietly plod on in my bedroom, paper after paper, book after book. I did sit the following June and I did get the blue pass letter that September. Intermediate over. Bring on the finals.

CHAPTER SIX
Finding the girl: finding the path

1960-1966. First lost love. Second love and Ben Hur. Promotion, leaving the farm. Marriage and West Hallam. The final blue paper – qualified. Wonders of the Co-operative Society. Ilkeston and picture palaces. Of boozy chess and growing vegetables; taming the clay.

After the extreme shyness amongst girls at school and the egregious attempts to date the one special one on the school magazine, my early attempts to have any guise of a girlfriend were both bumbling and cautious. Cautious probably because, and certainly influenced by, my elder sister. She was hot and wild and out and about in the tight slit skirts and high heels that were all the rage in the early 1960's. Perhaps this was not her inborn self. There had been no like-kind history on either side of the family as far as I knew. At an early age she certainly had been interfered with by at least one older boy who had come to play at the farm in the summer months.

Whatever the cause and if there was one at all, she was out of control and a big and constant worry to mum and dad. She would not stay in. She would not dress decently. Even if I had the time to or was it opportunity, I was not going to add to their worries. That is, I wasn't until Betty came along. There had been girls before. I had taken Glenys from the railway office to the ABC cinema in Nottingham several times and I really, really liked Linda who I met on the train with her pretty printed dress, laughing eyes and sheer excitement. The Saturday afternoon help on the farm for my dad was even broken for Linda as I set off by bus for Chesterfield and then a second bus beyond to meet her parents and take her to the pictures in Chesterfield. We saw Pat Boom in April Love and held hands and snogged. But no further.

My friend David Cantrill had recently started to learn bell-ringing. He was tall and fair and good looking and one Sunday evening at church introduced me to Sandy "a friend of my new girlfriend". These two girls came from Sutton-in-Ashfield where he had met them. A foursome was arranged at Sandy's house on a cheerful little street in Sutton to listen to some music on her record player. This was repeated several times when her parents were out and somehow we two couples got separated in the two small downstairs rooms so David could spend some time alone with his girlfriend. Sandy was warm and cuddly and much more experienced than me but the furtive circumstances and the sickly overpowering perfume just put me off. I stopped going.

Then it just happened. Like a bolt from the blue. Arriving early for bell-ringing on a Sunday evening I was met at the belfry door by this tall, leggy, blond girl with the most beautiful face I had ever seen. She had finished with David and wanted to be my girlfriend. I looked like Paul Anker and ever since she first saw me she couldn't stop thinking about me and she wanted to be with me from now on and for ever. It was as if the world's greatest illusionist had stepped onto the stage and spirited away the box labelled shyness, the jar labelled caution and all other girls in their pretty dresses too. I just knew instinctively that this was it. My pulse was racing, my heart was thumping and as

I reached for her hand she came straight to me and we hugged in silence. Enter Betty and my world turned upside down.

It was just unbelievable. This ravishing girl who could have stepped off the front page of any fashion magazine and had her portrait as the enlarged centre-piece of any photographer's window display, wanted to be with inconsequential me. Me, the railway clerk, the farm labourer, the rural bell-ringer. The no-hoper with girls. She had no inhibitions. I had no inhibitions. This ugly duckling turned swan. The all-in-one once-and-for-alltime confidence booster. We could not keep our hands off each other. Her face vividly flushed, her whole body shaking, she would pleadingly urge me "not to do anything silly". Me, whose sister was running amok and who would shortly become pregnant by a sixteen-year-old apprentice builder, was being given a stern talking to by dad after he saw us going into one of the farm buildings and ending with "she is only fourteen you know". We did try to cool it and we did pledge to wait until we were older. But how much older?

The big difficulty we had and maybe a blessing was how to meet. We were totally reliant on buses to bridge the five miles or so distance between us. As a further obstacle, her parents were not to know of the relationship and indeed I never met them. All I did know was where she lived and that she was adopted and did not know her natural parents. This probably explained their refusal to let her meet any boys but this would never have stopped Betty. She was a master at subterfuge and had girlfriends to visit and churches to go to. We met mostly on Sundays, my heavenly day since that first time but she would appear as a surprise sometime in the week and be waiting near the bus stop for when I rode past on my way home from the railway station. Best of all, she would get a secret message to me that she could board my train at Kirkby Bentinck station and travel with me the one stop to Tibshelf.

She would have to have caught a bus to get there from where she lived and would be holding her pet poodle. When this first happened it caused a sensation with my fellow travellers. This beautiful tall young lady with her poodle getting on to travel with Smithy and then walking with his bike back to the farm. Word got back to the office where I was counselled in one quarter to be "very, very careful" and advised in another quarter to "go for it or you'll regret it". Betty had no money at all apart from pocket money but somehow she managed to buy me some wonderfully touching presents that I treasured for many years. A silver coloured cigarette case, a yellow cravat, several sets of cuff-links and best of all a "45" record Acker Bilk and his Paramount Jazzband "I got my love to keep me warm". Each time I took her to the end of her avenue to meet the curfew, the ache would start and it continued until we met again. There would never be anyone else. But there was.

In the pre-billing office at the EMEB it was the practice to have the electricity consumption calculations checked by a second person and if a mistake was found to record this according to the initials of the perpetrator. One of my very first jobs was then to speak to that person and go over the calculation that led to the error in the hope that this would not be repeated. Most of the errors seemed to come from the initial "JP" and so it was to June Painter that I spoke most often.

She was a red-head, very bubbly, bright and laughed a lot and somehow different from the others. I asked her for a date and we went to see Charlton Heston in Ben Hur. We were both in some sort of transcendental whirl and went for a walk afterwards down towards the Nottingham arboretum. We held hands and it was incredibly exciting. We agreed to meet again outside office hours and I told her about Betty and said I would end the relationship with her.

I met Betty in Mansfield Market Place at lunchtime and told her there was someone else and perhaps we had had to wait too long and perhaps there were too many obstacles. She cried and cried and slowly walked away with her beautiful head on her elegant long neck bowed. I never saw her again and even though I have had the love of two good women since, there will always be regrets about time and about life and what-ifs. I had just finished reading a book by Connie Clausey "I love you honey, but the season's over". It concerned a circus leaving town. God forgive me. She would have met a man who gave her a far better life that I could have done.

Years later I returned to the office in Nottingham after lunch and a colleague said there had been a telephone call for me from a woman who had seen me in the car and who did not leave her number but would ring back. I waited but she never did. It would have been Betty.

Leaving the nest : making a nest

Two things happened more or less simultaneously. June and I had been courting for about three-and-a-half years. Because of my studying, we could not meet often. Some lunch times, the occasional evening but mainly limited to some part of a weekend depending on the papers I had to get off. There had been a few exceptions like the summer when she and a friend worked as chamber-maids at the Imperial Hotel in Blackpool and John and I were washed out of camping in the Lake District and so visited Blackpool on the way back south. This produced a few days when we met in the week, in the evenings and, as it happened, actually under a pier. But this was rare and my increasing determination to carry on with the exams was creating a blockage beyond which it was hard to see. This frustration had started to make June cry and I had to do something. At about the same time, a job vacancy was posted internally for a promotion to a Grade 3 in financial accounts at the adjoining district of Ilkeston and North Derbyshire (the job that Stan was doing in Mansfield). I had been told unofficially that if I applied, it was mine.

So the decision was taken. I would apply for and get the job and we would plan an August wedding. We would tour the vicinity of Ilkeston on the scooter and find a house in which to start our married life. If I did pass the Intermediate Part 11 - which I didn't think I would - I would take eighteen months over the Final 1 to allow for the disruption and if I got that, would crash Part 11 in six months so that the whole programme would have been completed in the theoretically shortest time, namely four years. The condition was that June would take over all the household finances and paperwork and leave me clear to concentrate on the new job and the studying. A starry-eyed vision of the future from young sweethearts wanting to find a way to be together full-time. Looking back, the chances were at best 10%. But we did it, bang on schedule.

We were deliriously happy. The house we found was in the pretty village of West Hallam and just two to three miles on the Derby side of Ilkeston. Semi-detached, it faced the cricket pitch and was 1930's built of solid red brick with a small rose-filled front garden but a large back garden abutting fields and over which was a view of a grassed-over pit tip and beyond, on the horizon, a windmill. For me it spelt independence and a new life and for June, who had wanted to buy it as soon as we first saw it and who lived in a rented miner's house in a back-street of Kirkby, it was a dream come true. The cost was £2,250 and on the basis of my new and fantastic salary (£840 per annum) I managed to get a 95% mortgage through the local solicitor's tie-in with the Leek United and Midlands Building Society. I chose to stay with this small personal-service society for several house moves afterwards. They were excellent.

The 5% deposit with legal fees, conveyancing costs and

the one-off indemnity guarantee fee, took literally the whole of my meagre savings. The triumphalism was in actually pulling off the acquisition of the house that June wanted on first sight. That there was nothing spare never really mattered. There was no central heating and in fact not a single electricity socket upstairs. During the first winter, we trailed a power cable up the stairs from a downstairs socket to feed a three-bar electric fire. Even so, ice formed on the inside of the bedroom window. The only furniture we had to start with was a double bed (which was June's from home) and an oldish settee with two chairs given to us by June's mum and dad from their sitting room. Our first two purchases were a small kitchen table with lift-up flaps made of melamine and a portable radio. Both came from a shop on Church Street and bought on hire purchase terms - one-third down and nine months to pay off the balance with interest.

At the wedding on a gloriously sunny August day when John had been best-man, the bell-ringers gave their services free and the spread of food had been supplied and prepared by June's mum and her friends in the Bentinck Miners Institute, Kirkby. Uncle Leslie, who didn't drink, was the star of the reception party by consuming several beers and proceeding to whisk most of the ladies present clean off their feet for each dance. Wonderful.

My new-found friend from the Mansfield Technical College business studies course chauffeured us afterwards to our new home to start the honeymoon. That first night was very special. We were both virgins. Next morning in a semi-daze, we walked through the village, across the fields to a pub on High Lane, West Hallam for a lunch we could not afford. A few days later we actually did go away for a honeymoon. Roy my old boss at Mansfield had in the meantime got a much more senior job with the Eastern Electricity Board in Ipswich. He invited us to his house for a week with Josie and their two children. The highlight was one day on our own at Clacton. Roy paid for the train tickets, funded our stay and discreetly gave me £5 to get home. I paid him back from my first new-job pay check. Is happiness temporal? Certainly it needs no materialistic props.

A newly-weds routine developed. We were very close. June got a clerical job in the Ilkeston Cooperative Dairy which was located almost alongside the electricity offices that I now worked from and we did the main shopping together once a week gradually learning the prices and experimenting with what we could and could not afford. Ilkeston proved to be an old-fashioned working-class sort of town with its main shopping street leading up a steep hill to reach what passed for a market square adorned on one side by a most magnificent church and on the other by the ubiquitous Cooperative departmental store.

The co-op, like its counterpart in Mansfield, commanded the prime position and had the biggest single building from which to feed, cloth, educate, entertain and offer banking and savings services to the working populace at large. Not only did it put on winter-time lectures and slide-shows of sunnier days at the Youlgreave well dressings, not only did it put on dances and concerts but it brought the likes of David Whitfield to town to perform his latest hit. A far cry from Newton Church Hall and Kirkby Bentinck Miners' Institute. In addition, this venerable institution paid back its profits in the form of dividends to help the working man and instil the idea of thrift and saving in his children. For those who wanted to move a little faster, albeit within their means and within the constraints of the rather harsh consumer credit terms of the times, the accounts office on the top floor held out the prospect of hire-purchase or deferred credit terms for the larger ticket items it had to offer. Repayments were due weekly or monthly and a steady queue at the accounts office counter testified to this occurrence. On top of all this, a full banking service was on offer and the first cheque-book usually originated here. Interest was paid by the Cooperative Wholesale Society Bank on current account and so a prudent man would have every reason to stay within the fold. My friend Tony has done so to this day.

Not that the co-op's tentacles were restricted to this most dominant four-square building. Aside from the dairy which had its own vertical integration downwards to the farmers such as my dad and upwards to the creameries and cheese-makers, down the road was the Co-op Travel Centre (still active today) and almost alongside my new office block was the Co-op Garage repairing and retailing the new Ford Consul and Classic. That too has gone from strength to strength gobbling up weaker brethren over time. If all this consumer control proved fatally exhausting, the answer lay in the hands of the Co-operative Funeral Director who was and still is the biggest player in the land.

There were other shops to explore. Greaves the Furnishers at the bottom of Bath Street with its window display of richly coloured fabric sofas and matching chairs and especially the deep thick cushion seats with dark-wood arms. There was one never-to-be-forgotten day when we arrived home from work to find this very set has been installed in our lounge upon thick new carpet that was not limited to this most important room but extended to the hall, on the stairs and the upstairs landing. It was like landing in heaven. And we had saved up for it. It was not on hire purchase.

The chemist on Church Street holds fond memories not for its contents that failed to match the green and red jarred hermetical ambience of Crofts of Tibshelf but for the sign vigorously displayed one lunchtime during roadworks outside its front door and with an appropriate large black arrow "prescriptions will be dispensed up the back passage". The same black humour or ignorance must have led the father of the barber I found in a back-street to send his fourteen-year-old apprentice son, some forty years earlier, to cut the hair of a newly deceased and previously long-standing customer and alone. "Just started when this head made a deep gurgling sound and stuff came out of its mouth. I yelled in fear of my life and ran out of the house as fast as my legs would carry me. Over these past forty years, I've been so glad to be cutting the hair of people like you who are alive". After such a story, I always went back hoping for more and did not find a more interesting barber until my early days in Singapore.

Ilkeston in these early independent mesmeric days was more than just shops. Two cinemas competed to show the likes of "Godzilla Versus The Thing" or "Laurence of Arabia" and from which we would disgorge along with Tony and his new wife Margaret and file into the nearest pub. We had a system. He went into one bar and ordered two pints and the girls' drinks and I did the same in a second bar. It proved to be the only way to get two pints in before the throwing out time of ten-thirty

. But the highlight was the annual fair when all the streets leading to the market square and the square itself were closed to house the merry-go-rounds, dodgem cars, and hot-dog and candy-floss stalls. The town held one of the oldest charters in England and within this was the right to this annual take-over. Needless to say the central attraction, the big wheel, was erected right outside the main entrance to the Coop. Apt I thought.

To have any hope of passing the exams in the time-frame of our plan, a disciplined routine was called for. We had to be home and had our meal in time for a seven-o'clock start to my studying. I had to do three hours minimum each weekday so that with five on Saturday my twenty-hour week programme was covered. About three nights a week after the stint I would run to the Punch Bowl for two pints and cogitate on how it was going.

Saturdays required the most dedication because I had

always worked on the farm all that day and being by nature an outdoor fiend and missing my dad, the books were a poor substitute. It must have been even more sacrificial for June. Alone each evening and no Saturday daytime together. Not once did she complain. It was a truly joint effort. Playtime was Saturday night and we made Sundays sacrosanct. Drinking and gardening. The combination of sanity.

Our first foray on a Saturday night was by chance not too adventurous. It turned out that my new and immediate boss, Norman, was treasurer of the works social club and this was situated in playing fields mid-way between home and the office. Since June and I had been regular visitors to the Mansfield club, it was an easy transition and one which allowed me to get to know Norman better socially. He was an incredibly nice chap and had the misfortune of a club-foot due to catching polio when very young. He was a qualified accountant and quiet and competent. He was a patient trainer and was the key reason that my early days in the new office was not the baptism of fire it could so easily have been.

Although the section was the same as at Mansfield and indeed the district was larger, the atmosphere at Ilkeston was completely different. The people were friendly, helpful and the whole team seemed very happy. I started to realise that it wasn't the actual work type or even volume as such that caused back-biting and politicking, but the people. And the attitude and approach of people depended mainly on the person at the top. The head of our section was Albert. He worked hard, had come through the ranks and was highly respected. He had no airs and graces and was extremely kind to me as the new boy. Norman's counterpart was Jack and a bigger contrast with the bullying man at Mansfield it would have been hard to find. With the two lady clerks, Myrtle and Grace, it was a very happy ship. In their unknown way they contributed much to my efforts to concentrate properly at home. If at the month end anyone couldn't balance, everyone helped and was happy to do so. The last to leave would be Albert, the boss. What a yardstick to measure future work situations by. What a lesson in motivation.

As this was his stamping ground, we were gradually introduced by Tony to pubs in the vicinity as a variation from the social club. These Saturday nights were a foursome as he had a young wife Margaret and we all got along well. She was pretty and I thought very sexy and together they were an attractive couple. They were the first friends of our married life and since he worked in the Derby office of the electricity board and they were just starting off in their first home in Ilkeston, we all had much in common. As it turned out however, there would prove to be one important difference between us.

Whereas June and I were remote from our families, not so much by distance as by communication in that neither of our parents had transport and neither had a telephone, Tony and Margaret bought a brand new house right opposite his mother. Partly because Margaret worked in Ilkeston and partly because she and Tony's mum got on very well, there was much interaction between the two houses and maybe this led to his creeping feeling of being stifled.

But, there was no hint of this as I tried, usually in vain, to match his ability to down pints of bitter in The Candlestick at Mapperley or The White Hart at Stanley or the Rose & Crown at Smalley. Afterwards we invariably ended up at our house and as the girls talked Tony and I played boozy chess. It occurred to me that on the odd times we played whilst sober, I lost, whereas on these late Saturday nights I almost always won. This could have been due to the superior ability of my brain to concentrate for longer after a hard day, alternatively it could have been the direct result of an inferior ability to drink pints.

During the first year, my friendship with Tony was cemented by our decision to study together on Saturdays alternating between our two houses. Whatever our joint or several input to these days, there developed one disparate ingredient. Lunch. He cooked a full hot meal with three vegetables. I did beans on toast with a pickled onion, my only dish. A testament to June's unequal contribution to our domesticity. This happy arrangement leading as it did to our evening out, had to end when I passed the first part final and Tony didn't. I always knew this was due to nerves and not to knowledge or dedication and I was to learn much later that the ability to hold one's nerve at a crunch time comes near the top of value assets. It is particularly helpful when preparing for and attending a board meeting, but that was a long way off.

Sunday was the day off and we observed it with all the religious fervour of a fanatic. What had not got done by Saturday afternoon in the twenty hours of Foulks Lych was just too bad. We went back home on the scooter to either Kirkby or the farm and usually both or explored around where we now lived. The Forsyte Saga gripped the nation. It was strange going back down Red Barn Farm lane, almost as if I had never been there. Perhaps the huge wrench of leaving had left a scar that could only heal if I was now a visitor only. And yet nothing had changed. My mum still cooking and cleaning with the quiet energy and dedication she had always had. Still very much playing second fiddle to my dad who was still milking and feeding the cows, still rearing the pigs and fowls and still railing against officialdom, politicians, royalty and the world at large. But he was still making ends meet, bringing up my sister's first born and second born and a third on the way and mum with plenty of top-notch wholesome food and always a beef joint for Sunday lunch or a chicken that had passed its best. Carrots and broccoli and apple pie and custard. But we were visitors now and my brother Alan had left school and worked the farm with my dad going out to get his first pay packet at the age of fifty.

No more the sole helper to my dad, killing the cockerels we had reared since they were day-old chicks fetched in boxes by the service bus from Chesterfield agricultural market on a late summer Saturday morning. They with their glorious but short-lived life of fornication with the laying hens until the final few weeks of incarceration in a pigsty to fatten-up. Dad and I entering in the dark to catch two more for the quick flick of the neck single jerk treatment. Mum and I dressing each one by plucking out the feathers after dowsing in a bucket of hot water and then drawing the insides of the intestines and private parts. I always marvelled at the smallness of the penis and the attached tube considering the massive urge emanating demonstrably from that quarter. The gizzard, heart, liver, kidneys and finally the corn-crop from the neck end all had to come out. The inside was washed through with cold water and the legs and wings tied to the body with string. I had to then weigh the bird and referring to my home-made ready-reckoner of price per pound and ounce, to stick on the cost to the customer. This cash bonanza getting the family through Christmas and into the new year.

For years and years into the future I would dash back when the telephone call came from my dad "haymaking's started, can you give us a hand?" But, in reality, my life, our life, was elsewhere and the tie was broken.

Back in West Hallam Sunday was also gardening day. Those spring and summer evenings digging and setting with my dad in the bottom garden were in the blood and no amount of studying or new independence could stop the replication. And replication it was, there was no origination. The methodology from the farm garden was followed slavishly, often with an aching heart. The soil was heavier with more clay and lacking the annual infusion of cow manure barrowed from the cow-house but the crops and technique would be the same. Then and still.

That first autumn and winter the whole of the long back garden was dug with my dad's long-owned spade that he gave me as his parting gesture and the following season we had potatoes, peas, broad and kidney beans, carrots, beetroot, spring and winter cabbage, onion sets, Spanish onions, spring onions and even my dad's favourite purple-sprouting broccoli. This piece of ground was, I reckoned, un-worked since its days as a meadow. It rewarded us accordingly. I felt proud to be providing for us and those first gardening Sundays proved a perfect respite from the books. Later the gardening would allow me to think, the greatest luxury in life, and remain sane.

Aside from consolidated accounts and income tax and profits tax and the taxation of foreign subsidiaries, I began to wonder if in delving the depths of these final examination papers, Foulks Lynch was pushing me into the wrong professional qualification. Surely I would end up a lawyer. Mercantile law, the law of bankruptcy, liquidation, administration, receivership, executorship, intestacy and equitable distribution. Subjects never even heard of never mind having even a spattering of advance knowledge before the tutorial paper arrived through the post. A wonder world of definitions, of cases, of textbook references of worked examples. Plod, plod, revise and re-read with more underlining of print in green and red than any self-respecting book should endure.

During the last three months of my crash course attempt at the part 2, final, I gave up ringing bells with Dr Futer's team at the beautiful old parish church at West Hallam. This was a bad and sad mistake. I was never to return to that hobby that gave me my first real mental challenge and insight into the variation in lifestyle and background of others drawn to this most virtuous art-form. It gave me my first real girlfriend, pulled me through my first real job interview and taught me the absolute vitality of prolonged concentration. And I dropped it for the real world.

It may seem like a pious collection of well-honed cliches but once the euphoria generated by the final pass letter started to wane, I began to feel that if one wants something badly enough and sacrifices time on other things to concentrate on that single goal, then notwithstanding a start point less advantageous than fellow competitors, it is possible to win through. Having left school at 15 with no qualifications, here I was at 24 a qualified accountant never having failed an examination. At that time, I could see no reason why any obstacle should hold me back. I was wrong of-course.

CHAPTER SEVEN
Organisation and Methods

1966-1969. VW Beetle to Ford Anglia. DIY disasters. A baby arrives. Goodbye accounts – hello efficiency. Mapperley Hall HQ and the sparky team. Racism and morality in a London eye-opener. Ravenshead and clever Mr England. O&M studies and my own team. Welcome PA Management Consultants and farewell dear friends. The enemy for life from tragedy and the near-affair.

June and I took two inter-related decisions. We would start a family and would need a car. We reckoned we could afford it because she wasn't paid very much working in the dairy office and so there was little income to sacrifice and we had become accustomed to living fairly frugally during the two studying years of our marriage. It had been no hardship. We were very happy so we might as well go for a baby now and enjoy our children whilst we were young. It was a sort of self-reward for our plan having worked out. She came off the pill and I booked driving lessons with the cheapest advertiser that turned out to be a retired policeman living just around the corner in the village.

He used his own VW Beetle and at fifteen shillings a lesson his precise and disciplined coaching worked out just fine. I went for the shortest time he thought possible - fifteen lessons with a double one on the day of the test - and he seemed to lose his cool somewhat when I passed first time. He insisted on driving back to the village himself from the test centre. It irked me a bit but I didn't care, it was one more of our plans ticked off. I did not tell him that I had passed my first driving test aged sixteen on the farm tractor and my second aged eighteen on the scooter despite in the first case missing the instruction to do an emergency stop and in the second falling off out of sight of the examiner.

The portents, especially exaggerated by a desire to minimise both time and cost, were therefore good. It was a shame the car was a Beetle since I absolutely loved it but knew we couldn't afford one because they held their value so well. It was sturdy, reliable, masculine and different from other cars somehow. Maybe one day we would get one. What we did get was a rather old but good condition Ford Anglia from someone who worked at the co-op dairy. It was £280 with £95 deposit that was met with £20 we had and £75 borrowed from my dad. This was the first and only time I needed to borrow actual cash from him and it was repaid at £5 a month. Some time later when doing his farm accounts I discovered that he had had to sell one of his bullocks to get the money for me.

The exam results had arrived in early September and by Christmas June knew she was pregnant. As the spring drifted into summer and June got bigger, I grew my vegetables and learned from our elderly neighbour how to look after the many rose trees in the front garden. We had a concrete garage delivered from an advert in the paper. It arrived as a series of concrete slabs and metal bits and concrete tiles and ironwork with the metal door. I was utterly baffled as it just lay on our driveway but did manage to check off the pieces and quantities from the erection diagram. It was correct apart from some triangular metal pieces and having telephoned the company, the sales lady was most insistent that they would have been packed but having pressed the point with my newfound confidence in such worldly matters, she with much reluctance agreed to re-send these bits so that assembly could start.

A few days later a lorry of the same size as the original one arrived to deliver the missing items that turned out to be a dozen or so metal purlins that went from front to back of the garage as the main roof support. They were in fact the main metal items of the construction and duplicated the ones delivered first time around. What I had seen and described as a small triangular section was now obvious to me as a purlin in end-view. I received this second issue with good grace from a slightly puzzled lorry driver and later that year used them to support my kidney bean row and as clothes line posts.

Passing a paper on executorship law is no qualification for reading DIY diagrams and time has not eradicated this deficiency. I tried one term at carpentry at night-school but managed only a not very handsome bookcase whilst the chap on the bench next to me manufactured a whole bedroom suite. A Christmas present of a metal wheelbarrow took all Boxing Day to assemble and then re-assemble due to the wheel not being fitted first. It looked fit for purpose initially but without the key ingredient of the wheel was useless. A lesson not lost regarding certain people, but later.

The self-appointed project of painting the external wooden window frames and doors of the house plus the metallic door of our new garage a lovely bright tangerine was about half complete when June went into labour. She was calm and serene whilst I churned inside as we drove to the maternity hospital in Derby. I was turned away about 10 pm because "nothing much will happen before morning – 'phone in early". It had been a gloriously hot day and it was now a balmy warm night. It felt so strange in our home alone for the first time and worrying, worrying. The following morning brought news that something had very much happened during the night. June was no longer in the maternity hospital but in Derby City Hospital having been rushed over in the early hours of the morning due to "complications". But the good news was I had a son and mother and baby were doing fine.

I drove to the hospital as fast as I dare to find June holding a baby with a strangely elongated head with red weal marks. It's hard to split elation from concern. Wonderful, wonderful, June was fine and we had a son. Yet, the baby looked abnormal. Had we done something terrible and was this the price? After we hugged and some of the emotion was spent, I learned that the baby's umbilical cord had been wrapped around the head three times and as June pushed in childbirth so his pulse had weakened. This resulted in a dash by ambulance to "a proper hospital". The shape of the head and the weals were due to the use of callipers and "the head will return to normal soon". I held Christopher for the first time and vowed silently that we would always stay close. I had so much wanted a son and now my heart was about to burst.

That evening Tony picked me up in his beautiful big green Austin Cambridge and we went to the White Hart at Stanley to wet the baby's head and afterwards we ended up at his house drinking his home-made wine that, even after much beer, didn't taste too good. Driving to the hospital next morning two things were obvious. My head would burst before my heart and I was definitely heading for the right place. Making a baby was one thing. Surviving the self-inflicted punishment was another.

The big break came as another internal job advertisement. There were twelve boards on the distribution side of the nationalised electricity industry. Some vacancies were advertised solely inside the appointing board but as jobs became a little more senior so it was usual to have an industry-wide trawl for talent. This was such an advertisement doubling as an announcement. Our board had recruited a deputy chief accountant from outside the industry. He would head up a brand new unit to be called Organisation and Methods (O & M) because the deputy chairman, to whom he would report directly, was initiating an efficiency drive throughout the board. The vacancies, also being placed in the national press, were for electrical engineers, an operational research specialist, a commercial officer, a secretarial specialist and an accountant. "A multi-disciplined team approach to improving the way the board operates". Anyone could apply. Interviews would be at board HQ at Mapperley Hall in Nottingham.

The prospect of learning about how the very wide variety of functions within the board operated individually and maybe how they came together appealed to me greatly. I discussed the advertisement with Albert. Having only just qualified he thought I may not have the accounting experience they were looking for and also counselled that if I were to be successful, it would take me right out of technical accounting, at least if he understood what the objective of the new unit was. I thought about this a lot. What I couldn't get out of my head was that every single subject studied in the ACCA papers and each detailed derivative of that subject was proving to be totally unused in my present job. Perhaps I could make a mark on company law in a solicitor's office and I felt very confident of becoming a tax specialist in a professional accountant's office but had I really put all those hours in just to be qualified. If I could get a position in this new unit it might serve a dual purpose namely the possibility of applying some of the knowledge picked up from the study papers but also getting known. Much as I still liked the job at Ilkeston and the people and the location was perfect for our home and the new baby, would I be buried alive? Would I just aspire to Albert's job in ten years' time? I had to apply.

The whole group of us were to be interviewed as a team using techniques imported by the new boss Mack Pullon from his Nottingham City Council background. This was explained at the 9am briefing session and we would be involved for the whole day. It started with our being asked to listen to a reading from a newspaper article about fairly technical environmental factors affecting the world and then we all sat various forms of intelligence tests. Just before lunch, and as a complete surprise, we were asked to answer questions on the text that had been read out in the first place. So, as it transpired, we had a memory test too.

We lunched in some style in the HQ boardroom and I was aware of being observed closely not merely on small talk and our backgrounds and so on but also on actual conduct. This was not a worry to me. My mum had been brought up in a large house with many children and where sitting down to proper full meals including high-tea on Sundays was the customary thing. She brought these standards to the farm and eating properly was normal to me. Even had this not have been so, the Boxing Day teas at aunt Doris's house could not have been survived without etiquette and decorum and my Great Aunt Pem was a stickler for table manners and the absolute overriding necessity of obeying rules. Even in her very old age when we two played Canasta on a Saturday evening, observance and conformity were everything.

But this was no card game. In the afternoon a series of discussion groups were formed with one person from the HQ staff in each group. As we were breaking up to leave at about five o'clock, Mack himself took me to one side and said he would be in touch. The following day he came to the office in Ilkeston and spoke to Albert and offered me the job as the accountant on his new team. It transpired that there had been 80 applicants for the job.

It occurred to me that I would be entering a different circle when at the start of our discussion on salary and start date, he offered me a cigarette from his very posh cigarette case. It was the custom in our section to throw cigarettes at one another. He also ticked me off for saying yep instead of yes. HQ here we come.

As a new team, we all sat in one big office in Mapperley Hall. It was a young sparky team drawn from different backgrounds. There was an electrical engineer, John Trigg brought in from the Nottingham District of this board, Tony Papadopoulos an operational research man from the North Western Board in Manchester, Chris Notley recruited from BICC as a commercial specialist and Phil Aimes a secretarial professional also externally recruited. The one common thread was an interest in efficiency/improvement studies.

The books and articles thrown at me to absorb dealt with areas from previously unknown territory. organisation and methods theory, work study, management theory, time management and I was to go on a six-week specialist course put on by the Royal Society in London. All this was a million miles from my professional studies and nothing whatsoever to do with accountancy or law or taxation and I was fascinated and very excited. Apparently a much bigger step than anticipated had been taken and it dawned on me that this really was a career switch. It did not look as if there was any figurative work to do at all and I felt strangely unconcerned about this. It appeared that the fact that I was qualified was all that mattered. Real and new-found enthusiasm hit me from a prospect, however remote, that I might actually be able to look at a situation of which I had no previous knowledge and apply some theory and make changes that would improve somebody's lot.

The external course was to provide a number of first-time experiences. Located in Regent Park Crescent it was to be my first working time stay in London and certainly on the northern fringe as distinct from the West End. Through lunch-times and evenings I was to become familiar with Regents Park, Euston Road, and the streets around the British Museum and Russell Square. These areas would become much more familiar in just a few years' time and my stay at the National Hotel was similarly to herald more time in London's bed-and-breakfast factories that I could ever have anticipated or wanted.

It was a first on meeting people from completely different backgrounds on a one-off project basis rather than office colleagues. Most of the course attendees were from local authorities and so I was to learn about the, usually it appeared disharmonious, relationship between themselves as officers and the elected councillors. At any rate, I learned sufficient to be put off from ever entering that world and it brought recollection of my dad's distrust of "little tin god" officials. There were a few very senior police officers. A chief inspector invited me on a vice squad evening out that I declined and there was a certain superintendent who was, a few years later, to gain some national notoriety for alleged internal irregularities at a certain town on the south coast under his control.

There were also some foreign students, mainly from African countries, and I was to hear a first racist taunt when one of these was missing after the mid-day break and someone suggested he'd gone home for lunch. Funny observation in its way but clothing a very obvious sting and deliberately opening up what had previously been a harmonious group. That's the problem with this stuff. One can't quite put a finger on it. One can't quite be sure it wasn't just a silly little joke. And yet, it is meant to strike home and either get you on side or hurt, and it does. An unsettling experience given that my only contact with non-whites had been the tutelage from a very polite and cultured Indian in my first job and the happy banter with the young African labourer in the railway workshop. Here in this much more erudite place and against blacks with books who had been sent to learn about efficiency studies there was directed some, albeit feeble, ridicule.

I got home at weekends but this was the first time June and I had not been together in the week. The first week away wasn't too bad with exploring to do and drinks with some of the lads on the course but as time passed it got hard. I was unhappy and lonely and it was not fair on June with our baby son. But having taken the job and in learning new skills, I knew we had to put up with it and stick it out. What I didn't know was that this was merely an apprenticeship.

During my upbringing and on both sides of the family and with friends and acquaintances, I had never been conscious of any goings on, of any unfaithfulness or even of any marital unhappiness. There had been the whispers and innuendo in the railway office but I never really believed it. Yet, here on this course was a young and newly-married girl who during the six weeks was befriended by and overcome -it seemed to me - by a large North-Easterner. I watched the seduction develop until they were consistently missing the afternoon lessons. I often wondered what happened once the course ended. Did she leave her new husband? Did he leave his wife and children? Did they never see each other again and if so was it just sex? If so, that was new to me too. In my naivety I actually did not think that people acted that way.

Still, at the culmination of the course my recommendations for improving the administration of the Bedford Constabulary HQ office went down well. I tried to make my verbal report to the group amusing as well as cutting but doubted if the ideas for change would be implemented notwithstanding incorporation of the new techniques learned so assiduously. Whatever those Home Counties policemen may have gained from my assignment on their patch, it was a certainty that I had learned more about life than efficiency processes during those hallowed six weeks.

John G. Smith

Moving home and moving out

Of the members of this elite group tucked away at Board HQ, the friendliest was John Trigg the engineer. He proved the most conversant with the board's procedures and practices and therefore most helpful with my early assignments. In particular though, he had taken advantage of one feature of the benefits package attached to a job promotion. It transpired that provided it was accomplished within six months of taking up a new position, the board would pay for removal expenses and sale agent and legal fees incurred in a house move.

Astonishingly it did not matter that the move might be within the same board or might not actually reduce the home to office travelling time. Wow. So he had moved his family from a heavily built-up area quite close to the office to ten miles away where a new community was being carved out of a very rural and wooded area called Ravenshead. Having heard me moan mildly about the drive from West Hallam involving the crossing of Nottingham from South West to North, why not also move to Ravenshead especially as many new houses were being built and the board would fund it. The distance would be about the same but the journey much more pleasant and countrified.

So we went to see a sample of these new houses and were introduced to the developer, a large important looking man in a sheepskin coat smoking a big cigar. He invited us into his own new house in the desirable area of Chapel Lane. It was a palatial place of awesome design having the lounge upstairs to take maximum advantage of the huge window overlooking the fields within the greenbelt beyond and towards Blidworth village. The only issue concerning his new development on Vernon Crescent, of which we were privileged at this early stage to take our pick, was could we afford the price of £4,950.

Though small, each home would be maintenance free and furthermore incorporated some technical innovations such as a ducted hot air heating system that eliminated the need for ugly radiators - of a kind that we were one development behind having at West Hallam. Such a leap into the future was bound to add to the investment potential of this development. A very clever man was Mr England. So much so that a few years later following his sudden departure from Ravenshead a rumour spread that he had managed to arrange his business affairs such that he sold the properties from one ring-fenced company and bought his materials and services through another.

As would happen again and again in the future at crunch financial times, I went to confer with Tony on the tricky aspect of this possible move. An ex-colleague from the office in Ilkeston, Terry, had promised to buy our place at West Hallam for £2,400. This would eliminate sale agent fees. Needing a deposit of 5% on the house in Ravenshead, and given the single premium mortgage indemnity insurance plus having to fund the price gap, and looking at my new salary net of tax and the household utility bills and other outgoings, Tony was able to prove beyond any shadow of doubt that the move into that house at that price was just not on. We could not afford it.

Next day June picked the extreme right hand house looking at the development from Vernon Crescent and I called the agent to book it at the full price. It was an act of sheer bloody-minded bravado. To hell with the numbers we were on the up and up and we would back ourselves. We moved in early December. Christopher was just over three months old and it was snowing heavily.

The Organisation and Methods Unit might have been set up on a multi-disciplined team concept but somehow all my assignments turned out to be solely that, just involving me. As a pattern, it occurred to me that this was the case with each of the others too. But a difference was emerging.

John Trigg and I were noticeably getting assignments that had been handed to Mack by a senior officer defining a problem and wanting a specific set of recommendations within a pre-defined timescale. Mack's job was to agree the terms of reference and supervise progress. Once the changes were agreed at his level, the stages of implementation had to be scoped and progressed. He reported to the board on these improvements.

John looked at numerous engineering procedural problems and I examined the work content and methodology of the wayleave staff - ironic harping back to my dad's disdain for this breed of man - and re-organised the central purchasing function. All well and good but the others had taken on more macro-type studies involving productivity of the manual workforce and general operational research. Whilst I was travelling around the board's many work depots and offices gathering facts, talking to managers and staff, flow-charting procedures and simplifying routines within a final report for Mack to edit, the rest were largely HQ static and on assignments that never seemed to end. It was not unusual for the most senior amongst our ranks to spend literally weeks designing a multi-part form set to fit into some routine or other and then to pass it around the rest of us for comment. John and I, in our different ways, started to get restless. We discussed it during our by now customary drinks session in the White Hart at Blidworth of Friday nights.

Our rebellion never got off the ground because of a very surprising event. Although he had only just got his feet under the board table, so to speak, Mack had been appointed as the new chief accountant. This was a big surprise to everyone at HQ and had put the nose of each of the deputy chief accountants right out of joint. The precarious position of our unit following the departure of Mack had barely been understood by the time I got a call from the most senior of these deputies - in charge of financial and management accounting - to see him at the accounting HQ in Foxhall Lodge in another area of Nottingham. He explained that a new unit under his command was being established to examine the efficiency and workings of the board's entire accounting function. I was to head that unit working from a new office in Foxhall Lodge and could recruit my own team. I would be promoted to Grade 6 and if the work of the team was successful, I had a great future with the board.

This deputy chief accountant was close to retirement and the recognised patriarch of the status quo. I could tell he had no belief in what he was setting up. That he would fight changes tooth and nail. He was working to Mack's brief, probably some form of quid pro quo. Was Mack re-setting his O & M Unit under his new control structure? I imagined so. He did not contact me directly. I accepted the job with enthusiasm relishing the inevitable resistance from the old guard whom I would now be in the middle of. What I did not know was that bigger things were afoot.

This was the time of "In place of strife". The new socialist government under Harold Wilson and, on the industrial scene, his bulldozer Barbara Castle. This was a time to knock aside the old conservatism, to dump the old-boy networks, to herald in the white-hot heat of technology and above all to set about improving Britain's lamentable level of productivity. Nationalised industries were not to be excluded from this thrust, indeed, they were to set an example.

So, we shall welcome to the board PA Management Consultants working to terms of reference set at the Electricity Council level and delegated to each of the distribution board's deputy chairman. Our man in this position had recruited Mack and placed him after a suitable period as chief accountant. He, in turn, had restored a form of internal efficiency unit. I now had another qualified accountant working for me and an administrative back-up staff in our own office suite right in the middle of the HQ accounting big-wigs.

We had various studies underway with a noticeably higher level of resistance than from the general management reached from the Mapperley Hall projects. The head-cod of internal audit thought I would be well advised to look at each of the other branches of the accounting tree before his own since the audit procedures had been thought through thoroughly and were themselves a check on inefficiency. One of the other deputy chiefs thought I should take a close look at internal audit as they were well resourced but he couldn't recall any significant benefits resulting from any of their reports.

Then the call came from my new boss. The external consultants wanted a secondment from "the inside". It was felt that I would be the best choice. Recommendations from their preliminary work had already been accepted and "Field Study" groups were to be set up at strategic points throughout the board and the, so far secret, objective was to achieve such an improvement in productivity amongst the manual and skilled work force that a significant shedding of labour would be possible in due course. It would require a fair amount of travelling and I would, of-course, have to learn how the consultants worked. I accepted without hesitation and after a general briefing from the team leader Tom, I was introduced to one of the working consultants Tim to whom it was gauged I would best relate.

And so, as I chewed this over with John Trigg that Friday evening in the pub, it transpires I have made some form of seamless transfer from O & M assistant to the board's only inside man with the external consultants. For good or ill, who could say? But one thing I now felt certain of as I downed my third pint and lit up another cigarette, my career path had changed. I was in the business of change. Since leaving Ilkeston, I hadn't even thought of anything even remotely attached to accounting never mind done any technical work. If the wrong things had happened to me, too bad. The die was cast. We decided to leave the car in the car park and walk home. It was a clear cold night. I felt good and happy and my little boy was growing and I wanted to see him fast asleep and just give him a brief summary of what was happening.

The consultants were impressive. Their initial weekly reports were pithy and punchy. There was much figurative and graphical content and a story of great potential for improvement emerged. Twinning with Tim worked well. I fed him names and structures and systems and procedures and some politics, he fed technique and methodology but more vitally the discipline of working to a specific brief within a tight deadline and beating that deadline with just enough spare to re-think, at least once, the recommendations that flowed so naturally from the work done. It was an intensive time. There were courses, mainly on management theory and communication skills at both the board's training centre at Ashover in Derbyshire and at the Electricity Council's centre at Horsley Towers in Surrey. I was put through public speaking training and entered in a competition held at the De Montford Hall in Leicester. The latest books on management were digested together with PA's recurring technical briefings.

Once blocks of fact-finding and analysis were completed, so the formal studies started. Of the old O & M team, only John Trigg became part of the new regime. He was selected to head one of five work study teams and complementary teams were formed to undertake clerical work measurement. Members of each team, which were geographically spread throughout the board, were selected from volunteers from any rank who chose to take PA's "Alpha 9" intelligence test and passed it. The same test was open for those wanting to be trained as computer programmers for the forthcoming IT development that would complement the efficiency drive. These tests threw up some interesting mixes. In John's team for example there was a costing assistant from my old office in Mansfield, a meter-reader from Mansfield and an area engineer from Ilkeston. Each of these was destined eventually to have quite senior staff control roles. It was a time of egalitarianism and talent was coming through. Equally the old guard was slipping away although few of them knew, mired in their fur-lined little ruts.

Enmeshed and enthralled and at the depot in Boston, Lincolnshire, a call was relayed second-hand from Tony's office in Derby. Would I meet him at a pub in Ilkeston at eight o'clock that evening and he couldn't be contacted before then. Never before and rarely since have I seen anyone more agitated. It all came out in one great rush. He was leaving Margaret. He intended to disappear. Tomorrow morning after she had left for work he would load his car with just his own personal possessions, his telescope, HiFi music system, clothes and drive away. He did not know where. Only his bank manager in Derby knew and he had promised not to inform anyone.

Tony had resigned and served his notice and his final pay would go into his account as normal. He just couldn't stand Margaret, he couldn't even bear her feet to touch his in bed. His life was intolerable. He was at his wits end. He would leave a note. He would contact me in a few days time but I was not to let anyone know where he was. Not Margaret, not his mother and not his younger brother. No one. I was dumbfounded, not even suspecting that there was any problem between them let alone a crisis. Did Margaret know what he was planning? No. Did his mother? No. Bloody hell! Little else was said. He was shaking and deathly pale. We had another drink and I made him promise to make contact as he had said. We shook hands and I left.

June was as baffled and upset as I was but with a difference. Over those Saturday nights around West Hallam she and Margaret had become good friends. Margaret was nice and happy and they had built up a wonderful home. They had far more things than we did. What would she do? She had to be told. We sat long into that night talking it through. Eventually it was agreed that I must support Tony and let him do what he planned. I felt in my bones that the alternative would spell tragedy. I was also beginning to feel that the looming events would take more managing than any of the management situations in the books, technical papers or live in the board.

The first call came from Tony's mum. She had found the note. If anyone knew where he was it would be me. I told her the truth. I did not know his whereabouts. June and I went over to see her that evening. She was very distressed but mad, very mad. I must have known what he was preparing to do and I must know where he is now and it was my duty to tell her so she could make contact and sort things out. He must be unbalanced since this rash action was right out of character. He needed help, surely I could see that? If he made contact with me then I was to tell her straight away. I refused to promise. She is now in her late eighties and has never forgiven me. Margaret just never stopped crying all evening but at least she wasn't accusing, just heart-broken.

The garden at our new place was hardly a provider of solace or a facilitator of hard physical graft to hide behind. It was a typical new development outdoor space. It did exist but for someone used to the farm garden and my large clay infested area at West Hallam, it was barely an apology. I did put flowering shrubs in the front, Philadelphus, Ribes, and Rhododendron and I did put down a little lawn at the back and left some space for an extremely small vegetable plot. There was also a small garden shed that I erected but not for the puny tools needed for this pocket handkerchief-sized plot but instead the cage birds I had persuaded my uncle Leslie to let me have a go at keeping. There were Java

Sparrows and Peking Robins but now I was seeing Tony's pale face amongst them and so I took them back for their greater freedom.

I took Christopher on long walks in the pram, sometimes all the way to the gardens and lakes in Newstead Abbey. I talked to him a lot and tried to imagine where Tony was and what he was doing. A week after he left he 'phoned. He was staying at a pub in Kidderminster. He had pointed the car southwards and subconsciously headed in the general direction of the Cotswolds. Would I come on my own and see him the following weekend? I could give him some news.

His mother had contacted the police but for them it was just another domestic but they could list him as a lost person after a certain time had passed. She had contacted his work only to be told he had left in a normal way and they had no idea he had anything underhand planned. She had set on a private investigator but there was no news as yet, it was much too early. Margaret had not gone back to work. His mum was very upset with me, she was convinced I knew all about his movements and indeed had done from the start. But how was he?

Two men who kept the pub had been very kind, he was slowly recovering his composure, he had no regrets, he would not be coming back no matter what. He needed to look for a job. Tony was in one of those warm, hospitable coaching inns that would become so familiar as I tracked his life through the Cotswolds over the years to come. White exterior walls broken by solid oak timbers painted jet black. The innards of this Kidderminster inn did not betray its long, long past. The floorboards were creaky and undulating and the walls, particularly upstairs, had angles any architect or mathematician would have been proud to have played a part in creating against the laws of gravity and stability.

The inside of the pub reminded me so much of the farm

and everything left behind and the Christmas day afternoon with dad poring over the deeds newly arrived from the National Westminster Bank after the compensation from the M1 people had paid off the mortgage. Those original four cottages dating from the early 1600's and belonging to the Lord of the Manor residing in Newton Old Hall. All the time that had passed since, all the peoples from birth to death re-learning from their elders, repeating, duplicating but thinking they were each unique. Derbyshire or Worcestershire it was doubtful if much had been different. They would have loved and love would have turned to hate but would they have left? Where would they have gone?

Ordinary working people couldn't just, as my dad might have said, "bugger off". They were born and bred and worked and died in the parish of their birth, at best in a neighbouring one. So had Tony taken a modern option? Is this what the motor car, job mobility, qualifications, the ability to build and knock down and re-build a life is about? If it is then it's also brought selfishness and cruelty. Or was it more cruel to stay and have to stay, with life a lie and growing hatred leading to growing danger? But there had been great danger to Tony and there still was. There was some danger to Margaret. Does the risk of current danger proving to be short-term have shorter odds than creeping long-term danger fuelled by hatred in the togetherness state? It is complicated and as yet unknown territory. But it will be the forerunner of worse and more personal things to come.

In this almost surreal situation drinking with Tony in the battered old bar, my dad's regalement about "bugger off" was especially poignant. The two joint owners of this wonderful place are obvious poofters of the first order, though whether they love each other is, to my mind, thrown into doubt when one of them sets about trying to persuade Tony to go to bed with him. It all makes me feel a bit sick and if this is what disappearing brings, I vow to stick things out - so to speak. It brings back memories of the queer on the Nottingham train and I wonder if it's a sign to think about moving on again. I do not envy Tony.

In the weeks that followed we got many calls from Tony's mother. She now believed absolutely that I knew where he was and threatened to tell the police and her detective as much. Whether she ever did so, June and I never knew. We visited Margaret several times and she recovered slowly, going back to work and starting to hate her lost husband. Eventually, Tony did call his mother and slowly, slowly over time she forgave him. She never forgave me. Tony and Margaret never spoke or met again. He just kept his car-load of personal possessions, she had the rest. So much for materialistic worth. So much for materialistic glue.

Years and years later we heard she was re-married to a policeman and lived happily in Nottingham. She would still be a very nice person, attractive and sexy but what has that got to do with anything? In what proved to be an interim phase, Tony became management accountant at a carpet manufacturing factory.

Back at the Board, things were going well. Travel here, travel there, meetings here, meetings there, recommendations in, recommendations approved, action plans in place. June was pregnant again. She was happy and fulfilled and I kept coming across this girl at HQ at evening meetings. It somehow happened that I started taking her home and suddenly it was more. We started meeting secretly and it would have gone all the way except I couldn't perform. It felt like a secret sign because I wanted to and she was completely lost in it. The only person I ever told was John Trigg, it came out one Friday evening. Our friendship was never the same after that and although meeting up for our boozy nights was more difficult once I started moving away, still it was me that always rang him, never again did he invite me out. I think I admired him for that.

It had to end and it did and it really hurt. I realised too late that liaisons are easy to make and hard to break and that it was something my ego could well do without. I came down to earth with an almighty bump and saw June through different eyes. I woke up sweating in the night and went over and over in my head what had nearly happened. The conclusion was blindingly obvious. It was time to move on again.

CHAPTER EIGHT
Management Consultancy, here we come

1969 -1972. Leaving EMEB for Price Waterhouse. The big mistake. A London scene then Dexion at Hemel Hemstead. A second baby and a move to Bovingdon. Chris in hospital. Raleigh bikes and Tube Investments of Matrix fame and Dynamic Dave. Ironbridge, Jack Mytton and Brian Rix. Enter Prince Rupert and the great pain. Of Allis Chalmers, gall stones and a Swiss retreat. Men of cake. A new life 8,000 miles away.

I asked Tim how one got started in management consultancy in the private sector. He felt that an interview with PA could be arranged but his name must not be linked since he was debarred from approaching client staff. And so I walked through the hallowed portals of the PA HQ in Albert Gate off Knightsbridge and opposite Hyde Park. The interview was civil enough with two men wearing suits of a quality that it occurred to me I had never seen the likes of before, not even adorning Mack. I think it was my schooling that was the cruncher but anyway before leaving one of them suddenly remembered that the relatively few accountants they employed - most I should understand were engineers - were all chartered not certified and he had been reminded that they had a policy of only employing chartered accountants and not those from the other accountancy bodies. Sorry about my wasted journey but would I like to collect my expenses from the general office on the way out. I think Tim was more upset than I was although he tried not to show it. How long he stayed with PA I never knew but some years later someone told me he was on the board of Walkers Crisps. He left with me something more enduring than crisps. To the managers and owners, every business is unique. Agree with them but know in your heart that every business is fundamentally the same, act accordingly.

The consultancy bug had however bitten. In the very next week's Accountancy Age were large advertisements for management consultants. Of these, Coopers and Lybrand and Price Waterhouse & Co listed amongst others an office in Nottingham. I tossed a coin and it came down heads for the latter. The interview was at an address that was to become second nature over the next nine years, Beaufort House, Newhall Street, Birmingham.

I was to learn that all Price Waterhouse & Co (PW) partners were known by and were to be addressed as, their initials. So it was that I was ushered into the presence of BJB. Bernard Brock was an extremely personable, cultured and, like the PA directors, well-dressed and groomed man. We seemed to hit it off from the start and I can remember nothing of the discussion except that the defining moment occurred, without any doubt, about half-way through the proceedings when his secretary came into the room full of apologies to say that there was an urgent telephone message for me. I think that BJB and myself were impressed in equal measure. It turned out that I had left the PW number with my assistant in Nottingham "in case of dour emergency". One of the new members of my team had decided he had such a cause celebre. Unplanned as it was, it worked perfectly to authenticate how important I was and of course of the vital work I was undertaking. Obviously PW, in its current search for new talent in its rapidly growing consultancy practice, could hardly ignore such a young thrusting go-getter.

The second interview with the senior partner, EWB in London confirmed this fit and the only matter to resolve was the starting salary. Before leaving Old Jewry I was told that an offer of a position of management consultant would be made and then completely taken aback by "and what salary do you think you should start on". The dilemma was probably because this was my first foray into the private sector. In the nationalised industries salaries were controlled rigidly by means of scales attached to grades.

Years later I was to appreciate that this was an open salary policy so that provided the grade of any individual was known, and it was, their salary could be pinpointed quite accurately. Therefore to be asked, in effect, "what do you want?" was not merely a rude introduction to a closed salary policy but it served to throw me completely off-guard. What there ought to have been was a fast-forward button but that devise was as far off being invented at that time as I was from graduating to the other side of the table and understanding the rules of the game. As it was, I thought of my present and newly increased salary added a mental ten per-cent and rounded up a bit. It was accepted immediately.

As my train pulled out of St Pancras station and I re-read the offer letter as handed to me on my departure from PW's consultancy HQ, my feelings overwhelmingly were of elation. Here was the most prestigious accountancy firm in the UK offering little old me a job in their cream specialisation of consultancy and as a full consultant, not a trainee or junior version, but the full works. Who knows where it might lead. And, I wasn't actually a chartered accountant (PA take note) just a humble certified one. I did wonder a little about the salary, how I might compare with anyone coming in from the private sector. But then, we all start from different places. The big thing was to make a success of it. I was dreading telling them back in Nottingham. Better have a drink and work out how to do it.

It was the biggest mistake of my life. It was the biggest mistake anyone could possibly make. I cannot conceive how I could have been so mind-blowingly stupid. In this grubby little pub in this grubby little street and two doors from my grubby bed-and-breakfast so-called little hotel, I was turning it over in my mind. I had had this marvellous job with EMEB and was, I felt sure, being fast-tracked for a really senior position once the efficiency push was well under way and, furthermore, I had already had one interview for a really senior financial job in the North Western Electricity Board). We had our new house quite close to the office, our son was now talking and firing questions from all angles at a really rapid rate, I knew all the people involved with work including the PA consultants and was well respected and in spite of this, I had given it all up. For what? For a job that I knew nothing about with people for whom I had no empathy since they were proving to be mainly public-school, university degree educated southerners who commuted home each day leaving the likes of me stuck in this bloody place.

The writing was on the wall from the very first morning in the London office when I was told that "there are no immediate plans to base any consultancy staff in Nottingham". The advertisement that I had responded to simply listed all the main firm's office locations. The vast majority of the staff in the firm were on the audit, tax and insolvency sides and were actually employed as a separate entity. The Nottingham office had come about by buying a local practice called Mellors Basdon and then changing its name.

The consultancy side was new and because many of the most senior long-standing partners had reservations about the impact management advice might have upon established client relationships, the new set-up was ring-fenced as Price

Waterhouse "& Co". The suffix being the indicator. There were actually only three partners allocated to this new activity of which BJB was one and only two designated initial offices, namely London and Birmingham. I had been interviewed in the latter because it was closer to where I lived and BJB happened to be visiting at the time. I got the decided impression that the founding rationale had been to garner advice fees that had been spotted as drifting from existing clients to the likes of PA Consultants, PE Consultants and others.

These pure consultancy firms had multi-disciplined teams and only some consultants would be accountants. PW hitherto had employed only accountants and furthermore they were trained in professional offices with no industrial experience. The new group being set-up under "& Co" would have engineers and so on. It was true that I was an accountant but I had been picked specifically for my industrial experience. All of this came as a shock. I had thought I was joining a huge organisation with vast experience in management consultancy. Instead it appeared that I was in almost at the birth and it occurred to me that the powerful old guard might have a vested interest in enforced infant mortality.

It was turning into a hot summer. I was uncomfortable, lonely, unhappy and a country-boy fish out of water. EMEB did not take deserters back and I had no contacts elsewhere. What a fool I had been.

The system of getting work to consultants was taciturn and catch-22ish. Names were displayed on a planning board posted in the main administrative office and by first date of availability or time blocks of availability. The purpose was so that the manager of an assignment could match an available person to his need to staff a job. But, of course, the manager's own reputation rests on the quality of the work done and in that regard his choice amongst equals will always favour the devil he knows. So, the manager goes for the consultant he has supervised before and who also knows how he, the manager, operates. There is no need to justify this choice, it is merely a question of placing a job name against the consultants name on the date slot required. Simple, except that if you happen to be a brand new John Smith with no particular specialisation, you are likely to remain unallocated. In the daytime there was the archive filing in the basement and in the evening promenading at the Royal Albert Hall, walking in Hyde Park and one trip by tube to Kew Gardens but not a single person to speak to from leaving at five-thirty until next morning at nine-thirty.

Then, right out of the blue, the office manager pointed to RPT inked in against my name on the planning board. Was this a partner not previously heard of? No, apparently it was a client and would I contact the manager one Jim Cook. I most certainly would.

Jim was a tall man with large rimmed spectacles and who talked with a pronounced nasal influence. He had spotted "that you have nothing to do" and his lead consultant Tony Wheeler could do with some help so he was grabbing me after having spoken to BJB who, in turn, thought I would be ok. My joy at this surprising initiation was tempered with no little anxiety. Tony turned out to be a well educated, well groomed city gentleman complete with bowler hat and umbrella and RPT turned out to be a marine engineering consultancy located in the heart of the city with some sort of fee-billing problem. I recall little of the actual work but rather the civilised city start time of nine-thirty am which in my railway office days would have been about mid-morning, the city lunches and the city after hours pints. Tony and Jim were from completely different backgrounds to me but, and perhaps because of this, we all got on extremely well. From time to time, Jim would pull me off this job for an odd day to "look at a little problem" somewhere else.

One of these forays was at the Crown Agents and this was destined to become a major account for him to manage and make his reputation. Later, Jim would become Secretary to the main firm partnership. I was starting to feel a little better. I could do the work, the variety was immense and there was a noticeable lack of formality. The culture manifested itself as being thrown in at the deep end with minimal guidance or briefing and success or failure turned largely on self initiative. Perhaps I was reading this all wrong but for the time being this suited me well. The loner had, maybe, fallen on his feet after all. Even amidst the prestigious fields of PW & Co.

The real break came entirely due to Jim. He had been taken by the audit partner to meet the MD of his client Dexion in Hemel Hemstead that manufactured slotted angle and other products that made up storage racking systems. Out of this meeting had come terms of reference and a consultancy budget for investigating the cause of a substantial loss on the book value of year-end stocks. The amount was sufficiently substantial to have made a material reduction in reported profits and neither the audit tests nor the internal accounting staff had found reasons for the physical stock to have disappeared.

Jim had agreed sufficient fees for two accountant consultants and one computer specialist to spend six weeks examining possible causal factors. If insufficient progress was deemed to have been made then the management would re-examine their options but if likely causal factors were highlighted then PW would be asked to implement the recommended remedial action. It followed that whilst the initial brief was important in bringing in a new client, the real benefit would flow if the MD was so impressed by the diagnostic work that a much larger assignment ensued. Jim already had his first two consultants earmarked and now following the work at RPT had decided to put me in as the third man. Whether BJB and or Jim actually knew and then didn't care and whether the client was informed or not and if informed similarly didn't care, I was not aware but it certainly struck me as having extraordinary confidence in someone such as myself who had never even stepped inside a manufacturing plant never mind having the faintest idea how one functioned. Still, I was an industrial accountant so that would have to do. If it was going to be the deep end it might as well be one hundred as six feet. Without the technique to swim, the act of drowning would be the same.

Before we arrived on site I had time to think about the fundamental problem. The more I thought back to how accounts are put together, the more I looked back at the Foulks Lynch factory accounts papers and particularly the way job and product costs were compiled and used, so the more it became clear that the item stock can at best be regarded as a balancing figure. It is what is left after all the ins have gone in and all the outs have gone out.

Since any manufacturing process changes the form of the physical in to become a physical out it must follow that the conversion factors must be absolutely accurate for what is left to be that which is expected and shown in the books. This must be so even if all pricing differences have been eliminated successfully. Having tested this theory on John Trigg, he propounded a concept that I interpreted as roughly meaning mass in (say x) must eventually equal mass out (the same x). I wondered then if not having worked in a factory was such a disadvantage, in fact might it be an advantage especially if this one key underlying idea could be kept as the guiding light? In such a large plant working as we were told the full twenty-four hours every day, we would have to see the wood for the trees, so to speak.

It had been agreed that the computer specialist would test the processing systems, the data holding records and the pricing controls operating within the standard costs used. The lead accountant would look for deficiencies in the actual physical stock counting systems and records and at the product costing compilations. I plucked up courage to tell Jim that rather than just help in these and related areas, I wanted to apply the techniques learned at EMEB and attempt to flow-chart the factory paperwork system from purchase order to final despatch.

The objective was to uncover breaks or mismatches in the flow and dig out any points at which estimates or assumptions entered the pipeline since these could dilute the principle of what came in must go out, no more no less. To his great credit Jim agreed and also to the idea of submitting a short punchy report at the end of each week to the MD setting out progress and initial conclusions - the trick picked up from PA. Probably more by fluke than design, little of help was coming from the main areas of work whereas from my fact-gathering around each department two principal findings started to boost the standing of the management, and the weekly sessions on my short reports were building rapport, and one deficiency was looking possible.

On the positive side, the basic paperwork system was looking sound and the standard costing system was catching most of the price, usage and efficiency variances. However, some spot checks at different stages of the work-in-progress seemed to indicate that some and maybe all of the production engineering standards were underestimating the amount of inherent waste in the material conversion processes. This proved to be a controversial conclusion because it implied criticism of a technical department and in a final report I was forced from the PW vetting side to add that the sampling that had taken place "had no sound statistical base".

The assignment did continue after the initial six weeks but with just me. Most of the engineering standards were re-worked with consequential uplifts to product costs and selling prices. As the work deepened and as testament to the importance of getting the most senior managers involved -another lesson from PA, I was spending as much time at the HQ in Wembley as at the factory in Hemel. It transpired that I had earned a nickname in the PW London office of Maigret Smith which had a touch of irony in that after the drinks party on the day I left, the factory transport manager took me to one side and in apparent all seriousness said "till the day I die I will never believe that your real name is John Smith".

The first real job with PW had gone well. The cost to June and later to both of us was, however, high. On a dark, damp and dismal early November morning I was woken in my London bed-and-breakfast-factory room with the news that June had gone into labour. Rushing to St Pancras and catching the first train to Nottingham, I arrived home by mid-morning in the middle of the activity going on upstairs with June, the midwife and June's mum. June had opted for a confinement at home and I was most certainly not allowed to be present in the actual bedroom. Pacing and pacing the lounge, suddenly from upstairs I heard June call out my name and out popped Craig our second son.

What a contrast to today when the presence of dad at the birth is mandatory, or so it seems. Here dad was very much an outsider. On reflection, this dad was more suited to his time. Unlike his elder brother Craig had not presented any complications at his coming and nor was his face damaged. This very happy and emotional day ended with me catching the late train back to London. Another stark contrast to today. Paternity leave. What?

It made sense to move base and travel by car and the Brakespear Hotel just off junction eight of the M1 was a palace compared to the London dumps. But my long week away from home from early Monday morning to late Friday night was taking its toll on June with the new baby and a two-year old child. She was suffering from post natal depression too.

Because expenses charged to my assignment were piling

up with the hotel and car mileage costs, I left the hotel and took two different lodgings in private houses. The first in Hemel itself and the second in Berkhamstead but neither was successful because the good ladies in question also had a family and my erratic time of getting back from the factory disrupted their routine and to be fair to them, each had wanted to produce for me "a nice evening meal". Invariably that meal had to be warmed up in the oven and was not at its best. As winter drew on and the job got more involved a better solution beckoned; rent a place so that June and the children could come and live with me and we would be a family again. The lady in personnel at the factory found us a bungalow for short-term let in Bovingdon. Perfect. Well not quite.

The bungalow was fine when we viewed it, if dated, and not much different to my aunt Pem's that had become so familiar during the egg delivery and after school odd-job childhood days. It even had a similar sort of coke-fired boiler in the kitchen. But soon after we moved in the weather turned for the worse. It became very cold and started to snow and continued to snow. The picturesque road in our newfound picturesque village became difficult to negotiate and our slightly uphill drive became a real hazard notwithstanding my shovelling morning and night. As we soon discovered though, this was as nothing to the inside of the bungalow that had suddenly turned itself into a refrigerator.

My, by now, well recognised deficiencies in the handyman department manifested itself in an inability to keep the wretched boiler alight throughout the night and since this turned out to be the only source of heating, there were cold starts to the day and cold water. With a baby a few weeks old and a two-year old, this was not clever. Even this assumed insignificance when Chris skidded and fell on the parquet floor in one of the bedrooms, screamed his little head off and couldn't get up. June stayed behind with her crying baby and I made the heart-rending trip to Hemel hospital casualty department. The x-ray revealed a fractured tibia and he would have to stay in.

The very worst aspect to the whole sorry affair was that when we both went back to visit, he was suspended from the shoulders downwards on a traction mechanism so that all his body was in space. We were told that at this young age such apparatus was necessary to facilitate the mending process. Well, maybe so, but he looked so uncomfortable and miserable and June and I were both very distressed. What made it worse was that Craig would not now stop crying. Perhaps due to the coldness of the bungalow and more likely our predicament but, whatever, we had drifted into a crises heightened by our absolute need to be with Chris in the ward for most of the time. In my agitated state, not helped by my conclusions on the basic problem in the factory being challenged vigorously by the production engineers and by a mathematician in the PW head office, I had to do something. Think. Think.

My mum and dad agreed to come down and take Craig home with them. It was the only practical solution but left a nagging empty feeling of failure. This was the first time since our marriage that either June or myself had even thought of asking for, and certainly never wanted, any help from anyone of any kind. They came down by coach because the London service had a dropping point at Hendon and I could get there to pick them up. This produced the first bit of light relief in days. On Hendon High Street, the main A41 heading to and from London, and near the bus stop were many people busy shopping on a late Saturday morning but no mum and dad and yet I was told the bus had come and gone on its way to Victoria Bus Station. Looking around I spotted a large pub across the road and it took no working out. Inside and in the far corner they sat, my dad with his pint and mum with her fruit juice. Never had I been so pleased to see them.

Mothering is a largely unspoken, un-rewarded, natural and highly skilled phenomenon. Even before mum left with our baby, he was quiet and peaceful and she had done something to his protruding naval that would prove a permanent fix. That help at the crucial time ushered in a gradual change of fortune. I eventually mastered the boiler and we were warm most of the time. The snow started to ease and the car got up the drive every day. Chris came home. The bitter cold weather turned warmer. Birds started to sing and the spring bulbs appeared. We walked this pretty village and started to get to know people and best of all, we fetched Craig back.

Another little plus, although at the time there was no inkling of how good it would ultimately turn out to be, was meeting Ian in the local pub. What started as a game of dominoes, ended with his business card. He was the local representative of an obscure insurance company called Australian Provident Mutual (AMP). Amongst my many anxieties at the time was driving in the highly congested areas of the home counties - a massive difference to back home in the sleepy East Midlands - and daily on the M1 with no life policy cover. I wanted short-term but significant cover so that June would be O.K. if anything happened to me. Ian sold me three separate policies, each with high initial cover but which declined as the years past until ceasing altogether. I was happy with this notwithstanding that the premiums doubled once my sky-high blood pressure readings filtered through after the mandatory medical. It took twenty years to remove this qualification from the medical history records.

These three policies later became convertible to fixed term whole of life and not only matured over twenty-five years later with considerable capital gain but also brought a de-mutualisation bonus to those select few UK holders of this little known Australian insurer. Like the policy taken out in the railway office, it represented a reward for endurance and had its element of good luck but more seriously was the product of a genuine and sincere desire to save, both to build resources and to guard against bad times ahead. As with the Ilkeston Co-Operative Society ideals, these long-term and prudent plans gave testimony to an epistemology now largely confined to history. Today we can't even make a paper profit on our home as the only real asset we have without cashing most of it in.

With the factory job in Hemel now recognised within PW as a success, I had the confidence to talk properly to Jim. The reason for my being attracted to them was the local office in Nottingham. My family needed to get back home and I could not be included in the large amount of work still needing to be done in Hertfordshire. Within days I was on the planning board for a team to go into Raleigh, the largest cycle producer in Europe and based in Nottingham. An incredible stroke of luck and timing.

I was sad to leave all the people who had become so familiar in the factory in Hemel and its modern open-plan offices. Sad to end the daily bet with the graduate management trainee seconded to me on what colour knickers the girl at the desk facing us would come to work in tomorrow in this era of mini-skirts and no modesty boards on desk fronts. Sad to miss the morning round of the tea-trolley and biscuits and actually sad to miss Hemel itself where at the weekend we went with Chris and baby to feed the ducks on the lake in the park. But it grew the hard shell that is consultancy. For years ahead it would be a case of get in, get stuck in, get out, my own philosophy well suited to the lone ranger. At least that plant went from strength to strength with a final sadness that within the last week I have read it has finally closed some thirty-five years and no doubt millions of storage racking systems later.

Now established as a factory systems expert I would be passed to the control of the senior consultancy manager in Birmingham, Henry Butt. He had picked up an assignment, again through introduction from the audit partner, whose client Tube Investments was the leading engineering business in the UK and listed amongst the top 100 companies. The Nottingham cycle manufacturer, Raleigh, was one of its divisions.

This was the era of vertical integration as well as conglomerates and the day of concentrated focus was yet to dawn. The largest division of the parent company manufactured sheet and tubular steel and a natural outlet for tube steel was the cycle frame. The cycle division based in Nottingham had the identical problem to Hemel namely a large loss on the valuation of the annual physical stock count. The difference proved to be one of scale not principle. But scale matters especially if it is accompanied by complexity. Seeing the wood does depend, to some extent, on just how many trees there are and it is not stupid to conceive that the wood might never be identified with sufficient accuracy to effect the proper solution. It is one scenario if things work out or balance in accounting parlance, it is entirely another if they do not and if for example a supposed profit is reduced severely by a surprise stock loss. It signifies an error but where does that error lie? How do we find it? The same fundamental issue as with the storage racking maker but now the scale!

The site in Nottingham was so large that riding one of its bicycles was the only efficient way to get from one part to another. There were over 6,000 different cycle specifications and over 50 different brand names. There were complete units and completely knocked down (CKD) packs for export all over the world for assembly at the receiving end. At this, largely, pre-computerised time there was over one hundred people working in the production control departments. It is all too easy now to overlook the huge gains in efficiency and productivity brought about by computer and related technology and of the inevitable consequential reduction in back-office manning levels.

Barn door to balance sheet

Today, the production tracking done by that huge department might well be handled by two people and software and perhaps my three week's work in charting all the material flow was a precursor to some future systems analysis and ultimately an ancestor of that software? At any rate, it got some concentrated work started and soon there was quite a PW team in place.

What is more striking in retrospect than any of the actual consultancy work is how sheer complexity is a harbinger of trouble, mainly unnecessary trouble if a key virtue had been understood as the elegance of simplicity.

If a business grows by acquisition as well as, or as an alternative to, indigenously then from a marketing standpoint there may well be a big shout for brand and product specification retention to maintain customer loyalty and for after-sales support. To a degree and for a time this will work as sales and marketing hold sway, but at a point the downward pressure on production and engineering will tip the scales and rationalisation and standardisation will be called for. If this need is not seen in time then the danger of losing control is real. Add to this a history of sound and substantial British engineering at a time of lower-grade imported competitor products, and the availability of the main material in-house at a transfer price that may or may not be at arms length, and there is the potential to cook a poisonous stew.

There is another factor. Old businesses build a culture and supporting sub-cultures. Like the medieval trade guilds, this establishment can outstay its time. At this plant, on this one site, were no less than nine separate dining areas for lunch. Each had its appointed hierarchical spot. What price this for finding out what is really going on in such a vast place?

As consultants working directly for the financial director of this division, we were privileged to attend the directors' dining room. Having recently read Jean Plaidy's Royal Road to Fortheringay, I was struck by the court of this assembly. It held advantages for us in developing our work but few that were obvious to the directors save food and privacy. As in all self-made social groups there was the introvert, the extrovert, the serious soul, the clown, and all paid homage as ever to the boss man when he was around. In short, a thoroughly false environment and not one in which I ever heard a considered debate about the business.

It struck me as testimony to our tenancy of life when a few years ago whilst walking alone through a tiny pretty village in Nottinghamshire, I noticed a small red-faced man walk slowly from a front door to put rubbish in his outside bin. This man had been a most senior director of this huge world-renowned cycle producer with his top-of-the-range jaguar car who held court in the dining room and who carried such great responsibility for a business that would slowly die.

Or, even sadder, the old man in front of me queuing in the fish-and-chip shop. Now in his mid-eighties with bent back and failing eyesight, he even so recognised me as his Sunday evening drinking friend in the local pub years before when he was running a very successful industrial boot manufacturing factory that had been in the family for generations. It was sold for a considerable sum to a large conglomerate and he was left to his fly-fishing. I do not know why but as we parted in the car park he mumbled "all those years and what did I achieve". If there is a moral it is that we should not be too proud of what we do or of who we are, it will not last.

What was lasting was our relationship with the parent engineering company and whilst engineering and computer specialists were taking over cycles, I was being moved to a new division that to me had the paradoxical label of Standard Products. Really? This was to be a first for inviting in external consultants and a different sort of assignment. The objective was to determine the relative profitability of each or each group of like products so that decisions could be taken on retention or shedding and possibly on re-setting selling prices.

I was left in no doubt by the financial director that the whole division was under pressure. The job was to be based at the division's HQ in Coventry on Flechamstead Highway and almost opposite British Leyland's Triumph motor car production factory. A greater transition from the service industries to this the very heart of British manufacturing it would have been difficult to find. The actual factory was known by its principal brand Matrix and was destined to become famous for its involvement in the Iraq super-gun affair.

I was not to work alone. A consultant from the newly formed Manchester office was coming in as a costing specialist. He had much factory experience and had been recruited from the hosiery industry. He had apparently been involved in writing the selling proposal and had pushed a relatively new costing concept. His name was David Tittle or soon to be dynamic Dave. He was small in stature, had a head that on first sight appeared rather large for his shoulders, was red-faced, somewhat bumptious and meant business. He knew exactly what to do and how to do it. He spoke a colourful language and had certain turns of phrase absolutely new to me. He thought a particular issue was best picked up here, carried over there and plonked down where it could not possibly be overlooked. I sort of understood, but not quite.

David thought I should get hold of a book published just three years earlier. "Using direct costing for profit and product improvement" by Myron M Miller and Robert R Viosca. It was a big book, self-assured, authoritative and very American. It taught the theory of the nature and behaviour (behavior) of costs and was also my first introduction to the concept of added value. It would indeed become my bible for the next two years or so and its ideas would indeed be thrust upon the unsuspecting standard products division whether they knew it or liked it or not. It soon became clear that our personalities were very different and that we handled people in a different way. In this arena of change and with much scope for personal initiative, it was a recipe for disharmony and potentially for disaster. As a result, we split the product groups into two chunks and went our separate ways.

For a time however and until David persuaded Henry Butt, still my boss, to let him rent a house in the area for his wife and children to come to, we spent many evenings together in the same hotels, in the same bars and watching the same films. He introduced me to the new spaghetti westerns and we wallowed in The Good, The Bad and the Ugly, For a Fistful of Dollars and For a Few Dollars More. I think David was Clint, but I never did work out who I was supposed to be. Once the work in the main factory was well under way, we split for good. He stayed in Coventry and took a factory at Brechin in Scotland whilst I got a plant in Leicestershire that manufactured broaches for drilling oil and more interestingly the factory in what was then Madeley and is now Telford in Shropshire. This was the measuring instruments unit that made literally hundreds of varying types of calliper and slip gauges and other measuring devices.

The Shropshire experience in general was infinitely more memorable than anything in the factory except for the day when I asked the factory manager why a certain bright young man whom he had seconded to me had dropped out of university rather than stay to get his degree. His answer related to the girl this secondee was about to marry and was delivered in the unrivalled deadpan twang of the black country "'is knob got the better of 'is 'ead". A different time and place and years later in Miami and looking for a bolt-on acquisition, I politely enquired of the potential seller why he originally married a wife whom he constantly lambasted "cos I wus young, dumb and full of cum".

The journey by road to Madeley was bad. Unlike the mainly south westerly trip to Coventry, this was due westerly and as such crossed a number of the predominantly south to north arterial roads. Compounding this was the use for a large stretch of the infamous A5 (the old Roman Watling Street) with its seemingly unending succession of built-up villages and their road speed limitations and linked by the lethal use of three-lane highways. Such a road was obviously built to trap the under-cautious and so remove one more motorist from the congested system. It worked by jamming the inside lane with heavy lorries trundling towards the north Wales ferry terminal and by having an ostensibly free middle lane for the fast and overtaking car. Unfortunately, of-course, a driver in the opposite direction had precisely the same idea at the same time. Result : swerve, slide, crash. This death trap reinforced the sense of the life insurance policies originally guarding against the perils of the M1 but meant also that commuting daily was out of the question and thus the Monday early am to Friday late pm weeks continued.

The suggested lodging house was a quaint old pub in Ironbridge, the village named after the first such structure in the world and cast by Abraham Darby in 1779 to span the River Severn and so start the Industrial Revolution. My personal industrial revolution was faltering, not due to the sleepy tourists that wondered at the ironwork but rather the non-sleeping locals with iron constitutions. After the fourth consecutive night of talking, shouting, singing and general merriment right beneath my bed, in fact so much between the floorboards that perhaps I had haplessly stumbled on some equally old Shropshire custom of noise transposition, I plucked up courage to ask the landlord whether he had some sort of dispensation from the normal ten-thirty pm licence closing time. He told me that there was no trouble with the law and that the local bobby usually popped in about midnight for a few jars. It was not so much this information as the way it was imparted that caused me to check out. I decided that I would either die from sleep depravation or something worse.

This brief spell in the quaint pub led the factory staff to recommend a more select one albeit farther out towards Shrewsbury, the Mytton and Mermaid at Atcham. It turned out that one Jack Mytton had been a local character renowned for his size and drinking prowess and that I was about to tread in his footsteps. Real as part of the Jack Mytton Way as it links with part of the Shropshire Way and metaphorically as it reflected drinking pints in the bar watching the local farmers and their hangers-on concentrate with great skill at fives and threes, the domino game. What with Ironbridge and Jack Mytton and the farmers, I was beginning to wonder if the whole of beautiful Shropshire was floating on alcohol.

My becoming a regular at the Mytton and Mermaid was rewarded with the largest bedroom ever remembered on a world scene of hotel and hostelry staying. It was vast and overlooked the river and the rolling meadows, I loved it. So much so that it caused me to move on again, this time in cussedness. Returning after one long factory day my things had been moved to another and poky room because "of the return for his annual one-night stand in Shrewsbury of our special guest". Who? Brian Rix of the Whitehall Theatre farces fame.

The consolation was waiting for his return from the theatre performance. Actually a very late return as his E-type jag had apparently flashed past the pub and carried on half-way to central Wales. Brian Rix chatted with others in the bar about his experiences and in particular the horrendous car crash in Spain that had severely injured his wife. She had been saved by the roadside treatment from a surgeon on his way to a bull-fight and the crash had also involved another well-known show business personality whose wife had been killed. Farce and tragedy in close order and also he was devoting his life now to a mental-health charity for personal reasons.

He was a very serious and sincere man and my puny contribution was to collect sponsorships on my first long-distance walk for that charity. Even allowing for this chance meeting, I was sufficiently peeved at being turned out of my room as to leave for further upward progress in the lodging stakes. This time I would search for a place myself.

The job was going well and everyone in sight was doing direct product costing like their life depended upon it. With the expenses budget well in tact, now was the time to splash out, so let's go to town. The town in question was Shrewsbury which is historically fascinating having retained much of its medieval street layout and a load of fine half-timbered Tudor and elegant brick Georgian houses. The old town centre is confined within the horseshoe loop of the river Severn and is a maze of narrow twisting streets, courtyards and interlinking alleys. The town is associated with many famous people including Charles Darwin who was born and educated there, Clive of India was both mayor and MP, Lord Hill who was the Duke of Wellington's general at Waterloo and Benjamin Disraeli the Tory prime minister.

However, my interest is more in Prince Rupert the name of the dominant hotel fitting all the criteria of the old town and with its ancient façade, ubiquitous oak beams and creaking floors. This prince came to grief fighting for Charles 1 and I'm about to do the same but less consciously. The hotel is very comfortable, the food is excellent and this place is a positive oasis after the hurly-burly of the factory day but after an evening meal comes this incredible pain. It's like a bolt from the blue. No forewarning at all. It's as if the ghost of Prince Rupert has cornered me in the courtyard and stuck his sword into my right lower side. I am literally doubled up and breathing hard and frightened.

Forced into a crouching position, I thought about calling for a doctor now but instead made slow progress to the bedroom and sat and hoped the pain would go away. By keeping very still the sharp stabbing eased slightly and after about an hour there was definitely some improvement such that I could stand upright again. After about two hours it had gone altogether. Thank heaven for that and I thought the food here was good. Given my history of stomach trouble, the inability to digest milk and that really bad bout of indigestion after eating pork on the Electricity Council course in Surrey, it ought not to have come as such a complete surprise. Yet that pain was definitely something else.

Shropshire was such a beautiful county. June had been over for the weekend and we'd been onto Wenlock Edge and driven round the Wrekin and explored Shrewsbury but once more the job was coming to an end. Back at the HQ in Coventry to present the final report, I bumped into David again who, after several months, was also about to finish. Aside from swapping notes he announced that he and his family were off to Singapore. Where? Had I not seen the vacancies posted on the PW Birmingham office notice board for consultants in the Singapore/Malaysian practice? He had applied, been to London for an interview with a visiting partner and was going out to Singapore in a month's time. Wow! He thought I should think about it. We could meet up again in the Far East. Well, why not?

Henry had been promoted to partner. The first consultancy one outside London and a feather in the cap of the Birmingham office. No more Henry, step up HAB. He now had his own manager, another Smith but more posh and in fact a Peter Cuthbert-Smith and he in turn had allocated me to a brand new client somewhere out near Stamford in Lincolnshire. Another factory job to match my by now established reputation as a factory problem solver.

Barn door to balance sheet

Essendine was fifty-five miles from home and reachable by car daily. However briefly, the hotel-living life was coming to an end. Craig was now two years old. Perhaps I would get to know him. Perhaps I could pull my weight at home for once. Perhaps. The effort of daily travel would be more than offset by the mileage rate claimable. Provided my not very magnificent car did not blow up, there was even a decided possibility of making a legitimate profit on the journeys. Musing over this possibility, my spirits were lifted higher when arriving at a most improbable place for a factory.

Essendine turned out to be a quiet and isolated little village set in rolling countryside a few miles east of the A1 and north of Stamford, the lordly Lincolnshire citadel. What a dream of a place and about as far removed from the industrial Midlands as it was possible to be. Not only that, the frontal office block was modern and, like Hemel had been, open plan apart from the directors' individual offices. The plant itself was enormous with single-story sheds separated by wide-open yards. It was a complex recognised immediately as designed for modern productive manufacture.

The ownership of the business had been originally British and its name still reflected the heritage as the producer of high quality agricultural tractors of a size and price bracket far removed from my dad's little grey Ferguson. What had caused the demise I never knew but it was now firmly American and I was met by a surprisingly young and very American MD called Ken Glass. His job was to get efficiency and make money. He had been sent over here to do it and do it he would. Not from tractors though. They had long gone. The product was a range of heavy four-wheel- drive earth-moving loaders. The company was Allis Chalmers.

Competition in this market was severe and from an American brand leader and increasingly a Japanese entrant.

It was absolutely vital to set the right selling prices for each of the models, and to do that to know with a high degree of accuracy what the build cost of each was. The old system of average pricing and labour estimates just would not do. For this plant to flourish, he had to know the true cost of each model so that proper decisions could be made on the viability of the range. This was particularly vital since I should know from the outset that every single machine was exported. They were too expensive to break into the UK. Most of the production was destined for the Middle East.

Unspoken but apparent from this quick-fire succinct briefing was that he personally had commissioned the consultancy and his future was bound up in its successful outcome. A breath of internal fresh air to complement the external ambience. In my, so far, short factory experience there had been all too much political manoeuvrings but here was a single determined leader. My overriding impression was that if I got the study right then he would push it through. Maybe not too much democracy but what the hell. By the way, the financial director is in this office. Been here for ever. Solid as a rock. Don Hemmings. He will give you all the resources you need. Good luck.

Don was a very different sort. The most obvious visual differentiation was age. Well into his middle years and greying slightly, he had the air of quiet calm but my presumption that it would be from this quarter that opposition or stalling would come was soon dispelled. He supported the study and had specifically wanted PW to undertake it due to close links over many years to the audit partner in Birmingham. I got an early impression that if there had been any disagreement on this with the MD then because the terms of reference were primarily financial, Don would have got his way.

As time passed this proved to be apposite first because he communicated directly with the financial vice president in Milwaukee and secondly he commanded obvious respect from the line managers throughout the plant. This contrasted with the trepidation felt about the lone ranger who had rode into these Lincolnshire plains from out west and who hustled them into weekly "NETMA" meetings. It took me months to find out that this was actually an acronym "nobody ever tells me anything". No doubt the acronym alone explained the foreboding, no doubt it was intended to. Don did not want detail on how the job would be done but did think a weekly briefing on progress would be useful - my by now old PA learned practice - and he was seconding George in the cost office to me on a full-time basis. This was the first job that I had been selected for to work on alone and to mess up in such a sublime climate was unthinkable.

And yet there was a discernable undercurrent. The offices were large, modern and studiously quiet. The factory was well laid out and stashed with machinery. The loaders were huge and apparently well engineered and manufactured. Best of all the workforce, albeit drawn from primarily the surrounding rural areas, had a reputation as being made up of experienced productive operatives who worked for modest labour rates as other local engine-making factories also gave testament.

Then why had this young American come in? Why were the earth-movers not competing with Caterpillar. Why was an outside consultant here asking all these questions? And who might deserve to court the attention of Ken Glass's undoubtedly developing hit list? There was another thing and it would not have occurred to anyone except perhaps the new MD. The anti-egalitarian cycle-factory-director-versus-the-rest syndrome was in play. I had by now honed my theory on detachment of managers actually producing ignorance of what was going on that in turn deluded, then misled and might eventually create a seriously false sense of well being. Coupled to the gentlemen's club chit-chat, were things just a touch too cushy?

The walk to the directors' dining room was particularly embarrassing as it required passing through the canteen used by everyone else. So the people that I had spent all morning persuading to fill in my new forms, or carrying out physical stock takes unusually frequently, were now being by-passed to reach the senior eating room as if they were secondary citizens. Not good for them and not good for me. Furthermore, the food was not the same and everyone knew it.

The directors and senior managers had four courses of silver service with drinks before, during and if they wished afterwards. Don held sway and the conversation became, as with the cycles men, predictably non-business. Whilst I was not then, or ever have been since any saint when it came to alcohol, my situation of youth and position of PW consultant and not least of being watched constantly by a growing band of those involved in the project, made me stick to orange juice during these luncheon interludes. This could not be claimed of certain others and personal revelations sometimes ran freely especially from the two who had served overseas in the war. It became increasingly apparent that for all the horrors and as survivors this period had been the highlight of their life. It only took a few gin and tonics to go over this ground again. And again.

Ken Glass did not attend the dining room. It was rumoured that he ate sandwiches in his office and drank water. There was another stand that he was consciously or sub-consciously making. Unlike Don, who had forty-something Barbara a quiet and respectively married secretary posted outside his office to politely sift the would be entrants and distract them with due homely chatter, Ken had recruited his own Girl Friday from beyond the factory and office family circles. She was very young, very attractive, had legs that went on for miles and wore the shortest possible mini-skirt. If Ken was about to shake up the place, well then so was she. Toward the end of the lunch-time homily the name of Jane often cropped up and one couldn't help but single out the personnel director in this regard and especially a linkage to his name that really was Fullerlove. He related a story of how Jane had been taken by her boyfriend that summer to Egypt and he had been offered thirty-five camels for her. Jim wanted to give something to Jane, rather than for her, but it wasn't a camel.

The task of actually compiling product costs was progressing quite nicely and helped, as it turned out, by a fluke piece of rare inspiration. One lunchtime, because it was someone's birthday, the directors' dining room was skipped for the pub and because he too had fond memories of the war years I started to recount to Harry who was in charge of the cost office how my uncle Ernie once told me that to break a particularly boring spell waiting for something to happen the sergeant had issued brushes and tins of paint and told the men to "go bloody well paint anything that moves."

I was thinking aloud to Harry that applying the same logic we should "cost anything that moves" and not just what the standard factory processes had always been taken to be. To my great surprise this obviously hit a chord because in no time the word had got round the whole factory "consultant says that that moves must be costed". And so it was that people from all sides came to me with information about little sub-works and little labour jobs done and bits of material used that before they had nowhere to record. The shopfloor paperwork grew accordingly and with my pinching the standard costing principles from the slotted angle experience and the direct costing methodology - not forgetting the differential cost centre recovery rates - rammed down my throat by dynamic Dave in Coventry, the job swung into top gear. So much so that I persuaded Don to budget for another consultant for six weeks to start a programme of compiling standard times so that good labour variances could be extracted and to review sales price variances.

After this unintentional push to my work, a warm glow developed for old Harry and it got positively hot when thinking back to Herbert in the railway office. Whilst Herbert had perfected the practice of sleeping in an upright seated position albeit with slightly drooped head, Harry saw no need for such surreptitiousness. Called to one of my vital afternoon meetings on sticky issues of cost compilation and no doubt assisted by what I now realised was his regular two or three pints each lunchtime in the pub, and which happened to be within the grounds of the factory, he simply fell asleep. Here is me wound up like a tort spring valiantly helping along this fulcrum of the great British export drive and acutely conscious of my extortionate charge-out rate from PW, and Harry the head of the cost office has the inner confidence and self-assurance to nod off.

My original entrance to Essendine had been on the low key side, in time to put my Ford in the main car park and await the arrival of the notoriously early American MD. About mid-morning on the due date and with a pronounced swirl of gravel straight into the MD's parking spot came a brand new gleaming white Mercedes. Enter John Eaton my new short-term assistant. John was a good ten years older than me, handsome, worldly and rich. Seems he had been recruited by the Birmingham office as a property consultant but this little job should be within his scope. Three cheers for Peter Cuthbert-Smith and Henry, they had got their new man on charge from day one. After my brief explanation of what needed doing and a whirlwind tour of the offices, John ploughed into the factory. From that instant I lost control of him completely.

At first things went really well. Everyone liked him and got swept along. They soon knew he had been a successful property developer in Birmingham and made pots of money and had really retired but being so young needed to keep the old grey cells turning over and so was doing a spot of consultancy. Great. He added a good deal of spice to the lunchtime dining table and his skill as an accomplished raconteur was soon obvious to the established and, it has to be said, somewhat older members of the club. The problem, and as the days past a growing one, was that the subject matter of a quip might not have been best suited to this audience. He had been looking at the sales side and particularly the varying prices set for different overseas markets. This led to a general discussion on selling and ultimately the make-up of sales people. John proffered the view that a top salesman could always be identified as the one hair-arsing around the place with an order book in one hand and his cock in the other. There was a longer than usual silence and Don stared at me with rather cold eyes.

A bit of well meant coaching would probably have saved the day had not a couple of the directors been to see Don on a coordinated and common theme. One reported John's pre-lunch visits for a couple of pints of Guinness to the factory pub and the second, and the killer blow, was from the director with responsibility for the drinks cabinet within the dining room that John was discovered rifling after everyone else had left. Don had a discreet and low-key word with Cuthbert-Smith and the following week the dashing John Eaton was no more.

It was a big shame. I had got to like him a lot. He had been not so much a breath as a veritable gale of fresh air and in fact I had never met anyone like him before. We were destined to meet again but in very different circumstances and ones that proved far more amenable to his culture.

By now things were happening on other fronts. The pain that first hit in the Prince Rupert in Shrewsbury was recurring and noticeably starting to twinge around four-thirty each afternoon. It was definitely getting worse and the car journeys back home after work were becoming more and more uncomfortable and the only way to get any sort of relief was by leaning to the right and screwing up my lower abdomen. This not only made for a difficult driving position but it got as I could hardly concentrate.

June and I both new that something had to be done but I just couldn't afford to have time off work especially as my final report on the assignment at Essendine was nearing completion. And yet by now nearly every evening from about seven o'clock onwards and for at least two hours all I could do was sit as still as possible, ride out the pain and wait for it to ease. I could no longer help with the boys' bedtime routine and I was getting increasingly cold whilst the bouts were on.

It came to a head when one evening with pain more severe than usual I somehow slid to the floor and in a crouched position just could not move. June called out a doctor and he gave me an injection and next day there had to be a consultation. No question of going to work. Luckily and by chance the appointment was with the senior partner of the local practice who had perhaps come from a long line of such specialists since his name was Leach. He was not the best liked of his peers due apparently to his custom of telling it how it was. Not the most diplomatic certainly as was borne out by the conversation with the patient before myself and as it drifted through the paper thin walls of his surgery "suppose I would be feeling tired all the time if I walked about all day carrying a three-stone bag on my back". In today's more politically correct and litigious times the poor patient would no doubt be given a diet sheet and sympathy. After close questions centred mainly on timings of attacks of pain relative to eating, the excellent Dr Leach concluded "small suspicion of gall stones". He added that it would be a bit odd if the impending barium meal confirmed his preliminary diagnosis because it was the "F's" disease "female, fat and forty" whereas I was male, thin as a rake and not yet thirty. Was he preparing me for some other possibility?

The diagnosis was, however, confirmed and furthermore the stones were not numerous and small that might pass with urine but few and large that definitely would not. The consequential anxiety would have been multiplied tenfold had I known then about the dilemma facing and solution endured by Samuel Pepys. As it was, the only option was surgery and by the way the waiting list for such a common ailment was somewhere between nine months and two years.

June and I talked it over at length. Maybe it would be possible to lose myself in some other job for such a waiting time but definitely, definitely the consulting could not continue. The work was too intense and myself as a person too much under scrutiny. So what to do? Henry came over on one of his rare supervisory visits and promised to discuss the matter with his partners. The deal came back within days. Bypass the NHS and go privately. The firm would pay for the surgeon and the anaesthetist if I paid for the in-patient care side. That way the risk of cost run-a-way lay with me since their liability would be known at the outset but if my stay in hospital was longer than expected due to any unforeseen problems then I would have to foot the increased bill.

Both the offer and the way it was structured took me completely be surprise. PW went up in my estimation enormously. It might be a large firm but it could move fast and Henry had shown he was a really good man to work for. He was also as I was to learn over the years a true gentleman in the genuine old-fashioned meaning of the word. The appointment with the consultant surgeon was on a Monday morning. He offered fifty percent off the list price because I was not insured - by now I was getting used to deals - and this Thursday to come in for a Friday morning operation. Bloody hell.

Two apparently unrelated but destined to be intertwined

events developed within PW in parallel with my stones problem. First was news from Henry that in line with the rapid success of the consultancy venture outside London and his responsibility now for the whole of the Midlands offices and not just Birmingham, the main firm partners in Nottingham had, later I would learn reluctantly, agreed to have a consultancy presence within their midst. This coincided with the promotion to manager grade in London of a chap who happened to have a girlfriend who worked for the library at Nottingham University and so this Richard would be found an office in the Nottingham firm as the first East Midlands location.

I should appreciate that this was obviously good news for me in that once some work came in, I was the local chap to do it. Great except that as a second development, what Henry did not know and nor did his London based colleagues was that I had just filled in an application form for "UK consultants wanted by the Singapore/Malaysian firm". Dynamic Dave had been right, more requests would flow from that quarter and I had seen this one and having gone through the discussion phase with June on the lines of "if I ever get rid of this pain let's change our life", the plunge had been taken. If it came off then good luck to this Richard but a bit late for the one who had thought he was being employed there in the first place. He would be a few thousand miles away.

Somewhat closer to home but also driven by the emergent theme of making the most of today just in case tomorrow won't let us, was the purchase of a touring caravan and booking a holiday in Switzerland. Destined, due to impending events, to be doomed to one trip only, a towing caravan has to make the most of its chance and so this certainly did. It had been acquired as an act of pure impulse. Walking to the shops one Saturday morning with Chris and Craig (and being informed en-route by an old man that "you've got your hands full there young man") we passed a house on whose driveway stood this clean shiny caravan with its for sale sign. I went in and bought it. June was a bit surprised but she could see its potential as a passport to freedom and we had had our problems on the more conventional holidays mainly due to eating. Not me this time but Chris. The problem being that he wouldn't. That is to say, not the food the hotel or wherever provided. As a result, any prospect, however remote, of non-public displays of meal-time angst was to be viewed with relish and relief.

Having plunged into the almost unfathomable depths of tow-bars and heavy-duty flashing lights and things to lock the wheels when stationary and a gadget to keep the towing bar upright if the car wanted its freedom, we set off to tour the perimeter of Scotland including at one point the Isle of Skye via ferry. This was not an intentional journey but merely that having set off north on the A1 we seemed to just keep going in a sort of anti-clockwise direction. The highlight was probably driving through the northern outskirts of Newcastle in heavy traffic and hearing the announcement from the backseat that "there, that's Teddy gone". Towing a caravan with no experience and no proper vision of the rear there could have been no question of our stopping or turning back and so we never did discover what happened to Teddy or indeed whether there had been a multiple pile-up somewhere in our wake.

The idea behind Switzerland was to plan a foreign holiday but on a shoestring. The advertisement spoke of the boat train from London Victoria all the way to Montreux on the shores of Lake Geneva and then a funicular railway up to Gstaad. Of-course neither June or I had any notion that this was the in-season land of the rich and famous or that later it would be immortalised amongst the British as a stamping ground for the hedonistic Liz Taylor and Richard Burton. To us it was just a cheap way to get to somewhere that looked very beautiful and on a self-catering "stay with a family in their chalet" basis.

With getting my fill walking in the Derbyshire Peak District on a regular basis, it wasn't actually the Swiss mountains and valleys that had been a draw for me but the journey by rail. I still had deep pangs of the railway past and sometimes still regretted leaving that life. But mainly it was something to look forward to if ever I got rid of this bloody pain that now I dreaded the onset of as much as the attack itself. If only we could all come out on the other side in more or less one piece, then life would be wonderful again.

So June took me in the late afternoon with the real-leather grip bag, the leaving present from Ilkeston Electricity, packed with pyjamas, dressing gown, underclothes and toilet bag and we'd left Chris and Craig behind and I was worried but had no choice and feeling very, very low. It was the NHS old Victorian General Hospital in Mansfield that turned out to have some private facilities upstairs in a side wing. I was sharing a room with one other man who was very sick. There were some pre-op examinations and shavings and early the following morning an injection to make me sleepy and a drowsy trip on a stretcher down some corridors, down in a lift and through some swing doors into a large room where I recognised the anaesthetist who took my hand and hit it quite hard before pushing in a needle.

Sometime later that day or the next day the very sick man was still there and urine was shooting out from him in an almost vertical fountain towards the ceiling and there was much coming and going and a tall thin consultant came back and there was going to be another compete blood transfusion and I drifted off. The trouble was I couldn't move. I had tried but a sword or a knife or a spade or something was sticking in my right-hand side and I just could not shift at all. There was at least one tube coming down from a gantry thing and sticking in me and at least one other leaving me and going towards the floor. The thirst was unbelievable and there was some water in a tumbler on a little table near my left hand but try as I might I just could not reach it. I decided that if I ever got out of here I would make the very best of life, to make every day count, to be whatever the opposite of mean is and I desperately wanted to see Chris and Craig and I knew I was crying but I couldn't do anything about that either.

Conceivably it's late in the evening and the sick man has visitors. His wife certainly and it looks like two children and some others. There is blood in a plastic-looking pouch thing hanging above his head. He is very still. The next day he is better, sitting up in bed and talking to me. He is an airline pilot and lives as we do in Ravenshead but on Church Drive in a big house on the right-hand side going down. He is forty-seven years old and was in perfect health until near the end of their holiday in France last summer when suddenly he felt odd. They returned home early and he has been in and out of hospital ever since. They say he has pleurisy. When he gets out this time he will give up flying and go for an easier life.

Drifting through the days is one thing but I just cannot sleep at night. The nights go on for ever starting with the people going into and later swaying out of the drinking club just down the road that I can see through my window and carrying on with the noise and the lights and now there are more visits to the airline pilot from the consultant and a good deal of related activity. I am trying not to cause any trouble but I keep slipping down the bed and getting into a slumped position where I can hardly breath.

Some of the night nurses are very kind and when I press the little button do come and pull me back up. But there is one who is different. She tells me in no uncertain terms that she is very busy with the main wards and I will have to wait, and when she does come is very rough and seems to yank me up the bed. If I want she can give me an injection to make me sleep, and she does. What it did was to bring in the green dragons that circled above me and dived and returned and dived again. Then the pain built up in my lower gut. Not the constant deepening one of the stones but a stabbing one that went away and then returned a bit worse than before. A very kind and tender more elderly nurse said I had to get rid of trapped wind and inserted a tube or something in my rear end "to help you out."

How and when did it come about? I am no longer in the room with the pilot but a larger room and there are two other men. They are less serious cases and in fact both are in for hernia operations my by now favourite kind nurse tells me. The one just arrived is a very jolly chap but a bit loud and boisterous for my liking in this strange floating state where I keep sinking low and feel like crying again. He wants me to know he is the steward of the local golf club and it takes little working out that it is the nineteenth that is his favourite. His many male visitors are likewise full of bonhomie and whatever the rules leave behind a liberal supply of booze.

It's a shock to my aching system but June tells me I have come through the "op plus 2 day" and she can bring Chris in to see me if I feel up to it. The following afternoon I have two visitors and I am trying to tell them that tomorrow I am expecting a VIP to come in but they do not seem to understand or care that I am referring to Chris. Rather, my dad has got one of his famous arguments going by taunting June's dad about miners and how they get paid too much for what they do and they shouldn't get their free coal allowance etc, etc. As a coal-face worker all his life and now starting to suffer from the dust, Jack Painter is easy prey. They come all this way to see how I am and both by bus since neither has a vehicle of his own - too much traffic for the tractor - and this is what happens. I listen to the bedside bickering with irritated frustration and literally and temperamentally sink lower and lower. Never mind, I'll get my VIP visitor tomorrow. Why don't they just bugger off?

My friend and ex-colleague from EMEB John Trigg had agreed to fetch me out on day ten and although he's driving normally I keep hoping that he will slow down with every bump in the road sending a punch into my midriff. But, then again, I do not want him to slow down, I want to get home. My freedom was the more poignant because of wanting to say goodbye to the recovering pilot. I suppose the nurse had no option in telling me. He had died the previous night.

No words can express the joy of getting out and it's really strange about the other two visitors I had. One was this chap Richard whom I had not met before but who wanted to introduce himself to me as the impending new boss in Nottingham. He was pleasant, well groomed and fairly typical of the breed I now recognised as the thrusting young up-and-coming managers of PW management consultancy. He had brought me a book as a present. For some years afterwards the thought processes that lay behind giving the book to me were puzzling. Then as we got to know each other better, the mystery was solved. He may simply have thought that I had, or might have, a certain sort of sense of humour or maybe he was simply unthinkingly and selfishly stupid. The book was in the shape of a headstone. It was called "The little book of grave humour" and was made up of epitaphs.

My second visitor was equally a great surprise. John Eaton came bounding in with his sharp flannels and blazer and tie just as if leaving the pub at Essendine on a hot summer evening. He had to see how I was making out and he so admired my decision to have the operation because the greatest dread he had in life was having "to face the knife". Thank god I had never thought of it like that. Also, did I know that fifty percent of all who came in like me went out on a cold slab at the back!

Still, it was great to see his beaming face and to think he had come all the way from Birmingham and we only met a few weeks back and he'd been sacked off my job. Human nature is strange. My best friend lived just down the road and I had neither seen nor heard from him. John Eaton also brought a book. Alistair Maclean's Bear Island. That was better. I feel almost well again and especially when he relates the story of his secret affair. What secret affair? You know I stayed in that posh hotel on the A1 just south of Stamford, well she used to come to me there after work. Her idea and although she'd had a hysterectomy the sex was fantastic. Who, who? Well, the name came as a shock and about the last person I would have guessed at and it wasn't Ken Glass's dolly bird either. An apparently happily married quiet women like that. Seems white knights or at any rate a knight in a white Mercedes still excites a certain type of lady. I felt another pang as he sauntered off. This time it wasn't physical, more emotional.

Even during the six-week's slow and painful recovery period things were again happening. A reply came back from Singapore enclosing a contract. If signed, an eighteen month secondment could start from early July. They did not need to interview me, my credentials were fine. Dynamic Dave in play again? June and I discussed it again with mounting excitement. There were lots of nice touches. First, the salary though quoted in Singapore dollars had not only a conversion rate but examples of costs so that it was possible to work out a form of standard of living in comparison with the UK.

It was a continuous period of work but with six weeks holiday at the end that could be taken as salary if wanted. There was a government compulsory superannuation scheme but with this being a fixed term contract and short of the de minimus level, such deductions together with the firm's payments would be returned and so acting as a form of compulsory savings scheme. There was also a discretionary bonus scheme. A car would be needed and the firm provided a loan repayable through the salary. A place was available at the excellent private school for children under twelve years and at the international school for any older, and the firm had reserved places at the Tanglin Club.

Health care was entirely private via deductions again through the payroll. For the first month, the firm guaranteed to find as the initial accommodation a *leave bungalow* to help with settling in. I was to learn later that all this detail had been composed from experience by the excellent manager Tony Wilkinson. But for now it was too good to miss and it had to be the incentive to get over the operation. I signed and the move was on.

When you can only walk in a painful half-stoop and one step at a time and holding onto anything handy for support, it's easy to lose self-esteem even when exciting things are stacking up for the future. As the drugs wear off so the real aching soreness kicks in. To actually see oneself again is a shock. Just trying to get washed and dressed takes all morning and my clothes hang off me. I discover that I am back to the same weight as on my wedding day, ten stone six pounds, and with a wry smile to myself think of the futility of the stodgy lunches at Ilkeston and the superb dining at Mapperley Hall, at Raleigh in Nottingham and at Allis Chalmers in Essendine. All sacrificed to the stone and John Eaton's knife.

The scar is five inches long from my mid chest diagonally to my lower right-hand side and there is what I am told is the drainage hole lower down still. Later on I shall tell the staring eyes at swimming pools and in warm tropical seas "barracuda – South China Sea". No-one believed me but I felt better. It's also easy to kid yourself of recovery. Soon after I could walk upright again and unaided, I set off for a gentle stroll down the road, it is snowing but that's fine until the swaying and dizziness starts. Hanging onto a wall and with no-one around it will take all my strength to get back home. And I thought I was better. Going four hours after eating with no pain is a wonderful thing, but I am not ready for the real world yet.

Henry hears about my secondment to the Far East in six months time and is disappointed but wishes me well. In the meantime, once back at work, will I go back to Allis Chalmers where Don Hemmings wishes to discuss a new assignment and since I have had experience in finding steel and cycle frames and machine tools and four-wheel loaders, would I like to try my hand at finding cakes. Cakes?

It was rumoured to have been embryonic on a golf course. The chairman of United Biscuits had discussed with his counterpart at Cadbury certain issues associated with his small cake business. Before the round of golf was over, or so the rumour went, both men could see the merits of putting their two small cake businesses together. There would be synergies of scale, and best practice would prevail. Everyone a winner. Whether conception took place that way or not, fact is there is now one combined business and there are not many happy bunnies around. Procedures are a mess, cake is going missing and less money is being made now than when the organisations were separate. Anyway we've got the job and you are down to do it, when you are better of course.

The expression small proved euphemistic and relative. If the largest chocolate manufacturer in the UK had a cake side and the second largest biscuit manufacturer likewise, such a sideline will be less large than the mainstream activity. However, combine the two also-rans and up pops the number two to the UK cake market leader. In absolute terms the new venture was enormous with a HQ in Worcester and factories in West London and Glasgow and logistics predicated to the characteristics of a fresh product with a pre-determined and limited shelf-life and at a point in time when best before had just been implemented. Interestingly to me, this latter feature had itself resulted from a consultancy study the kernel of which I had been allowed to study.

From the initial pulling together of the most senior managers, it was easy to work out that the fundamental problem lay not outside but right inside this meeting room. Biscuit men to the left and chocolate men to the right and biscuit man agrees with biscuit men and chocolate man agrees with chocolate men. Biscuit views and chocolate views differ on every issue. My secondee this time is older than on previous jobs and is well versed in this cake game. His proper name is Elkington but everyone and it must include me knows him as the Elk. Together we roam the moorlands of factory and distribution points and delivery vans and offices and the bars of central Worcester with Don Maclean's American Pie blasting out from each and I hear the hourly chimes of Worcester Cathedral that must be sited right outside my bedroom window. But we are getting there and I'm starting to appreciate the tiers of a market that will prove useful years later in line management. In this case we have patisserie to better supermarket to poorer supermarket to little shop to market stall and finally to pig farmer. Add to this the returns and damages and the potential to swap lines within a van and trays between vans and accounting for stock may become complicated.

Now that there are more reliable manufacturing costs for the four-wheel loaders Don, back at Essendine, wants some other things looking at but he prefers to wait until I get back from my Far East contract and in any case on his last visit to the States there was talk of structural changes afoot that might affect the UK plant.

We take the Swiss holiday and it is a wonderful convalescence and I am now strong enough to take some quite steep mountain walks with June, and carrying one of the boys on my back. It is a magical transformation and we can buy white wine in the morning and dunk the bottle in an ice-cold mountain stream fed by the melting snow a few hundred feet higher. We can't communicate with the owners of our rented chalet who live downstairs because their language is German, a surprise since we thought we were in the French speaking sector, and when we both try to draw a kettle it produces only amazed German gestures.

On the main line train back, an Italian mamma gives Chris a huge chunk of home-made cake which he succeeds in spreading all over the carriage floor much to her great glee. She compliments us on having such a small boy who can speak such perfect English, and so fast!

Two weeks later my brother Alan drove us to Heathrow. Two adults, two small children, two suitcases. The car has gone for cash, the house has gone to an agent to rent out and Tony has taken the caravan and will pay for it in instalments whilst we are away. Sorry but we will not make his wedding and so I cannot accept the invitation to be best man. He is back with the electricity industry and this time the Midlands Board. He has met Pam who works for the Generating Board and their new life beckons. So does ours and we board the BOAC Super VC10 via Rome, Abu Dhabi and Colombo to Singapore.

CHAPTER NINE
Singapore

1972-1974. A hot sticky welcome to an island of surprises. Malaysian hill resort. Cockroaches and mosquitoes. Benjai Hill. The night market and the Tanglin Club. Kranji War Memorial but orchids and butterflies. First day at school and first assignment. The ANZUK forces' mess and of consultants' ethnic mix. Trips to Kuantan and Penang. Female mahjong. Sembawang Shipyard with Cycle & Carriage. A surprise arrival. Robinsons burns down. Marital cracks appear.

At least getting off the plane whilst it refuels in Sri Lanka gives some hint of the pressure cooker to come but nothing can really prepare our unwary selves for the sheer extreme of change. Read up all one might but there is no real forewarning of the bash to the senses that eight thousand miles south-easterly brings. It's amazing just how bright the daylight is. One of the first things will have to be getting us all fixed up with proper sunglasses and of-course Chris and little Craig are proud to wear their huge plastic examples. The brightness is actually dazzling.

Then the smells. Absolutely nothing in any of the literature mentioned that the nose was about to be raped.

It's sort of aromatic and pungent and obviously, well, present. Back home, unless something special was happening, like cleaning out the pig-sty or hen-house after a long winter or walking through the new-mown hay or entering an indoor swimming pool, it seems to me that there must have been no actual awareness of smells as such but here it's a positive assault to the nasal systems. And if animal smells are at first obnoxious, it's peanuts compared to the first taxi crossing of Singapore River. Later, led by the children, we will all learn to hold our noses as we approach but this first time is the ultimate nostril and then memory implanter. Years later it will be re-lived in Bombay but for now this is the smell of all smells.

Another inescapable first impression is of noise. This place is heaving with decibel-creating activity. Aeroplanes, cars, trucks, boats and people. Masses and masses of people. And what variety. This density and mix makes London akin to the Derbyshire hills. We knew in advance that two-and-half million people lived on an island the same size as the Isle of Wight but I had also read somewhere that the whole of the world's population could be accommodated on that island, albeit BO would be a problem, and so it did not really strike home.

It strikes home though when the taxi drives down to the city and up Orchard Road. There are people of every hue everywhere. Solitude here will be gold dust. But then I'm thinking well we came here for a different experience and only recently having been given a life, then maybe a life-changing one too. So O.K. it's going to be strange getting used to some things but just look at this garden. Positively nothing back home like this. A yellow-breasted sunbird has just landed on a bright red hibiscus and is using its long curved beak to, presumably, extract nectar. And more extraordinary still, some form of insect has just flown across the lawn with lazily flapping and enormous wings. It must have been a butterfly but if so it's from the land of giants and black or very dark blue and look there's another and bright yellow. There are pots full of orchids on the balcony. Orchids! What an absolute treat. We will definitely be able to settle here.

This is the land of "Wow, did you see that?" A young Chinese man is riding a bicycle down the road in heavy traffic. On a rear pannier is a live pig fastened down with string. And on the subject of live things, a woman shopping on the night market and just in front of us wants a chicken. The stallholder pulls one from a wicker cage and holds it aloft for inspection. The customer accepts and the vendor duly chops off its head. Until that split second it was of-course very much alive, now it is very much and twitchingly dead.

Pushing Craig down the road on his little cart, there are children of mixed race dangling a piece of string or wire or something down a drain. Just as I pass, they haul out a snake or eel or similar, long, thin and wiggly. It gives me the creeps all day long. Back on the night market, a sign announces a hair-cutting service that I am badly in need of. As June walks on with Chris and Craig I enter the cabin to find a very large Sikh-like man sporting a huge black beard and moustache.

Sat down and suitably robed and accompanied by a discernible "pssst" sort of sound, I am handed a well worn tatty looking girlie magazine with strict instructions to bury it in my robe should anyone else enter. It is far too early in my personal learning curve to appreciate the magnanimity of this gesture in this near-police-State but six months later would certainly have met with a decline. Still, for now the well thumbed girls are quite nice.

One tends though to lose a certain amount of interest in the most absorbing of magazines when without warning or permission hot towels are wrapped around ones head and the scalp is suddenly slapped repeatedly and quite hard with a giant's bare hands. The performance was not over with the unwrapping either. Clasping my head in his vice-firm huge hands he pulled upwards and yanked it to the left. The audible cracking sound was such that for all I knew the neck was broken and so the anticipation of the impending inevitable jerk to the right was mesmeric.

Thereafter I used a more conventional barber installed in a shopping complex who obviously had learned that there was a market amongst ex-pats for charging somewhat more than his night market colleagues. And it was very important to keep ones hair cropped. The pop star Cliff Richard thought he would visit but the authorities at the airport took one look at his flowing mane and thought otherwise. Go back to the decadent UK young man, and he did.

Devising methods to defeat the prevailing morality was clearly something of a pastime. Young couples walking to one of the very few areas of open ground on the island on a Sunday afternoon had, for that time of day, a surprising yen for literal assimilation. That is to say each loving couple wanted to carry the broadsheet Straits Times. A stroll round the MacRitchie Reservoir soon revealed that the love was not of the paper but of under it. The young male bloods cocked a more blatant snoop. Each Saturday night they boarded the bus that travels up the island from South to North to leave the republic via the causeway to the liberal Malaysia. What went on in Johor Baharu was, by ex-pat rumour and the occasional confession, something else entirely.

It is a sight that is, regrettably, not uncommon here now with the causal issues steeped in grid-locked traffic and no doubt other contemporary sociological factors too deep for my understanding but at that time in that new place it was a further "wow" factor to see from the taxi window a brownish coloured gentleman proudly holding his penis and urinating in the open roadside gutter. Took me back to the days working in the fields but even there it was done with a degree of decorum with back turned and facing a hedge or tree.

And what a contrast between these bucolic thoughts and the traffic flow in this hustling bustling noisy city-republic. Like so many other things to be witnessed and experienced over the next eighteen months, here is an extreme of contrasts. The old hanging on to its traditions or clinging on to its first entry into a modern state and the new as thrusting and as advanced as anywhere in the world at this time.

You can see it in the transport mode. There are cars here bigger and sleeker and sometimes brasher than we have ever seen before. From the USA side have come Cadillacs and Buicks and Pontiacs and Lincolns, from down under the huge pick-ups and convertibles surely designed solely to move from Sydney to Darwin not Singapore City to Changi and now as built up from their CKD form - as I shall learn from direct involvement soon - the shiny and the ultimate in new Chinese *have made it* status symbol Mercedes 280SE.

And yet as the throw back to a time not so long ago when the British really did still control this place, most of the taxis are black, occasionally green, Morris Oxfords with a spattering to herald the invasion to come of Toyotas. At the bottom end the Japanese, despite the history and the ingrained hatred from those middle-aged or older, have already taken a strangle hold with the Mazda and the little Mitsubishi Colts and an odd Datsun. In the midst of all this come the trishaws whose skinny fit owner/peddlers appear to think nothing of crossing a main road with four or five lanes against the flow of traffic. It is an incredible act of bravado and the occupants do not seem unduly bothered either.

Later on we will be encouraged to get involved in an unofficial and mildly alcoholic-induced trishaw race. But there is a fair bit to come before that. Of course, the cyclists and their multifarious burdens are everywhere too as are the open-backed trucks which, along with normal loads, can sometimes be seen full of Chinese banging and clanging drums and symbols amidst coloured streamers. It looks like a great celebration and it is. Not of the living though but of the recent dead. Chinese funeral processions are not the same as ours.

The oldish Chinese ladies hit me next. Not literally since they are too busy pushing wheelbarrows filled with hand-mixed cement up wooden ramp inclines to the top of a wooden square tube into which their obviously precious and certainly heavy load is dropped. Or else, once these wooden surrounds have been removed to reveal the created concrete column, leaving the barrow with a male building worker who is cladding the column with bricks or tiles. I know about this construction method through absorbed observation and sheer wonderment at the inverse logic.

Why aren't the females doing the lighter tube building or brick-laying work? Why aren't the hulky males doing the heavy mixing and wheeling tasks? It is a conundrum explained by ancient culture and these ladies have been brought over from mainland China specifically for the task. They are known as black and whites because they all wear black predominantly but with a white waist-band and a white head-band. Denis, who will enter this story a little later, tells me not to be taken aback by this particular aspect of culture shock.

In a rare moment of relaxation he gets a little light-headed and tells me about a popular joke circulating amongst the new breed of educated second generation Chinese immigrants to Singapore, such as himself. Roughly translated, it concerned a Western ex-pat who courts and entertains and buys expensive presents for an oriental beauty but who is distracted temporarily and whilst so distracted a wily Chinese gentleman "slips her one from a rearward direction whilst the ex-pat is not looking". It is a joke with deep significance.

Some time later a very old and very small black and white came up to us in the supermarket stooped slightly and touched Chris gently on the cheek. In her pidgin English she said simply "ee so white". It touched me too and very deeply and I thought of my mum now so very far away.

Still the biggest surprise is the weather. Being no more than eighty miles from the equator it ought not to be and yet it is. It's the humidity as much as the temperature. Go to find the car at the end of an evening out and it will be dripping in water but this is not due to rain but to condensation and a corollary is that it barely cools throughout the night since the moisture in the air holds the heat. Someone said that a Western ex-pat lives on borrowed air for the first six months. That is probably about right in that after a time of nonchalantly wondering what all the fuss was about, there is a stage when it hits.

An advertisement on TV summed it up. It was for one of the hill resorts in Malaysia that was promoted as "cool as an English springtime". Not having appreciated this luxury back home, now there were times of panic. Will we ever get cool again? How do we get cool? How can we continue to stand this heat? It brings it further home, as if there was any need, when it is so noticeable that the local Chinese actually sweat just as we do and when the local ladies of all strata walk around holding paper-made parasols to fend off the direct sunlight.

Such a climate brings a whole new dimension to an appreciation of the insect world. Unlike back home, grasshoppers can actually be found. Indeed, it would be difficult to miss one having as they do a penchant for dropping in on any outdoor activity and waving their long green legs in agitated frustration at their space having been invaded. If these beautiful creatures are at one end of an invading spectrum, then the dreaded cockroach is surely at the other. What is more, they are not content to merely stay in the grass. More likely and without even a by-your-leave they will arrive via an erratic flight path and drop like a Harrier Jumpjet straight onto your plate of food. They are big, hard-backed brown with protruding antennae and come from Hell. They are skin-creeping devils and one night one landed on Craig's face whilst he was asleep in bed. The screams still reverberate. And that was just me.

At least grasshoppers and cockroaches and the like have the merit of visibility. The longer-term real enemy is the mosquito. It is invisible. It really does creep up from somewhere behind and get you although it will be tomorrow before you know it. Tomorrow comes the swelling and the itching severe enough to drive the white man mad. Not to scratch is to resist an urge as great as any to befall any man. To scratch is to leave a scar of testament to this tropical idyll. The good news is that the malaria carrying variety have been driven from the island and to mitigate against any risk of a return, the bad news is that one of the most serious offences it is possible to commit is breeding mosquitoes. It's bad news because as an ignorant foreigner the likelihood is that you would not know the crime had been committed. All that has to happen is for the inspectorate to find on your premises static water. Another wow. A second invisible enemy is a small insect that is perfectly at home in the Malaysian jungle. It's an enemy because it somehow emits a sort of whistle that gradually increases in pitch until ones eardrums burst.

Arrive and work

We were met at the airport by dynamic Dave looking pretty much the same as when we last met in the PW Birmingham office. He certainly was not all bronzed and sun-tanned as I had expected but he did have huge sunglasses and a wild looking bright flowery shirt. He looked fit and healthy and was obviously pleased to see us. It was over twenty hours since leaving Heathrow, we were jet-lagged and the children were tired and ready for a proper sleep. He whisked us through the hordes of people and outside to his car. It was a Sunday morning and we were here and within this tropical wonderland we were travelling, although unknowingly at the time, along the spine of the Island and called rather splendidly the Bukit Timah Road. My meagre and subsequently acquired knowledge of some hauntingly viscid Malay words teaches me that it means *hill of tin* derived from the mining of that material turned into the useful and decorative pewter ware.

A word learned much sooner was *awas*. It meant - there is a huge pothole in the road and this sign is so close to it that you have already fallen in so next time you won't forget to drive much more slowly will you? The Bukit Timah carriageways north are divided from those going south by what is euphemistically referred to as a drain. In reality it is a wide and deep v-shaped trench that during our early weeks stays just that as a mysteriously extravagant waste of road space. When the rain comes however it is transformed into a massive and rapidly flowing torrent of water and the Straits Times will nonchalantly report that Lee Hong Kim, or some other unfortunate, was "swept away in Bukit Timah last night."

Turning off Bukit Timah somewhere to the north we turn into what is obviously a very posh residential area that could be on a different planet to the crowded hustle and bustle that has been our introduction to Singapore. Having entered Benjai Hill we are driven through open gates and up a private drive to a low-slung, colonial style and very attractive bungalow set in extensive gardens.

Unaware at this point that we are about to be spoilt as entrants to residential life on the island, we have it seems taken up a six-week temporary residence in a *leave bungalow* - just as the contract promised - that actually belongs to a senior Swiss executive of some important corporation and who has taken his family back home for their customary summer holiday. Not only do we inherit his home but all five of his staff who are lined up as in an Edwardian costume drama to greet our dishevelled arrival.

This is clearly no soft ataraxic landing since there is a large welcoming party also. David's wife Christine is here with the three little ones who are very excited to see the new arrivals. We learn later that, convinced that no children would arrive from their early years of marriage, twin babies had been adopted only then to discover that at last Christine was pregnant. The three were to become firm pool-side playmates of Chris and Craig and Christine would become a close friend to June and would teach Chris to swim before his impending fifth birthday.

Seeing them all there happy and smiling and full of life I could not help but recall a discussion between David and myself in some bar in some Midlands hotel or other about the upsides and downsides of being away from home all week and my proffering a view that at least the absences kept the marriage fresh. Yes well that's the trouble isn't it, sex. Sex? Well I mean Friday nights. What? Well it's so bloody predictable. So then that's what must happen after a week of differential cost centre recovery.

The welcoming party included David's boss Tony Wilkinson and his beautiful and most intelligent wife Gay and many from the office who were to remain a fog for some time yet and the food and drinks went on well into the evening and as Tony left he casually mentioned that his colleague who was the other manager in the consultancy unit would pick me up at eight-thirty the following morning for a first introductory meeting with the client scheduled for nine o'clock.

The colleague's name was Scott and no he hadn't been at this welcoming party. He was a rather serious man and chose not to socialise. He was in charge of the project that had just been won and that I would be working on. It was to do with the merging of the island's two telecommunications bodies. So, no little settling in period then. Get right down to it with the serious one. I know absolutely nothing about telecommunications, I am a manufacturing factory specialist aren't I?

Scott Pirie was, I was guessing, aged about forty, maybe late thirties. He was somewhat stern looking with a decidedly professional bearing exaggerated by being very slim, bordering on skinny. The slightness of his frame was accentuated by what I would come to appreciate as the accepted business uniform namely lightweight slacks and a tailored, usually brilliantly white, shirt with the obligatory top pocket for holding paper money. Senior men wore a tie. No more jackets ever unless there was some formal evening occasion but this would be rare. Might possibly need a jumper for evenings, not of-course for outside because the temperature will not drop but for the ice-cold air-conditioning in various places. I see.

Basically there were two types of ex-pats here. Those that chose to take advantage of having an amah (servant) and join the whirligig of social life and those that wanted to make money. He and his wife were in the second group. He had come here from the Middle East where he had worked a contract to a similar end. He mentioned the firm's senior partner, Philip Grundy, several times and there was an innuendo of *like kinds* and in fact his main job currently was looking inwardly at the firm. I see.

As regards the assignment that had been awaiting my arrival, it had arisen from a major and significant political decision. The young bright and ambitious new Minister of Communications in Lee Kwan Yew's government had been to Harvard. There he had conceived the idea of a single telecommunications body to run and develop the island's services. This had been agreed and was to be implemented and as there was, as I would appreciate over time, no opposition party to have to bother with, the programme could go ahead immediately. PW had won the contract. He would manage the job and I would do it.

The significance of the decision stemmed from Singapore's geographically strategic location. Satellite beams were bounced off the receiving stations on Sentosa Island that was just off the south coast of this the main island on their way to and from Europe and Australasia and Japan and the USA. It was the perfect staging post for telecommunications and these services were so important to the island's revenue that they were under the control of a government department called the Telecommunication Authority of Singapore (TAS).

All the executives were of-course civil servants. The technology and equipment in use was state of the art stuff and the work was highly profitable. PW had been told that out of every one dollar of revenue, ninety-five cents was profit. By absolute contrast the domestic telephone network was run as a public service but along the lines of a UK public utility - so now I see for the first time how a bit of my c.v. might have struck a cord. It operated intra-island only and although a small fixed charge was levied for the equipment, there were no call fees.

The rationale had been to stimulate usage and especially amongst the newly arrived Chinese and Malay workforce as an adjunct to economic growth. In this regard it had been highly successful. The problem was that it was consequentially starved of revenue and therefore a big loss maker and had had little or no new investment since colonial times. The equipment was old, the service was poor and the managers, who were ordinary employees and not civil servants, were known to be de-motivated. The organisation was known as the Singapore Telephone Board (STB). So there we have it. A prestigious profitable external provider and a deprived internal one. Solution: simple. Put the two together. I see.

The first thing we have to do is get some wheels. For

the boys, and on our very first venture onto the night market, a small pedal car and a bike with stabilisers. For us and from an advertisement by an ex-pat going home the one car absolutely suited to the driving conditions here plus its nostalgic pull back to West Hallam, we have to buy the VW Beetle. It's green and considering the road progress here, particularly down the Fullerton Road, along the Esplanade Drive, Collyer Quay and Raffles Quay, is well suited to being just a grown-up version of riding the dodgem cars at Blackwell wakes in the early years at the farm.

Remarkably though, the car is also in good condition considering that it is quite normal to nudge along the vehicle in front should it not be advancing properly and the outsize solid metal bumpers of the people's car is ideal for the job. Later on we will realise that the lack of air-conditioning is a serious deficiency, but for now it's the perfect purchase. The car loan will be paid back over the contract period, painless.

The next big step is the Tanglin Club and somehow, again as promised in the contract, it is open for a new PW employee notwithstanding there is a waiting list. It is expensive but necessary to socialise with the, largely, UK ex-pat residents and to swim to keep cool and to occupy the wives during the husband's working day. Wives, it seems, are not allowed to work even should they want to or, as we would discover, actually need to. A tiny minority who have an exceptional skill such as Gay Williamson's speech therapy, will be exempted. Other essential ingredients of the Tanglin Club are the playing of tennis on the tiered courts and to eat in the plush restaurant and to take satay and drinks by the poolside. Mind you, Scott and his wife are not members.

In the early weeks we made little use of the excellent Tanglin Club because, no doubt like countless other ex-pats before us, the lure of this new land and the freedom from most domestic chores proved too tempting. On Saturday afternoons and Sundays we were tourists. At first staying on the island to visit the crocodile farm and marvel with no little distaste at the masses of the creatures lurking in what appeared to be quite shallow water in a series of ponds. Fascinating for the boys but causing us to think twice about purchasing any of those fantastic crocodile skin articles in the gleaming glass and chrome shops along Orchard Road. Back in Nottingham a crocodile briefcase had been a conceivable aspiration, now and here it was already looking abhorrent. Belts, shoes and handbags and even full sets of travelling cases were somehow fashioned from these forlorn creatures.

As time passed evidence would build that the whole approach of the Chinese as a race towards animals was different to ours. Did it stem from them still being much closer to nature? Bucolic in an urban framework? Or, were they cruel by nature? Was it just being open and honest about the use of animals albeit with liberal insensitivity? In the Snake Temple visitors were actively encouraged to hold and stroke the creatures that you note are not slimy but dry to the touch. Only Craig would and there is a photograph to prove it.

Dogs were kept in cages and if barking is any sign of pent-up frustration then these domestic animals were amongst the most frustrated in the world. June had a letter of complaint published in the Straits Times under the editor's bold heading of "Dog Tired In Namly". It made no noticeable difference. Dogs can't read and the established Chinese residents either stuck to the Chinese press or were not going to change their animal husbandry to suit the odd ex-pat upstart in their road.

Later still and further afield, a tarantula spider would be casually displayed in a garden centre presumably as an invitation to buy it or *buy-it* if ones sandaled and sockless feet interrupted its progress. At the zoo in Kuala Lumpur the snakes' diet was spiced up with live mice and rats that could be nonchalantly observed slipping down the throat and, at least on the horrendously hot day we were there, a full-grown tiger walked amongst the paying customers without any apparent sign of a tether, a keeper, or come to that a care in the world. Scared us a little though.

Meantime, the live chickens continue to have their heads cut off in the market. All a far cry from my dad's sweating distress as he tries to hold steady the head of a cow that has knocked off its horn as I try to bind it with cloth to stanch the bleeding or desperately nailing railings inside the pigsty because the big sow has started to roll onto and squash the newly born piglets, or his tears when the new puppy dies of distemper.

Other trips out are awe-inspiringly wonderful. After the Chinese gardens and the botanic gardens, the aquarium and the two reservoirs, we find the still isolated and palm strewn sandy beaches off Changi on the extreme east coast. It will be four years after leaving this place that I shall devour with passionate self-interest the excellent novel by J G Farrell The Singapore Grip and through it learn something of the commercial and human scale tragedy of the island's fall to the Japanese in 1942, ironically the year of my birth. I was blissfully unaware of Wavell and Percival and the infamous Gordon Bennett and that the notorious prison that held so many British and allied soldiers for over three years was within yards of where now the local boys on the beach were intrusively, through no more than ignorance, marvelling at our still white skin.

The obituary for Sir David Griffin in the Daily Telegraph tells of his hospitalisation on the fateful day February 15 when the city surrendered. Sent first to Selarang Barracks, Griffin reckoned from the starvation rations and the violence meted out by the guards accompanying PoW working parties that the Japanese intended to dispose of the bulk of the prisoners by "natural causes". He noted that men were eating cats, dogs, mice, cockroaches and strips of blanket. He spent three years and seven months as a prisoner, the first eighteen months in Selarang and the rest in Changi, built to hold 600 criminals but housing 5,800 PoW's. He would write "The prisoners saw them (the Japanese military) as they really are, and to their life's end their loathing for the wicked race will never die."

And we will lounge privately here, swim off here and fly paper kites from here. What a difference in just thirty years from the atom bomb but still with the ingrained hatred of the Japanese amongst the indigenous middle aged. One day a Malaysian taxi driver in Johor Baharu makes an unscheduled stop at a crossroads just to the north of the town. He points out with a shaky voice the site of a mass grave of men and children. The women were retained. He knows we are British and will not take a fare. This experience causes us to visit the Kranji War Memorial off the far north of Bukit Timah just short of the causeway. This most moving of sites has, at the head of the rows and rows of crosses with names and crosses without, vertically mounted slabs listing all those lost in the Far Eastern campaign.

Under the Cambridgeshire Regiment is the name I hoped to find, George Wilson. One of my mother's elder brothers, George had left behind a new wife and a son John, later to become a school headmaster, but never returned. The family believed he perished on the Burma death railway but here in the office was written proof that this was not so.

Because of the abject cruelty of that ordeal, only one man from the villages I grew up in returned from the death railway and he drove the dustcart collecting trash. One step up from being treated as such but a poor return for a hero. Perhaps uncle George, as he would have become, was the lucky one in that he was aboard a ship that was torpedoed in Singapore harbour. Almost all those on board were lost. I took a photograph of the page in the memorial book and of the plinth and sent it with a letter to mother. It seemed the least if only thing that could be done in, and sent from, this immaculately maintained and infinitely sad place.

What developed into my favourite attraction was the Mandai Orchid Gardens, at first for the orchids themselves but indelibly for the butterflies attracted by the flowers and the flowing water between the plants. They were so magnificent in flight, in colour and most astonishingly in size. This triggered off a little hobby. Discreet enquiries led me to a back-street Chinese chemist prepared to make-up what I had read as being the necessary *killing bottle*. What was actually in this screw-top wide-necked bottle I never actually knew but it was not the sort of artifice to be left hanging around nor sniffed at with anything more than swift curiosity.

To a butterfly caught in a net and then dropped into the bottle without human contact - important for preservation according to the book - and on screwing down the lid, it was instantly fatal. This quick manoeuvre was vital to the wings not being damaged. A balsa wood board and some pins were the only other materials needed to set for a metamorphorised creature. Later on the pins holding the wings outstretched can be removed and the butterfly is transferred to a display board for mounting within a glass frame complete with its little bag of chemicals to ward off any enquiring insects. So effective is this that even from my bumbling amateur indexterous hands came a presentation case now thirty-seven years old.

From a combination of early Sunday morning trips to the orchid gardens and much later from a hill resort in Malaysia came labels such as Appias nero figulina, Torinos tepander robertsia, Moduza procris milonia and Catopsilia p. Pomona but the star was not caught by us but was purchased as the much rarer and incredibly beautiful Rajah

Brooke's Birdwing.

If the yellow sunbird flitting from flower to flower in the Benjai Hill garden was a taster, then the banquet was called Jurong Bird Park that we found tucked away in the sparsely populated south west corner of the island and constructed as a single but multi-shaped and huge bird cage. Here were hundreds of tropical species of birds of all sizes and colours and with elevated walkways to appreciate their flights. There had been and would continue to be culture shocks in relation to the approach towards and apparent treatment of animals. But the orchids, butterflies and birds were redemption.

Christopher's first day at school opened a floodgate of memories. A forceps-squashed forehead, walks around West Hallam in the early hours of an autumn morning trying to get him to sleep, his torso suspended from an iron framework in a Hemel Hemstead hospital, the VIP visit to my hospital bedside at my very lowest point, an Italian mama's wonderment at his fast perfect English and now the old Chinese lady touching a small face simply because it is so white. And here he walks from the car with his little case holding the mid-morning drink and snack into the private and rather posh Tanglin School for ex-pat children in the bright sunshine and warmth of a nearly eight-o'clock tropical autumn morning. Does one have to hit the lows to get the highs? Is it appreciation from relativity?

In my heart on this morning it is manifestly absolute and I feel glad we made big decisions. I could still be growing in EMEB and we could be thinking of moving to a bigger house in Ravenshead. Glad we are here. It's thought provoking that the school hours are eight to one, and you would assume a throw back to colonial times and lazy afternoons out of school and in the shade; it is also thought provoking that as we crawl up the driveway in a stream of enormously sized and expensive cars, we look out on holes in the ground in which live families whose children will not be taken to Tanglin school.

It was supposedly an innocuous encounter with a tiger by a visiting Sri Vijayan prince, who mistook the animal for a lion, that gave the name Singa Pura or Lion City. During the eighteen century the British recognised its strategic position as a halfway house to reach, feed and protect its growing empire. Against this background, Stamford Raffles founded modern Singapore in 1819. In 1832 the island became the central governing body for the Straits Settlements of Penang, Malacca and Singapore.

With the opening of the Suez Canal in 1869 and the advent of telegraph and steamships, Singapore became very important as a centre for the expansion of trade between East and West. Following the Japanese surrender in 1945, Singapore became a Crown Colony and after self-government in 1959, became an independent republic in 1965. The two and a half million population of forty years ago had grown to four million by the turn of the millenium and of these some 77% are Chinese, 14% Malays and 8% Indian. So now as when we were there, the ex-pat community was a 1% ethnic minority. Albeit an elitist one.

So elitist that we had to have our own amah because although wives could not be out at work, neither ought they to do domestic chores because of the heat and humidity. It so happened that Christine and David Tittle's amah had a friend and we interviewed Kim who seemed perfect and stayed with us throughout the contract. She became a very good friend and part of the family. So much so that on her one day off, Sunday, she always appeared reluctant to go home and often came back early.

When we prepared to leave the island, Kim wanted to come with us and I made some enquiries but Singapore was not exporting people at that time. Although initially her English was poor, she understood my question made soon after joining us as to who she might vote for in the forthcoming general election. "Lee Kwan Yew, if I no vote

Lee Kwan Yew, he know". Some mild enquiries left an impression of a form of cross-referencing system. Best not to push the matter but the point would be cemented by quiet warnings that at cocktail parties or other meetings with senior people it was wise not to pass adverse comments or judgements.

Following that election at which the ruling People's party headed by Mr Lee was returned with something like a 98% majority, the leader of the main opposition party, an Indian, found himself incarcerated for a time. Not that imprisonment always proved necessary. According to reports in the Straits Times, criminals brought in for questioning had a habit "He fell from an upstairs window whilst trying to escape interrogation" (at the main police station on Robinson Road). It was common for a picture to appear on the front page of that paper showing Who Got Me - or similar - lying dead on the pavement outside some building having been shot by an observant policeman. He was usually about No 7 or thereabouts on the wanted list and blood transudation would invariably embroider the picture.

All this accidental or deliberate retribution by the Republic's officials must have contributed greatly to the efficient functioning of the State at this time of rapid economic growth and social change. Not that the judiciary was likely to be much of an impediment to the speedy discharge of the rule of law, at any rate based on the sagacious conversation flowing at a dinner table just before leaving the island. The senior judge present gave every impression of being rather close to the government.

As regards matters economic and social, a slightly more balanced picture of the progress and state of the island and its neighbours could be found in the South East Asia Economic Review, published afar but available and one had to marvel at the ease in which the Singapore Housing Board persuaded the indigenous Chinese and Malays to move from their hitherto Kampongs and the like to the high-rise tenements springing up along Serangoon Road. Mind you, Kim never seemed overly keen to return to her high-rise. Of-course financial incentives were in place to move home just as there were heavy tax disincentives to breeding more than two children "a two child family is perfect" or so the television said. Mind you again, road tax went up steeply with the value of the car owned. Perhaps this added to the kudos of the Mercedes 280SE. There were plenty about.

It was a bit like the chocolate men versus the biscuit men, with a twist. The twist was Mandarin. The Elk in Worcester had a great line in cockney rhyming slang "lovely Bristols – cities – titties – get it?" but with him and without interpretation, one could usually work something out. Try working it out when your meeting switches to Chinese. What could be deduced is that we have reached a highly contentious issue and the length of time in Mandarin roughly equates to the degree of contention.

After the introductory meeting with the TAS officials on one side and the STB executives on the other and a more thorough briefing from Scott Pirie, I decide on the tactic adopted successfully in the UK. But will it work here in this culture on this sort of assignment? In my mind I rate it as highly risky. I have not done an organisational job before and back home such work would only be given to the most experienced consultants. I am a factory man used to diagnostic probing and implementing new systems. I have not knowingly even seen a senior civil servant never mind re-organised one and my familiarity with telecommunications is nil. If these deficiencies come to the fore, myself and I assume the PW management who sold the job will not fair well. Still, to me the risk is worth taking. I must get to know what is really going on. So, although he is some layers above these managers, I ask to see Mr Goh Seng Kim.

The Minister of Communications has already appointed

Goh Seng Kim to head the new telecommunications authority. He has risen rapidly on the international side although still a youngish man. His secretary ushers me into a large wood-panelled room at the very top of the TAS building. He moves from behind a large desk, walks to me and shakes my hand and beckons that we sit opposite each other on a suite of couches in one corner of the room. He orders tea.

Goh Seng Kim is not the epitome of a thrusting young executive. He has a serious face, a calm bearing and speaks quietly. He welcomes me to Singapore and hopes our stay is a happy one. I do have two small children and a wife with me don't I? He has a young family too. He knows Britain well and has great respect for the managed transition from British rule to their Republic State. He welcomes the fact that I am new to the island and consequently know nothing of the history and politics of the two bodies about to be merged.

He is quite unconcerned that I have no background in telecommunications. It is outside objective input that this job needs. Had I known how to show relief, it would have been impossible to hide. As it was I merely sat opposite sipping tea and listening to this most cultured man express his hopes for the future, his worries for the transitional process and above all I am trying to comprehend the sheer scope of the task he had been handed. He thinks it will help if I understand the composition of Chinese names because the politeness of using the correct salutation is important especially to senior people.

The first name is the family name, in his case Goh. Therefore in formal address he is Mr Goh. On fairly formal occasions but amongst people who know each other, it would be normal to address the person by using all three names so he would be Goh Seng Kim. But, as we two will from this time be friends as well as business colleagues, then in our chats together with no-one else present I would address him as Seng Kim. Seng is the generation name so what I will find confusing at first is that males and females of the same family have the same middle name. The third name is very personal. It is used only within the family or by very close friends. A Westerner would never address a Chinese person solely by the third name.

We discuss the assignment. There will be no preconceptions. The organisation structure could be based on technical function, on management function or even geographical area combining functions. The crucial need was that it would work practically and be suited to the next five to ten years of what was forecast to be heavy growth in the networks' traffic. There should be no sacred cows and no-one's present position was inviolate. Obviously many executives would be surplus as duplicate roles were identified. This was not to influence the study. This would be his problem.

He wanted only to name two bright stars, one from each existing organisation, which he did. I would probably find their input invaluable. Yes, we could meet regularly, he would welcome it. My lasting memory of this first meeting with Goh Seng Kim was his use of a term never encountered before or indeed since. It was *digit*. It meant a person in a role. The perfect de-personaliser.

Our honeymoon period at Benjai Hill was coming to an end. The leave bungalow with its garden and orchids and birds and butterflies had to be vacated. We could have moved to the ex-pat ghetto of Orange Grove Road but I wanted to go native. To flavour some, at least, of a Chinese community albeit one assumes a reasonably affluent one since the working class were in high-rise blocks to where we certainly would not be going.

It was not one of my better decisions except for Bob and Sue Curtis. Bob had advertised their rented semi-detached house on Namely Drive off Sixth Avenue that in turn was off the Bukit Timah Road. They and their three children were moving to a cheaper place to get within his new and reduced serviceman's allowance. The house was in a good district, had enough space, was light and airy and even had a small lawn and orchids on the veranda. It was a good find and we took on the one-year lease. Only later did we twig that our across-the-road neighbours had in a cage multi-dogs that barked some of the day and all of the night. His fellow residents going down the road had similar attributes.

It turned out that we had as our next-door neighbour an American oil-rig worker and the reason we'd seen little of him since our moving in was because, as he explained as I washed the car one Sunday morning, he worked "six weeks on, six weeks off" a rig off the Indonesian coast. It was an off-putting first encounter because having asked my name, just in order to be friendly as Americans tend to be, he semi-convulsed with a "what, John Smith? You're telling me I live next door to John Smith? Don't ya know every crook in the States is John Smith? Wait till I write the folks back home" Nice one. And to think we could be safely tucked away in Orange Grove Road.

But Bob and Sue - never Sue and Bob - more than made up for it. Bob was seconded from the RAF to the ANZUK (Australian, New Zealand & UK) forces who still ran the military air operations on the island. Still was the pertinent condition because the brief was to hand over to the Chinese personnel over a final two-year period. In the event, the bright young Chinese officers had "cottoned on" much quicker than anticipated and as a result Bob was apparently "not too pressed". In fact most days he played golf and most evenings he participated in the officers' mess.

Originally he had trained as a fighter pilot but failing to make the grade had become an air traffic controller. I was to learn that back home he had been a Flight Lieutenant although here styled Captain Curtis. Later back in the UK he would rise to Squadron Leader and then in Germany in charge of the RAF side of a base, Wing Commander. Right now though this good-looking, fast-talking man of military sharpness and vocabulary was quite a tour-de-force. As a character and comedian he was to light up our social scene. Someone he liked would be *couth* and a stupid question was inclined to make *my brain hurt*.

He was a hit with the ladies and had a one-line conversation stopper at any cocktail party if family situations could be worked in. His father was Archbishop of Mauritius. Not that that was quite as impressive as it may appear. Being a humble rector in a Lincolnshire parish and seeing an advertisement in the Church Times, he applied and got the job. Still, Bob had been to Mauritius and could talk eloquently of it and had photographs of the religious pageantry.

He described the *silliness* of the games held in the mess but on our first invited visit it was obvious that he not only enjoyed the fun but was a wholehearted participant. We witnessed the running of The Derby that involved horses' carved wooden heads being pulled along ridges by tethered rope from one end of the room to the other by girl-power. Officers' wives each turned a handle on a spindle to haul in their appointed nag as fast as possible. The first one home won. Of-course the main draw was the betting and given a liberal amount of alcohol, the resultant excitement must have borne some resemblance to the real Derby. Was it great or was it sad? Grown men and women with not much to do and far from home.

Later on and beyond this mess some instances would crop up where the facemask of pleasure in the good life would slip. After that first experience, Bob got into the habit of picking me up now and again for a night out at the mess. Despite always being made welcome, it was hard not to feel a gatecrasher into a very private party. It was a closed world of jargon and banter and particularly hierarchy so that whatever the social scene, rank appeared never far from the surface. A really senior officer was always a really senior officer, it was somehow obvious as soon as he entered the bar. And, judging by the pickled complexion of a fair number of faces, drinking as a pastime was not the exclusive province of either the here and now or merely Singapore.

Bob had not been alone in aspiring to be a fighter pilot. Those that had got through and were active were the crème de la crème and were lauded as such and never paid for their drinks. To me they exuded no special qualities apart from youth. I was young but they were younger. To listen to the recount of mock battles over the Straits was to eavesdrop on excited schoolboys after an unexpected win over the visiting football team. A world where the young man was the best. He knew it, they knew it. All the rest as a supporting cast.

Was that why the rest drank so much, a lost dream, or just manly bravado in a cloistered world of exclusivity? Bob told me that barrels of English beer were sometimes flown in specially and because of the climate here and the treat of it, once word had got around it was best to polish it off fairly smartly. Such passion often resulted in an unsteady and speedy drive back to Namely and coffee aplenty before his final leg home. Apparently on these drives back from the mess he sometimes suffered from double vision. Coffee came up as a feature of his story of an excellent night out with a few of his work friends that culminated at a small hotel on Orange Grove Road that specialised in Irish coffee. It developed into a sort of competition. They ended up having twenty-seven *each*.

Bob and Sue became genuinely good friends and gave us sound advice on things like caring for the children in this climate breeding strange complaints like monsoon blisters (that by Chinese superstition could form a complete ring around the child's body and if so were fatal), where to eat the best Chinese food, where to go for a quiet drink and later on where to aim for in Malaysia as we ventured further afield. With half a thought back to Tony and his new life in the South West of England, I was now forming a view that the real relationship within a marriage might well be different from the one on display even allowing for Bob's vocal acclamation of the additive role a big toe can play in a sexual marital relationship. Macho Bob and his quiet calm capable Sue in the background.

But Sue was at the extreme end of the male/female spectrum. The female end. She did not drive a car, that was a male thing. She wore her hair long and had long flowing dresses. She was very feminine. One night having drinks after a meal she whisperingly confided losing her virginity aged nineteen working in a hotel in the Channel Islands, told me about an event at now aged twenty-nine and relished the prospect in store at aged thirty-nine. Quite a girl I thought.

We did keep in touch, the two families that is, and some years later stayed at their home in Wiltshire at the time of the summer solstice. Bob and I went for a pre-dinner drink and sat in a vine covered coach- yard of an old pub in Glastonbury. I was thinking about the ex-pats back in the Singapore days, and especially the older ones who had got senior jobs that demanded they stayed there and about them living a lie. A well hidden lie but a lie nonetheless.

It took a peak into a private room at their luxurious colonial style home to see the pictures of the Malvern Hills and the old school photographs to start to detect it and two too many brandies at the end of the evening for the veneer to peel away. One senior partner of a firm who had married an Asian girl and for all intents and purposes was a permanent resident actually shed a few tears when describing his old village. It was not embarrassing just sad.

But as I listened to Bob reminiscing, his time had not been a lie, on the contrary a real truth. Whilst it had lasted he had been important. In fact, until the formal hand-over, he had been in charge of the military air control system. He could put his name down for being strapped into the co-pilots seat for a g-force dog-fight over the Strait of Malacca. He could "hop in a plane and zip down to New Zealand for the weekend". I was to be told that it would be a fight to get back into the first division having chosen to take time out in the fourth. Looking at and listening to Bob I just wondered if the ancient and beautiful and peaceful Glastonbury and Wells were not for him the reverse. Still, for now all was well and the three children were in private schools courtesy of the RAF. Pre-dawn tomorrow he planned to climb the Tor with his eldest daughter to witness the sunrise on the solstice. A new day, a new year, a new life. Later they moved to Germany. And all this from an advertisement to rent a semi in Namely Drive.

Slowly, almost surreptitiously, the secrets of domestic and international telecommunications revealed themselves. How can situations so different be so alike? Mack has me fed to the Assistant Chief Accountants at EMEB to have a look around and Goh Seng Kim politely, charmingly feeds me to STB/TAS. I am developing a theory that will strengthen over the years that in the management of business process nothing is unique. People are unique and so what is in their head is. But their head tells them what they have experienced. Other people's stories and what they might read about could be an influence but it is a mistake to think it is an influentially changing one. One thousand pounds for every *unique* business described to me over the years would have resulted in comfortable wealth.

Given honest technical advice and accurate diagnosis of the prevailing culture and the patience or good fortune to feel for the timing, the most impenetrable jungle can be conquered. Goh Seng Kim's two bright young men, Mr Fho on one side and Ng Chee Meng on the other gave me or pointed me at all the technical knowledge needed at the organisational level. The top structure was ultimately agreed as a hybrid of technical services and whole-enterprise management functions.

The qualification for each senior position was laid down and after a series of meetings, *digits* were found that best fitted these needs. Specific quantified objectives were listed for the top two levels of management both for the first year and for three years. It was when we got to the information that would be needed to determine whether or not these objectives had been met or looked likely to be and to the underlying procedures to produce this information that, along with other jobs, more staff had to be drafted in. So PW recruited and in due course along came Denis Yew, Chan Cher Boon, Lawrence Seah and John Bishop.

Denis Yew and Chan Cher Boon came first. They were both Chinese and about the same age but otherwise, and as I would appreciate over time, very different sorts of people. Some of this difference lies in a name. The explanation of names received from Goh Seng Kim needs developing. An ethnic Chinese might adopt a Christian name. For example Yew Kuan Chew might become Denis. Thereafter to a non-Chinese employer or friend the Chinese generation and personal name will be dropped in favour of the combined Christian and original Chinese family name. Enter Denis Yew. Why should this happen?

To become more Westernised, more acceptable to a non-Chinese fraternity, certainly. But possibly a bit deeper. Suppose you have antipathetic feelings towards a form of totalitarianism or you would like to read a less governmentally prone press or you would welcome less censorship of foreign television programmes (excepting of course the Dave Allen Show that somehow gets past the scrutiny notwithstanding its sometimes irreverent content that one assumes the authorities fail to understand) or you think the playing of the national anthem each time the main TV channel starts up is a mild form of brain-washing or even that you might just want to leave the island but cannot, then going for a Christian name just might be a form of protest.

The name distinction was, however, no more than a modern handle on an ancient cultural divide. Denis's family had a trading business of long standing and as either derived from, or as a result of what we would now broadly regard as, a middle-class cultural background. Proof of this lay in the spoken language. Denis spoke mandarin which, apart from being the official language of China since 1917, denoted someone in the Chinese Empire who was a member of a senior grade of the bureaucracy. Denis therefore came into the Western world with pedigree.

By contrast Chan Cher Boon - note no adoption of a Christian name and this was deliberate - spoke hokien, the language of the working classes and in particular of the southern regions of China and of Hong Kong. Cher Boon had got to where he was by study and sheer hard work. He was not only a qualified accountant but also a qualified lawyer. He eschewed many of the Western deferences. He would succeed as a Chinese man with a Chinese soul.

When on separate occasions Denis and Cher Boon came to our home for an evening meal, Denis ate exactly what we did. Cher Boon left the chicken and asked for the skin that was devoured with relish. In the office Denis would accept a boiled sweet or toffee whereas Cher Boon sucked Chinese sweets that are sold by the pavement vendors. These sweets are indigestible by Western guts. By study and learning, Cher Boon's spoken and written English was excellent. Denis's was rather poor. Denis and Cher Boon communicated in Chinese by the characters that are standard throughout the dialects. They could not understand each other in verbal Chinese.

At the front, or rather the back, of the tome "Classical Chinese Paintings – Selected Masterpieces of all Dynasties – Compiled by Professor Lin Ta-yung" presented to me on leaving the island, are the signatures of each member of the consultancy staff. All except one bring out a name in clear English. The exception consists of three Chinese characters, those depicting Chan Cher Boon. Whether resulting from a subtle plan hatched by Tony Wilkinson or Scott Pirie in the higher reaches of management or whether by dint of timing and how workloads fell, it transpired that Cher Boon always worked for Dynamic Dave whereas Denis worked for me. In context, that was about right.

Denis had a most beautiful wife, April. Beautiful not merely due to her angelic facial features but because of her paleness of skin. Such paleness is the sheer epitome of beauty in a Chinese lady. They already had their own home especially built to their specification and two young children. Denis was one of the very first Chinese to become a full member of the Tanglin Club. April had her own domestic staff and had returned to work full-time. The day of the new-breed indigenous Chinese couple fully integrated in and comfortable with Western culture had arrived.

Denis would leave PW and set up his own trading company and as the years passed trade extensively with, and own, ceramics factories in China and Malaysia. He would export ceramic products all over Europe and would visit us in Nottinghamshire in a car driven by someone I embarrassingly mistook for himself. In fact it was his little boy now grown into the spitting image of the young Singapore Denis.

This little boy and the little girl had both been released from the by now more liberal Republic of Singapore to attend university in the UK. As we sat and drank tea on a Nottinghamshire lawn this hot July day, a more Western scene it would have been hard to conjure. Yet, they all worked for Paramount Arts and Crafts and Denis and April still lived on Greenleaf Road, Singapore and when we went out for dinner, Denis would *take* rather than *have* the chicken and April would still supervise the decorum of her flock in the manner that only cultivated Chinese ladies seem to possess. I had met them between leaving Singapore and now, but that is a tale to come. Cher Boon came once to our UK home but at a time when I was abroad on business. He stayed the night and June 'phoned me in Australia to say she felt odd and had locked her bedroom door. Rumour had it that he went back to the law and emigrated to Australia. My guess would be that he did stay in touch with Dynamic Dave.

Lawrence Seah was a computer expert and came into the team because all these integrated procedures we were coming up with needed a technical buffer between what we wanted and what the mysterious and formidable Indian head of mainframe George said could be provided. Like Denis, Lawrence had taken a Christian name and was, of all the Chinese we met, the most keen to integrate with Western ways and learn how Western companies did business. In his case there was a further impetus. He confided in me during the badminton lesson that he organised at his local Chinese school.

I took Chris and Craig to watch the local kids play badminton en-masse on a Sunday morning. The intensity and the skill and the speed were breathtaking as literally hundreds of courts were erected to further the national game. During our later journeys through Malaysia the evolution was obvious as in every little clearing by the kampongs and wherever two trees were the right distance apart, a piece of string connecting the two was all that was necessary to create a game.

And again years later on his sole visit to our UK home and notwithstanding that Craig in particular was by then playing badminton to a good standard, we still could not take a single point off the slim darting Lawrence. But he and his wife had a problem. A child with a rare blood disorder. Despite diagnosis locally, they were desperately worried that the required specialist treatment was not available on the island. He wanted me to know that if they got dispensation to leave on these medical grounds, then they would do so. And a few years after we left Singapore, they did. We met in Manchester's China Town but the final destination was not to be here but Canada. After a relatively short time the immigration papers were approved and slim, smiling, chain-smoking Lawrence and family had gone.

Then there was the escapist rebel. John Bishop and family arrived when we were well into the second half of our contract. He was a product of PW in the UK and had met Diane when she was a single parent with three small children. They were a lively, fun loving and adventurous couple and we two families spent one joyous weekend driving up the East Coast of Malaysia and staying overnight in a ramshackle hut at Mersing before taking a put-put boat to one of the off-shore islands for snorkelling.

John and Diane boasted openly about their fantastic sex life and its *instant* success. They were big eaters, noisy and happy and the kids followed suit. But John did not fit well into the somewhat conservative disciplined mode of the Singapore firm and would become the first ex-pat to break his contract and join a Western business outside the profession. June and Diane became special friends and would keep in touch over all the years that followed. June proved good at maintaining contact with the Singaporean set. With the sole exception of Denis Yew, I was not.

But then and right out of the blue, I was sent an e-mail address. Blue to red as this large smiling face bounded across the large open plan office of the plush suite in central London on the late morning we had agreed to meet. Straight into the pub across the road then to his favourite fish restaurant for a wine drenched long lunch over which came out his life story post those long lost days.

John Bishop was now successful, very successful. He had a large salary for a one-day week with a mid-cap company in the construction and renovation market called Morgan Sindall and for whom he had over the years become a very senior director responsible for acquisitions and general development. He would soon retire on a good pension and have share holding benefit but had several non-executive directorships lined up, one of which was as chairman of a largish company about to go public.

He and Diane (Di) lived in a large house in Surrey and they had other properties both here and abroad. So the rebel had made good. But it had not been a smooth passage. They had had a second stint in Singapore and they had also lived in Bermuda from where John had done business around the USA. But they had eventually settled into a life as up-market hoteliers back here but had "bought at the top and sold at the bottom". They ended up penniless and in rented accommodation. For some folk life is smooth and relatively featureless. That distant breakfast in Mersing was as good an indicator as any that the steady life would not be the lot of John and Di.

Denis had become more than a work colleague whose reports I toiled over to turn into something submittable. He explained many of the nuances of Chinese thinking and the heritage of the dynasties and of the mainland geographical provinces. He showed us the rose-wood furniture imported from the mainland and described the pots and jewellery and fabrics. We learned the technique of using chopsticks, keeping the ends perfectly level by knocking them down on the little stand provided to keep the business ends off the table and holding the bottom one still whilst the top one was worked by the index finger and thumb as a lever and passing the ultimate test of picking up button mushrooms.

Experience had shown that until this practice was perfected the taking of any morsel of fish from a rotating central plinth of the table would be no more than a triumph of hope over attainment. He wanted the two families to book a rest bungalow for a weekend in the cool air of the mountains north of Kuala Lumpur. Not as far as the Cameron Highlands but just as high at two thousand metres above sea level. So we drove the two-hundred-and-fifty miles to KL and continued to Robinson's Hill with its single road traffic-light controlled summit. The term rest bungalow is a euphemism for a luxurious stone built retreat built for the British rulers and now reserved, if required, for the Malaysian senior officials to get their (as advertised on TV) *cool as an English spring* get away. It came complete with log fire and chrysanthemums growing wild in the garden. We ate, drank, talked and relaxed in our cool luxury for a life refreshing two days and I caught a few butterflies. All in all a great Denis idea.

We made two other main trips afield during the contract period and both, as it turned out, were to have health warnings attached. The first was a recommendation from Bob Curtis of officers' mess fame. We should drive up the East Coast road of Malaysia to Kuantan and stay overnight in a beachside hut (as it turned out *the beach of passionate love* or so the translation would have it) to savour the perfect white sands and if the season was right, witness the turtles coming ashore to lay their eggs.

But Bob and Sue and children must have been more worldly and prepared travellers than we. The journey was too long, the humidity too great given our non-air-conditioned beetle and there were too many rivers to cross slowly by rickety floating barges. The roadside boys selling water melon was a respite but it was the non-functioning of the mosquito nets at Kuantan that was the final straw. Chris was being bitten the worst, perspiring profusely and getting very distressed. We were close to panic with no prospect of any medical help and so in the early hours we packed everything back in the car and set off on the long trek back to Singapore. It taught us a lesson and was to be our final foray alone into the unknown. That which sounds good and looks good may not be. Search for the hidden snags and have a get-out plan. Adventure, yes. Misguided enthusiasm, no. Of course this lesson should not be lost outwith the

Malaysian jungle. It applies to other jungles too.

Why do the Chinese spit so much? Whilst they are not in the same league as latter-day professional soccer players who all participate in the concurrent private competition of gob of the game and the winner of which presumably gets a nice big ball of phlegm as a flying start for the next match. Why, for that matter, was this part of the world known as white man's grave? The answer lies mainly with congestion of the lungs, in turn a product of humidity.

So it was unfortunate that the nagging soreness in my chest and the more and more prevalent wheeziness leading to a doctor's diagnosis of "slight bronchitis" got worse just as we left for the only break allowed in the contract. Our one week off was to be spent in Penang off the North West coast of Malaysia and partly in the sister club to the Tanglin Club. This beautiful island bastion to the British colonial past and just off the military base at Butterworth was a good choice with the George Town fortifications and E&O Oriental Hotel (too expensive for us) and funicular railway as built by British engineers at the end of the nineteenth century and trishaw rides and just lazing by the pool. Such things are, however, not best enjoyed when coughing up blood.

But lifestyle changes are not made without a few things not functioning right. As the chesty things started to clear up so this pain came to my right-hand side exactly it felt where the gall-stone operation scar was. I had been so sure that my gut problem had gone permanently. Whilst being suspended almost upside down in some contraption after having taken a barium meal, the *what now* worry was not helped by the vocal opinion of the supervising doctor that I was "a bit young for cancer". In reality the problem would have been caused by my internal acid factory kicking in. Itself not helped by Singapore's very own Tiger Beer. A high ranker on the richter acid scale.

And there was a silver if not alkaline lining to the

remedy of June's problem. After very heavy periods and a lot of pain, several inspection visits to the excellent St Margaret's Hospital resulted in an operation. When she was well enough to leave, the highly polished and quietly spoken Paul Tan took me to one side and explained " I have tightened a few things up inside and am returning her to you as a virgin". Another example of the Chinese humour Denis had tried to portray. Like the work colleague who had a friend whose hobby was collecting insects in the jungle and who as a result caught some dastardly internal thing that needed a rectal inspection. Whilst performing this, the Chinese doctor asked if the patient had his mouth open. Yes replied the surprised man, why do you ask? Because all I can see are the trees through the window replied the witty medic.

We found we had to work at play. If there are little or no domestic chores to perform, if gardening is limited to tending the pot plants and cutting the small lawn that anyway is composed not of the fine English grass but the coarse tropical variety, if walking other than short distances is out of the question and given a built-in child minder/baby sitter, then the issue of using up leisure time begins to loom large.

With a growing band of work colleagues and friends and all in a similar position and of a like mind, except of-course Scott Pirie, we are gradually sucked into the whirl of social activity. June's new found friends play bridge and Jim Bell the senior tax manager in the office gives lessons. It takes little time for her to become as good as any of these girls who, along with husbands, swap homes for regular bridge evenings. So June teaches me and soon we are in the bridge circle. Drinks and nibbles and Acol and finesse and opening three no trumps and Tony Wilkinson showing off a bit by serving Japanese wine warmed in a pan. But always, always use Jim's neatly typed up rules of engagement otherwise your partner will not know what you intend.

The story of Jim Bell is rather sad. All of his professional life had been spent in the tropics "can't leave now – blood's too thin" and he was a competent tax specialist in this scene of expats and cross-border trading companies that demanded this expertise. So he had made good money and saved it and his prestige was enhanced by being an acknowledged top flight bridge player. He taught and played his evening's hands accompanied by a regularly topped-up brandy that never ostensibly affected his judgement.

Near the end of our stay he started to bring photographs of his luxury villa being built to his specific design in Northern Cyprus, the place chosen for his retirement in mid-1974. In early 1974 the Turks invaded. Jim and his wife lost everything. Over thirty years later Julia and I visit Kyrenia having depressingly passed through the checkpoint and the guns, and the waiter back in Paphos tells me that reciprocity is still being "considered." Too late for bridge-playing Jim I fear. Long since gone misere.

The Tanglin Club had a series of tiered tennis courts that when not acting as a magnificent cascading waterfall following the afternoon's downpour, provided our Friday night's sport. We had teamed up with Chris from the audit side of PW and his wife for doubles under floodlights and the incredible luxury of having ball-boys on hand. Aside from the actual game, it was a very professional set-up. The star performer was Chris's wife who had perfected a *Maureen*, her name that I attributed to the deadly concealed drop shot that won most rallies and always the deciding game of the match. Whether it was actually intended remained a mystery and often formed the basis of discussion when we retired to the bar and restaurant afterwards.

The Tanglin Club restaurant had one superlative dish never matched anywhere since. They had a genuine whole English Blue Stilton served by a scoop from the centre. It was, and still would be, worth cutting out an entire meal for. Many years later I asked some old friends who had by then been in South Africa for twenty years what they missed most about England and the answer was Blue Stilton. The miniature one sent over for Christmas got the response "heaven." As a home-thoughts-from-abroad craved for unavailability, Blue Stilton must rank alongside Marmite. There must be a good business opportunity waiting for someone.

There was a suspicion of being lured into an activity by someone proficient in order to be, necessarily, a second fiddle. Jim's bridge, Chris and Maureen's tennis and now John Bishop's ten-pin bowling. He had this strange type of action that started the ball nearer the gully than the logical centre of the lane and was delivered out of the side of the hand rather than simply the front. The result was a sort of curved spin that nevertheless hit, as predicted, just to the outside of the centre pin and scattered the lot. Not unreasonably this is known apparently as a strike. John had more strikes than the rest of us had hot dinners and talking of which eating out transcended all of these sporty groups. There was cook your own from thin strips of meat at the Russian Troika, wet your own from the Steamboat restaurant, podge your own at the Happy City Chinese ten-course banquet, eat your own at the Tony Wilkinson's recommended "cheap and cheerful" three-course Robinson Road special lunch or the sandwiches dipped in tomato ketchup (good for the heat), pot-up your own at the steak and kidney place overlooking the bustling harbour (third busiest in the world after New York and Rotterdam, or so it was said) or best of all, wag your own oxtail at the specialist place. All in all a gourmet's paradise even ignoring the fare at what were some of the most luxurious hotels in the world. Alternatively one could eat noodles from a roadside stall on the way to work or shellfish on the night market.

Swimming was the most favoured and time absorbing

pastime. It suited the weather and playing with the boys especially once Christine Tittle had taught Chris how to swim in the Tanglin Club pool. He adopted an unusual style. One that involved three or four strokes underwater then coming up for air and then repeating the process. It was all the same effective if deceptive in that on returning to the UK it tricked a well wishing spectator at the scouts' swimming gala to jump in the pool fully clothed to rescue him. But we had great fun fighting water battles and racing and having diving contests that scored my belly-flops no more than five out of ten. Looking back it is these activities as continued during the thunder and lightning storms or watching the rats scurry past in the drains that seem a bit off.

The one activity that remained a sole female pastime was mahjong. This secret world of painted tiles and weird expressions like *three winds*, as if one wasn't enough, was a favourite at the club during the daytime. Seng Kim told me that amongst the Chinese it was, however, very much a male thing and especially at Chinese New Year when the serious gambling kicked in and when it was not unknown for the treasured Mercedes or even a business to change hands. As far as I ever knew, the Western ladies stakes were lower.

Once the telecoms job was well underway and Denis and Laurence were writing and testing the systems, I was given a few other assignments. One of these sprang from another legacy of British rule and engineering construction, the Sembawang Shipyard in the far north of the Island. A new 40,000 DWT dry-dock was to be built to further the escalating activity of overhauling the tankers that plied their trade from Europe and the Middle East to the Far East.

Like telecommunications, this work was a direct result of strategic location but as I was to learn later this facility would not be without its competition. Southern India had a claim as an even better half-way house. But for now it was all about systems and, in the PW context, financial controls. Whatever may be thought of the achievements or otherwise of the colonial era, an outside observer such as I was could once again only marvel at the legacy from the British to the new Republic.

A large busy shipyard together with all the infrastructure, plant and machinery and order book and goodwill just handed over. My only lasting memory of the time spent in the yard was of the outsized, red-faced captains and other senior officers who emerged from the office early in the morning after having lodged their bills of lading or whatever other paperwork accompanied the job of stewardship of the giant craft. Having been told of the great distance needed to change the course of a tanker let alone stop one, a silent prayer that the large men of the sea had started their indulgence in liquid refreshment after docking rather than before, seemed apposite.

No such anxieties were heralded by the serious men of the Diethelm Aluminium Extrusion Plant. The sober countenance of these Swiss gentlemen were the very epitome of my mind image of the exact clean race that we had brushed against on our little holiday before setting out for this sweltering domain.

But then came the chance to get immersed once again in the mixed Chinese/Indian/Malaysian culture that I had learned to enjoy so much in the telecoms world. Cycle & Carriage was the perfect name for the perfect indigenous Chinese business because it explained the transition that is possible by alert management in changing times. Cycles and carriages had indeed been made and sold in cycle and carriage times but now it was Mercedes time and betwixt it had been the developing forms of transport. A factory in the north of Singapore Island received CKD packs directly from Germany (just as the Nottingham factory exported its cycles but note it had not diversified upwards in the transport business) and assembled and painted and trimmed the result to create the gleaming white Mercedes 280SE, the pride of the successful emerging nation of new Singaporians. As further proof of business acumen, a second plant assembled the Mitsubishi Colt from Japanese CKD packs.

My job was to introduce systems of cost capture from the shop floor activities and building to the final product. One interesting variation of the very similar work done for Allis Charmers at Essendine was trying to accommodate instructions in each ethnic language of the operatives. It was one thing to describe in English what is intended to be put in this little box on this form, that itself was capable of numerous interpretations, as I had learned. But try doing the same thing in four languages and one –Indian – just like Dutch that needs umpteen more letters than any other to say the same thing. Anyway, the results must have been broadly O.K. since soon I was flying weekly to KL to do much the same job in the truck assembly plant in Petaling Jaya. This dual activity became very tiring but the compensation was being able to explore the wonderful city of Kuala Lumpur, accepting the jungle cocktail on checking into the posh hotel overlooking the racecourse and marvelling at the liberal and open array of *services* listed on the checking-in form. Somehow it symbolised the absolute difference between free Malaysia and the hidebound Singapore. I did not avail myself of these services but I know someone who did.

White Knight to King 6, check

It was late afternoon when an incoming 'phone call in a booming voice with a slight Birmingham twang opened with "how are you doing you old bugger" followed by the distinctive laugh that could only come from the one person I could not have been more taken aback to hear from or, to my own surprise, more elated. "Where are you" I somehow gulped. "Downstairs waiting to see you, we got in this morning". Enter once more John Eaton, the ex-property developing consultant maverick sacked from my job in Essendine and who had taken the trouble to come to see me in hospital and cheer me up.

Over a few beers that evening the story of his boredom in the UK came out and knowing of my escape (as he put it) he had approached the big accounting practices in Birmingham specifically seeking an appointment in Singapore. To his own surprise, as much as anyone else's, it seems he got a contract eventually with a firm smaller than PW in the UK but actually much larger in Singapore due to their long association with numerous governmental bodies on the island. So here he was complete with wife and two teenage children and as ebullient as before.

This John was to add a new dimension to the experience. He swept in as a sort of long lost friend although in reality we hardly knew each other. It was his character and the circumstances of our previous encounter that somehow created a special relationship. At any rate here was someone right outside the PW circle and whose activities would be different to those we had experienced. Where there had been caution, here was risk. Where there had been conservatism, here at a stroke was liberalism. Where there had been solid employment, here was an entrepreneur.

I never really knew how it happened but there had been some sort of big shake-up in the consultancy department of the practice he had joined, Peat Marwick Mitchell (now it is one of the big four accountancy practices in the UK and known as KPMG). It had followed a scandal that at the time was well reported. What emerged, and in no time at all, was John in charge. To reflect this status, his salary went through the roof as did the associated contractual accoutrements, not least the living accommodation reflected in a move to a splendid bungalow in its own grounds. And from what I was told during our occasional lunch-time meetings, the confidence in him was not misplaced. His pitching for new work was both aggressive and successful and involved some real estate dealings. His language as ever was colourful and descriptive. He appeared to specialise in "shit or bust" meetings. John loved the fast, noisy, business expansion climate of the day. He said so over and over again and it showed.

Although I had not known this whilst in the UK, John's main hobby was sailing and on the entrepreneurial front, he took me one weekend to see a large wooden yacht that lay at anchor off the north coast. With the now customary throw-away nonchalance he explained that after a "session" at the yacht club he had bought this wonderful traditional craft and had just commissioned restoration work. Before we left the island, that work would be finished and the yacht sold at a considerable profit. On other weekends he was determined to get me crewing on the dingy he had bought purely for sailing. John had joined the small and not exclusive East Coast Sailing Club and it became a different and quieter alternative to the Tanglin Club for some of our Sunday afternoons.

June and the boys would stay on the sandy shore whilst I followed instructions on when to lean out to sea and when to duck as we came about on the tacking manoeuvres. It was a wonderfully new experience that I absolutely loved and made a vow to pursue once back home. A vow never fulfilled so these tacks to the Malaysian coast and the spinnaker-hoisted rushes back have had to last me a lifetime.

It was when we were settling on that quiet stretch of beach one such Sunday afternoon that we spotted a skinny couple also at ease at the far end in deck chairs and reading. Although they were not easily recognised behind the sunglasses and towels, June and I worked out that it was Scott Pirie and his wife. So they had joined a club after all.

Not of-course the expensive and extrovert Tanglin Club or better still the prestigious Island Club (where Lee Kwan Yew the Prime Minister of the Republic played golf) but the cheapest and remotest yacht club where they would be most unlucky to be spotted by anyone let alone someone from PW. So we let our little secret stand and Scott and his lady retained their privacy except that being outside the PW fold it seemed in order to point them out to John as we pulled the boat ashore one afternoon. His unique perspective on life was again displayed with the choice observation "can you imagine them making love? It would be like two skeletons rattling"

So here was John. A late arrival and instant success. A money-making adventurer. It takes someone special to drop into a completely foreign scene and make a mark quickly and with panache. Why cannot life be perfect, why does there always have to be a spoiler? There had been that incident at Essendine. When we met at the ice-cold almost blacked-out Britannic Inn on Holland Road, there would be the three fingers held out sideways to the waiter to demonstrate the depth of the whisky in the glass before the "half as much again" water. When we met at lunch-time some Fridays - unlike me John did not work Saturday mornings - for a sandwich with tomato sauce he never left with me but would stay "for another" and there was the impression that his week was already over. The yacht club was very social and the afternoon sailings always ended "with a session". We were invited to his bungalow for a cocktail party and as we left he put a full bottle of vodka in my hand for being "such a good friend". Vodka? I didn't know you drank vodka Mr John Eaton, but then there is probably quite a lot I don't know. His teenage children hadn't settled well and wanted to go home and then they had settled too well amongst the spoilt ex-pat brats brigade. That brigade that for fun, and for something to do, bent forks and spoons at the Tanglin Club before showing them to the polite and well brought up waiters.

John's wife was an exceptionally attractive woman. Soon after they first met they made love in a corridor on a train returning from the continent. Not as exhibitionists but because they just couldn't keep their hands off each other. But things change over time and had changed. Now he could meet her off an aeroplane from Spain and "She would be radiantly full of some Spanish sod." Or was this booze talking? Cause? Affect?

For some reason I never understood, the employee personal tax arrangements in Singapore were modelled on the American not the British PAYE system. This resulted in an annual visit to the Inland Revenue office to agree and pay the past year's tax. The last I heard of John was a rumour that he had jumped a ship headed deeper into the Far East and had not paid his tax bill. Never knowing if this was true or not, I have often wondered over the past thirty years what happened to him.

Tropical storm clouds gather

The old colonial wooden-built Robinsons departmental store was burnt down one morning and we rushed from the office to the beautiful Raffles Square to see its death throws. Over twenty people were trapped in the lifts and perished along with the tradition. The teacher of French at the Chinese YMCA turned out to be an English Bohemian who was, helped by his wife, building a boat to sail to the New Hebrides. But these were in turn tragic and interesting blips in a bigger picture. I was worried about June.

The climate was genuinely hard to take and especially for someone like June who was fair-skinned and found perspiring difficult. This was not helped by my pushing for trips initially around the island and then Sentosa and then into Malaysia. It would have been better during the daytime to have stayed either in the apartment, even without air-conditioning that we had learned to turn off due to the problem of acclimatisation, or in the shade at the Tanglin Club. But no, I had to explore. At any rate until the lessons were learned. Then there were the child illnesses of blisters and bites and breathing. These things are more worrying for a young mother than a chap busy at work.

And the thing that I dismissed as a flippant aside but was clearly building up in June's mind as a major issue, namely the constant attention of Kim our amah to the two boys. It was not that she resented the help. June knew as well as anyone that it was essential in this climate. It was pandering to the kids, making them lazy. In a phrase that became more prevalent "spoiling them". Specifically, when a toy was thrown aside, Kim was there to recover it. When food or drink was tipped over, Kim was there to clean up. But how do you tell a maid not to?

Then there were the reports from the letting agent back home on the not very satisfactory situation. First, no let at all when we had been assured of a 100% time coverage. Next a bad tenant who eventually left leaving repairs and cleaning to be done. My concern was getting enough income net of the letting costs to cover the mortgage. June's was more deep-seated. Her home was not being treated properly.

A further angst was why it was that of all the couples in our position that we knew, only we had not had and nor was there any prospect of, a visit from our respective parents. Whereas I was angry given our offer to pay for the flight tickets, to June it was more like abandonment. And there was the letter saying that her dad had had a little stay in hospital with a mild chest problem. For a coal-face miner that was not unusual but still she would have liked more details and to have been there.

The symptoms were obvious but I pushed on regardless. Letter after letter to family and friends back home and the comprehensive lists of when sent to whom and when replied to. The almost religious listening to the Archers radio programme as it was played in omnibus every Sunday morning. The overwhelming importance of booking the Christmas telephone call back home and in the latter months of the contract the ticking off of the days on a large calendar in the kitchen. As blind as I was, surely one could not have overlooked the episode when Christine thought June might consider joining her as a Samaritan and the interviewer for the volunteers suggesting that instead June might consider continuing to talk to her.

In spite of all this and like dynamic Dave nine months earlier as his contract was nearing the end, when I was approached about starting off a consultancy practice for the firm in KL and as a manager, I seriously wanted us to go. More salary, a firm's car, my own office to start up and in a place I had got to know and really liked. So I was shocked when June put her foot down and flatly refused. We had our first serious argument and it was probably to have far-reaching consequences not least in signalling our fundamental differences. But for now I was smarting with failure and we got the travel agent in our block around to plan a return route home. Ceylon, Seychelles, Nairobi and the so very drab London underground with its dark - coloured shabbily dressed customers. Oh God, what next.

CHAPTER TEN
Price Waterhouse : an Indian odyssey

1974-1978. Back home, low in spirit. Coarse fishing and sub-cultures. Home made wine and emigrating friends. Re-joining the old firm. Develop the home and sell. A new broom at PW. Duodenal ulcer and Black Sea dysentery. Southern India, consultants' wives, the Moonlight Saunter and Swan Hunter unfortunates. Elephantiasis. Ravi arrives at the Malabar Hotel. Sweet tea and dignified people. A bumpy end. NEC Birmingham, management games but disenchantment. Up the housing ladder. A wasted life? The family takeover. Inheritance.

I was showing Ray the little pink tablets in the box that I had just collected from the chemist. The sort of sporadic flutterings of my heart, palpitations I suppose, had made me feel really strange and a bit frightened. Coming on suddenly, there seemed to be no pattern as to how long it would last or having stopped when it would start up again. Activity didn't appear to be a factor, indeed my heart would race away most often whilst sitting quietly and most probably thinking about coming back from Singapore. After a few questions, the doctor suspected the cause was the sudden change in temperature. I wondered if

I was doing a psychosomatic backflip, at any rate worried as I was it recalled with a wry inner smile the reaction of the travel agent to my unconventional planned route home. Tashkent, Istanbul and Ajaccio. "The temperature in Tashkent in January after your time out here will probably kill you all". And so we had gone for the commonplace and well publicised jungle route.

It's usual for young mothers to make friends. Just the day-to-day circumstance of taking the little ones to playschool and fetching them back and swapping mothering stories and the taking and the bringing back from the parties. But Ray was different. Maybe Ray and not Rachel said it all. Not bothered about fashion or being skinny or keeping a prissy, prissy house – if there are cobwebs in the kitchen so there are cobwebs in the kitchen. If it's meal-time, well throw a few bits and bobs in a pan. But with hamsters and gerbils running amok and a dog on the settee and a cat on the window-ledge and demijohns of fermenting wine bubbling in the airing cupboard and fishing reels drying on the boiler, her home was a flop down have a coffee happy and contented sort of place.

So although she was June's now re-found best friend, her kitchen was my first gravitation point. Un-thought-through and unplanned I was telling Ray how low I was. June was instantly very happy, back with her mum and dad and sister and the wider Kirkby family and Chris and Craig were in school and making new friends but for me it was cold and empty and dark and dreary and my heart now even physically seemed to rebel from the reality of being back.

Even Henry, my old sponsor, sitting in his large oak-panelled lined office with the suite of leather furniture and original paintings had not been exactly welcoming. I did understand didn't I that he would have to formally interview me for a job. I did appreciate didn't I that legally the UK firm had been left in favour of the Far East practice and it was up to me to get back in if that was what I wanted and of course things had moved on.

Whilst I had been swanning around in a tropical paradise, the firm had expanded beyond all expectations. The little specialist group was now a multi-disciplined large one. I was saying to Ray, well, did I really want to go back? I had already learned that dynamic Dave did not. He had joined a hosiery manufacturing group back in Manchester. I was thinking of starting out on my own. Contrary to what Scott Pirie had prophesised, it had turned out that it was possible to have a good social time in Singapore and save money. These funds (remitted to Jersey until the tax year end) added to the compulsory return of the State superannuation scheme fund and my terminal bonus and the car sale proceeds - amazingly the same amount as paid eighteen months earlier - had created quite a nice nest-egg and notwithstanding the problems the rental income had just about funded the mortgage whilst we were away. This meant that I could probably finance a consultancy start-up although, as yet, I had no idea how to go about it. Also, the new salary offered by Henry was about half that earned in Singapore. What to do?

Roy, Ray's husband, was a practical man. Dexterous. The very antithesis of me. His job was selling grinding-wheels and over many Sunday evening sessions in the pub, I heard all about the sizes, properties and machine-tool applications of these appliances but my disposition was such that I learnt next to nothing. What I did gather was that he obviously worked on some sort of performance basis and had a regular group of loyal customers notably amongst whom was Rolls Royce in Derby. It must have been so because he actually *put in* no more, on average, than two days a week. How this occurred really interested me and I found myself questioning him closely on it in case, out of pure self-interest, it should prove useful in the world of factories and incentive schemes and motivation and the like. He got on well with his boss and I got little further than that.

Not that he was lazing around for the other three days. Ray was an orphan and she had inherited several properties rented out to students in Nottingham. Roy kept these in working order and apparently there was much involved in this and as I heard first-hand some of it was not too pleasant. Then again they had a towing caravan and each Friday was usually a pack up and get away day. Ray confided that she was not always happy to be so hustled but went along with it for the peace of a campsite by a river whilst Roy fished. And it wasn't long before he was picking up Chris and Craig to go with their two boys, Mark and Jonathan, on a fishing expedition.

Thus the world of coarse fishing opened up with the visits to the tackle shop for all those mysterious artefacts embedded in the conscious of the river-fisher but brand new to we ignoramuses. The tackle box with its outward hinging upper compartmentalised section, the weights, the floats, the lines, the reel and above all the knowledge. What fish and at what depth and so which line and how may weights with what float. How to strike and how to land and from my perspective the two worst skills. How to get the hook out of the fish's throat and how to untangle the unfathomably knotty line on a perishing winter morning.

Looking back on this experience of coarse fishing there are a number of really interesting aspects. Like bell-ringing, one such aspect is of sub-cultures. One minute a bit of society is a closed book or even a complete unknown and the next you are immersed in the whole social milieu. The language, the custom, the tradition, the experts and the also-rans, the old-fashioned and avant-garde, the absolute dedicated and the casual participant.

This coarse fishing is a sphere of independent patient loners impervious to four a.m. starts, wiggly pink maggots and the foulest of weather. He and his rod against the unseen sleek one in the secret depths. But bonhomie and, match-play aside, full of needful information of what is taking, what is stocked or what is dead water. If one took, say, just the UK then how many discrete sub-cultures are there? Has anyone tried to list them and what proportion are cross-cultured as distinct from intra-cultured?

Think of the butterfly collectors, the bug collectors, the bird watchers, the fossil seekers, the prize tomato growers, the orchid enthusiasts, the embroiderers, the Hammond organ players, the ball-room dancers, the model boat enthusiasts, those that restore my idealised steam train. The list must run into thousands. Each single member of each single sub-culture could spend the whole of a lifetime solely within the warmth of the chosen haven. Then, you or I might be wholly ignorant of the entirety of their world. The most impressive feature of the media is how, at a moment's notice, the BBC or similar can rustle up an expert in, say, bovine encryption because a cow has been found writing with its front hoof in the soil in Shropshire.

Another interesting diversion is to consider what it takes to get young children really involved in something. So involved that they move on themselves and indeed eventually actually resent the interference of adults. It is to do with active participation in something with an intrinsic physical dimension and the more bits and pieces, that is variables, the better. The absolute converse of the special, expensive, elaborately wrapped Christmas present that is back in its box or broken by Boxing Day. Fishing fits the favoured profile perfectly. It requires study, developing skill, gradual accumulation of tackle and, never to be underestimated, an element of competition. How clever of the publishers to release the ABC guide to fishing in weekly instalments. It fits the pattern. Give a child just two or three things to get involved in and provided there is enough depth to each and directly connected practical activity, the "I'm bored" will be banished for ever.

Then there is environmental tutelage. Not many young

ladies get into show-jumping or dressage when they are in their middle teen years. By then, if at all, jumping fences and the like is as natural as getting up in the morning and having breakfast. Why? Because from the age of three the innocent sweet little darlings have been dressed in jodhpurs and the rest and with their back as straight as a ramrod are confidently riding their own pony round the showground.

Whilst there will always be a minor percentage drop-out (break-out?), the vast majority of children will grow into the precise environment they have been fed on. The child taken to the cliff top car park to see the view and taken home again is your future passive tourist. The child taken out of that car and given the first pair of small boots to put on and walked on the cliff path for five miles and shown the bird life and told the names of the wild flowers and fingered the rock formation, is your future rambling adventurer.

So, as a parent, which way do you want things to go? It is of-course why social strata self-perpetuate. But if you know you are most likely setting a blueprint then there is nothing other than maybe finance and imagination to prevent picking a preferred course for a child that is outwith your own experience. I may have never played golf but if I observe that golfers have a lifetime's enjoyment from the game and a few make a fortune playing professionally, then there is nothing, other than the fees, preventing me from entering my child as a junior at the nearest club. Chances are that I will not, but I could. A second shot might be that a close golfing friend might do it instead as happened with Roy and the coarse fishing. In one sense thinking this through is depressing because we are all capable of pre-mapping. But it is not as depressing as was the unlocking of the human DNA and knowing that we are all chemically cloned.

Fishing was by no means Roy's only outdoor activity, in fact he was leisure-time's perpetual outdoor man. He was a serious fell-walker and indeed his idea of a Christmas present for Ray was, and actually was, a new pair of walking boots. But even this pursuit came second to where it had all started and from where most of his long-standing friends came. Rock climbing. His idea of a winter break was to go off with a group of like kind and climb peaks in the Scottish Highlands or, I remember one February, on the Isle of Skye. So that was Roy, no interest in TV or sports or cars or other women (he called Ray "the dragon" – affectionately I am sure) but camping and fishing and walking and climbing and always the mongrel dog rescued from the PDSA. Little wonder then that his younger son Jonathan is now a leading world expert on scorpions having published a recognised work and making regular appearances on South African TV to enlighten the viewers on the arachnid venomous creature.

I had taken Roy to the farm several times and once he had helped with the hay-making but on this occasion he spotted the damsons. Actually the trees that grew at the extreme east end of the stackyard and almost certainly planted there originally as a windbreak (and the east wind in winter could be bitterly cold, my dad used to say there was nothing to stop it between there and Siberia), were not strictly damsons but what were always known as bullies. Looking years later in "The Fruit Expert" by Dr D G Hessayon it is clear that they were bullaces. The information note says "Search all the catalogues and you will find a supplier, but it really isn't worth growing". Somehow, and sentimentally, it sums up the farm. Not quite what it aspired to be. True damsons are black and small and round but the bullies were larger though not as large as a plum and more elongated.

When we wanted proper damsons we went to the village of Astwith on a steep inclined road down to Hardwick Hall. It was said that the trees flourished in that place due to their uniquely sheltered position; elsewhere the local climate was too cold. None of this stopped us using the bullies. My mum made wonderful jam and, mixed with our Bramley apples, made pies and stewed fruit. The problem was that these bullace trees fruited infrequently. For perhaps four years there would be no fruit at all and then on the fifth a veritable abundance. So it was when Roy clasped eyes on the trees. His idea was, however, not jam or pies but wine.

With my dad looking forward to the final product, we set to and picked the whole harvest, three sacks full. Using a recipe I found we meticulously cut up and de-stoned the fruit and put the whole lot in a large bath that Roy found from somewhere. Adding warm water and several diced oranges and lemons, the lot was covered for so long and then the magic touch. The pith was put into the sacks that in turn were suspended by rope from the main cross-member inside his garage. Underneath was the bath of juice and each day we gave the sacks one more twist to extract more liquid.

After about a week and when it seemed all that would come out, had, we used his tried and tested fermenting skills to start off the innumerable demijohns. Every conceivable warm spot in their Heavytrees bungalow was occupied with a glug-glugging jar and eventually and after the sugar content test suggested the right point had been reached, we bottled. Incredibly there were over eighty bottles of beautifully clear, light-sherry coloured wine. And sherry is an apt term since, in the event, it was more akin to fortified than table wine and we soon learned to drink it from small rather that normal sized wine glasses. At least our household and my dad's did. I sometimes wondered if Roy was as conservative especially having regard to his often excitable state when we met on the following few Sunday evenings. So the bullies might not be worth growing but sometimes in this life one has to suffer to get the best results.

Over the next few years June and Ray became ever closer until they were probably each other's best friend. Ray meantime had started teaching hair-dressing at a college in Doncaster and so was driving the beloved van a good thirty miles each way each day. Not that that changed their somewhat eccentric lifestyle. But something was about to. As is often the case, there was no single but a series of transforming events.

The sideline of rental income was stuttering for some reason and flats were being sold off and not replaced. Roy got made redundant and after two or three re-employments with hitherto rival firms making grinding wheels, appeared to have hit a void. He wanted to start his own business or join an old climbing friend in his engineering business but for some reason neither happened. Mark, his elder boy, was proving to be a little slow at school and some problems were coming from that direction.

But the biggest factor was Roy's brother and especially following a visit to attend the funeral of their father who had died suddenly after being apparently fit as a fiddle and independently located in a Derbyshire village. The brother worked for a successful and affluent businessman in South Africa and I started to hear about all the opportunities his brother could see for opening a factory manufacturing to suit Roy's product knowledge. That is a range of grinding wheels to feed the growing manufacturing industries in not just South Africa but also the neighbouring African states.

It was a wonderful opportunity and the brother's boss could finance the venture giving equity to Roy in exchange for his technical knowledge and selling skills. So Roy went over to Johannesburg to check things out and came back with a plan. This plan involved getting all the product specifications for the wheels he now believed there was a demand for in South Africa, talking to potential material and chemical suppliers and assessing any UK demand from that overseas location at the price he could calculate for the products. But also the plan embraced selling the rest of their rented out property interests and Heavytrees so as to advise his brother of the funds available to purchase a property over there. Whilst their main household effects were en-route, they would buy a small flat or similar and hold on to it as a fall-back UK base. It was all quite perfect.

Roy had regained all his joie de vivre, the boys were excited and had studied the atlas and all the interesting new place names and been shown pictures of the native big game animals and the colourful birds. There was only one problem. Ray did not want to go. But she would go along with it when the time came, Roy was sure.

June and I drove the whole family including Flossie the latest mongrel to Heathrow. Flossie could on no account be left behind. The shipment of her alone cost £400 which in the early 1980's was a staggering sum of money and she would be in quarantine over there for six months after arrival. In the front seat with me was June quietly crying, in the back seat with Roy was Ray very noisily crying. The final goodbyes in the departure lounge were dreadful and not least as a throw-back to the wrench from Singapore some eight years earlier. Although I would not appreciate it at the time, it too was to have a profound affect on June. It would be twenty years before I would see them in their new home territory. June would not be there.

Back with the old firm

This misplaced arrogance in the hallowed halls of PW Birmingham is really getting at me. Even the senior audit partner, never mind Henry, is questioning whether I can perform "back in the First Division". I can't even be bothered to try to explain about the work relationship built up with Goh Seng Kim and I suppose it would be best not to say that he is a far more cultured, developed and senior man than anyone in these corridors of ugly brummy accents could ever even hope to aspire to be. Or mention the leaving dinner given in our honour by Mrs Kuma the newly appointed finance director of the merged telecommunications body or of the senior judges who she had invited also in our honour.

I will not mention than June and I are now reasonably competent bridge and tennis players and can hold our own on most civilised society occasions and have probably eaten in better restaurants than most of them could even dream about. And, geographically, are certainly more worldly than any of them in our age group. Instead, and with as much acerbity as I can muster, I tell Henry that it's what I put on our shoes each Sunday morning when, in his pre-rejoining appraisal, he proffers a view that I lack a certain polish for the rapidly growing UK consultancy business. One wag in the office comments openly on my new blue suit especially made by the Chinese tailor on Orchard Road for my return to England (two pairs of trousers to the one jacket); he suggests I look like a budgerigar.

What galls me most is that there is not a single organisational study on the planning board in the office. Is that due to the quasi-blackmail teeth of "perhaps we had better get our consultancy side to take a look at this before we come in next time" not biting so deep as to reach the most important business aspect of all, that is, structural? Furthermore, there is no presence now in the new Nottingham office because their new man there has also decamped to Singapore.

So much for the provincial spread of the new consultancy service and yuppie for the audit partners keeping their clients free of the new-fangled efficiency and systems things. And to think that I'll be dealing with this bunch of pricks when I could be setting up my own office in Kuala Lumpur. So the decision is this, do I press on pretending I want my old job back or go it alone using my new-found capital to fund a start-up? Safety versus risk. Those two opposing armies that will bedevil me all my life.

In the event the job offer was a formality pending only my being knocked down a peg or two. The fundamental reason was Don Hemmings out at peaceful Allis Chalmers. Ken Glass the young thrusting American MD had moved on, head-hunted to run the huge diesel-engine manufacturing factory in Stamford. The business of making heavy earth-moving machines had undergone a metamorphism with the American owners selling a 50% stake to the largest Italian manufacturer of these huge beasts.

The new joint venture needed a mature steady pair of hands and Don stepped up from financial director to fit the bill perfectly. He in turn was waiting to see me and so I slipped back into the factory groove as if time had stood still. I liked and respected him and empathised with the new-found export growth prospects. Whilst not presenting much personal progress, it would be a safe landing and the boys were young and June was happy again and I ought to want a steady income. So, at least this time, safety first. Also, I was still fascinated with the disproportionate qualities of revenue and capital. Revenue is spent. Capital should beget capital and will only be revenue in the long run. Until now my theory had been just that but now that for the first time some capital existed there was an opportunity to apply it.

My idea was to invest the capital by expanding our recovered but small new house in the hope of accelerating a jump in the property ladder but to get best possible value by cutting out the builder's profit. The snag of-course was that unlike Roy or John Trigg before him I had no practical skills at all and that fact eliminated any thought of a self-build. What I could bring to bear was energy, strength and my weekends and so having thought this through I went for a pint with my brother-in-law Mick.

Mick had been an apprentice bricklayer with the local builder Fred Stone (my aunt Pem's bungalow was called

Barnston named after the barn in Red Barn Farm Fred's surname since he had build it) but by now was pretty much a generalist builder having worked for a number of new-build firms. He had four children and, as was customary at the time, a non-working though still fashion conscious and flirty wife. He could use all the extra cash going and my sister actively pushed him into weekend overtime or extra-firm work. After all, she could always take the kids to the farm to be looked after and fed.

The bargain was struck. I would pay the top labour hourly rate and would fetch him early every Saturday morning and return him Sunday evening. Travelling time was included and he would eat with us each Saturday night before he and I went for a pint to recover. He would work out the quantities of the various materials and order them - twice as it turned out for the large window pane that we smashed on fitting - nd do all the skilled jobs except the joinery and electrics that he would hire in and I would do all the labouring including all the hand mixing of the mortar and cement.

We annoyed the neighbours on both sides and especially the one I nicknamed Laughing Jack on account of his permanently melancholic countenance and who formally objected to our non-matching colour roof tiles and the extra effluent that would naturally follow the expansion (more people would be staying at a larger house, presumable the product of some obscure logic) and that would pass under his property thus raising the possibility of a blockage under his land.

We also had much difficulty passing the exacting standards of the building inspector on the water test of our new drains. It seems the water once blocked at one end should stay put but somehow by the time he arrived on the scene, it had drained away or partly so. Management consultants never encounter such problems. But eventually the project was completed and it had taken a whole year from Easter to Easter.

The house was one-half as big again as when we started. New living room, kitchen, bedroom and bathroom and garage. Neither the idea nor the execution was unique, hundreds of thousands have done it but it does provide an excellent example of capital to grow capital whereas revenue dissipates. Being bricks and mortar brings to bear the attendant factors of supply and demand, with the inequality skewed to demand, and the tradition in the UK of home ownership but these do not dilute the principle that investing in something tangible (motor cars aside) ought to grow or at worst hold value. I am convinced of this.

Revenue spending is for essentials, however that is defined, and leisure spending is short-lived and must be covered by recurring income with spare for when the rain sets in, which it will. We had bought for the impossibly high price of £3,950 and spend the ex-Singapore capital of £4,000 on it. We sold almost immediately for £16,250 to part finance a quantum leap to £23,250 on a 1950's house badly in need of modernisation. The capital programme had started.

Whether or not I lacked polish and notwithstanding the doubted ability to adjust to the first division, things were going well. The credit went to Don Hemmings and the extent to which my involvement with the rapidly expanding Anglo-Italian plant was getting deeper and deeper became suddenly apparent when I was asked to give a paper to new recruits at the London PW training centre on *client satisfaction*. Someone in administration had come up with the startling statistic that I had undertaken nineteen separate assignments for a single client.

To lighten the morning I got a back-room chap to play the Rolling Stones's *Can't get no satisfaction* as they all trouped in. It was unconventional, broke the ice and gave me a counter-theme with which to start. More important to me, it was intended to send out a message of rebellion. Rebellion because whilst accepting in my own mind that the opportunity to work for this factory could only have occurred because PW was the external auditor and I, as an adviser, had been fed through that entrée, the very presence of PW now was an irritant. I grew to resent the visits of my manager Peter Cuthbert-Smith.

Peter knew nothing about the manufacturing of four-wheel-drive heavy loaders and his questions were superficial, irrelevant and a waste of valuable time. I still believed that a short, sharp six-week probe by an observant and quick-on-the-uptake outsider who was prepared to go down the line and listen would always beat six months effort by the line management if only because the incomer sees fault in what to the native is normal. Go to any hotel, town or village or sub-culture gathering for the first time and prove it. But, and it's a big but, my tastes were changing. The realisation dawned. Inside was my real slot. Not outside.

Fees and profit and getting on with clients matters. At any rate they are the hallmark of success in this game. And so in successive years after getting back from Singapore in the annual promotion or nudge round, I became senior consultant, then manager and then senior manager. As ever though, not without a cost. There is a new man in Nottingham and he wants me wrested away from the jurisdiction of Birmingham to be his cutting edge.

C.C. was the senior partner of the Newcastle office and comes with a reputation for ruffling feathers. More than that, he sits on the main firm's steering committee in London. Things have to change in backwoodian Nottingham. Profit has to be made, old hands have to go, young thrusting managers have to be brought on. For a start he chain smokes cigarettes even throughout the lunches he starts taking me to at the urbane Victoria Club where only the successful business men and professionals and retired rich go.

The club of red and brown velvet and leather that has a man to park the jaguar "leave it on the double yellows outside", a man to hand out the towels in the lavatory and a snooker room on the top floor with a live feed for the horse racing results and in the hushed eloquent ambience of the basement, the only casino in town. But C.C. hasn't moved into town. He has taken Barrowby Hall in a quiet village thirty miles away close to Grantham and aside the A1 for ready access to London by road or rail.

Chris Collett is telling me that I need to understand that the times they really are a changing for UK business as a whole and the PW firm must adapt and move on. Fees from audit and tax work by dint of regulation and thus compulsion are not enough. The firm must be in the vanguard of pushing industry forward. We must help our clients grow, develop, be more productive, use more technology, acquire. That is why my role is so vital. The audit side will get me in, or else. He has reviewed the income from non-regulatory work over the past year and it amounts to "ten percent of fuck all". Wow! I think back to the shock I similarly gave the teacher back at school. A man with spunk.

The reciprocal shock I give to C.C. is the news that I am ordered to take some time off. After a nice lunch with him of braised kidney prepared in a way that only the chef of the Victoria Club could, the pain starts like literally being stabbed in the back. Before with the stone it was below the rib cage and any recurrence of the cause of that problem, I had been warned, would be with kidney stones. Eating kidney did not, so far as I knew, create stones and in any case even my scant knowledge of physiology taught me where the kidney region was (hadn't I proved it with poor Ted in the railway office?).

What on earth was there to give pain in the middle of the back? A pain that now recurred constantly and seemed to develop into an internal vibration that demanded absolute stillness not to make worse and a creeping coldness and not wanting to speak to anyone but just get into some quiet corner and suffer alone. The tests proved my body as a master class in acid production. Long hours not bothering or not being able to eat and often indifferent food when I do. Constant travel. Leaving home early Monday morning, getting back late Friday night. Waking in a strange place and wondering first which hotel this is and then what town and then what job. And not to do with booze either. Can't afford to drink much, too many balls in the air, too much to do. And this is the cost of push, push, push and rapid promotion. Craig is six, nearly seven and I don't even know him. I have a duodenal ulcer.

The specialist medical consultant practising from the Ropewalk in Nottingham recommends an operation that he would undertake himself. It involves cutting the vagus nerve that he explains is the main trigger for acid production. There are a couple of snags. First the operation might be plain unsuccessful and secondly the vagus nerve actually serves a useful purpose in that acid is needed to break down food ready for digestion into the gut. I am probably such a proficient acid generator anyway that there will be instant success and indeed things that I have always shied away from eating due to indigestion will suddenly become acceptable. Paradoxically, in this case, the ulcer will have been beneficial once of-course the operation has been successfully carried out. But, under these circumstances,

the second snag could arise with age. As a body ages, so less acid is produced naturally. With the vagus nerve severed, there could come a time when too little acid is made. This would create its own problem albeit down the line, so to speak. Best if I think about it and certainly talk to my own doctor before taking a decision.

The only other contact with the excellent Doctor Leach from the local surgery (he of the instant and correct diagnosis "slight suspicion of gall stones" some four years earlier) had been the dramatic early Saturday morning knock on the door in the summer of the year we returned form Singapore. The test results were back and he had to inform us personally and urgently that Craig had dysentery. Christ! The culprit was probably a kitchen at a hotel on the Black Sea resort of Mamaia.

The idea behind taking a holiday in Rumania had been to get back to some heat. This had been achieved par excellence. We were room-bound from midday until about five pm each day and the still sweltering night time heat was helped in its effort to make sleeping difficult by the most voluminous and noisy bullfrogs in the world and also by the hotel disco that had no volume control and was timed to suit only nocturnal creatures that, small children in particular, are not.

The only practical daytime activity of lounging on the beach did not prove to be a wholly satisfying experience either and for several reasons. First, the raging trots enforced positioning just outside the communal lavatories that, on the artificial beaches, was not the most welcoming of places. Then there was the presence of the ample ladies of the vicinity who did not bother to cover their bodies between taking off their day wear and putting on their beach wear and vice versa. Nor had these flatterers of the female form adopted the, one had previously thought, standard practice of shaving under their arms and in some other places. Nor could they be relied upon to be completely discreet when performing certain bodily functions. In short, this was not St-Tropez.

We did, however, manage a trip to a first class wine tasting event. First class in that the seven wines were intended to be drunk and not tasted and in the sense that one was equally filled with nationalistic pride in noting that on the return coach trip, it was the Germans that first broke into inebriated singing followed by the Scandinavians and only a reluctant last, the few British of us. This proved that our native race is comparatively both the least exhibitionist and the most impervious to alcohol.

This little trip away from the coast and the wonderful chalk portraits of Chris and Craig done by a local artist in the lounge area of the hotel, proved the two bright spots in an otherwise dark adventure. It got no better with the bumpy decent into Manchester by the aged Russian aeroplane, the failure of the car to start and me trying to sort out Craig's rear-end discharge whilst June vomited from the car window on our trip back over the Macclesfield Cat and Fiddle route. So the news that Craig had a really serious medical condition that must keep him off school indefinitely and that we were to receive a daily visit from a public health officer did nothing to vindicate my decision to go to the Black Sea in the first place. Now we were seeing black in Ravenshead.

Healing the ulcer and off to Cochin

My appointment to discuss whether or not to go ahead with the operation on the vagus nerve was not, however, with Doctor Leach but with the new and handsome Doctor Dawson who apparently everybody likes and who is always behind with his appointments because he talks to the patients. Handsome he might be but this morning he looks pale and drawn and his opening gambit is to tell me that he too has a duodenal ulcer and that this is one of his *off* days. He draws a little diagram of the basic shape of the digestive tract from stomach to duodenum to small intestine to large intestine and explains what basically happens when food hits the sore on the lining. It's wonderfully simple and suddenly it feels like I can begin to understand the source of the problem. This in itself and the fact that I am talking to someone who has the same problem somehow perks me up and this breaks into a form of relief when he proffers a view that there is a real alternative to the operation. After the gall-stone experience, I am listening hard.

I could attempt to heal the sore myself. This would involve going on a liquid only diet for about five to six months. Such liquid would have to be inclusive of all the essential minerals, vitamins and other supplements. Had I heard of Complan? Seems it is a proprietary food-drink. Taken every two hours of the waking day it would provide all the ingredients necessary for life whilst letting the sore repair itself through not being bombarded by ingested food. On no account must I take any form of alcohol or tea or coffee and soft drinks must not be of the acidic type such as orange juice. I lamely asked what I could drink. With the first smile this morning came the triumphant reply, water!

And so the experiment begins. Two-hourly drinks made up whilst at home either by June or myself and varying the flavours to add some variety and at work by my secretary Marilyn who has developed the habit of hitching up her tight skirt and sitting on the corner of my desk at lunchtime to discuss how I am doing and telling me her life story. A story of Scotland and husband and now me trying hard to concentrate past the slim white freckled legs that ultimately lead up to the red hair, I suppose, or am trying hard not to suppose. Trying hard to resist.

Like the stone, it is travelling that presents the real test. Two-hourly breaks to make up a Complan drink is not exactly compatible with client visits and hotel stays. Neither does it fit well on the beach in Newquay or Looe with the buckets and spades and swingball and boats and crablines. Once again June copes fantastically well making up my feeds as if she had acquired a new baby which in large part, at this time, she had. As time passed, the theory was to progressively move to solids and here we were lucky to find a book written by an American who had been through the process and found good advice wanting. He called his development towards eating solid food again "The Ulcer Diet Cook Book" and it became our bible for a further six months or so.

First the butter fudge, then the mashed potato, next the pulverized boiled fish and now if there is no pain, go buy a meat-mincer and use the finest setting to grind the softest meats. Soon we can have a small mixed meal but progress slowly and carefully. This is not a diet to lose weight, there is little of that after the liquid only phase. No it will cause weight gain but no matter, the object of the exercise is to gradually return to something like proper eating.

When there is a set-back, halt and revert to two steps ago. Try again and then again. Gradually progress was made and, imaginary or not, an itching started deep inside as if literally a wound was healing over. But never again, at least not until the new designer drugs came on the market, would it be possible to contemplate eating any strong green vegetable or an orange to add to the long-time banned fatty foods cut out with the stone six years before. After the cure I took my team of consultants to the local Conservative Club for a game of snooker and had my first half-pint of bitter. The consequent deep burning of the acid gave a, almost forgotten, shock that I with much help had learned to be without. No fun here. Alcohol will have to wait.

I did see Doctor Dawson again due to the need for some specific advice. Was it safe for me to go to India? Henry had had me over in Birmingham again helping put together a proposal under the auspices and within the budget of the Ministry of Overseas Development (Judith Hart at the time). Most probably due to Henry's, by then, personal reputation for local government work, the assignment had been won. The job was to attach sound financial controls and operating procedures to a large capital project being partly funded by the UK government in Cochin in Southern India. The capital scheme itself was ambitious and with no little risk in that it involved a twin objective. First to construct a modern shipbuilding and ship repair facility and as development proceeded to build within the new yard an ocean-going tanker.

Maybe it had helped a little with the proposal that my c.v. contained the work done at Sembawang in Singapore. Anyway, PW would operate as British technical experts under the aid programme and in relation to the financial soundness of the new yard. Out there in India we would find technical experts already acting as advisers on the actual ship build. For our assignment Henry would be the director in charge and he wanted me as the manager. The timing was just at the end of my healed ulcer phase. Peter Dawson - for we are now on first name terms - was sure I should go. He had travelled all over India with his wife and his ulcer and has had no ill effects and there was no medial reason why spicy foods should upset the healing process. Just be careful and pack the suitcase with plenty of fudge. In my joy I couldn't help thinking *of the sugary type one assumes*.

The job could be priced as to three working consultants and their wives/partners to join later plus the manager and director and due to a stipulation of some indigenous Indian involvement one of the consultants would come from PW's affiliate firm in New Delhi. The little team of UK consultants had been put together in true PW style not due to their absolute suitability for this assignment but because they were available on the planning board. Nevertheless, this should not matter as the work itself was not thought particularly difficult, merely that the local situation would be unusual and anyway I had worked in the Far East and not least with many office workers of Indian decent. So that would be OK and in any case Henry and I were both down as workers and whole blocks of the intended work schedule had been promised as down to us personally.

John Newbold was from the London office and young, good looking, fashion conscious and a good talker. Stuart

Price was different. Drawn from Newcastle he was older, worldly, a cigarette chain smoker and an out-and-out hard grafter. The plan was for the four of us men to go out and get settled and start the job with our Indian colleague joining later. Henry would return after three days but I would stay for the first two weeks. If all worked to plan, then a further two weeks after my return, I would go out again taking the girls with me and work for a further two weeks. Thereafter Henry and I would alternate but with a handover few days to co-ordinate progress.

The inaugural visit was interesting from the standpoint of both the actual journey and the extreme of climate change. Cochin was reached by a connecting flight from Birmingham to London, then Heathrow to Bombay for an overnight stay in the Centaur hotel and the morning flight to Cochin with a refueling stop at Mangalore.

It was sitting by the pool at the Malabar hotel in Cochin on Tuesday evening drinking an Indian gin and tonic and watching the sun sink rapidly down on this absolutely perfect Indian sky and waiting for my booked telephone call to June that the memories of the past two days or so hit me almost as if I was the outsider watching a wide-screen film in multi-colour and set in a different time. There is the Bentinck Miners Welfare in Kirkby-in-Ashfield and its Sunday lunchtime and I sit having my first full pint of bitter after the healing and June's dad Jack, one of whose regular drinking places this is along with the Summit" Institute and Frankfort working mens' club, is asking about my forthcoming journey. What is remarkable is that there is a good two inches of snow outside blotting out and making almost scenic the car park and football pitch beyond. And here it is hot though cooling rapidly and one can actually see the sun dropping to the horizon just to the left of the Malabar itself.

This ancient but proud hotel built of wood and set on stilts is as if plucked straight from a Somerset Maughan or

Graham Greene novel or maybe is the small sister of the original Raffles in Singapore, that is no more. How long will this survive? And Henry driving too fast in his Triumph Stag and deliberately in the middle of the motorway in case of a skid in the snow to either left or right and waiting for the snowplough to clear our runway before taking off from Heathrow. And landing at Bombay in the early hours and making our way through a heaving mass of humanity in an inhuman density of clammy air and the small Indian boys clambering to take our bags to a taxi for one rupee and crossing from Bombay island to the mainland and the type and intensity of stench that surely only the Singapore river could have matched?

And the beggars knocking on and clawing at the windows of the taxi as the driver has to stop in traffic or at the traffic lights. And the absolute contrast of the calm and efficiency of the reception staff, all clad identically in their light brown uniforms, as they allocate the rooms and carry the baggage. And the slow passage down the west coast of India in the forty-two seater Avro turbo prop, made in India to a British design, that needs to refuel half way and as we disembark to get some (hot) air at Mangalore, the elegantly well dressed Indian lady who climbs back up the steps with, as it soon becomes clear, an urgent need to pass water. It becomes clear since the water in question falls immediately from the underside of the plane and splashes onto the steaming tarmac quite close to where we are all standing.

The first sights and sounds of Cochin are truly enthralling. The immaculately dressed official driver who picks us up in the official highly polished and spotlessly clean car and who has to drive carefully on the evening run back because it is particularly difficult to dodge the lorries on the pot-holed roads in the growing darkness because they do not have lights. It is not that the lorries do not switch on their lights, simply they do not have lights to put on.

In the office and on the roads we have picked up quickly, because we have had to, that the two most important pieces of silent communication in Indian are diametrically opposed to that that we have been accustomed to. A horizontal shake of the head from side to side turns out to mean yes. A vertical nod means no.

Another incident of initial mis-communication occurs on only our second night in the hotel dining room when the manager suggests we should stay after the meal because there will be entertainment. A lady artiste will perform *the moonlight saunter*. About eleven pm and by which time we are all in great danger of falling asleep in our chairs, our drowsiness is stirred by the sudden onslaught of loud piped and very Indian sounding music from somewhere behind the curtains. Out glides an ample lady in flowing kaftan and commences to serenade us with a couple of numbers accompanied by three male musicians dressed in traditional costume who have somewhat mysteriously appeared from the rear of the little stage area. During the third rendition the artiste starts to remove an outer garment and then another and then another until she is most definitely taking off inner garments.

It is no exaggeration to say that we little group of British technical aiders are, to use a more modern parlance, gobsmacked. Here, in about as southerly a major town in India as it is possible to get, in the best hotel around and on an everyday sort of weekday night we are witnessing a striptease? It seemed to be with an air of apology that the manager came over to us after the show to explain that under the prevailing laws of this the Kerala District, the artiste was not allowed to remove all clothing "some little items must remain." He then tempered this applied morality by informing us that should any one of us wish to take tea "or something similar" with the artiste "or one of her friends" in our room after any show, then that could be arranged. I seem to recall that one of the consultants gave my room number to one of the artistes one evening but I must have been too tired to hear her knocking.

The primary purpose of my second trip to Cochin was to assist the programme as working manager. The secondary purpose was to act as escort courier. The girls were joining their partners and I was taking them. Any drama that might have been anticipated from such an unconventional and gruelling journey undertaken by three complete strangers held itself firmly in check until about two hours into the early morning of the overnighter in the by now slightly more familiar Centaur hotel in Bombay. John Newbold's rather glamorous and city-wise wife was banging on my hotel room door shouting hysterically that she would have to, have to, positively have to stay in my room. She was terrified. Something absolutely horrid had dropped onto her bed.

Down in Cochin meantime things were starting to gel. Stuart and John were deep into procedures and controls and getting excellent help from the local office staff who spoke impeccable English and to a man were proving to be very well educated. In this context *man* is an exact term since no females were employed, even the secretaries of senior executives were male. I was to learn much later that the general level of literacy and numeracy in Kerala was deemed to be the highest of all the Districts of India. It was also communist controlled though that may have been coincidental.

Much had been learned from the shipbuilding experts and not least how to *work* the bar in the lounge of the Malabar. The only drinks that were deemed safe were Indian bottled beer and Indian gin with, guess what, Indian tonic water. The beer had proved easiest to crack, not literally. A bottle of beer in the bar at hotel prices was expensive especially viewed on a long-term basis. That is, every night for months on end, basis. By contrast, a crate of the same beer bought at a local store was dirt cheap. The solution to this paradox had been to reward the barman for his stowage of our crate under his bar. It had taken a bit longer to inject our bottle of gin into his system but over time it had proved possible. How naïve a simple country boy such as I can be in the ways of the world. But we learn as we go along and soon, back in the UK, I will need to acknowledge these and more sophisticated bar fiddles.

Evening refreshment aside, a good deal of sympathy was building for the new-found friends. Our boys had it cushy. Girl friends arrived, good hotel and food, specific short-term project and trips out at the weekend. Not so the shipbuilders. Their lodgings budget did not stretch to the Hotel Malabar and nor to journeys afield but such stringency paled in comparison to the contractual terms of their employment. Each man was on a fixed-term eighteen months stint. No family and friends and no returning home in between time, short of breaching the terms of the contract and all that that would entail. Some were finding it very hard and the contrast with ourselves was as between a little heavenly interlude and purgatory. It was going to be responsible for a least one marital breakdown and in the general context was bordering on the inhuman. Does anyone at Swan Hunter still care?

The trips out were purely wonderful, not that it was necessary to even leave Cochin for the car to stop whilst an elephant walked majestically past hauling some huge load or see running parallel to that road on the iron road an even greater load being hauled by my beloved eight-freight steam train. All these things have happened but in a flash and in this far-away place I am back in the sheds at Middle Furlong Road gaping in awe at this massive powerful engine. It has taken India with its coal and iron and sheer economic need to keep the monsters working. Three cheers for India and there are tears in my eyes, I can't help it.

As if striking an improbable contrast, why is it that soon

after dark each evening a bundle of clothes on the ground will signal a silent sleeper? The alfresco sleeping place could be in the grounds of the Malabar, on the boardwalks leading to the bedrooms, on the sidewalks of the town and even on the open roads themselves. The answer is simple. These people have no fixed abode so they sleep in this hot humid atmosphere just where they choose to end their day. As at the start of the new day they wash under the standpipes alongside the road. Very simple, very practical, very dignified.

This weekend we have hired a driver to take us to the hills. But hills is a euphemism. There are, by UK standards at any rate, major mountains inland from Cochin. It is possible to rise to over six thousand feet and indeed necessary to view the plantations of tea and peppers and a whole host of oriental spices. The air is cool, the views breathtaking and it is reminiscent of Northern Malaysia and Switzerland impossibly merged into one.

Because we must stay overnight, we experience how the privileged colonialists lived and it would seem still live. Tucked away in the sheltered downland lee of these magnificent uplands are the hill stations. This one has its own cricket pitch, tennis courts and rambling shaded garden. The owner/residents have a natural air of breeding that can only make us feel inferior; a tiny insight into what life in India must have been like for certain of we British before independence. And the first experience of the invited evening meal.

It is not so much dinner as drinks and "freshen that up?" and drinks and freshen that up and so on. If one was hungry to start with then best forget it as the booze flows and the conversation gets louder and louder and as you were instructed to arrive at eight then why is it now eleven and still no food? When the curry does arrive we are all pretty much past it and immediately after it has been consumed, everyone leaves. They just say goodnight and go.

This is not a *in the hills* phenomenon for it will occur everywhere we are invited into senior society for dinner. Good for drinkers but hard on the constitution especially one weakened by an ulcer. Luckily I still have my little stock of fudge to nibble at. But to gripe would be uncharitable as this weekend break is a spectacular event and the girls are treated to an elephant ride whilst the boys take tea in the shade of the banyan tree.

Oh, the contradictions of India. It is suggested in the shipyard that one Saturday we take a trip even further south on the coast to Trivandrum and to a recommended eating house but the memory is not of that. A beggar is tracking us as we walk along the quay and he is propelled by his hands on the roadside because his torso is perched on a small board on wheels. He has no legs. My mind is in a quandary. As with the boys at the airport or those running alongside the taxi in Bombay or those bedevilled souls who drag their grossly enlarged limbs in the sufferance of elephantiasis (this affliction had been named for me by a well groomed Indian gentleman at the cocktail party thrown to welcome us and who turned out to be a doctor "It is caused by nematode worms blocking the lymphatic vessels you know". I ventured the view that it was fortunate that we were all taking the anti-malaria tablets. "they won't help in the slightest, its airborne and as with all of us you will either catch it whilst here or not") what is the best thing to do?

I see three options though there are no doubt many more or variations on a theme. One. Physically and mentally ignore these people. They shall not exist. Walk by on the other side. Two, philosophise. There but for the grace of God. In this life there are the haves and the have nots. The rich and the poor. The healthy and the sick. The sound of body and the afflicted. In any case, what can I do? Nothing I do will change things one iota. Three. Just give something. Is that a cop-out to make me feel better? Maybe but in some small way it might help this one person for just a short time.

Of-course it is an easier decision on the Strand in London or in the underpass at Waterloo bridge because we are told there is no need for anyone to beg in England these days. In fact, they are all fake beggars and after a day's shift with their sad little dog on its grub infested rug, they up sticks walk around the corner and get picked up by a smart car. So that's O.K. then, no need for a conscience here and actually it's obviously making things worse if one promotes a fake. But that does not compare with India. I have just given this wretched human being balanced on his tatty trolley a few rupees. The man leading us to the reputed eating house castigates me for "encouraging them". Well, you decide!

We quicken our step because a small boat has just landed at the quay and rumour has it that the principal occupant is Leslie Philips, the comic actor, returning from on offshore island and he may be going to eat where we are. Oh good.

Deeper into the assignment and on a subsequent visit I have to explain our work to two visiting VIP's. Politically it will make sense to involve our Indian consultant colleague in this. After all, this is a joint Anglo/Indian project. Ravi had arrived within a few days of ourselves and had made an immediate impression on the staff at the Malabar. He was less like a common-or-garden journeyman consultant come to do a job than a film star fresh from Bollywood and demanding the sort of attention his adoring fans would expect. Not so much Ravi as such, more the entourage of glamorous wife, baby and nanny. Their accommodation was not acceptable. There was no separate room for the baby and nanny and in any case the beds, decor and fittings were not of the standard they were accustomed to in Delhi.

When one is about to settle for several months and in such a close community, this initial impact is not ideal. Ravi had a similar hard-landing impact on the clerks and other office staff at the shipyard. He was used to big city ways and operations and technology and all this was something of a comedown. The theory of an Indian consultant on the job as well as the laudable one of leaving expertise behind was that he would know the Indian way of doing things and thus enhance efficiency and would render communications easier and generally get the outsiders more accepted. In the event, the caste was different, the dialect different, the expectations different and it would have helped if Mark Tulley's book No full stops in India had been published before this assignment had been planned. If his initial integration into the study could have been smoother, at least he proved to be a worker and he did build a rapport with Stuart and John and by the time the VIP's arrived we at least presented a team.

There were two of them and each was somehow different from anyone I had met before. He was young, tall, slim and impeccably dressed and from the Foreign Office in London, he spoke little and asked few questions but had a good look around and left on the Friday evening. She had escorted him from Delhi where she worked for the British Embassy. Extrovert, bright and bubbly, she was full of enquiry and took extensive notes and did not leave on Friday. Instead she wanted to go on a trip along the famous Cochin inland waterways to see how the waterside people lived and fished and worshiped.

Whilst the rest were drinking and eating below decks, she and I talked a lot on the upper deck whilst sunbathing and taking in the sights. I was trying to fill in the pieces of a jigsaw that was all too vague back in the UK. I had learned just a few years before that the repair dry dock facilities the British had built in Singapore had drained off the commercial life-blood of those in what was then still called Ceylon that had itself been wholly British hitherto. These Singapore facilities had been handed over lock stock and barrel when the island became a republic.

Of-course the ability of bigger tankers and container ships to travel further from Europe and the Middle East enroute to the Far East and Japan was a factor, but how big a factor? Otherwise had we not just built up to hand over to kill off to again hand over? I was mentioning this in the context of this British overseas development aid for Cochin. Henry had told me how difficult it was for the British yards such as Swan Hunter, Harland & Wolfe and Vosper Thorneycroft to get new shipbuilding and ship repair work. Wouldn't this new facility in Southern India add to that difficulty? My VIP sun-bathing companion could not really say.

A few years later I arranged a rendezvous with Ravi's wife on St Pancras station in London and, as promised, she handed me the little package of semi-precious jewellery we had corresponded about. I wanted to start a business importing these and kaftans into the UK. Like other business ideas at this time, the venture did not materialise. I had convinced myself of the overriding importance of the day job. Wrongly.

Later still, Ravi sent June and I an invitation to their Christian wedding in New Delhi. We did not go. Another mistake. Someone I should have made a lifelong friend and business associate of, and in a place holding much feeling for me, therefore drifted into the shadowland of history.

Cochin may one day be renowned for its shipyard, who knows. It has, however, always been famous for something else, tea. This is the second largest wholesale tea market in the world and the merchants and buyers come from all over to sample and place their orders on behalf of the blenders and packers. We now know this because our men in Cochin have become friendly, courtesy of the Malabar bar, with a senior manager of one of the biggest growers.

The high point of this friendship is the promise, if customs do not spot it, of a brick parcel of the freshest tea we will ever taste to take home on our final departure. I was particularly proud of my parcel of freshly picked, dried and cured tea mainly because, knowing of their fondness for tea, I had decided to give half to mum and dad as a present from my time in India, there being little else to choose from except the little wooden elephants that somehow did not seem quite right. My dad was a champion tea drinker and to prove it used for his indulgence a white mug that held a full pint. Having smuggled my bounty through HM customs with no little guilt and it having travelled some eight thousand miles or so, and then waiting with hardly concealed eagerness for the praise that would be heaped upon this never to be repeated first edition treat it was, to put it mildly, quite a blow to hear mum's verdict of "we didn't really like it, it was a bit sweet". The felling of the mighty world traveller by a piece of homespun Derbyshire honesty!

But at least a present in a reverse flow had hit the mark. A boy working the reception at the Malabar had asked if I could possibly buy for him in the UK, and bring back, a torch. Not just any torch but one identical to that somehow acquired by a colleague. At that time the fashion in the UK was for a huge instrument all encased and sealed in rubber with the on/off buttons also embossed as rubber. It was no big deal as they were in plentiful supply back home but when I refused any payment by giving it as a present it was as if all the festivals of a lifetime had occurred simultaneously. I often wondered how long it lasted and if he could get replacement batteries, perhaps it is still treasured albeit long outdated. Perhaps it cast some light on Anglo/Indian relations. At least the rubber would have been coming back home.

The arrivals to see the consultants and the local shipyard office staff and the departures and the return visits and the catching up, the sounds and smells of India, the decorum and dignity of the people at all levels, the old working steam trains, the working elephants, the fiery curries, the midnight saunter, the beggars, the mountains and the tea plantations, the inland waterways and the Indian beer and Indian gin and tonic, all made a big impression on me. My brief Indian adventure had something no other journey could ever hold. It was due, I think, to the people themselves.

Perhaps we would be as humble and grateful as they given that this place and time in life was ours? Perhaps not. I was thinking as I did my final packing of the Indian doctors and nurses at the hospital in Mansfield and of just how far they had come, not physically but metaphorically. Because that must be the real test, not where he has reached but how far he has travelled to get here. The shifting of call-centres to India in the implementation of the current global market does have another side. An Indian side. The jobs might be fairly basic and repetitive but they are clean and ennobling jobs and a passport to family support and development. The employer will find no lack of talent. My later work will find Indian nationals amongst the top echelon of computer software engineers. I will also sell a British business to an Indian group and be told by the go-between that "India is booming Mr Smith, booming."

But leave we must and I will be last having presented the final report. Even the admiral of the yard complete with his little stick of office comes to the final cocktail party even though, as predicted by the office staff, he arrives last and leaves first. As January had progressed to May and with the air getting steadily stickier, this India has one last surprise. Barely had the small Avro reached its cruising speed than it starts to lurch alarmingly. The man to my right says we have flown into the first monsoon of the season and for proof the plane falls violently then rises and moves sideways and a passenger up front who one assumes had not fastened his safely belt shoots upwards and bangs his head on the cabin roof. He yells and blood is pouring from his head and the sole stewardess tries to help but her body is cartwheeled in the air and now another passenger is trying to fasten her in a seat. I think I must have passed out for a while but when I started to watch our antics again, it inexplicably occurred to me that my PW issue briefcase that had been bulging with the final working papers and books and had been wedged firmly between my seat and the back of the one in front, had gone. My life was about to end anyway.

At the cocktail party I had been invited to in Bombay, to fill in the time before the big aeroplane arrived from Australia en-route Heathrow, I relayed the flight experience from Cochin including finding my brief case in a little luggage hold at the back of the aeroplane and adding as bravely as I could muster the rider that I had tried to take some comfort from knowing that if the problem had been really serious in flying terms then the pilot would have climbed above the weather. "Oh no" responded the listener, "the Avro can only fly up to fourteen thousand feet".

I ought to have taken in what a Mrs Gandhi was telling me about her family relationship to the famous dynasty and about whether I could call and see her son who worked at Nottingham University. But I did not. Back at the airport I had two or three super large real Scotch whiskies and did not bat an eyelid when the senior steward of the Boeing 747 picked up the internal 'phone to the pilot and said "all 411 safely on board, ready to depart." Seems we are full to capacity due to some cancellations locally in India because of the weather.

Raising the profile, getting the jobs

Whether attributable to Henry doing some form of covert promotion on the back of the Cochin job or whether as a direct result of the customer satisfaction talk earlier I am not sure, but I am joining a national *circus* of courses by the

PW main firm for clients and on the technical subject of CPP (current purchasing power) accounting. The idea is one from the profession as a whole and is intended to help finance directors compile a set of accounts that will sit alongside the conventional historical basis ones but eliminating the effects on the numbers of inflation. All comparisons will be fair because figures will be reduced to the current purchasing power irrespective of the timeframe of happening. It sounds technical and it was. Also, it never caught on and thirty years later we still digest historical information. But at this time the heavy sessions and worked examples need to be spiced up with the role of the management consultant. And as it will be spicy, it will fit nicely into the graveyard slot, that is, the one after lunch when the audience is more prone to dosing off than digging in.

My choice of the most doom-mongering economic statistics of the time is intended to send the message that their MD had better send for PW consultants or else all is lost. It did generate a number of worried questions and post-session talks, so it must have struck a chord with the worthies as far south as the London School of Economics and as far north as in the Adelphi Hotel in Liverpool - where the Grand National runners used to parade. More notably, I was mixing with a team of lecturers that included the firm's technical partner and a certain other London partner who was to leave and make his name in industry only to lose it in ignominy, not unrelated to current purchasing power. Some say that life is a lottery.

It is starting to dawn on me as I get a bit more senior that PW is a form of amorphous being with tentacles and feelers and subterranean communication channels and, above all, its operations internally are subtle. I am being talked about but no one is going to say and I am not going to be told. Apart from the lecture tour, it is things like being introduced into a discussion forum that meets occasionally at Nottingham University and at which the odd junior minister turns up, that give the game away.

Meantime, Henry has landed another plum assignment. Birmingham City Council has decided that it should build a National Exhibition Centre (NEC) on its territory. It will pull business away from London to the second city and might even one day host the Motor Show. It will have its own infrastructure with a link road from the new M6, it will drive development of the smallish Elmdon airport and most importantly it will have its own railway line and brand new station to be called grandly Birmingham International. It will have at least six halls of varying sizes and will be capable of staging events from the gigantic to the intimate but, as is being explained to us by the Deputy Chief Accountant in charge of the project and as we can see, as of now it is just green fields. Each hall will have a number of pods and a pod is where food, beverages and booze are dispensed. Each pod will be connected to a central counting house or cash office.

Birmingham is a powerhouse of industry. The new NEC will give it a commercial heartbeat. Our role is to design and introduce all the operating procedures and controls concerned with the financial and cash aspects. This is not just a big job in terms of scope but very prestigious in that PW already had a strong relationship with the city council that cannot be tarnished and the project will be in the public spotlight and the finances open to public scrutiny through the council minutes. From the outset it had all the hallmarks of a tough ground-breaking project and of which our work formed only a small part.

Before the grand opening ceremony, the responsible Deputy Chief Accountant would have died and the chief project manager would have suffered a breakdown. As with most if not all major infrastructure driven construction and operational projects, that which is self evident and even taken for granted once it is working smoothly, bears no visible evidence of the planning, toil, frustration, set-backs and abject failures incurred from its conception to birth. Once it is done then it is done, at whatever cost. Today it is barely conceivable that what is the NEC Birmingham was once just rolling Warwickshire countryside. But it was when Henry and I first met that Birmingham City official there. "We can't even get a cup of tea yet". Instantly I am back in Cochin and recalling the tip from a well-meaning traveller "seventy percent of the world's population is right handed, so in a place like this, always lift your cup with the left hand". Thirty years on and in the coffee shop at Tesco, I drink a left-handed cup of Americano. I am right-handed after all.

The team was a brand new one. Colin Whiteside came up from Bristol, Don Miller was newly recruited in Birmingham though from South Wales and it would be the initial assignment for my first recruit in Nottingham, Chris Downes. We will pull in computer men as we need them and Colin will scour the world market for the best electronic point of sale (EPS) equipment. A study that will prove useful in a later life en-route to launching a new product. The NEC will prove to be a long, detailed and hard grind assignment involving, as it did, actual implementation of our recommended methodology, hardware and software and Bristol Colin and Cardiff Don are in for many months of Midlands' hotel nights. To break up the slog, I try to inject some fun events.

There is to be a management game run by Nottingham University and we enter ourselves as a PW Nottingham team. I am MD, Chris is finance director, Don is production director and Colin is marketing. As it develops, Chris is the star turn and keeps on churning out reams and reams of data so convincing that we all feel obliged to go along with the obvious. And we reach the final round. The economic climate is confusing. It could be best to play things safe and price moderately, but then again there are strong pointers to customer price sensitivity and maybe the theory of marginal costing -remember direct standard costs in the dynamic Dave era? - should be put to the test and Chris has some wonderfully powerful numbers on a conceivable outcome of pricing just above the margin. Conversely, we might misjudge the willingness of satisfied customers to pay a full economic price. At the final crunch round we decide to price up and even inflate the full selling price. That we have won and by a considerable amount astonishes us as much as the other finalists. In fact we have cleaned up the market. Two of the other four finalists, Rolls Royce and the Gas Board, have gone bankrupt. It did wonders for the morale of our PW but also NEC team and enhanced our stock in the office and our team photograph appeared in the Nottingham Evening Post.

I was beginning to think that the riskiness of having to take line management decisions was more exciting than advising with all its caveats and fence-sitting. One silly little game is no guide, but still. Less wonderful than playing at management was the ignoble event emanating from accepting an audit manager's invitation to a boys night at his rugby club. Better to stick to the occasional snooker evening or even the lunchtime striptease that is now all the rage in certain city centre pubs. At least there, as with the midnight saunter, a coca-cola bottle was just for drinking out of.

Whilst managing the NEC job, I am looking after work for a chain-making manufacturer with plants in Walsall and Glasgow, learning about presses and shears down in Reading, deep into medical devices in Kirkcaldy and other things. It is a busy productive time and we are having to recruit more staff. This has not gone unnoticed by Don who, having finished his part of the NEC job, went up on the dreaded planning board. It clearly held more dread than usual because a letter arrives which, although postmarked Ealing W5, has originated in the Somali Republic. It sounds a long way off, and it must be, judging from the time the letter has taken to reach me. It starts off in Berbera on the Gulf of Aden on 4th June and ends in Mogadishu on the Indian Ocean coast on the 12th. The London postmark is the 24th and it is date stamped into the Nottingham office on the 28th. This is still the era when all the incoming mail is opened by the partners at their morning and so called prayer session even though, as in this case, an envelope might be marked personal. But Don would have known that having spent his NEC office time there.

He obviously took to heart my idea of importing jewellery from India and keen not to be outdone is offering to bring back some jewellery from Somali that is described as "a bit different and quite reasonable in quality and price". Since, in the event, he did not, I cannot vouch for this statement. I can, however, empathise with his grouch about the intense humidity and his view that whilst Mogadishu is basic enough it is Utopia compared to Berbera bereft of electricity (but, Don, it is less than twenty years since electricity reached Red Barn Farm) and Europeans . Travel and work environs beget relativity. In my earlier letter to him I must have tried to cheer him up by saying that he was missing "nowt" because he is responding that due to the "Somali lovelies" being prohibited from associating with foreigners, he actually does miss "the Marilyns of this world". She as in my secretary with the long white freckled legs that Don must be salivating over in his hot sticky bed. Whilst writing on the 7th June he is listening to the BBC's World Service and noting that the Queen's Jubilee event has spawned a whole industry of commemorative memorabilia and wonders whether the year should be extended indefinitely to boost jobs and so bring down the rate of unemployment. He is less than enthusiastic about the Queen's speech at the Guildhall and says it was about warm icebergs and other stuff he couldn't understand. He ends up by saying that a letter to him from Julia (Henry's secretary) refers to a lot of people leaving the Birmingham office whilst I have set two more consultants on in Nottingham and he assumes therefore that the Midlands Region HQ will soon move to Nottingham. He is, of-course, being sarcastic.

Not for the first time or the last, Don has got things just about right. Nottingham is taking off and it has much to do with the senior audit partner who has been as good as his word. He is forcing the other partners and managers to open their audit client doors to we consultant types and including the tax and trust specialists. And, a major event is about to unfold. Prior to joining my team, Chris had worked in the cost office of a large Nottingham based manufacturing company. He had heard from ex-colleagues that a significant problem has been unearthed during the annual audit and it appeared to relate to a disparity between the value of the physical stock count and the book stock. He thinks that the reputation of PW and my personal experience with precisely this problem at Dexion and Raleigh could persuade the business to use us. I am sceptical. It is unlikely that an outside firm, whether PW or not, with no prior knowledge of this organisation or this industry will be allowed to compete against the consultancy services of the existing auditors and that is assuming the management cannot sort it out themselves. But I am wrong. Word gets out that a competitive tender will be placed for a wide-ranging study of the factory procedures and processes. I write to the Chairman suggesting a free three-day pre-proposal survey and to my surprise the idea is taken up. That is the background to my meeting Dr Bill Pilkington, the chairman of a group of leisure based businesses of which the errant Bell-Fruit Manufacturing Co Ltd is one.

This is the first big assignment that I shall manage that has come from cold selling, though hot intelligence from Chris, outwith the PW family. No one in the firm has even heard of this leisure group never mind earned any fees from it. So, landing this multi-manned and somewhat open-ended assignment and right on the Nottingham office's doorstep is regarded as something of a coup. Luckily the start of the work is delayed and therefore coincides with the rundown of the NEC project. This means I can get Colin on the team again and use my two new consultants but I also need a London based specialist engineer and a computer expert for parts of the work and I put in a special plea for Don once he is back from Somali. I need a thinker. The team goes in and the Nottingham consultancy fee budget balloons.

It is clear from the outset that I have been parachuted in behind enemy lines and straight into a political minefield. No wonder outsiders are preferred. What we have here is a group chairman trying to uncover the inner workings of his main manufacturing business that is firmly in the grip of a long-standing and autocratic managing director. He can use the stock loss problem to dig deep into the factory and with the full authority of Cope Allman International, the London based controlling plc group of which he is a main board member. The book loss on the stock is so material that the obstinate MD will have no option but to agree. Of course, that is not the same thing as this recalcitrant man welcoming myself and my team with open arms or advising his managers to cooperate fully and tell the truth the whole truth and nothing but the truth.

Don soon got ensconced in a subsidiary joinery manufacturing plant where no little of the eventual main problem came to light. Neither this nor his African adventure served to dent his incisive intellect. At a key progress meeting chaired by Dr Pilkington, Colin had used a Rugby Union metaphor in making a particular point. This had prompted the chairman into a brief aside about his past prowess in that sport culminating with the information that he "used to kick for Nottingham". Whilst we all nodded in appreciative awe and Colin moved on with his report I noticed Don writing a note that he carefully folded in half and had passed from hand to hand until it reached me. Obviously he wanted to add something to Colin's dictum. The note read "What a coincidence – I used to wank for Somerset". It was at the final progress meeting as we all trouped out that Dr Pilkington in a quiet measured tone suggested that I rang him sometime.

The discontent had been growing in direct proportion to the creeping regulatory control. Working papers had always been formally set out on the main firm audit side. This seemed right because the audit was a legal requirement and the work had to be scheduled such that a peer review could be undertaken expeditiously. But that was audit. None of us would have touched that sort of work with a bargepole. Yet, working paper rules and structures were invading the advisory side too. We had to go on courses to understand how to put together working paper files - one two-hour lecture was entitled "managing the intray" - and we had to make time to allow someone unconnected with an assignment to check that no stone had been left unturned. It was like asking a true entrepreneur to stop thinking for a bit whilst the world caught up. At any rate, I thought so. I was happy actually doing jobs. I worked for the client not the firm. All this checking of paperwork and asking non-productive questions of the real workers was getting on my nerves.

It came to a head at the evening cocktail party where important partners from London joined the partners from the provincial office to meet all the staff from senior managers to the janitor. I had already been rocked by the sight across the room of a tall, immaculately groomed lady whom I took to be Spanish. I didn't get to speak to her but I couldn't take my eyes off her. Amazingly she is the wife of one of the audit senior managers. Amazing because he is short in stature and introvert, even rather stern. She looks to have Mediterranean blood and never have I seen eyes so dark and large. Wow. But the party breaks up and that does it. If we are all great chums and the firm is egalitarian really then why are we all heading up the road to the pub whilst the partners to a man have gone off in the opposite direction for an obviously pre-arranged dinner? I am really pissed off. I am out of here.

As I walk up the hill all I can think about is how much I will miss Henry. My business father over these past years. He of the big jolly smiling face and making a V sign in the background of our group photograph, he of the Indian whisky, he of the pained imploration that I gain polish that I threw back in his face but should not have done because he meant well, he who will be reduced at the behest of the London set to being the provincial local authority expert and who must retire as all partners must at age sixty and who, although I could not possibly have envisaged it on this night of mixed emotions, will only have seven years to live after that. So the Christmas cards that never stopped from Babs and Henry are now from just Babs.

Up the housing ladder

The best thing about the house we have moved to is its position. Everyone says that this factor in terms of value is by far the most important, so that is O.K. Sheepwalk Lane is one of the better addresses in the village although to use the collective term village is to glamorise what in essence is a confluence of several ancient little settlements with estate infill from the likes of Costain builders and the cowboy responsible for our last home. Not that long ago Larch Farm, Kighill and Fishpool were small settlements in a heavily wooded area on the edge of Sherwood Forest and supported by the character-filled Hutt hostelry that is now a hideous managed house devoid of all remnants of history save its tatty bric-a-brac. Once its oak panelled walls were a staging post between Nottingham and Mansfield and it provided proper food, drink and shelter.

My mum can remember being brought to what is now known as Ravenshead when she was small. It was a scattering of small pig farms and there were pigs running wild. Our new home is elevated from the lane and set back some fifty-five yards or so. It is this aspect and the equivalent length of the rear garden that is the attraction. June spots the site and knowing that gardening is in my blood from the farm, thinks we can make it work. The house has been empty for nine months and with one unattended coke boiler in the kitchen is very cold inside and damp. Judging by the experience at Bovingdon, this will have to be the top priority. My ability to make a coke boiler function for twenty-four hours a day is dubious. Needless to say, because we are more than fifty yards from the gas main running down the lane, the supply will have to be paid for. This is the hottest summer on record and the contractors find the hottest few days of all to work inside fitting the new central heating system. To a man they sweat profusely. I feel sorry for them and for the sheer irony of the contrast from the ice-house we first visited.

Over the years this solidly built 1958 house with its massive concrete lintels, rock-hard bricks and thickly timbered roof trusses will be turned into a modern amenity home for a family to grow up in. A humble start but potential, as they say. This building is actually identical to the two neighbouring ones. In its heyday the National Union of Mineworkers (NUM) was a very wealthy organisation. Its purchase of original paintings had occasionally hit the headlines. What was probably less well known was the investment in property. Even for a trade union, it is not a bad idea to put surplus funds into bricks and mortar and having done so why not let your top officials rent the dwellings whilst the capital grows. For the purist it might seem a bit of a mixture of labour and capital but if the mine owners could put their employees in rented accommodation, why not the organiser of labour?

So the NUM, no doubt with their colleagues on the local council in the know, bought certain chunks of an about to be developed place then split between two parishes but one day to have an identity of its own. This particular piece of ground was large enough to carve into three plots and be in such a prominent position as to justify housing their top three officials. The NUM President, who was not merely well known locally but was a leading moderate in the Labour Party at the time, had now been re-housed into a retirement bungalow also owned by the NUM and located in the plush Berry Hill area of Mansfield adjacent to their HQ. As a result the house he had occupied for many years was to be sold but the conveyance was complicated by the need for all twenty-something trustees to have to sign on behalf of the owners. If was further complicated by the agreed consideration having to be split at the last minute as between the price for the property and the deemed value of fixtures and fittings and carpets that were apparently owned personally by Mr President.

Those things that one has some skill in doing and take an interest in are best done personally. The rest are best left to others. I systematically set about removing the rear garden lawns and Jack, June's dad, helped with the cutting by spade into slabs to be stacked soil-side uppermost to rot down for recycling later. Over five hundred rose trees, mostly neglected, ill-pruned and woody are taken up and the best specimens re-planted in the front tiered garden. There is to be a large vegetable garden and I shall indulge myself with the crops we used to grow at Red Barn Farm. The manure will come annually from the nearest farm. All that my dad and I had had to do was wheel it by barrow from the cowhouse. No such facility in close proximity here although the hostile neighbouring villages do refer to the developing Ravenshead as sewer city on account of the preponderance of cesspits in the early days. There will be an orchard with Laxton Superb and Worcester and Bramley apply trees and a damson and a plum and a pear tree. There will be soft fruits; raspberries, strawberries, blackcurrants and redcurrants and gooseberries. I will grow sweet peas for my mum and try, though never succeed, to grow chrysanthemums as good as Jack's concave and convex specimens.

But as for the building works that will have to be paid for as cash becomes available supplemented by three mortgage increases. There will be two flat roof extensions to make a playroom for the rapidly growing boys, an aspirational quiet room and a Singapore duplicate shower room. Fireplaces will be removed and the chimneystack re-built to make safe, the whole house will be rendered and painted and all the windows will be replaced. It all takes time and money but eventually it will be done. The capital plan continues and it might well involve another move, maybe this time into the grounds of Newstead Abbey. Except June has had enough. Enough is enough. The prospect of another upward movement made her feel physically sick. It will be another six years before I will know this.

A sad, sad end

Uncle Edmund is ill. He has taken to his bed and will not get up. This is surprising news because it seems no time at all since great aunt Pem gave me a photograph of his retirement presentation. On his sixty-fifth birthday he is dressed in his railway issue trilby - replacing the bowler hat - and top coat and receives the gift with a fulsome smiling face of no wrinkles but full of jollity for a life-long job well done. The year before he had received his gold watch for the fifty years' service on the railways. I have a second photograph of him standing on the footplate of a train engine actually instructing a new recruit. It has a date stamp; my thirteen birthday.

Uncle Edmund had consciously and deliberately led a steady life using his after-work hours to read and study. He had never married - not wanting to get involved my mum said - and never owned property - not wanting to have the hassle and not wanting to take any risks I thought. He always had a young man in tow to run errands and to talk to (was he a latent homosexual I had often wondered) and most importantly he had been prudent "you need money if you are going to live to be a hundred."

So what was this illness all about? I had some catching up to do. Whilst I would always be grateful for the start he gave me in the railway office in Nottingham, for the walking holidays that triggered the greatest passion of my life and for the perception that it is possible to overcome a poor education with hard work and personality, still we had drifted apart. This had something to do with my absence abroad and just working but more to an incident on a train journey together when he ruminated on the life of my dad culminating with the statement "George is no businessman." It was probably true but coming from this man who had refused financial help at the time when the farm had to be purchased from the Duke of Devonshire's Estate or be lost and indeed had contacted his sister, my aunt Gladys, to say "George is going bankrupt and if you have any money left in there, get it out."

Aunt Gladys had told me about this message personally and so I knew it to be true. I took it personally as a red rag might be to a bull. In any case, had he not brought up a family on thirty-four acres of poor land with no more than six milking cows and sundry bits and bobs? It had been left to aunt Gladys herself and my dad's youngest sister my aunt Ruth to put up some money and save the farm. I began to consider the possibility that his early help to me had had an ulterior motive. Best to forget about it and put some distance between us.

Ever since his retirement, uncle Edmund had come back to Newton to live with his aunt, my great aunt, Pem. In theory it would be a perfect arrangement. She was now in her late eighties and needed a certain amount of looking after but according to him "still eats like a horse and in fact lives for her meals" and he gets free board and lodgings in the comfortable if old fashioned bungalow and can look after the garden to his heart's content, growing his dahlias from their polythene covered frost free start to the October full colour show, and tending the rhubarb crown and the Christmas roses and the herbaceous borders. He can play the organ at Old Blackwell church, give private piano lessons from the parlour, pick up his local connections and generally enjoy a studious retirement on medieval England and the reformation. Money will be no problem.

In practice, things had not quite worked out that way. She was getting old but still had a clear mind and with it a sharp tongue. She was used to being alone with him as an occasional visitor on some weekends. My dad called every Saturday morning with the milk and eggs and did her little jobs and they got on very well. Now Edmund and Pem were on top of each other in this little badly designed bungalow with its many doors leading every which way. Whether because of this or due to age, she was getting increasingly codgerty, not least about his dog, an overweight Jack Russell that barked incessantly.

He took to sitting in his dressing gown until late morning smoking his pipe and complaining about her habits. These complaints were falling increasingly on my mum who had been called in to help. She was now doing all the cleaning and washing and attending to great aunt Pem who was starting to suffer from incontinence "the place is beginning to smell."

By this time my mum had her own problems. The rheumatoid arthritis diagnosed a few years earlier was getting worse and cleaning up after an increasingly frail old lady and an increasingly grumpy man, was taking a toll. My dad should have put a stop to it but it was only a bit more work for mum and he wanted his aunt Pem looked after. Edmund wasn't doing it.

Taking over the organ playing again should have been a joy and perhaps it was but there were soon rumblings of discontent. It must have been a big come down from Leicester cathedral to Old Blackwell's St Werburghs parish church and whether due to the transition or not, murmurings from the established families' dominated choir suggested that "he plays too fast, pushes it along a bit too much." Was it just that or the falling out with the vicar or maybe starting to take over from the long established choir master? The photograph taken back in 1956 at the dedication of a new pulpit shows from the stern faces of most of those present what sheer opposition an establishment can mount against an outsider. These insiders at that time included a suitably formidable-looking great aunt Pem and the one-armed bell-ringing wonderman Arthur Smithson.

Whatever really happened he soon left, only to pop up again as the regular organist at Tibshelf church where, after a time, the same pattern was repeated. So these episodes left him disenfranchised from the two local churches and their established cliques. It proved a big step towards him becoming a recluse offset by giving only the occasional piano lesson. He took to walking alone through the village and stopped visiting any member of the family. Not once after retirement did he visit the farm. He relied for information on what bits of news my mum might have, not that that was much since she was no socialite either. The once revered head of the family was head no more. He wasn't even the head of great aunt Pem who stuck rigidly to her own routine.

Slowly, patiently, my dad had taken over. It was he who 'phoned around and it was he who had asked me to find a home for aunt Phyllis when she could no longer work as a companion and it was he who went to Sutton on the tractor to see her and shop for her. My dad never forgot the inequitable bringing up. Times many he repeated what his mother had said at the Sunday tea-table "there is only one egg, it's for Edmund."

And then the rot set in. Literally as it happened. It had started with a raging thirst and ended with sugar diabetes. It was firmly under control until he took to his bed and wouldn't get up. By the time my mum had got really worried about him and my dad had telephoned me, it was patently out of control. They had not managed to get a doctor to see him, home visits were not the flavour of the month at this time. It was not a lot like Dr Finlay's Casebook that was so pleasant to watch on a Sunday evening with the dashing Finlay or the lovable old Cameron dropping in the instant their housekeeper, dependable Janet, received the call for help and sitting by the bedside enjoying a wee drop of the hard stuff whilst arriving at a correct diagnosis leading to a complete cure. It was more like Dr Doolittle's Wastebook, that is to say if you are well enough to get to see me then there can't be much wrong and if you are not then the best thing is for you to stay put and die in peace.

With these thoughts in mind, it was not with the best of humour that I conversed with a said doctor on emergency duty. On entering the Barnston kitchen his opening remark was "I have just left a nineteen year old man dying of cancer, that is where my priority is." If it was intended to make me feel as bad as uncle Edmund looked, then it succeeded. And uncle Edmund's riposte that "help comes from the most unexpected quarter" did not ease my guilt either.

In Chesterfield Royal Hospital they first removed one rotten foot and then the second. Those feet that had tramped across the north Yorkshire moors in the Holiday Fellowship "A" group and had been stood upon to deliver the evening entertainment monologue and had flowed across the pedals of the church organ, too fast for some. On the Wednesday evening he told me there was some talk of having to remove up to and perhaps including the knees. But first they had to attend to a virus that he had picked up. I looked up at the television screen hopefully and loudly playing to the whole packed ward and I asked him if he thought our man would win the Formula 1 championship this year. He said he didn't know, he had no interest in it. He said he had asked my mum to get his solicitor into the ward because he wanted to leave her £1,000 for being such an angel over the past few years. I left with the cheery remark "see you on Friday". He said "I do not know where I will be on Friday." He was right. He died during the night on Thursday. This independent, clever and hard working man who had planned to be one hundred years old was just seventy three and he hadn't had time to instruct his solicitor about his final wish. Fifty years plus on the railways and eight years of lonely and pretty miserable retirement. It taught me a lesson.

His will was very simple. He left only one specific legacy, £500 to me and the rest was to be held in trust for the benefit of his sister, my aunt Phyllis who had worked all her life but had always needed help. She had some strange type of nervous disorder that was never really understood or diagnosed. She would, for instance, take perhaps ten minutes to put on her hat. She fiddled and fiddled with it because somehow she just couldn't get it right. She wore lipstick and smoked cigarettes and was a companion to old ladies.

The trustees appointed by the will, in practice my dad, could if they wished use the capital for her benefit as well as the interest. None of the capital was spent. My dad looked after her like the true brother he was for the next thirteen years but she was destined to die another lonely miserable death primarily from starvation. All she would eat in the end were cornflakes dry from the packet, and gradually less and less, lying in her cold and forlorn flat in Huthwaite right across the road from where my mum had been born in the big house that now no longer existed having made way for the road widening scheme.

And so it was that in 1988 uncle Edmund's will could finally be distributed. It was as it had been back in 1975, just over £14,000. Quite a tidy sum back then but not so much at this time. How much it was back in 1975 can be judged by the fact that I put £250 to the £500 legacy and bought June a brand new car. It seemed to me that he never spent money, as prudent as our present chancellor isn't. But neither did he set out to make any. There is another lesson here. This is not a mistake I intend to make. The beneficiaries were to be those of his brothers and sisters living at his death or their children if by the date of distribution these peers had died. In fact two had and one had predeceased him and so was out of the reckoning. Not that it would have bothered aunt Gladys who would not have wanted Edmund's money after the rupture over her dear husband, my wonderfully eccentric uncle Leslie the birdman who had painted the street green and stored the surplus at the farm.

She had a stroke and was left speechless although she tried very hard and cried with frustration. Uncle Leslie was perfectly fit when it happened but then was inconsolable and whilst she was in hospital he suddenly died. My dad had a theory about tablets. Through the previous generation, the redoubtable original John Smith, aunt Gladys was quite wealthy and I made a special request to see her will because she had told me on several occasions that "all my money comes to you." Under the terms of her will everything had been left to her adopted daughter Marjorie and the will was in perfect order. Just as well because by then they were living with Marjorie and her husband Mike in Bolton in separate accommodation developed from the garage and paid for entirely by aunt Gladys. She showed me the time slips prepared by Mike for his and others' time and all nicely priced up to add to the materials.

Of the five still alive at the time of Edmunds death, Phyllis would have left four except that two had predeceased Phyllis. Uncle Harry, who had also been an engine driver before starting a garden nursery business that failed had also succumbed to the family genetic weakness known for short as *the sugar*. He did not lose his feet but his testicles and his dignity with his penis lying on top of the sheet with a tube coming out of the end. He joked "Daisy says when we next get to bed they will not be able to tell us apart." He liked a joke did uncle Harry and he was exceptionally good looking. I think my mum always fancied him and he came to the farm often on his bicycle. In particular he was called for when pups had to be drowned. My dad could not do it but "Harry will". They went into a sackbag and into a bucket of water and were held down with a brush.

As a very young man he had been sued for breach of promise but meeting aunt Daisy had put a stop to all that sort of thing. She left a husband for him and took along her son and they had a further son together. This second son, who was now inheriting his dad's share being one quarter of what Edmund left, "lives in cloud cuckoo land" or so Harry told my dad. Harry and Daisy were a true love match and not long before he took ill I stopped the car on the way to the farm and watched from behind as they walked hand-in-hand to the pub in Sutton and thought how happy they were together. After he died, she was packing up to go to her first son who lived in Australia but the bags never went anywhere. She died within six weeks of Harry. My mum said of a broken heart.

And then aunt Doris, with her red cheerful face and bluster and who my dad loved to bait with his choice treatment for all Royalty "stand 'em up against a wall and shoot the buggers", slipped quietly away to join her beloved librarian Harold at the churchyard at Teversal. Their two children took one eighth each. My dad and aunt Ruth who had been the two youngest children and were now the only survivors duly took a quarter of the estate each. To be precise £3,654.38 each.

And so it had taken until my dad's seventy fourth year for him to come into any real money and ironically it was exactly one month after he had inherited his quarter share of aunt Phyllis's estate. More ironic, however, was the amount. Like aunt Gladys before her, aunt Phyllis had in fact through inheritance and by not spending been wealthy in her own right. Her estate had been slightly more than uncle Edmunds these thirteen years on and so my dad had received £4,066.73. The final irony was that the lad from cloud cuckoo land had done as well as anyone.

1988 then had proved to be something of a landmark for my dad. He had lost a sister who had worried him all his life and on whom he had increasingly to spend more and more time and effort. His eldest brother's estate had been finalised and for the very first time he had some capital apart from the farm itself. But he did not know that this fated year had a final card to play.

CHAPTER ELEVEN
Bell-Fruit

1979-1991. An off-beat start. Learning the ropes. 1968 Gaming Act and a new industry. Getting the culture right. Rapid promotion and corporate politics. The loan business. New blood and a tragic death. Bulgaria needs us. A world tour but Australia lost. Of bolt-on acquisitions and new electronic products. The Dutch travail. Vikings and Bilston and private clubs. More acquisitions. Smiley Mr Zodeh. Pension pots. A group take-over to swinging times. The dangled MBO. Takeover.

I did not even mention the subject of my call. Would I come back and see Mr Johnson who would be expecting me. "So Pilkington wants you to take over from me does he? Well it won't happen. I am having the changes made. We are the biggest manufacturer in the UK and we have the best engineered machines and I do not accept that the new-fangled electronics will take over. Furthermore, I have my successor already groomed for when I am ready to go, which I am not." On relaying the essence of this brief and one-sided meeting to Dr Pilkington, he needed some time and would get back to me. When, after a few days he did so, "would I pop back and see Gordon Dean on the Operations side?" I might recall that he had pointed him out to me at the Victoria Club and "it is the Operations that make the money."

You could call it an interview. You could call it a chat. You would be wrong on both counts. It was more of a get-to-know-each-other, will-we-get-on-together, you-will-be-branded-P's-man sort of session. Especially the latter as P's men have come and gone in the past and always with ignominy. The setting was unconventional. Ushered into his large office, this large man with a pale handsome face (mistaken, in a few of his tales, for Kurt Steiger the German film star) did not rise but remained at his desk thumbing through the Daily Express.

And why did I want to change jobs, well because for various reasons I had had enough of the profession and wanted to go into line management and now aged 36 it would be my last move. "Last move!" he nearly exploded as his big frame shook and some colour came into his cheeks. He was 57 and did not consider he was stuck should he want a move on. I tried a diversionary tactic - the military metaphor would be learned from him, only later would I recognise it as such - observing that at any rate he would soon know if he would live to be an old man in that according to actuarial mortality figures the average English man that reaches age 58 will live to be 75. He was more than unusually taken with this notion. Pressing a button on his desk console "Val come in with your pad". Still flicking over the pages of the Daily Express, he dictates a very brief letter to me. It offers me a position as Operations Assistant reporting directly to himself with equal status to his regional directors and therefore including a new Ford Granada 2.8 automatic car. He adds a bit to my present salary and hopes it will be enough because I am already on more than his directors are. And that was that.

It is now a well established trait this penchant for a bad career move. No sooner had my notice been submitted and the hierarchical cold shoulder been wielded than the rumour surfaced. I was on the forthcoming partner list. The comfort found in not wanting to be part of the elite and in half believing anyway that the rumour itself was most likely a subtle form of retaliation, was wearing thin as I stood by Val's desk in the outer office wearing my new suit and shiny black shoes to hear that "as far as I know there isn't an office for you or even a desk and Gordon's in Holland and not back until Thursday". Thoughts of returning home were tempered by wondering what I would do having got there.

Help, as it often does, came from an unexpected quarter. One of Gordon's more junior assistants Chris Gunther sitting in the office next to Val suggested I go and see the "Operations in the field". This good idea tempted mild retribution to this ill-mannered and incompetent Gordon bloke. I enquired as to the most distant division and after a brief chat on the 'phone to the director there, set off for Pewsey in Wiltshire, a place destined to be forever etched in my mind as Gordon's metonymy "sleepy hollow". Not that comatose would describe accurately the bearing of Roger Channing the all-powerful and profit generating Southern Divisional Director in question.

So numerous were the telephone interruptions and the vital outgoing calls and the bursting in of a vast array of staff on deadline matters that barely could a single question of mine be answered. Whilst the evening meal and drinks in the Seven Stars were great and we two got on well together, I returned to Nottingham befuddled and baffled with no more idea what went on in the field operations than on that first vacant morning.

To get to know how anything really works in business whether it is a service industry such as I had just joined or the telecommunications set-up in Singapore or the numerous manufacturing plants of the past or building a ship in India, the short-cut route is to be thrown into it and to be responsible for definable outcomes. I could diagnose and think through what to replace with what and I could persuade people to do it. But could I manage? Deep down that was the conscionable niggle and that is what must have driven me out of consultancy into industry and that is what made me so insistent with both Dr Pilkington and Gordon Dean that I did not want to be on the finance side but in line management. And now Gordon was either taking me at my word or calling my bluff. My inclination was to the former since in this first month I had learned that this man was neither ill-mannered nor incompetent. That first morning had been just bad luck. He had to fly to Holland at short notice to address an emergency and he reckoned I was man enough to sort myself out.

What he wanted me to do was to go down to the East Midlands Division and take over, albeit temporarily. To my worries about getting stuck in a division when, if I was going to build a proper career it had to be at HQ, he promised a safe return after three months provided things were back on an even keel. It is one thing to give sound advice to management from the base line of privileged access backed by the reputation of a prestigious national firm. It is one thing to be able to juggle in ones head the complex detail of four or five different jobs. It is one thing to drive oneself physically and mentally to the limit. It is quite another to be put into a working unit of dynamic force that has gone wrong and be personally responsible for turning the situation around.

Because the geographical spread of this division encapsulates Burton-on-Trent which is the heart of the UK's brewing industry, so it had been the starting point for the whole business. A business made up of the clan *fruit machine man and boy*. Those that now manage have been engineers and know these machines inside out. Like coal miners and railwaymen the association with the workplace is infusive. There is no social gathering that will not turn to a discussion of the evolution of the generations of the machines and when someone mentions the first "fruit-drop", then eyes and not throats start to water. They know the product (though not this expression) intimately. They were in when the first Jennings machine appeared from the USA and they can describe in brilliant technical detail each model of the first range of machines produced in Nottingham, that Mr Johnson is so proud and protective of, from its coin acceptor to its payout shoot. In short, they know all about this business, except they do not. What they know about is the product make-up and its functionality on site and how it has evolved. That is not the same as understanding how to compete with the other operations that are now around and how to use effectively the new-fangled electro-mechanical machines.

The skill of diagnosis is analysis. It is deep and thorough number crunching and it helps to be an accountant with an added interest in maths and statistics. The skill of consultancy is separating this application of science from personalities who can taint and deceive and especially to be wary of the good talkers. We want the actual factual situation to be absolutely clear and we want to know how it got to this position and we have to have our very best shot at predicting where we are heading. Then the skill of consultancy is to make proposals for change suited to the culture of the organisation and presupposing that this culture has been identified accurately.

Good managers can do this preparatory work themselves. They usually do not. Sometimes because the day-to-day workload will not allow the space and they are insufficiently trained in delegation or have inadequate grey matter to find that space. Or they simply do not have the analytical ability to detect what is actually happening, not merely the woods for the trees syndrome but as basic as knowing what type of wood this is and whether it is flourishing or declining. Or there is a political motive for not being personally identified with proposed changes.

Such political motive need not be grubby, it can be

laudable and sensible. Goh Seng Kim in his sensitive position in Singapore at that point in time had all the attributes to personally find the right fit for the new authority and whilst it may be true that he would not have had the time to do so, it was very wise to get proposals from outside consultants. The only tricky bit was selling his acceptance of them. This principle helps in explaining in the specific why the Telecommunications Authority of Singapore is still, thirty years on, the largest such body in South East Asia and why in the generality the consultancy industry has grown worldwide far beyond the conceivable expectations of any of the founding fathers. What good managers must do is make the changes happen in a way and at a pace that suits the organisation. It can be revolution. It can be evolution. Usually it will be a bit of both but this skill, far superior to the pre-skills, is judging where the balance lies, at this time, with these people, in this set-up.

Arriving at the large and busy depot at Beeston I was not quite the greenhorn they were apparently expecting. As had been my practice now for years, I flatly refused to make any prescriptive comment or respond to any leading question or pass any judgement of any sort until I was satisfied in my own mind that I understood the financial situation of that which I had landed in. This somewhat dour approach was never popular and it did mean that invariably there was a very apparent slow start. It was not born of any textbook or any piece of PW training and it was probably indicative of ingrained caution or a lack of confidence or a mixture of both. But it had stood me in good stead over a whole variety of situations from the three thousand cycle specifications at Raleigh, through the eighty-seven products from a Wiltshire pig at Scott Bowyer to the mind-blowingly complicated assembly path of a colour printing machine used to produce a bank note at De La Rue. And so it was that with the silent indulgence of Gordon I had spent the best part of two whole weeks including a few whole nights analysing the performance of the geographical divisions.

To the manufacturing side of the group and, as I suspected now and in the future would get to know for certain, to the senior management of Cope Allman International the controlling plc, the Operations was a simple business. Whilst capital intensive, it generated oodles of cash and oodles of profit and could be used as a milch cow for more reliable and steady businesses outside this barely respectable leisure side. In fact, as my analysis and then synthesis showed, this was far from the case and there was a good brain holding it together and controlling it.

Fundamentally, the operation was a huge rental business or as someone unkindly observed years later, a huge furniture removal business. The modern mode of operation had developed under the legal and regulatory framework of the 1968 Gaming Act which had effectively put an end to the gathering momentum of unlicensed and gangster inducing activities of clubland. The single most effective move was to ban the ability of operators to share in the take of the machine. Instead a set fixed rent was to be the sole reward for placing a piece of equipment on a site and the win must be so small as to constitute merely a prize and not a gambler's windfall. The games played on the machine would be primarily for amusement and not monetary gain. Thus, at a stroke, Amusement With Prizes (AWP) machines came into being and a legitimate industry was born.

The business incentive was not how to rip off an addictive gambler but from a marketing standpoint how to keep players interested with only a small win incentive and from a financial standpoint how to balance the risk of capital injection with a small but steady recurring revenue stream and high labour costs. What had become apparent during the 1970's was that a new game, and that meant a new machine, had only a limited shelf life in a particular site. After that it needed to be moved on to make room for the latest invention. As a result, Bell-Fruit Manufacturing

Co Ltd had sprung up like a phoenix from the ashes of a cash register business and Bell-Fruit UK Ltd (Operations) learned how to make the new rules work. By the time I arrived, the former was the largest of its kind in the UK and the latter the second largest.

It was the constant stream of new models onto the market that added the first layer of complication to the operation. How many of which model from which manufacturer to buy and when? Then came how to decide on the grade of sites from the very best that will take the new machine to the very lowest that may be six moves down the chain. Then how to agree a suitable rent with the site owner (at this time dominated by the breweries) and how to distinguish quickly between good and not so good machines in terms of player appeal. This alone demanded rapid and accurate weekly performance information and especially since on the brewery sites, a manager of the pub where the machine was sited typically was entitled to very little of the take after rent and duty whereas a tenant might be entitled to fifty percent.

Public houses free of the brewery tie had one hundred percent. But the real beauty of a large operation such as this (40,000 machines sited) was that other equipment had come to be sited to augment the AWP's, notably pool tables and juke boxes. Finally there was a raft of single sites outwith the public houses and subject to different rules and therefore amenable to a different breed of machine. These were the private member clubs.

The functioning of the operations business as a whole was as complicated as anything I had seen before. There were marked differences between the geographical regions in terms of total machine estate, the mix of equipment type, the average rent earned, the costs per unit in absolute terms and, as a result, in profitability. The East Midlands Region ought to have been the most successful since it operated in the heartland of the brewing industry and had arguably the best balance of economic wealth of players of machines to the operating costs of the region. But it was not.

When I walked through the door that first Monday morning I already knew what needed doing and I knew who had to go. It helped that the engineers had staged a walk-out the previous Friday afternoon. It also helped that I had met the incumbent regional director at what was delightfully termed, in the straightforwardly simple style of Gordon that I would come to admire so much, the No 1 Meeting. This was the monthly meeting held around the board table in his office that brought together the regional directors, the finance director, the head of security, Chris Gunther with his book of statistics and Val to take the minutes. Now it also included me, the outsider with no knowledge of the operation or even the industry and whose future role could only be speculated about and who was Ps man.

This was Gordon at his military best. The troops were on parade at 8.30am sharp irrespective of where they had travelled from or stayed overnight at. All the *tactical* decisions would be taken by midday, twelve-thirty at the latest. The whole company (of men that is, not corporate) would re-convene at the Chateau steakhouse by 1pm and to relax after the battle with a few drinks. By the time the group got back to base, Val had done the minutes and each director was to return to his patch to implement the agreed action. No element of the bar or lunch table chat would be stood by but only the minutes reflecting the next month's brief. There was a good reason for this rule, but it would take me longer to understand it.

A myriad of operational detail was discussed at these monthly meetings but the principal decision was which of the tested new AWP models were to be purchased, in what quantity and for what divisional distribution. Since the average machine take of the existing estate influenced greatly the priority for allocation of brand new machines, it followed that a region with poor results found itself in a type of Catch 22 downward spiral. The suffering of the affected director was palpable and the behemoth Gordon was not the type to pull his punches. This was no one-to-one development forum. This was a public bare-knuckle fight and the East Midlands man was gasping for breath. By contrast, the West Midlands boss was positively gushing with self-esteem and on this morning he had taken the opportunity to have a number of side-swipes at "unproductive HQ hangers-on". After the 11am pee-break, Val re-entered with the (initially astonishing) tray of cans of beer. I thought I would help out and managed to give a quick shake to the can that our bumptious West Midlands colleague was now being handed. As he tugged the fastener open it obligingly mini-exploded in his face and onto his nice shiny suit. "I'll bloody well have to keep an eye on you" came the brummy response. A little early respect may not come amiss.

A financial crisis

Seven months to the day since joining, there is a call from P's secretary. Would I like to join him in his office? P is looking grim and Gordon asks for a sherry. Terry will be leaving. A heavy loss has been thrown up in the books of the holding company and something to do with financing overseas activities. As a first step to sorting things out, Louis Manson the group chairman had asked for the head of Terry. Gordon had specifically recommended me to P who in turn had the support of Louis for this internal appointment that would take effect immediately.

I hear myself protesting that they both knew that I came into the group not wanting to be on the finance side but to make it in line management and so far I thought things were working out. Yes, yes, they know all about that but a very special situation has arisen and there needs to be minimum fuss and Gordon thinks you're up to it. Perhaps I did not really appreciate the seniority of the position. Of-course I was well in tune now with the Operations under Gordon having been appointed the director of Central Services three months ago. That service alone controlled over 800 vehicles, had substantial capital tied up in off-site machines, carried major stock holdings of spare parts and was responsible for selling-on the used machines to the multi-site market of arcades and fairgrounds and the single-site free trade outlets.

As I knew, the Operation extended to six geographical divisions each under its own director but also there was the specialist business placing machines with NAAFI at camps all around the world where our troops were stationed. There was the large mainframe computer set-up and the accounts and statistics and marketing departments. But we are talking here about the whole of the Leisure Division of Cope Allman International Limited and of which P is the chairman. As well as the Operations, the division comprises the manufacturing business under Johnny Johnson as I very well knew (I did not know he was a Johnny), the central sales office in London handling not merely the UK but many overseas markets, the divisional office itself and the manufacturing plant in Australia and the Operation in Holland. There is also the cycle factory at Bilston in the West Midlands and latterly our attempts to establish an Operation in Spain, which brings us back to the Terry problem.

This position is twofold. First, the holder is the Leisure Division financial director which carries the same status and position in the hierarchy as Gordon and Johnny (resented by both, as I shall discover) and incidentally the same perks such as a 3.5 Rover car, a three-year rolling contract and membership of the directors' top hat pension scheme. Secondly, this director is automatically the divisional controller of the parent company alongside that of each other division. It follows that I would sit on the divisional board when it meets monthly in London and would have a functional boss in the group financial director.

I look carefully at Gordon now on his second sherry. I can tell he knows much more than he has told me. I feel strongly that it is a push up by him, not a pull-out by P. He is telling me silently that it is the right move. How very badly I had wanted to be a company director and had got there in a minor way a few months back but now this was a proper directorship. I am thirty-six years old and it seems a long way from the railway office and Mr Jenning's secretary click-clopping across the yard to the all too adjacent loo to herald the mare-like splash of her bladder's contents into the pan. I accept. As I leave the chairman's office with its side suite of leather armchairs and low coffee table bearing a copy statuette of Rodin's The Thinker appropriately as it turns out with head on hand staring at the floor, P says "welcome to the division John and from now on call me Bill, pop back and see me later will you?"

The announcement letter is a beauty. It reflects precisely the neat and carefully articulate political character of the Bill I shall get to know so well. Headed Senior Staff Amendment, it explains that Terry wishes to take up a new position outside the group and has therefore asked the board to release him from his contract. The personal letter from Bill concludes "You are aware, I'm sure, that you are directly responsible to me, but also have a functional responsibility to Peter at Cope Allman International Limited, in respect of all matters relating to the collection, reporting and dissemination of financial information, banking and other financial control procedures existing from time to time. I trust that you will find the work interesting and that the association will be long and fruitful." Bill asked me later if I had noted the concluding word *fruitful*.

A good hint of relationships, positionings and the ever present office politics at this time when group conglomerates were in vogue with their multi-tiered hierarchies came in a second personal letter from Peter. "This is just a personal note to congratulate you on your appointment as financial director of the Leisure Division. I notice that Bill's announcement did not make your title explicit but states that "authority for the financial control would be handed over to his successor ......". We must ensure that the appointment is to the Leisure Division board and is as finance director. Would you like to clear this informally with Bill first and if that is not the proposal, I will take the matter up at some higher level! I also enclose your official invitation to the Group Accountants Conference at Crick where I assume you will lead the Leisure Division delegation. I also enclose an invitation to the Group Finance Committee meeting which I have had to schedule at 8.00am Monday 6th November before the conference proper commences. I assume you will be taking over Terry's files which will give you some idea of the sort of things we discuss. My very best wishes for success in your new appointment which I am sure you will find continuously exciting and riveting." Ah, ah; somewhat different style here, bit lighter, bit more jolly but definitely with a few little hints. Anyway, here we go.

Gordon wants me to drive him to lunch. This is not unusual. The steakhouse used after the No 1 meeting is his canteen. It is only a question of who drives him there or sometimes he'll drive himself if he does not intend to return to the office but to go straight home. The other party will always be someone in his inner circle since they will be required to sign the bill. Gordon knows about personal taxation. On this occasion it is to be just we two because he wants to fill me in. I have learned to be careful at these lunches. Gordon drinks a lot. It will start innocuously enough, a couple of schooners of sherry from the wood and white wine with the fish.

Gordon is a careful eater and has a standing agreement with the waitress that always looks after him "one and a half plaice", that's right, not steak. The problem starts at coffee as that is "large Bells" time. If he goes back to the office, Val will purloin a bottle of this same Scotch whisky from one of a number of secret hiding places and lock his door like the trained bulldog she actually is paid to be. Bill knows what goes on but as the head of the biggest profit centre and cash generator and who can seemingly, at this time, do no wrong, Bill needs Gordon's support at most Leisure board meetings. It is also a fact that Gordon has at least one strong supporter on the main board.

What I need to understand (Gordon is talking cuddling his Scotch) is that Bill falls in love. Three years ago this smoothy Terry breezed into Bill's office. No-one seems to know from where but something to do with confectionery. His black patent shoes with the silver buckles and his bracelet bearing the name tag Terry knocked Bill clean off his feet. In no time at all poor old Dougie was downgraded to some kind of chief accountant and our Terry was in charge.

Poor Dougie though only in his forties now has cancer and hasn't long to last. Terry is a womaniser of the first water or should I say first semen since it's those stains we are still trying to remove from the back seats of one of our cars he borrowed recently on some pretext or other. He brags openly of all manner of conquests including the wife of a well known West Indian test cricketer. During the past year or so, our Terry has been swanning around Europe supposedly setting up the finances for a push into that hallowed turf. It has been obvious for some time that our Terry was pushing for a main board job himself and that Bill had lost all control of him. Now he has fallen flat on his face and I'm glad. Get stuck in and sort it out for all our sakes and remember this - "never play politics, I repeat, never play politics". Join me in another whisky "Vera – two large Bells, no ice".

Over a series of taxi rides across London and in his office in Hill Street in Mayfair, Peter was also keen to fill me in. What he demanded above all else was a clean set of accounts each month for the entire Leisure Division on time and with NO SURPRISES. The year-end stock loss thrown up two years earlier at Bell-Fruit Manufacturing had been a bad shock. This loan business was worse. If Terry could spend so much time away from his desk in Nottingham and get the whole group into such a pickle in Europe, then what might the true state of the divisional accounts be?

Bill was regarded at HQ as a dominant chief executive who pre-dated Louis on the main board and who often got the better of him in debates on strategy and who had been placed at a very young age at the head of the Leisure set-up by the man who built up the whole group Len Machin . If Terry had been up to any tricks, it might be in Bill's interest to cover it up. Bill had not asked for Terry's head, Louis had.

Then there was the legacy of the Viking cycle factory in the West Midlands. In the Leisure Division from the outset only because it was deemed a leisure pursuit, this huge plant had been closed down primarily as a result of a massive claim for compensation from a customer in the USA who had had the misfortune to have a fractured front fork penetrate his chest. The whole ethos of the bike had been that it was top of the market, super lightweight but at the same time super tough. The plant closure had left huge cycle stocks, potential claims overhang and maybe worst of all an empty 145,000 sq ft of factory on a fifteen year lease with likely looming and substantial dilapidation claims from the landlord. My first priority then was to make sure the accounts of the Leisure Division gave an accurate picture of the state of play. Secondly to help himself and Paul understand and then unwind the European loans debacle.

The perils of a functional reporting relationship were not hard to see. The likes of Bill, Gordon and Johnny were tough cookies. They were profit responsible and enjoyed a good deal of autonomy. In addition, the group financial director's time must be spread thinly. There were other divisions. At the heart of the group, and from where it had all started, was the Packaging Division with its many companies and its overseas interests, particularly in France. There was also an Engineering Division and a Fashion Division. In all some 160 separate businesses.

And yet, the importance attached to the job of divisional controller came from accurate financial reporting irrespective of the pressures on the line management. But if I found myself in conflict with Bill or Gordon or both, I was likely to lose the support that had put me where I was. Tricky, especially as Peter had gone out of his way to make me feel comfortable, had encouraged me to visit the other divisions and meet the controller and chairman of each division. Especially as I had made a few surprising friends by winning an after dinner cycle race around the table of that first conference and picking up a brand new, fifteen gear, Viking cycle as a reward (one less on the stock list to shift). Especially as Peter was such a nice chap, well educated and cultured, an ex partner of one of the large accountancy firms and a big buddy of Paul who in turn by all accounts was right at the very centre of power.

Peter had a limp and walked with a stick "cycling in the city, a car came too close and knocked a bit off me" and as an act of friendship and as demonstrable mollification, Paul would advise "don't run the risk of bumping into him, more bits might drop off." On balance it looked as if on any conflict of interest, it would be best to be aligned with Peter. What I did not know in these early days was that the relationship between Peter and Louis was already strained and that Paul would prove to be no more than a fair-weather friend.

Panic is a bugger. The mind is blocked. I have to turn my attention to *this loan business* but cannot fathom at all what has been going on. Where on earth to start? But start I must now that the financial legacy of Bilston has been agreed although the issue of what to do with the building remains but that is a commercial decision and I cannot, wrongly as it turns out, see myself being involved with. Gordon has agreed a faster write-off of stocks and I've now got two good accountants preparing the divisional accounts. Most importantly, Peter seems pleased and the board meetings as regards numbers are fairly smooth.

So far so good. So far so bad! Terry's reports of the currency movements on the loans are an absolute mystery. I cannot understand the figures reproduced religiously every month and worse still, I cannot understand the words they are clothed in. And the panic, I begin to realise, must stem from a deeper worry. If I even start to understand this situation, why would loans be taken out in Swiss Francs to support finance placed in Spanish Pesetas? That franc is the strongest currency in the world. The peseta is just about the weakest and getting worse, indeed if as Terry's report keeps saying the original exchange rate to the pound sterling was 141, the fact that it is now 180 and still heading south, shows to any half-numerate person that someone is in for a hiding and the pound is itself deteriorating against the Swiss Franc.

I recall that in Terry's summary and quick-fire briefing before he left (he did not stick around, far from it) some mention of "back-to-back loans". What on earth are they? I hear on the reliable grapevine called Gordon that the two HQ P's have just returned from another trip to Spain and that Bill's "tame ferret Ted " has just returned from Zurich. This Ted chap goes back yonks and works from the sales office in London. Officially he is the divisional credit controller and inter-alia chases debts arising from sales of fruit machines overseas. But there is no business in Switzerland, it is an illegal market. And Bill has been on the conference line to Ted with just me present telling him that now we have a "new bright controller and from today you report to him and at last there is someone to keep you under control." Why do I feel so uneasy? Louis, Peter, Paul, Bill and now maybe Ted . Am I the cannon fodder?

The constant probing clears some of the mist, but never all. I make seven separate trips to Madrid and always accompanied by Jeremy a member of the group HQ internal legal staff. He is a qualified lawyer but more importantly speaks fluent Spanish. Why was the Spanish company set up, who set it up, just how much money passed through it, what was it used for, where has it gone? I record faithfully and report back the detail of everything we are told having to take Jeremy's word for much of it. We progress to clear-up mode. That means use of different Spanish lawyers and the external auditors. Sometimes my head is swimming; it is hard to sleep even in the Amelia Castilla, even after the Spanish version of a measure of liquor. The Spanish company is closed down, no funds remain.

It is easy to add two to two and make not five but twenty-two. Evidence and proof are different to suspicions and maybe's. I believe I trace funds from Switzerland to New York but the trail ends, yet somehow Holland is involved. There is no pacification in late night mumblings about all commercial Spanish lawyers being crooks or in Bill's dictum that "no seriously rich man made his pile honestly". Was a manufacturing plant actually set up? Was an operation really set up? Did an operation already exist? The meeting I arrange with a kind of middle man referred to frequently in Terry's papers takes me to a private office suite in central London entered only by a security code. He is unhelpful and the session is short. I feel relieved to be out of there. Later he wants me to meet him at Zurich airport to exchange currencies, I refuse. Eventually the Swiss Franc denominated loan is written off.

Bill delivers what to me is really bad news. Peter is leaving the group. Louis had put a paper to the main board, the gist of which was that he had lost confidence in his finance director and it called for a vote. The non-executive directors voted with Louis and so did Paul. At the next Leisure Division board meeting Louis explained that the business of the loan write-off had been a disaster but he was more concerned about the *innuendo* that had surrounded certain aspects of some of the reports that had been submitted by Peter. He did not attribute direct blame to John Smith but was disappointed that he had contributed. I started to sweat and waited for the knife, but it did not come.

A mysterious middle man

It's odd how things turn out. I quite warm to this chap Ted . I begin to see him as one of life's lovable rogues. He likes his food does Ted and when I bring him in from the London lair and over the fillet steak "butterflied, always butterflied old boy" he starts to fill in the historical jigsaw. He was an original Len Machin man. Machin was the clever rough tough bugger who put the whole group together in the first place. Cope Allman was the name of a shell company, long since non-trading, that Machin got hold of and then started to back businesses he bought into. He did not care what the business did, if it had assets and made money and passed the tests his number-crunchers applied, then it was in.

This was the era of conglomerates. Hanson Trust was not the first. Len had been returning with his beautiful wife from a holiday in Kenya and on the aeroplane just happened to sit next to, and got into conversation with, this young man Bill Pilkington. Bill's doctorate was in mining engineering. Did I know that? He had been doing practical field work in Zambia and was returning home.

The next thing, this young wiz-kid is chairman of the fruit-machine group being put together in Nottingham and would you believe at the age of twenty-six. And, his wife Sue was once Len's secretary. When Bill first met me off the train at Nottingham railway station, I recall this tall, slim, handsome man, bald as a coot like now, with his raincoat neatly folded over his left arm. Instantly I knew Len had picked a winner. John, you need to know the background, you must understand the background.

Bell-Fruit *is* Bill. Len used to have these fantastic annual get-togethers of senior executives and their wives. One year it was in Jersey and Matt Monroe was flown in especially to sing Sinatra's My Way, dedicated of-course to Len. Eventually Len retired to his own island in the sun and somehow, God knows how, this little lawyer Louis got control. And yes I still visit Hill Street from time to time. Doing what, well bits and bobs for Bill.

It soon became clear that Ted's reporting relationship to me was at best nominal and at worst a blind. My telephone call to demand, yet again, his monthly report would elicit the pained response "can't finish it just now John, I'm in Cyprus today and due in Amsterdam tomorrow". What the bloody hell are you doing there? "Oh just collecting a few debts and clearing a few things up, Bill rang me yesterday, sorry forgot to tell you." And then his expenses that I decided to bring under control. Why are there so many taxi fares and not just inside but beyond London when he is allocated a fully expensed company car that is using oodles of petrol? And Ted, and I'm sorry to drop this on you, but I have found out that you cannot even drive a car! No John, that's right but my son can. And Ted, I have had one of the accountants here reconcile your foreign currency, for instance if we take all the pesetas handed to you this year and spent by you and then left over in your reported reserve, well you have managed to spend more than you ever received! Oh John, John, my desk drawer is full of foreign currency of all types, accumulated over years and years. I am just no good at these things. For now it is a nil nil draw.

Months later, when I am stronger, my new internal audit team pay a surprise visit to the London sales office. Terminology changes over time. We have found some *accumulated reserves*.

Ted was once a prospective parliamentary candidate, he brings a copy of an electioneering poster bearing a beaming and younger version of himself to prove it. It occurred to me that if he had got elected and if he had taken Churchill's place, and he would have put himself up for the task ahead, one could imagine a bemused Hitler ordering General Paul's sixth army west rather than east and instead of being encircled at Stalingrad, marching with white flags aloft straight into the North Sea at Zeebrugge.

In the divisional office there are a few other boys of the old brigade. One is called Allen and is best known for his paintings. The most famous is a cock pheasant in full colour regalia. It can be found as a print in many pubs and similar public places and as a tea-towel print and on tin trays. A far cry from his worth to us, one might think. But Allen has contacts and more important, had contacts. He is indulged and wrapped in cotton wool and need only pop into the office every now and again because he effected the first introduction to the second largest brewer in the UK and with whom our Operations overall holds some 40% of its entire estate of prime managed house fruit machines. That is quite some legacy and worthy of quite some reputation and of course he still goes to certain important meetings with Bill. This is the man who one day hands me a slip of paper with a name and telephone number and suggests it would be in my interest to make a call. My subsequent visit to London turns out to be an interview for the position of financial director of a very large printing and publishing group. I did not get offered the job but it did serve to help me see Allen more through Bill's eyes, that is, as somehow a bit special.

When, a few years later, Allen gives his departure speech it is the longest, funniest and most unconventional one that can be imagined for anyone to deliver to any audience at any time. There was not one word about how he came to be in the group, or what he had achieved or might have achieved, or thanks for this or thanks for that or any of the normal guff. We heard about his formative years in South Africa as a senior diplomat or military man, (I couldn't decide on the evidence which) and we heard about the dichotomy of his doctor over seemingly innumerable medical examinations in that the consummate amount of whisky he drank would dilate his blood vessels and thus be beneficial, but on the other hand his addiction to cigarettes would have the opposite affect. On balance therefore the one habit should cancel out, medically speaking, the other and so the odds were that he should live for an average and perhaps above average length of time.

It sounded a bit tongue in cheek and it was the harbinger of a whole plethora of jokes and in the event the prophecy proved inaccurate. Within a few years he was dead. Ironically, his final wisecrack was about a man who had died. His widow had to dispose of his tank-full of tropical salt-water fish. Finding no takers and in mournful desperation she attempted to flush the lot down the toilet. After a few goes the attempt was successful apart from one cold-blooded aquatic vertebrate that refused to swill away. This, is seems, was a flat fish that normally spent all its time swimming on the bottom of the sea and because this practice had evolved over the years it now had only one eye. This sole eye was obviously positioned facing straight upwards and was in the centre of its body. The distraught widow was positively haunted by this one eye staring up from the toilet basin and he cautioned all listeners to make absolutely sure that such an unfortunate event had never occurred in whatever place we found ourselves going to the loo. It was the sort of story that never leaves one, so to speak. But Allen was leaving and we were to be the poorer for it, not economically of-course but then what is a salary compared to a character.

The dust must have settled on the Spanish episode and Bill has decided to flex his muscles. Changes are afoot. He cannot get the modernisation needed at Bell-Fruit Manufacturing, particularly the technology switch to electronics. The biggest competitor is having more and more success and, being backed by the largest brewer in the land, has the financial power to buy the new equipment called for and the software engineers to create the new type of game. With fewer and fewer of our manufactured machines reaching the top of the earnings league table, Bill and Gordon are being drawn more and more into conflict. Bill wants the Operation to buy "its fair share" of the new in-house machines but Gordon wants to buy only the best performing ones from whomsoever makes it. When Bill's persuasion has won out, Gordon can prove site loss to other operators. Gordon will not shirk from reporting that this is so. Johnson is to go and the head-hunters are out.

Gordon is now sixty years old and Bill thinks he must be *underpinned* to plan for succession. Gordon disagrees on the grounds that he has good years to go and is capable of recommending his own successor, but gives ground partly because he wants Bill off his back and partly because he has problems in Holland and wants the space to sort them out. Bill plays his next card. He wants Gordon to have a strong financial director from outside. This is met with acquiescence. Gordon eats finance men for breakfast and he is no mean slouch with numbers himself. And now the final move. Bill shows me the Cope Allman International's (CAI) Succession Planning Chart that forms part of the strategic planning review. I am pencilled in as his successor.

It is important for me to get more commercial experience and so I am to be promoted to group commercial director. What does commercial mean exactly? "Anything we want it to". The fact is, the engineering division of CAI under Jim Cameron, is shrinking as businesses are gradually sold off. Within our expanding leisure division a good place can be found for two of their people. Their incumbent finance director can come to us and report to me and take over day-to-day matters on the accounts and their head of central services could take charge of all our vehicles. My new commercial brief will therefore still include financial control but now take over all the functional services but most vitally I will lead the expansion drive. I will be put on all sixteen of the subsidiary company boards including the ones in Holland, Australia, Germany and what was left of Spain. Also, the very successful operations company working with NAFFI overseas. Bill intends to retire early, certainly by the time he reaches fifty, he will not repeat the mistake his father made of working too long and then dying soon afterwards. He and Sue have settled well in Holbrook Hall in rural Derbyshire and the wise thing was to enjoy it to the full. So there we have it. Senior future all mapped out. The best laid plans of mice and men. For we mice scratching away in our little pen things were moving along nicely. For the men in London, storm clouds are gathering.

Johnny Johnson, as the press release formally notated, has been replaced after a fifteen year stint as chief executive of Bell-Fruit Manufacturing. The announcement of his successor (with a very happy looking Fred (aged 45) injected in the middle of a glowing eight paragraph career profile) is coupled with my own appointment as group commercial director. My write-up however extends to just two paragraphs and my mug-shot is more suitably stern and includes the last remnants of any hair on top a bulbous head but counter-balanced by long sideburns. The write up of the new boss of manufacturing included the perhaps surprising revelation that whilst working for a business located in Grantham, he played centre-half for the local soccer team. My eulogy contained no such sporting acclaim and indeed, although I hadn't mentioned it to Bill as he composed the piece, I could not even boast of having wanked for Somerset. Still, my mum and dad were very proud of what had happened and I put a little write up in the Derbyshire Times especially for them. It would come to light again much later in my mum's small tin box of treasures.

All the other new blood was pouring in too. From the depleting engineering division I inherited Keith Parsons as my new financial controller. Successful down-scaling is one of the toughest management skills to acquire as I shall learn subsequently and Jim Cameron and his now ex-money man Keith had been through the mill. Almost literally. To have weathered the storm and to now be placed in a key role in the go-go leisure division calls for political nous.

Keith Parsons had developed his own kind of language to clothe this nous. It was a form of language that was both verbose and complicated and any response, assessment or even opinion would be sprinkled liberally with soft negatives. It was hard to interpret and get to the bottom of what Keith was saying. He was a sort of verbal antithesis to Gordon. It was hard to pin down Keith or establish just what he stood for. In a largely technical and functional role it is possible to be like that indefinitely and it is why two so-called experts in the same field can disagree fundamentally and both get away with it. Keith had found a way to survive and would continue to do so. Until, that is, his chain-smoking cigarette habit caught up with him.

Of-course it helps to have a sponsor on the main board.

Keith clearly has engineering Jim like I might have leisure Bill. But how do mice know which of the men is the stronger? It is not a question of which one to back, the bets were all pre-laid. It is a question of where the power and future direction lies. That is why being a mouse is precarious. Attached to the right leg and one is zooming, attached to the wrong leg and anything can happen and this is quite irrespective of personal ability. I can quite see that Bill and Jim have done a deal, but to whose ultimate advantage? Did Bill need Jim's support to finally oust Johnson? Did Bill need Jim's support to *underpin* Gordon? After all, Jim and Gordon are close, this channel is the principal Gordon grapevine. I am now close enough to Gordon to know this for sure. The thing is, are Bill and Jim back to par or does one still owe the other a favour? I do know that Bill and Louis are disagreeing more and more and that Bill persists in digging holes for little Louis to fall into (it is hard not to know this when Bill has sent for me to listen in on the conference line and when Louise has opened up with his customary "Bill are you alone" and Bill's response "yes Louis, of course." For a thinking man and a reasonable chess player it is all a bit worrying. In accepting Keith, have I inherited a viper in the nest?

Perhaps heavy smoking was bequeathed by engineering turmoil because my second new man is David Soubry. David was a vehicle specialist and could be better used with us because our fleet size swamped all the rest of the CAI put together. Furthermore, this fleet of over 800 cars and vans was owned outright and therefore represented a considerable asset on the balance sheet as well as having a prominent presence in the operation costings.

The vehicle resource was not well looked after. Though long regarded as a central service to the operating divisions, Gordon's No 1 meeting often voiced discontent on vehicle choice and service and repair costs. The lead man could now retire (one of Gordon's despised "old boys who lurk in dark corners gossiping and causing trouble and drinking scotch they haven't earned") and David Soubry could take over.

David was not a plant or if he was he proved to be a most worthwhile one. He negotiated improved purchase terms by playing off the vehicle fleet suppliers and instigated significant upfront payments direct from the manufacturers that evaded the distributor chain. He also paved the way for outsourcing fuel and service supplies and was amongst the first in the country to experiment with LPG as a new fuel and to take advantage of the newly emerging car auction market for disposals. As important as these business things, David was a gentleman in the old fashioned meaning of the word and became something of a father figure to the young team that I was gradually putting together at the centre. As it happened he was also well connected and in particular in a doggy way. His most high-class wife Frances was a leading member of the beagle hunt fraternity and June and I spent one splendid evening at the annual ball held at Belton House near Grantham in Lincolnshire. Never before or since have I seen grown men in pink suits. It occurred to me that that alone must be the overriding reason why hares run so fast. What were the dogs needed for?

David and Frances had produced three children and one day he brought in a note from his daughter to show me. It was on House of Commons letterhead since she, even at this young age, was a researcher for Edward Heath. He was so proud of Anna and more so when she became a TV presenter and reporter and later she will do a small interview with me for the local TV on a new product launch. The Soubrys were sailors and David had his own dingy. All in all, a happy fulfilled family that lived in a beautiful Victorian house until the owning National Trust so hiked the rents as to enforce a move. That move was to an old cottage adjacent to the windmill at the top of the hill at Tuxford. To help fund the move, much of the antique furniture was sold and then David set about bringing the cottage back into a liveable state.

He had just returned from a motor manufacturers' jamboree in Monte Carlo when the pain came. He had radiotherapy and rather proudly showed me the pink coloured crosses on his chest. My new office was large with its own en-suite toilet and shower and feature columns and statues. We sat at ease in the leather armchairs and discussed the content of his various consultations and after two or three weeks he explained that things were progressing well and that in answer to his specific question of the senior medical consultant on how long the treatment would last and its consequences, he had got the reply "well look at this way David, go and book your next year's holiday." As this was high summer, the prospect of planning for next summer pleased him immensely and he was positively jaunty as he stubbed out his fag and left the office.

In late September David asked me to come to their orchard and pick some plums as this was an abundant season. We set up the ladders together and whilst me and Chris and Craig picked into the wicker baskets suspended from the "S" hooks, David went indoors to make a pot of tea. Frances strolled out and I remarked on the good news about David's treatment. She asked me to walk away from the boys and in the far corner of the orchard said "John, he is absolutely riddled with it, the position is hopeless."

He took his own styled cocktail of drugs throughout the autumn and sank slowly with never a word of complaint except to advise me quietly one day in his bedroom to "stop smoking." He died on Christmas Day and in his eulogy in the beautiful parish church of St Nicholas, Tuxford, the vicar praised, amongst other things, David's devoted service as a church warden. I had not known he was a church warden. But then that is David for you. Or rather that was

David. In the pub afterwards the group of mourners, that included Jim Cameron, was extraordinarily quiet for a wake. Twenty-odd years later I will visit Frances in the same old cottage next to the windmill. His photograph is still on the sideboard and Frances is still growing the vegetables and making the chutney. She is also, now and again, still crying.

New blood

Bill and Gordon have been quietly interviewing for Gordon's potential successor. They have agreed to make an offer to one Tony Darling and although he and his family will have to be re-located from Newcastle, Bill sees the potential in him to take over from Gordon eventually and as an ex-PA consultant and senior engineer in a rope-making manufacturer, has the added advantage (as I did, as Bill points out to Gordon) of not being imbued with the industry's bad habits; a new broom so to speak. Gordon thinks he is probably the best of a bad bunch.

The taste for new blood is positively draculanian. The job of financial director for the Operations is to be offered to a Mike Peace who comes from a large contract catering company. So here, for the time being, is the new order. I am going commercial whilst concurrently building a team to keep this growing division under control, Bill has his new jovial head of manufacturing and Gordon has an understudy and an experienced outside finance man. The perfect blend for a whiz-bang future.

One of the ways to boost the flagging sales of the manufacturing side and at the same time find an outlet for the models that have proved less than winners in the UK market would be to export. Not that finding overseas markets is easy notwithstanding the best efforts of the super sales director and his team in the London office and notwithstanding the diplomatic and bulldog-like follow-up skills of my friend Ted . For one thing, most of the markets are illegal and where this is not so, local fashion has dictated a size and style of machine far removed from the UK mould and/or the regulatory authorities have constructed such a web of approval apparatus as to make a theoretically open market as hard to penetrate as Geoff Boycott's batting guard. That is, not exactly impossible but practically very difficult and very time absorbing and costly. Specimen machines for the vast German and American markets slowly disappear down a bureaucratic black hole and the best way to gain a foothold in the Spanish and Dutch markets is, initially, almost certainly to buy into and then build an operation as a precursor. But let us draw a veil over Spain and come back to Holland. Australia is uneconomic to service from the UK and anyway is *club* culture but we will own a manufacturing plant located there. As for elsewhere, well spare parts might be sent to South Africa or Greece or other strange places that are aching for a follow-up visit from Ted but generally speaking, that is it. As a manufacturer, you either make it in the UK or you do not make it.

But then Bulgaria pops up. A salesman in the London office has been approached by a go-between with an unpronounceable and unspellable name who happens to know that the official Bulgarian Tourist Board (BTB) want to site machines not dissimilar to ours in their rapidly developing ski resorts. The proposition is that Western skiers would play the machines with tokens (a unique UK invention born of the 1968 Gaming Act) and to purchase tokens they would tender their Western currency but winnings would be converted to local currency. This brilliant idea for wresting the most desirable hard currencies from the foreigners had come from the head of the BTB who now wanted to meet ourselves. Only he, the go-between, was authorised to effect this introduction. This was the perfect opportunity for me to cut my commercial teeth and furthermore since I had worked in tandem with Jeremy in cleaning up/closing down Spain and since it was imperative we get the legals right, so a three-man team would be sent to break into this new market. Jeremy, me and Mr Salesman.

At this time the cold war is very much still waging and the iron curtain and the Berlin wall are still very much in tact and my first thoughts that the Eastern block might not be too keen to have us, occur as the pilot of the huge Russian Aeroflot plane takes too literally the instruction to overfly central London quietly. Cutting the engines is obviously an efficient way to achieve this objective and a belly-flop on the Thames now seems highly likely. I exchange glances with Jeremy and we are both thinking that bloody hell here we go again.

It was never explained why but our go-between is meeting us not at our destination Sofia but in Zagreb and that is where this noisy tub is taking us. It is odd how this parallelism occurs. Two months earlier, June and I and the boys had been to Ancona, the lovely Greekish but Italian town right beneath where we are now crossing the Adriatic Sea. And how did my commercialising brief lead to this basement bar/restaurant up the steep hill of ancient Zagreb in this country still known as Yugoslavia?

Next day we are led by our proud mysterious go-between off the Sofian tarmac to a waiting large black Russian car and whisked to the best hotel in town (Japanese named and owned and, I am reliably told by the head waiter, a trade-off for Japanese finance – well, well). I note that there is none of the notorious communist State red-tape here, so we are VIP's indeed.

The first meeting is unconventional. At 10.am sharp, the head of the BTB storms into the room at a pace and with a crash and a bang that certainly does justice to his large bulk. Without a word he slams a full bottle of Johnny Walker scotch on the table and looks we three trembling Brits steadily in the eye. As if to catch my breath, I then notice his companion. A most beautiful woman with that unmistakably Eastern European face and smile starts to talk. Her name is Svetla, she will be our interpreter, she will accompany us at all times, she has visited London many times and Mr Big wishes to share the bottle with us and when it has been consumed then we can talk business. OK? Ok with me Svetla, keep talking and smiling and maybe there really is a reason to be here after all.

As the bottle goes down Mr Big, through Svetla, explains that up to this time it has not been possible to allow Western holiday makers to visit his beautiful country because the purpose-built resorts on the Black Sea coast have been used solely by the important officials from the motherland and as far as the winter was concerned, well skiing had never been thought of as a useful activity. But things were changing. As part of the new five-year plan, Bulgaria could earn its own foreign currency within certain confines and sea-shore hotels and ski resorts were going to be built to serve Western tastes. I tried to interrupt the lecture by informing Mr Big that six years ago my family had visited a summer resort in Rumania and had experienced the excellent facilities (leaving out the bits about Craig almost dying from dysentery, the clothes being almost taken off our backs by locals desperate for any Western gear and the black market in currency conversion rates) and that I had been told at that time that Bulgaria had similar facilities. I feel sure that Svetla translated this riposte accurately but all it elicited from Mr Big was a solid stare.

Perhaps the best tactic is to just soak up, the propaganda and the booze that is. By the time the background had been covered and the bottle drunk, it was the lunch break. We were informed as such by Svetla as explanation for Mr Big standing up suddenly, shaking our hands and leaving. He would not be joining us for lunch as he was very busy and had to go to other meetings. Recollections of the lunch itself are dim mainly because it was preceded by liquid refreshment that all the BTB staff present were poured as standard. We all had a tumbler about three-quarters full of what I assumed initially was water. Actually it was Vodka. Svetla thought it would be best if we retired to our hotel in the afternoon as Mr Big still had much preparation to do on "protocol". She would meet us the following morning for breakfast. There were no objections on our side.

Whether it helped at all or not I cannot be sure but apparently Jeremy, as well as his command of Spanish, had a good working knowledge of Russian and it seems that this is close to Bulgarian. At any rate he appeared to comprehend much of what was going on and it was most impressive to see him reading the local newspaper over breakfast. I decided that if I was to have the slightest comprehension of anything then my stomach would, for once, have to come to my rescue and dictate that I abandoned drinking spirits in favour of their excellent red wine that I had heard about so often. Interestingly this went down well. First because it was actually very good and secondly because Svetla explained that the wine being served did not find its way to Western Europe. "Our best wine goes to the motherland" and it was good that I should want to taste it.

The approach to ones liver surviving the trip varied. Jeremy politely took what was offered but diluted it liberally with water whereas Mr Salesman decided that anything they could take, he could, although this did probably contribute towards some adverse reactions in that he got involved in a fight in the bar one night and looking back on it was lucky to escape relatively unscathed. Disappointingly, Mr Big did not return to the negotiation table and from what we could gather from Svetla, matters of protocol were proving more tricky than had been anticipated at the time our invitation had been issued. Aside from Jeremy's tan relaxingly earned on the sunbed at the side of the hotel swimming pool and some reconnaissance trips by Mr Salesman and I to size-up possible sites for our machines should at some future date they be allowed in the larger hotels in Sofia, four days of pretty much emptiness followed before I decided to terminate our initial exploratory visit.

Our go-between had evidently gone between something or other soon after our arrival and we never saw him again. As we waited in Vienna for a connecting flight home, it occurred to me that my initial incursion into the world of commerce had not been an unmitigated success. But something else was niggling away at me. Of we three Brits, I would rate myself as by far the least attractive to the opposite sex yet Svetla had made a very obvious attempt to stay close to me and particularly in the official car and I had found leaving her at the airport very difficult. Maybe I had read too many cold-war books to consider this a good thing. What was a good thing was that I should be back in time for our weekly bridge game with Alan of the PW office and his Spanish-looking beauty of a wife who I now know is called Julia. In the year it will take for the ground in Sofia to be prepared properly, Bill's determination to see me fully launched will involve pastures much further afield.

Around the world

The difficulty of making fruit machines at a profit was not limited to the UK. The factory in Australia was also in the mechanical to electronic transition. It was also in trouble. For some years, Bill had been in the habit of visiting his far-flung empire twice a year and as I would hear later, Louis occasionally went too. But the profit slide called for a good look at the *nuts and bolts* of the place and such was the reputation of Gordon that a couple of years earlier he had been sent out. Changes had been made as a result of his review but the feeling was that he had been a touch brutal. Not that that would have bothered ye typical Aussie one jot but the fact was that the MD was a Brit and (can I believe it?) an ex- engineering division ex-Jim Cameron placement - history does repeat itself and old habits die hard.

So our man in Aussie, the giant Cliff, had baulked a bit at the prospect of another heavyweight coming out from the UK. Gordon was doubly miffed at not being asked to go a second time. First, he relished a second go at Cliff but also a further go of a purely sexual nature with the lady he met in a bar who had told him that he "made her come" more times in one night than her husband had in two years. This was not surprising as the husband was apparently an invalid but it was expensive in terms of johnies (getting through a packet a night) and in terms of making up with Rene once the letters started to arrive on his return home. The lady in question would leave her husband for good if only he would return to Australia. Gordon kept explaining to his wife that this woman must be a crank but Rene was not impressed, after all hadn't she found a packet of you know what in his jacket pocket only a year before?

With my factory background and as part of my new brief, I would go this time and Bill thought it would be a wonderful opportunity to make a serious inroad into the thirty-day de-minimus rule. That rule devised by some official in the Board of Trade, with undoubtedly a brain the size of a planet but about as much knowledge of business morality as the local vicar, and successfully sold to the Treasury. It offered a sizeable reduction in taxable pay for those hard working export driven executives who needed to spend a load of time abroad in any one tax year bringing in the foreign currency and so reducing the frighteningly wide trade deficit. How this squared with sorting out a factory in Australia and having a few jollies en-route was lost on me but then so was the tax allowable *entertainment* of a business lunch with export potential in mind. Most lunches now had that in mind.

The thing was though that given my peregrinations in Bulgaria and Spain and thinking ahead about Gordon's problems in Holland, it could be beneficial to visit my old stamping grounds en-route and see how machines get sighted in the casinos allowed in Malaysia and round about, and on the way back I could do a fact-finding tour of the two states in America where machines are legal, that is Nevada and New Jersey. After all it would be no bad thing to give our New York lawyer a push on progressing the approval process. Well, yes. Why not?

So, much sooner than I could ever have expected, Denis is meeting me off the plane at the new Changi airport in Singapore, we are taking lunch at the Tanglin Club and then his gorgeous wife April is taking me shopping whilst Denis attends to important business. What a turn-up. And how odd to be walking in Kings Cross, Sydney (another King's Cross?), because the body-clock will just not function after this final eight-hour flight and sleep is impossible, and some young man dressed as a clown with a pure white painted face is trailing a ball of cotton wool on the end of a piece of string with a placard around his neck saying "fifty cents a smile". Is this real or am I still dreaming thirty-nine thousand feet up?

This sheer inability to sleep is unnerving. The eternity of the small hours has turned my eleventh-floor bedroom at The Menzies into a prison and I'm consciously using the stairs and ignoring the lifts in a vain effort to get tired physically. The two days in Singapore was supposed to prevent all this and why did I not suffer after the flights to India? Perhaps just thinking about it is making things worse. How can I get to the root of what's wrong here if this semi-dreamlike stupor persists? It is like a perverse magic trick that has gone wrong. No sooner does the banter start with the taxi driver than I could sleep for a week on the backseat or am I dreaming now? Is that really two men sitting at a table outside a bar drinking those midis of Tooths or Toheys pure acidic beer? It is only eight-thirty a.m.! But the daytime must be battled through in an atmosphere even more acidic than the ice-cold beer.

Beer that is downed at lunchtime and as the first shout at the in-house bar where all senior managers congregate after work. The computer tests I have set up on the raw materials and piece-parts held on the shop-floor and in stock are not helping my popularity and nor is my switch, Bulgarian style, to red wine. Someone muttered that I'll be ordering a bloody sherry next. Is this drinking a contributor to the problem with the factory or just an Aussie thing? Hard to be sure but aside from my sojourn in Eastern Europe never have I seen so many bright red faces, in fact half of the men look as if at any moment they will literally burst. And it is a masculine place. Most of the male population of Sydney pour into bars on leaving work and these are not pretty, aesthetic, female-friendly places. They are utilitarian beer-swilling faceless rooms reminiscent of the downtown Glasgow of my cake-manufacturing days. The barman tells me, after it all quietens down, that the skill is in pre-filling all his midi-glasses by the time the rush starts so that the process (my word not his) is reduced to grabbing and paying and definitely not waiting for the pouring out bit.

This sort of clinical attack on the leisure quantum is here again as I am taken around the clubs that house the fruit machine output of the factory. Back home the law allows for only two machines in a private club but in New South Wales that's tosh. There are hundreds lined up like soldiers on parade and the odd thing is a whole row can consist of the same model that functionally is therefore identical to its neighbour. But that does not stop ye punter, typically a middle-aged woman carrying a large handbag, playing only on one specific machine, *her machine*. And heaven help the woman who dares to sit at that machine with the handbag left dangling from the handle whilst the owner replenishes her cup of coins from the bar. They all play the same my love. They bloody well don't and anyway I've fed this one and I'll bloody well get the jackpot out of it. Clinical is the correct adjective. It does not look much fun. But it does explain why this club can afford Shirley Bassey and it does explain why we Brits get clobbered at cricket.

It's strange this serious dedicated approach to pleasure. Down this road where I walk during my lonely evenings are innumerable adult shows. Inside, the German-made pornographic film sequence stops and as the lights go on a girl appears through a side door onto a stage. To her own particular taste in music she performs an artistic strip-tease. Nothing, unlike the Indian *midnight saunter*, is left to the imagination and when the act is over, out go the lights again and the film recommences from where it left off. As ones eyes become accustomed to the dark, and in the blue glow of the entertainment, it is unmistakeably the stripper who is now making her way up the centre isle carrying her little bag and presumably en-route to the next hall. If one waits long enough, the next act will arrive in reverse fashion. One minute the centre of attention, the next – ignored. Prophetic.

How quaint, how pleasurable, how clinical and now how jolly is the little party headed by Cliff seeing me off on the night flight to Hawaii. No one says as much but obviously since I have not sacked Cliff nor made threatening noises generally and since they have all co-operated fully and as the exercises started will be pushed through and the results posted back to the UK, there is no reason not to be pleased with the visit, and of course I will now drink a few midis instead of the red wine. After all, how else can I even hope to get some sleep on this next long haul?

Strange how sleep itself has become something of an obsession over here. Never bothered me before even to the point where my life-long sleepless night could be regarded as normal. Not that I could ever predict when it would occur, it just did, and the long slow quiet hours would simply be put up with. A string of such nights though is different especially when you understand why but yet can do nothing to change the pattern. It becomes a sort of drip drip torture of the tired brain. Perhaps it's a form of nemesis that causes me to turn to a complete stranger sitting at the next table in this revolving restaurant high above Waikiki beach and inform him with worldly grace that "I have just had two Wednesdays, one in Sydney and now one here". Not taken aback one jot, he counters with "and I haven't had one at all, jumped from Tuesday to Thursday mate". It must be the lack of sleep.

It is so very very hot in Hawaii and the shorts and hat that have to be purchased in the gift shop downstairs have to make their own, and as I shall become familiar with, very American impression first by leaving no doubt even to the most casual observer that this is indeed "Hawaii" and secondly by being bright pink, a colour that would not have been a first choice but which nevertheless actually seems OK. The food is another set-back. The sensible order of a salad and steak arrives in two tranches (and the first will not be taken away until substantially consumed) and each would have been sufficient to feed the whole of Napoleon's army to sustain the march across Europe. But the greatest wonder of all and quite surpassing the pink shorts and the mountain of food and the external glass elevator to the revolving restaurant is the impact of delicate pink flesh on a deprived male body. I had seen many most beautiful girls, Chinese, Malaysians, Thai, Indian and others in my non-European working life thus far. All had one thing in common. Clothes. But here lazing on this magnificent beach was a quite different phenomenon. Small but beautifully formed and ever-smiling and evidently high-class, ladies from Japan. Ladies whom it seems care to wear next to nothing. Just think, I could have opted to have flown directly to mainland USA.

If there was no work in Hawaii (stop off and recover were Bill's exact words) there was a mission for Reno, as it sits high in the Sierra Nevada and as it is approached over Lake Tahoe flying high to the left of Stewart and Carson City. I feel my eyes water partly from the effects of the steep climb and now descent in the plane the pilot says "we affectionately call the rocket", but mainly from the memories of the Westerns relished in the Metro Cinema in Newton from the nine-penny front seats, and trying to make the four-penny bar of Sharps toffee last the whole film. It was always in Carson City that the baddy got his comeuppance. And the way this plane is falling out of the sky, this could be mine. If PW's business doesn't get you, then this one will.

The reason for the quick zip over the mountains is my second little jaunt. San Francisco. Well why not. Bill thought it would be a shame to miss it and especially not to have stayed at No1 Knob Hill and I am now thinking to have missed Miss Samantha Eggar who it seems is a famous British film actress checking in and demanding the best room for herself and the little dog. They do not have the best room available right now Miss Eggar and dogs are not allowed. She kicks up a hell of a stink and I instinctively feel ashamed to be British just, no doubt, as many Americans feel ashamed to be American after this tour of Alcatraz. No wonder Burt Lancaster took to birds.

Redemption comes in the beautiful breathtaking form of the Golden Gate Bridge. Ok, so Sydney is receding but its Harbour Bridge so pales by comparison as to be almost a white-out. Tony Bennett left his heart here and there is a danger I will too. The little cable cars, the Fishermans Wharf, the architectural change from ethnic quarter to ethnic quarter and the liberal freedom in the air. I think to myself that if you cannot create here, you cannot create anywhere. What a shame there is no one to share it with. For the first time in ages, I am very lonely.

And what has Reno to offer? Not a lot. A backstage look through the one-way mirrors at the stupid punters and can Sue advance my forward bookings by a day. She at least sounds pleased to hear my voice and yes she will and meet me with the car at Heathrow. She actually wants to. So let me see this lawyer in his 26th floor office in Manhattan and then catch the disappointingly slow train to Trenton. Surely there must be ways to further our machines through this agonisingly ponderous approval process but even pushing right into the heart of the New Jersey Gaming Approval Board only serves to confirm that it's not merely the technical qualities of hardware that has to meet the most stringent vetting in the world (this is the USA after all) but the qualities of we humanware. All the top management have to have an impeccable pedigree and, to support the case, the State's 850 question dossier has to be compiled for each person and furthermore the Special Investigation Team will need to be invited over to the UK to interview the applicants on the (UK) ground and be allowed to make any further enquiries they see as relevant from the detailed answers given. The applicant will pay all expenses.

The lawyer representing us cannot be sure why we were not informed of all this beauocracy at the time we received the machine technical specifications, but in these matters dealing with these sort of regulatory forces, it is best to take things a stage at a time. Maybe but there has to be a known end, there has to be a definable process. Placing slots in casinos in New Jersey and Nevada is not expected to be a licence to print money; we have to weigh up costs as well. Even assuming the boys back home can be persuaded to fill in the questionnaires, what is likely to be the expense of the investigators and then what else is involved? I carry responsibility for finance too you know. There is no open-ended cheque book to get machines past your authorities.

The balance between being aggressive and angry and being cool and calculating is hard to find and as I peer from this glass eyrie down on the ant-like traffic of Fifth Avenue it is hard not to speculate as to which side this overcharging stuffed shirt is on. There is supposed to be relatively free trade between us and the yanks just as between us and the Germans. There is something about this commercial lark that I am not quite getting.

Sue meets me as arranged and in this early morning light she looks and smells absolutely gorgeous and she wants to handle the drive back to Nottingham in the 3.5 litre Rover that is now the corporate recognition of my new enhanced status. It is great to be home and so close to those gorgeous legs. I have missed Chris and Craig like crazy. As we chat over coffee in this very British non-Aussie, non-American motorway service centre and catch up with events I just know we are both feeling things. Things that should not be. Things that cannot be.

Australian folly and bolt-ons

To those that can hold their ground and be patient, all things will turn in due course. The man that came within a whisker of firing me over the innuendo flowing from the Spanish loans affair has now written a personal letter. He feels that the recommendations in my Australian report are sound and tells me that Bill, through Cliff, will get them implemented. Much can be done to reduce the stockholding and improve profitability even if ultimately the business passes out of our hands due to the problems of control at this distance. The message appears sincere. I will take it as such.

Cliff made a little acquisition on the repair and restoration side of things called George Holdings and the eponymous seller who has stayed on board is being invited by Bill to come over and see how things are changing shape in our manufacturing business under its new head. Once that has happened, Cliff himself is coming for more or less the same reason if at a slightly higher level and it would be beneficial for said George to meet all the senior managers, including from the Operations side, to help knit together our growing Leisure Division. Perhaps events will be more social than strictly business but that will be no bad thing.

Social is certainly an apt description for this scene in the roof-top bar of the Albany Hotel in Nottingham where, by the time I arrive, one George is literally rolling on the carpet not in a drunken stupor but convulsed with laughter. When he has regained a modicum of composure he starts to explain what had set him off. To do so he asks each of the Bell-Fruit Manufacturing managers in this group to explain again the different roles played during the course of today in different meetings in different locations. The explanation proffered was just incredible. They had all met for this early morning meeting in the boardroom to go through an agenda on the vital subject of conceptual design only to reconvene minutes after it ended in another room under another committee heading with the same people and so on and so on until the day drew to its weary close and the chairman of all the meetings, the new boss man Fred, went home and the rest all retired to the haven of the Albany Hotel.

What George wanted educating on was if there was so much to discuss and decide upon, why didn't they just have one bloody big meeting in one place with one agenda and then get on with some work for God's sake? And he had come all the way from Australia to learn something! He was again reduced to peels of laughter that might well have been sub-titled as ridicule. I was aware of the rumblings in the ranks about Fred being all front and bluster and has Aussie George instantly put his finger on the root of the problem? Has the autocratic and austere Johnson been swapped for a super pseudo-democratic waffler? Can this man actually take decisions, what decisions have been taken so far and what were the consequences? I intend to dig into this before things go too far, meantime George can come home and have dinner with June and I. See what else he has picked up.

Bill has gone to inordinate lengths to make Cliff feel welcome. The private dining room at the Victoria Club has been booked and the special menu agreed as accompanied by really good French wine. Gordon and his divisional directors are there as well as all the Bell-Fruit Manufacturing heads of departments. It is a truly splendid occasion and the more so as Cliff is accompanied by his wife who no one here apart from Bill, Gordon and myself have met before and therefore there is much social catching up to be done. How does an English rose take to the Australian redneck etc?

At any rate it was truly splendid until the drinks finally hit her, him, both. This delightful couple have obviously learned to participate in true Aussie style so it must be the French muscling in that has upset the grape applecart so to speak. A disagreement between man and wife can start quietly and politely enough, but it can develop. Notwithstanding the advanced conversationally diplomatic skills of Bill and to a lesser extent Gordon and me, the storm is now raging and it's lashing the pair against dangerous group harmony rocks. Remember that Gordon had been out to Aussie to help things along and he in particular is not taking kindly to the little wife "being banished to the shit hole of Sydney." It's a big shame and I feel very sorry for Bill buttonholed in this most elegant of locations. He is supposed to be showing off his far-flung trophies. Instead they are being melted down and poured in public over his very bald head. Gordon is the first to leave the room for a pee but we all know he is destined for the upstairs bar and with a look at Bill, I am second. When did Bill and Louis decide to divest of the Australian interests?

There is an outcome from the Cope Allman International's Strategic Planning Committee. For the Leisure Division the answer is *bolt-on acquisitions*. At first I thought we were being asked to buy a nuts and bolts business which seemed strange when the manufacturing plant must go electronic or die and when the engineering division was being downscaled. Or maybe we could get a bolt from the blue, that is, something unexpected if unwelcome but as it turned out I should have been thinking more in terms of shooting one's bolt. A firm of outside consultants whose main claim to fame was that they were secretive had come up with two complementary ideas for growth. First, we could use our finely honed management skills to manage something different from what we did now but that was leisure orientated. Secondly, we could make more use of our present skills by applying them in different directions.

When I thought about this, the logic was obvious. We could have a bash at just about anything. And we did. Ladies dressing hair. Ladies going to the loo. Ladies behind the bar. I think the study group must have had a male bias. Of-course this thinking pre-dated the theories of *stick to the knitting* and *identify the core skill and cut back to it and concentrate solely on it* or something of the sort. It is important to be empirical. Make sure you have proved it is wrong before devising the new theory.

Meanwhile, Tony Darling wasn't having much success in taking over from Gordon. They all worked for Gordon. He knew it. They knew it. It did not help that Tony was the antithesis of an analyst and as I had established, the Operation was grounded in statistical detail. One had to get to grips with the nuts and bolts (there we go again) to get on the wavelength of the managers. Tony was more your marketing front man, a kind of latter day Allen but without the contacts, and so it was terribly easy for Gordon in open meeting to ask him a specific question knowing that the answer would be largely irrelevant. From a start point where Tony was super confident glowing with Bill's assurance that he would take charge in due course and through a phase when he tried physically to take over by direct contact with the divisional directors, he had been reduced to a bit player who would be asked from time to time if he had any marketing angle on this or that.

A pattern was emerging. Bill was not pushing Gordon over much on loosening the reins and in turn Gordon was buying a few of the latest Bell-Fruit Manufacturing machines to help out Fred. Meantime jovial Geordie Fred himself was being looked at somewhat sideways and aside from his management style his use of nicknames was getting on everyone's nerves. I told him if he called me Johnny just one more time, I would start to call him something not nice. What with Keith's politically correct language that no one could fathom and the new Mike Peace's apparent quiet deviousness, the new blood/succession planning from Bill was beginning to seem like a Gordian knot. Where is Alexander the Great coming from? But no matter for now, let the pot simmer for a while.

As regards diversification, what about ladies hairdressing. What? And if we want to expand the scope of the role of the service engineer, what about ladies' personal hygiene. What about it? And if electronics are taking over the manufacturing of fruit machines, why not apply electronics and technology and stuff to the Operations, show the brewers we are in the vanguard of development. Well yes. And, we could think about starting a new business from scratch using the brewery sites as a captive audience, a sort of test-bed for automating the bar perhaps. We could?

What a lot to think about. Where to start? Lets go back to the beginning, what's all this about ladies hairdressing?

I seem to be standing at the back for most of this flight to Cincinnati as that way one can smoke and drink and chat in reasonable comfort whereas we are packed liked sardines in the so-called seating area and I feel too much like an intellectual sardine to stay put for too long at a stretch in what passes for a seat. Tony Darling is fast asleep and has been for hours and is coming along because of his now well recognised specialisation of marketing. The next flight is infinitely more interesting because as the pilot helpfully points out, we are tracking the mighty river Mississippi on our southerly journey to Memphis. Looking down on that truly awesome river flow I am back in my bedroom at Red Barn Farm completely buried in Tom Sawyer and not even knowing yet that Uncle Harold has Huckleberry Finn up his sleeve. I am feeling home-sick, it's making me weepy. Not for the new life but for the farm life. Why didn't my dad buy more land and make a proper business of it? Then I could have stayed at home and taken over and done a proper job instead of this stupid world of commerce with its bigoted plotting bastards. What is the point of much of it? There is no-one to answer.

Fantastic Sam brings me back to reality. He would bring anybody back to reality, or is it fantasy? When he was young he had this brilliant idea about ladies hairdressing. It came whilst waiting for his mother in the local salon. The place was small, dingy, uncomfortable and the best girl whom his mum liked had gone and the appointment system was up the spout and what should have been her treat was just another of life's interminable drags. It should all be changed: he would change it. And so Fantastic Sams was conceived. It was based on a few simple marketing concepts that we needed to take on board if the business was to migrate successfully to the UK, of course after reading and signing the confidentiality agreement.

The most vital ingredient was separating the hairdresser from human persona. If a client gets to know the hairdresser personally then once that *operative* gets big headed and leaves to set up on her own, so the client migrates with her. Bad business. The clients visit a *chair* and that chair has a position name, for example Sunshine or Lulubelle or Betsy. That way the relationship is cemented but impersonalised, get it? Next, there is no appointment system yet no waiting. Waiting is the death knell. The staffing levels must match the client flow, get it? The salon is bright, airy, welcoming, cheerful and clients are greeted personally by the manager. Of course, it is no longer just ladies, but a whole family experience and for the kids there is the Fantastic Sam Fun Machine that for a few dimes goes mildly bonkers with all sorts of flashing lights, noisy happenings like hands shooting out and finally dispenses a small prize. Accessories are part and parcel of the business model. All the products are branded Fantastic Sams and it's a two way cut. The suppliers are required to package according to the brand and to price down for the bulk sales and the customers will buy $1 of hair treatment product for each $1 of hair dressing price.

The staff are highly skilled and cannot work for Fantastic Sams without the passing out certificate in hair care. This certificate is awarded by the Fantastic Sams Institute that each person has paid to attend on a full-time basis, get it? The business has grown from a single outlet in the same small town that Sam's mother went to, to a national franchise chain. Each year there is a convention attended by all the franchisees and Sam addresses the business partners and together new ideas are formulated. It's the Fantastic Sams family, get it?

Tony and I wonder over drinks that night if the marketing concepts will travel to an Anglo Saxon culture but get diverted by a casual chat to a man at the bar who apparently travels the world with the professional golf circuit. No, he isn't a golfer himself, he repairs the sticks they use (or whatever they are called) and yes it is a full-time occupation and let us make no mistake about it, a very profitable one and would we like another drink on his tab and by the way had we seen the report on television that evening of the near miss of two planes earlier that day close to Cincinnati? We check the story next morning in the Memphis Times (or similar) and according to the detailed timings, one of the planes could well have been ours.

We decide to treat today's session with Sam in a more light-hearted vein starting with the observation that Sam himself is more bald than myself and close to Bill and do we really need the meeting fixed up with his in-house lawyer to go through all the legal framework of the business. It is ironic that my eventual report to the board back home will not be overly optimistic and will lead to the venture being still-born whilst one of Tony's little side lines during and after his tenure with us will be ladies hair-dressing.

It is an ill wind one supposes. Talking of which, I plucked up courage just before we left Memphis (of which place itself we saw precisely nothing apart from the obvious observation that the blacks did all the menial tasks such as cleaning the cars and sweeping the drives and opening the post) to ask Sam how it was that he came to marry his first wife when throughout our visit he had constantly and unceasingly reviled her. That prompted a retort that is impossible to ever forget and may well serve as a lesson to all aspiring beaus " because I was young, dumb and full of cum." Goodbye Fantastic Sam.

A few weeks later I am to meet a very different sort of American who, in down-town Miami, is enthusing about a device that automatically dials your customer or potential customer and pretends to be you and records their response and then tells you what to mail out and to whom and all whilst you are asleep. Just like our electronic experiments to come soon, it is way ahead of its time and when eventually it does hit the UK market it is destined to drive normally balanced individuals like myself first into torrents of fury and then round the twist.

But for now on this swelteringly hot January day, I am interested to learn that poor New York is snowbound and the tourists are stranded and I am baffled by the game of and the frenetic betting accompanying Pelota and astonished to be eating black bananas. The stewardesses on Lakers Sky Train have a special attribute. They can fail to find any change for a twenty-pound note handed over for a whisky. They can fail many times over, as if it's a battle of attrition and the odds are that the punter will get fed up or fall asleep before the elusive pay-back is located. Sky Train my arse. Sky or ground, do it right or don't bother.

A bolt-on acquisition is to buy a business that expands the scope of what one does utilising some existing skill. The type of business will be different from the main one of course since if it wasn't then the deal would be a normal expansion acquisition to take advantage of perceived benefits of scale like cutting the combined overheads, buying in greater bulk and therefore more cheaply, and so on. Think of a bolt-on acquisition as a trailer or caravan purchased to be pulled by your existing car, as distinct say from a self-propelled mobile home. The point is that the car already exists and so the motive power is already there, it does not have to be purchased again to do the extra job of towing the trailer. The trailer itself needs no overhead of an automotive force, as the mobile home does, since it piggy-backs onto an existing force. Therefore we have *bolted-on* an extra resource to a present facility. As Fantastic Sam would have said were he not in Memphis but in Nottingham, get it?

Of-course if you think about it a bit more deeply, your original car was not specifically intended to pull something behind it whereas the mobile home was always thought of as a single power unit. I mean the car will pull the trailer, of course it will. But it will need some adaptation, a towing bar for instance, heavy duty light flashers for instance. More importantly though, the car will have to be driven in a different sort of way. Now it is not alone. However neat the connection, weight has to be pulled and this will require a different use of gears or if the transmission is automatic, the use occasionally of a manual override to the gears. When going downhill, some push will occur and this needs to be countered by a change of driving style. More fundamentally still, your car was not designed originally to be anything other than a car. Add something to be pulled and it will not be an efficient fit for purpose device and relative to something that is, it will labour under a disadvantage. Something else, if the performance of your car comes under pressure, say for instance it is not being maintained properly or it is just aging and in any case newer models are on the market with more advanced technology, you might find having to look after the caravan at best a distraction and at worst a retardant. You might even find yourself having to choose between the two as to where your attention is best directed and since you had the car first and understand it better, the caravan will take a back seat. Unfortunately for you though in this most competitive of worlds, your rival the mobile home man still has his foot on the gas (to quote Fantastic Sam again). He is very good at what he does, he has to be because it's his livelihood.

But we are all sold on the theory of better utilisation of existing skills. No-one, including me, has thought through the practicalities consequentially. It will take a new man altogether to advise us to "stick to the knitting". In the new millennium, we all understand the rationale behind focus, concentrating on that which one is good at, outsourcing to others the peripheral activities, passing volume activity to low cost countries and retaining high skill value added work. But this is the 1980's and the pedigree of CAI is of a conglomerate. If we can make the present skills sweat, that seems an excellent idea. And it actually originates from the consultants brought in to look at the whole group, not just our division, and they have a thumping (if secretive) reputation as strategic advisers. It might cross a few senior management minds that if the bolt-on acquisition policy fails, the blame can be laid-off. But it did not by any stretch of the imagination engender one single spark of opposition.

The research threw up a company deep into ladies loos. The key point is that our Operations workforce is split in equal part between *collectors* (female) and *service engineers* (male). We all know that the collectors are fully loaded. It is a difficult job mentally and even more tough physically. It is a young ladies' game because of the energy required and the girls must be good fast car drivers and extrovert by nature. Because of this profile, the majority will have small children so the job must be slotted in between the morning and afternoon school run.

Would you fancy breezing into a typical British pub at 9 o'clock in the morning to empty the fruit machine amid the smell of stale beer and fag fumes and noisy cleaners and grumpy landlords and lecherous draymen and then walk onto the street with a bag full of cash? It takes a certain and rather wonderful woman to do that. Having been out on the rounds with several collectors, I am a great fan and am actively trying to protect them from the excessive enthusiasm of our own internal security teams who are want to lurk behind corners and pounce on the slightest pretext. Such accosts can involve very personal searches. It happens to be one thing that Gordon and I disagree on. He is right to be hot on security but I do not like some aspects of how it is practised or the independence of the internal police. I feel the same about a separate personnel department. Managers are paid to manage. Human resources and security both fall within my definition of management. One day I will change things. Anyway, collectors cannot be asked to do more.

Not so engineers. Although we have our own radio waveband and base-to-mobile communications system, engineers have time on their hands as an inevitable consequence of the ad-hoc nature of faults arising. Collections follow a routine pattern and can be loaded with work but engineers wait to be called out and once out can get involved in lengthy diagnostics and repair. But the trouble is, the vast majority of calls are simple coin jams that may take mere minutes to fix. As a result, it is extremely difficult to set the optimum population of a machine estate for one specific engineer given the wide variation in type of fault to fix and especially in rural areas or anywhere with low density cover because travel time is also a key factor. All in all your engineer might be in the depot having a fag, still at home, visiting his girlfriend or doing a spot of shopping. We will have to accept all this because during the last hour of pub business each evening, he will be needed all over the place and we offer a maximum two hour response time to call out. Or, actually, will we have to accept all this? This is where bolt-on fits in.

This company in Surrey has built a big business servicing ladies toilets and of course a good place to start stems from the knowledge that all females above and below a certain age have a periodic event. Anything that is regular is predictable and can be planned for and therefore become a source of ready work. It is not difficult to persuade the toilet custodian to offload (today lets say outsource) this particular service as it has always fallen into the unmentionable category as I have discovered on a number of occasions when going through a typical profit & loss account looking for cuts, "never mind what that is, it is not cuttable."

All this is explained over a nice dinner in a gorgeous hotel in Castle Combe just south of the M4 and in the village that apparently was used to film the quay-side scenes of a popular Sunday evening series The Onedin Line about seafarers in the transitional era of sail to steam power. It's worth a mention in that the pretty spot is miles away from any sea. Not that the next meeting venue can measure up. It's their depot in East London where one eye is on your car outside to check that the wheels are not being nicked. The thing about the job itself is that it is quick and easy to execute and anyone with an established bunch of engineers can do it as an infill, so to speak, whereas they have much difficulty recruiting service engineers specifically for the task in hand. Our interest continues since having peeped at the books, here is a profitable outfit that maybe we might have a go at buying as a stand-alone.

In the event, it is a disaster. Just as it is mildly embarrassing when having a quiet pee for the woman cleaner or soap dispenser filler-up to breeze in, so it is for our hardened worldly fruit-machine engineer to enter the inner sanctum of the ladies' loo. Mind you, that is not what killed it. What did was priority and a mixture of the principles set out earlier. Not so much bolt-on as belt-up. Why should the service boss divert his precious engineer away from the hysterical wife of a pub landlord having a ten-thirty pm rant for someone to fix the one-arm bandit, to some poxy loo job that won't even be needed till tomorrow? And why should a service engineer take a call to visit such a loo at three pm when a pleasant time is being had with his girlfriend? Priorities you see. So the idea is dropped but not before money has been spent and productivity lost. Not to mention impairment to the high esteem that management had hitherto been held in. Sort of.

Meantime back at the ranch Bill has come up with a coup. He has stumbled across Reg Conway. Although in his early sixties, Reg is young at heart and bursting with energy. He has been in electronics and telecommunications and that sort of thing for all of his career and until recently was a senior director of a large company in that field, that is until a kind of retirement occurred. He had to be snaffled up quickly so in fact he has already been set on, salary, car, understanding on expenses etc but of course he will slot directly under me. Of course. The really big thing about Reg is that he has a thorough understanding of electronic data capture and if this knowledge could be applied successfully to sucking performance data out of our new breed of fruit machines then we could kill two birds with one stone, that is, impress our brewery customers and at the same time steal an efficiency march on our competitors. What will be particularly beneficial is that Reg has a good working relationship with the electronics faculty of Birmingham University that apparently has a first-class reputation in this area and positively breeds good software engineers. It's all very exciting and stimulating and opens up a whole new chapter.

Somewhere in the back of my head I think I hear a small voice that might be Gordon repeating what he said in the context of ex-Terry. "Bill falls in love."

This new chapter will go on for a few years and I will become inextricably entwined in it. At its peak, our new company LPE, of which I am MD and Reg is technical director, will employ twenty-five assorted electronic engineers and support staff and will be sponsoring batches of work at Birmingham University led by an Australian professor who is undoubtedly very clever and knows his stuff but who somehow never quite convinces at the key progress meetings. After umpteen prototypes or *marks* as Reg calls them, a working data capture unit is developed to the stage where our collector simply plugs the device into the back of the machine and after her shift takes it home not to make friends with the kids but to disgorge its contents into our special unit that talks to our mainframe computer. After many false dawns the achievement is a major breakthrough. We are the first in the industry to capture data electronically.

But nothing is perfect and in fact the whole industry

has been watching carefully. Pioneers are heroic but followers often take the biscuit. The brewers had formed a technical committee out of which a standard protocol had emerged. Was our technology compatible? Furthermore, rumours were circulating that the capture device itself might sit within the fruit machine and eventually be part of the manufacturing process. Of course the machines would be more expensive but that would be a capital cost (back to the old revenue/capital argument) and whether it could happen or not, doubts about funding our capture units were emerging.

It did not help that the workhorse collectors found the unit heavy and it was additional to all the other gear they carried, something had been added and nothing had been taken away. Why oh why must the pub managers and tenants and the site owners still insist on a printed paper receipt? The portable printer that our girls had to carry was becoming an Achilles heal. It kept on breaking down. Yes, we had done the donkey work but was there a pay-off?

Gordon was not a patient man and he was starting to square up to Reg. Deliver a workable product or give in. And there was a personal and deep-seated resentment building. During the war and as a young man, Gordon had been landed on the Southern tip of Italy and had fought his way to the North. Reg had been one of the boys in blue who should have made that passage easier but hadn't. Gordon had been riding his army issue motor cycle when it hit a landmine. His pillion passenger colleague soldier was killed outright, he was thrown clear and lived. Such things stick in the mind and Gordon had grown into a rottweiler. Reg was a terrier. The terrier will put up a good fight but ….. Anyway, Gordon had the power base of the whole Operation. Reg had a small new company and me.

What Reg did have was a personality. Bill had demonstrated once again his flair for picking a character. This little dynamo had made money in the past, testament to which was a splendid home in deepest Warwickshire now supplemented by a small bungalow near Nottingham airport at Tollerton to cut out daily travelling. The location was no coincidence since Reg was a pilot. He was a few other things as well. Whilst it is common for most of us to own a succession of motor bikes or cars or both as we drift through life, it is less common not to dispose of the last model. Reg had disposed of nothing.

In his stables in Warwickshire, they were all there, right back to his very first Jaguar,. Reg was a hoarder and still a collector. That is how he met his Nottingham girlfriend. She was the wife of a disabled man who had advertised his classic motor bike because he could no longer use it and needed the money. Neither could he use his wife and she needed the sex. The spark with Reg was greater than any from the classic bike and the little bungalow at Tollerton became Reg's second home in every sense. It developed into a loving and beautiful and mutually beneficial relationship.

There must be some correlation between the heartache and frustration of trying to get something new off the ground and opening up ones heart to a fellow sufferer. There is no other logical explanation for why Reg is telling me all about what is going on in his private world especially after this very bad day when it now seems virtually certain that our data capture unit will not become the industry standard and when Gordon has almost certainly decided not to buy any more for his estate. There is always a deep-down reason for any even vaguely off-convention action and Reg has found consolation in his new girlfriend because his real wife down in Warwickshire is an alcoholic. And a real one. Not someone who likes a drink, gets a bit tipsy sometimes, has difficulty coordinating sometimes. No, a real one. But Reg speaks fondly of her. She was an excellent mother, but the emphasis is on the past. She still makes a good meal for him when he gets back home and he laughs out loud relating the tale of when he flew back from Germany in the little single engine aeroplane that hit a bad storm and how his wife was lying behind the pilot's seat shrieking in terror as the plane bounced around the sky. But he is close to tears as he weeds the herbaceous border and uncovers another unopened bottle of gin.

He plays the classic guitar too. It has pride of place hanging in the small lounge at Tollerton. It melts the heart of his new girlfriend but he did not play it for me because we are never there together. I will be there with someone else. A different start point but the same faltering steps into a brave new world.

The second big new project for LPE was the electronic pub. Reg had been trying to get a meal in a restaurant and couldn't find a waiter never mind actual food. So the big idea came. Why not bypass the middle man and get directly to the source. Electronics could do this. There could be a keypad on, or better still built into, the restaurant table (the word tactile entered our vocabulary) notifying the kitchen of what dish was wanted and furthermore it could hold the prices so that it would concurrently be storing the bill. We huddle in a thinking session - brain storming is yet to be coined but it will come - and decide we know nothing about restaurants but a lot about bars to which the same principles could be applied.

We may not have succeeded in inventing a world beating portable data capture device but we did kick start the brewing industry into accepting electronic data capture as a concept so why not automate their bar and while we are at it, we could spew the takings data into an in-house computer and link it to the now accepted industry protocol electronic performance data stored in the fruit machines. When you think about it, we could even wire up the pool table and the pin table and has anyone ever thought of inventing an electronic dartboard? Bill is OK with all this, we can quietly wind down the data capture and divert the team to developing the electronic pub. After all, our clever little backroom boys have provided much quality discussion at the various industry committee forums, but we will keep our new thing quiet for a while.

Back to Aussie and going Dutch

One should not feel low on a warm summer morning away from the office on a lusciously green playing field but I'm watching Craig who is goalkeeper and as he spots me and turns to wave some inconsiderate runt of a kid kicks a ball past him and scores. Craig looks as if he is about to cry. It is the worst possible thing that could have happened just as I turned up. I shout across that it wasn't his fault but mine, but this is not why I am low. I am low because my rare hour of freedom is cupboard love. I am here to say goodbye. For three weeks anyway but it will seem a lifetime. With the expanding turmoil at work I live increasingly for Chris and Craig and for the weekend with its cricket and football and swimming and tennis and anything else we can get in. And I'm waving goodbye as I walk slowly away from the field and the lump in my throat is so large that I can barely swallow. It's no better in the VIP departure lounge at Heathrow, June was fine on the telephone but the boys were out playing and I missed them. Another expenses paid trip to Sydney, there should be euphoria but it got buried the day Bill and Louis asked me to go back for a second time. It does need sorting and it's good they want me to do it but it's the middle of July and the blackcurrants are ready for picking and more than ever I need my garden and my boys for my sanity.

There is an air of seriousness about this trip down under, even foreboding. Cliff's figures have not improved and the Victoria Club affair is still in sharp focus. This time the Aussie managers know me and where I fit in the scheme of things. The shadowboxing is over. The flights will be direct, no stopping off en-route, no messing about. It is fortunate that my leisure market researcher is back in Australia and has promised a few trips out. The Blue Mountains have been mentioned and so maybe this might balance the blue language and black atmosphere that I expect to encounter. The organist playing Bach at the Opera House stops in mid-flow to turn to tell his audience that only in Australia would one of their number shout out during his concert and the man on the beach with his wife and two small children trots off to the bottle shop and returns with a bottle of white, of red and of port that are nonchalantly consumed during the picnic for these two adults. Everything is a bit not quite right. Neither is the factory. It will have to go.

Spain has gone. Australia has gone. Cui bono. Those now in London I suppose. Seems to me if one has the courage, or is it bravado, to start something then it should be persisted with or at least turned into something sellable. Unless of course the market has gone and in these two countries it has not. But the people then are not the people now so like real politic, it's easy to blame someone else. Bill is saying that Gordon is not, as everyone assumes, a good manager. A successful one, yes, but it has been due to the right set of circumstances. If he was, would Holland be in the mess it is? No-one but Gordon has been in charge and in principle the operation is precisely the same as it is over here. Well we had better be involved before that goes the way of Spain and Australia, get over there whether Gordon likes it or not.

Well it's all very pleasant really. Gordon uses this small private family-run hotel on the canal side in Amsterdam. The food is good and the place is discreet. Well it would be, it was originally recommended by our super sales director in London and was his first leg on the frequent world tours of customers. There is much to commend a small snug private lounge like this with its well padded leather backed arm chairs. Who wants to be in the gaze of Joe Public in the big tourist hotels? It is definitely conducive to chat and we have been swapping life stories and I heard myself coming to the surprising conclusion that it was the purchase of my Vespa scooter that broke me from Newton life, the place, the people, the trap.

Mobility is geography and geography is freedom, well if not exactly freedom a bigger pond as they say; must be the whisky. But deep down I know I am right. Why has it taken so long to unearth this? Is it of any worth? Definitely. It started a pattern of value. Singapore, India, Bulgaria, Spain, Australia and here I suppose and it must, absolutely must, continue. Some would say pleasant too in this the red-light district with the amazing array of sex shops and impossibly sized dildos and the ladies in the windows. Is this a fundamental national characteristic difference between the Dutch and the Spanish I wonder. One is behind glass whilst the other is in your face, so to speak.

But it is different as we move inland to the heart of the Dutch Operation and through the villages with names impossible to pronounce and containing seemingly all the letters of the alphabet twice over, and contrasting sharply with the small neatly painted wooden houses with their small neatly manicured gardens. And after the mandatory site visits, that is, a glass of pure acid in each bar expectantly indistinguishable as owned by the monopoly brewer, I am looking at figures that don't add up and a property tax return more bent than Gaudi's Casa Mila. And is this the common thread? Has our man in Holland put his knowledge of Dutch and all things Dutch to really good effect, just like our ex-man in Spain? Has he been making continental sausage meat of off-site machines and on-site income? It is an apt conclusion to draw once one discovers that before marrying his Dutch lady he was an English butcher. I report to Bill that we will have to cut back to near carcass and then see if the trimmed animal can still run and gain weight under closer supervision.

Shedding labour in Holland is an easier decision to take than implement in this dress rehearsal for when little England gets sucked into the inflexible, employee biased and financially punitive European labour laws. Our man in Holland knows this and is going to make us sweat especially in relation to his own tender skin. But then, pitch-forking hay bales to my dad on the cart, winter digging the vegetable garden, walking from Edale onto Kinder without a pause and now knocking eight bells out of a squash ball, profuse sweating has always been a conquerable affliction.

With the geographical and new product external horizons losing perspective, Bill's eyes would inevitably turn inward. Suppose there is a hidden but large cost centre. Suppose it is located roughly in a patch where there is a super-profitable business. Suppose you want to raise the profile of a past mistake either cynically to have it taken away through sheer embarrassment or more constructively to partly or wholly solve the problem. Stand back because Bill has quietly planted a seed. It pushes its head above the soil within days and looks harmless enough. But it is growing unnaturally quickly and can you see that it has tentacles. They are already entwining and appear to be forming a word. That word becomes clearer and clearer until unmistakable. It spells out BILSTON. Bilston is in the West Midlands, the once heartland of British manufacturing from machine tools through to the machines themselves and the things the machines automate such as motor cars.

Our West Midlands problem is not to do with cars but with bicycles, tens of thousands of them. We can start with a disaster leading to an urgent need demanding attention. When CAI was put together as a conglomerate, Len Machin authorised the purchase of a cycle manufacturer. As to why, nobody seems to know. When later the divisions were being formed someone thought cycles equals leisure activity equals leisure division equals Bill; long before my time. These bikes were aimed at the higher end of the market. They had to be due to Raleigh in the middle and cheap imports at the bottom. The brand name was Viking and the niche was of a super lightweight aluminium constructed machine. The disaster occurred when the Vikings invaded America and an unfortunate young man hit a rut that caused the front frame to snap and the broken off forks to impale him, or so the claim stated.

It was not as if the single claim of itself was too bothersome, huge as it was. Product liability insurance cover was in place and the lawyers believed a final settlement would be for a much lower amount. The real trouble stemmed from the American fondness for publicity, especially of the bad news kind, especially of the litigious kind. Word spread like wildfire amongst the leisure biking community and sales stopped virtually overnight. By the time some response was prepared, the story was over. Aside from the large loss of jobs, directly in the factory, indirectly with suppliers and the demise of the dealer network, where did the urgent need come from?

The purchasers of the business had not only taken on a manufacturing facility but also a long-term lease that still had, at the time of the collapse, fifteen of its original twenty-one years to run. And it was expensive and it carried a dilapidations clause demanding a fair sized annual provision and the building had to be kept secure and it had to be marketed. Because these running costs were deducted from Bill's Leisure Division net profit each month on consolidation at HQ, they gave him a slight but nagging headache. There were no fellow sufferers on the leisure management side simply because they knew nothing about it. It was all part of HQ group accounts, nothing to do with them. Well, it hadn't been, but I knew about it now. I was being handed the Bilston account in all its glory. Somehow it had fallen under my commercial brief.

Sometime down the line - for now the seed has only just poked its head through - Graham's leader in the West Midlands, one Barry Jackson, sums up the situation in a typically succinct West Midlands manner "Where the bloody hell is Bilston anyway." A weakened Gordon is listening to Bill's idea. It is clever if a surprise and unwanted, and it could bring big benefits, but some dangers are obvious and Gordon is quick to point them out. Nevertheless, Gordon is being steamrollered.

What Bill is saying is that the most important aspect is benefit to the whole of CAI (I happen to know that Gordon has been on a salary sacrifice for some years to fund additional pension rights and now good increases in salary during his last three years are very important given the excellent final-salary-based pension scheme). Maximum CAI Group profitability is what we must all strive for. The facts are these. The Bilston plant has 145,000 sq ft of enclosed space on one level spread over five interconnecting bays with excellent loading and unloading facilities and masses of parking space. It has good East, West and South access from junction 9 of the M6 and North access from junction 10. True it has no office accommodation as such but there are toilets and things at one end of bay 1 and a huge mezzanine floor. Ok, it's not central Birmingham but it is central to the West Midlands patch. Look, the capital ingoing costs will be funded by the Group and the running costs can be capped to those at the present Midlands Division HQ and think of the efficiency gain on space and productivity. A brand new office for Barry Jackson for a start.

In today's speak, this would be spin. At that time to ex-Canadian settled, ex-American influenced, ex- Italian campaign war veteran Gordon, it was bullshit. To Barry when I led him to the mezzanine floor, it was "a foot of solid pigeon shit." Which it was. It was also on this winter morning freezing cold, colder than outside in fact. The cold was trapped in and grew on itself. A suitable epitaph for Bilston. A brilliant idea from Bill, a bitter pill for Gordon. But Gordon was weak. Sometimes there is no option but to give in. The plan was to go ahead and as Bill said to me privately afterwards, once the dust (or whatever) has settled maybe I might think in terms of locating a whole-company off-site store there (as distinct from just the working stock of the West Midlands Division) and perhaps even a main computer centre. If so, what else could occupy the other bays? Who knows. So we move costs around, we engineer financial change. It is best for CAI in the long run.

Bill has another very clever idea. Lunch time eating and especially drinking and especially involving Gordon and his merry men, is out. Out of the building, out of all reasonableness, out of control. My LPE has developed its Electronic Pub hasn't it? Well we will create a dummy mock-up in our offices. Create an in-house pub/dining room, call it The Three Bells (the Bell-Fruit motif). Wow! We will put on a decent standard two-course lunch and limit drinks to two per person and all for £1 per day. If the executive has a business guest, then no charge will be made.

The deed is done. No expense is spared. There is even our three bells company motif woven into the carpet. Initially, Gordon rebels. No-one but no-one will dictate to him his lunch-time pursuit and in any case much of his business is personal to his managers and not for the flapping ears of all the rest of the hangers-on. But psychology is powerful and Bill has the high moral ground and things get more and more uncomfortable for Gordon. Gradually he succumbs. It helps that the new lady barmaid has served to reinforce my theory developed over the factory years that no system was even invented that Joe Bloggs (or in this case Joyce Bloggs) could not defeat. This lady, duly encouraged, has redefined any existing British Standard for what constitutes a drink. Two of her drinks is no deprivation. For now the score is Bill 2, Gordon 0.

Club machines

The role of the sweeper-up is not a pleasant or glamorous one. If this commercial brief is to continue, I want a spell in the forward line. An initiative is called for. All the profit and cashflow is still coming from the Operation and my continuing analysis shows that a minor product has the major margin. There is an antidote to the mass-site market as owned or controlled by the big brewers. This is the small private club and steeped in its historic Englishman's castle liberalism The private club is home to a special sort of gaming machine that can pay out a big jackpot because Joe Public cannot get at it, at least not until he becomes a member whether as conservative, working man, bowls player or yachtsman.

The reason the humble club machine is extra profitable is not because it is cheaper to buy than its pub counterpart but cheaper to operate. It has a much longer life (less depreciation), moves around much less (lower unit labour costs) and needs no collection service (club committee money-man does this with vigour since it is his main source of revenue). The big snag is that a club *route* is hard to build up requiring much patience and much pandering to each committee and no little insight into a town's various societies. But where a nice route exists, we could spend some *goodwill* and buy out the local club route owner. The proposal paper gains support, funds are allocated and my club machine acquisition programme gets underway.

Setting out to buy their business is of counterpoint. You know nothing, they know everything. To them it is unique, to you it is the same. To them it was a hard accumulation, to you it is easy maintenance. To you it is only the future, to them it is more history than it is even the present. To them it is a good price, to you as an integrator, it is cheap. So routes are sought out, pursued and gobbled up and the fragmented market is consolidating under our banner. I travel and talk and charm. My man Clive Mackintosh follows up with hard numbers and methodology and realism. It works a treat and goodwill is so slow to be written off. And the selling characters are a life's treat.

The giant from Colchester whose waddling huge frame stops all conversation dead in the restaurant of The George at Stamford in Lincolnshire and for whom the staff must find a special chair and whose share-holding family are so cross-bred as to defy unravelling and whose drink is Pimms No 1 and whose car is a green Rolls-Royce. Later he will treat us to his hometown oysters and put us up in the oldest hostelry. He has made a fortune. He is a fortune. Or the craggy creep in Scotland who wants to contribute to my favourite charity and has a little something for me to take away as a memento of this visit. Or the man who meets me at a service station on the A1 and agrees to sell in thirty minutes, my fastest ever deal. Or the deal in Liverpool big enough to justify completion in the Isle of Man, the presence of Gordon himself and my Spanish-speaking legal colleague Jeremy from London and where, by five pm in the hotel in Douglas, our little group hosted by the euphoric vendor and wife have consumed nineteen bottles of champagne. It was pleasing to still be able to count to nineteen.

But then the true gentleman from the North East with the wonderfully self-contained club business who joined my management team to continue to run it and who, at the end of the three-year contract, handed me his customary lobster even after I had handed him the sack "I only got it for you, you might as well take it". And all because he did not quite fit the by then new corporate culture. Business is a bugger, I lost a very good friend, sod the business.

Contrast the heart of London clubland brothers who turned their sale proceeds into a ocean-going yacht and a, very up-market, fish and chip restaurant in the Jewish concentrated North Finchley and at which the male customer on the next table has just swamped his juicy chunk of fresh cod with HP sauce. Tradition, one supposes.

In time, we have the largest consolidated club business in the UK and it will form a key element in a High Court case that claims that consequential profit was overstated due to the depreciation policy. But that was to misunderstand the concept of *real* depreciation. If I took much from Bell-Fruit, what did I give? A club business, that's what.

With the help of the enlarging club machine estate, the Operation as a whole has gone from strength to strength and as Gordon's divisions absorb their new prizes, so he and I become increasingly good buddies of ostensibly equal rank. Not just club routes are acquired, the taste for growth sharpens. Bill wants an East Anglian flank and he warms up the joint owners of the dominant player based in Norwich. It is a story that has an interesting start, middle and end.

The start of the day-one meeting on their patch is delayed because Bill's Jaguar car, that I am driving, will not take the hill up to Grantham in flat Lincolnshire on this freezing snowy morning so, nil desperandum, we are off to the little Nottingham airport at Tollerton. Bill's urgent discussion eventually causes this young man of nineteen or twenty years old or so to take us out onto the tiny runway and I assumed to meet the pilot who would be warming up the two-seater. Not so. Our young companion is the pilot. Not that that is much of a worry since of course all pilots have to be qualified and experienced. More so is the way we are bouncing about in these dark and stormy clouds and the nonchalant manner in which our captain is studying an ordinance survey map stretched over his knees and his invitation to reach behind us for the crate of beer bottles and why don't we help yourselves?

By the middle game when the acquisition might happen and then again it might not (this one is big and we do not want to seem over-enthusiastic) we now know that one of the joint owners is actually Mr Big. Or rather Mr Norwich on account of his extensive and long-standing business interests in that city but more specifically because he is chairman of Norwich City football club. The timing of our talks coincides with a clash between the high-flying Nottingham Forest and the lowly Norwich City (called The Canaries - maybe since they are a small club and can only afford players that are cheap, cheap). It is a home game for Forest and Mr Big invites Bill and me to the away team's directors compound. Always having hated soccer, I found great difficulty in understanding the thicker never mind the finer points of the encounter and it did not endear me to this senior Norwich person and more importantly the man with the final say on our potential purchase, when out of pure instinct I went along with the crowd and stood up and cheered like crazy when Forest scored. Of course the Norwich box was not the crowd. It was merely a silent minority. Bill had the good grace to desist.

At the end we appear to be, unusually, rushing through the completion agenda in this oak-panelled, legal tome-strewn board room in a wonderfully appointed building abutting Norwich cathedral. Even Jeremy our London lawyer is having a job keeping up but at least we ought to get away in reasonable time and it's a pig driving from Norwich no matter where one is heading. As the papers are gathered, hands shaken and photographs taken, the secretary comes in bearing a tray holding a single cut-glass tumbler with liquid and ice and lemon. She says it is four-o'clock, her legal boss's gin and tonic time.

Anyway the king is dead, at any rate the two owners are. That matters not because they did not actually run the business we have just bought. Barry Vail runs the show and he will slip nicely into our set-up as an ex senior director of our main national competitor. Mind you, this particular Barry is used to his independence and he will have to report to Gordon and the very last sticking point before we agreed the deal was who would inherit the 7-series BMW that was virtually brand new and formed part of the company assets. Bill thought Barry could use it. Gordon saw it as a good car for himself, after all he was a sizeable man in stature. If no agreement is reached, the vendors would buy it back. Finally it is settled, Gordon will take it. The corporate score is now Bill, 2 – Gordon, 1.

The acquisition deals keep coming. It's an orgy. Devon, Scottish Highlands and Islands, North Wales. I am everwhere. I have two men full-time hauling the fish in. Bill's point is that we are only spending the money the Operation has made and is making. Somehow, wily old fox engineering Jim Cameron has got himself onto the Leisure Division board. He is talking about leaking buckets. Are we topping up the estate only to have it leak away at the bottom? Are we topping up because we haemorrhage? Nasty. But the quality end of the estate as a whole is going from strength to strength and not just due to the acquisitive growth. There are now not even token purchases from Bell-Fruit Manufacturing. Gordon cannot be criticised for buying from outside manufacturers. The manufacturing turnaround has not worked. Successful machines are not coming through. Bill presents his master plan for saving the factory. The board agrees to support it. Fred is to go. Louis sees no point in searching for another factory supremo, after all it's been Bill's baby all along really and his is the blueprint for putting things right so he should take direct charge, he will be appointed MD of Bell-Fruit Manufacturing as well as Chairman of the Leisure Division. Jim goes over to Bill and shakes his hand and jokes "you're in the direct line of fire now Bill."

John G. Smith

A new man at the top

Bill has a glamorous new and very experienced top-level secretary/PA named Miss Vicky May. All the boys are betting on the odds. She urges me into Bill's inner sanctum where Rodin's thinker still holds his head in his hands. This is a grave chat over coffee. Louis has been sacked. The non-executives have voted him out. The most senior of these is a long standing member of the main CAI board and a sitting MP and the senior partner of a firm of stockbrokers. I can only listen and recall being told by Bill some time ago how he had indignantly pilloried this man for his firm making a stock transaction mistake. This was not being accepted and was not going to be corrected and Bill was getting really angry. Mmm. Apparently Louis's replacement has already arrived -must have been on the cards for a while, how long? - and Bill was not at liberty to give his name yet.

The whole climate had changed. The whole culture had changed. Louis had been cold, not autocratic but more aristocratic, distant, aloof. New man Mike Doherty was preaching about getting involved, knowing the businesses well but at the same time empowering the people and sticking to the knitting. We did not need to go to London anymore for meetings, he would come to us. Quite a change. He reminded me of that breath of fresh cigarette smoke that wafted in to PW Nottingham from Newcastle. Tall, close up, wanting detail and another heavy cigarette smoker. How was he getting on with Bill? I could not tell. Now it was closed doors. Miss May had gone into her beautiful shell. Then it just happened, right out of the blue. Mike telephoned me. Bill was leaving. He would be back now and again to clear up but he had been relieved of his responsibilities. From today, I reported directly to him.

Years later my wife and I were sitting in our favourite

restaurant in Plumtree called Perkins, the ex-railway station quiet place tucked away from the hustle and bustle, the one Gordon had first introduced me to for an out-of –the-way lunchtime chat, when I spotted Bill and his wife Sue at a nearby table. There was no great rush to shake hands or slap on the back for old times' sake, just a polite greeting "didn't know you used this place" kind of affair. For the man who had taken me on, pushed me on, made me his appointed heir, extended the invitation to the Christmas gathering at Holbrook Hall with the choir on the front lawn, insisted I join him "for the best breakfast in town" when in London, insisted on me staying at Grosvenor House in London, The Menzies in Sydney, No 1 Knob Hill in San Francisco, it was surreal. More surreal was the fact that this was the first time we had seen each other or even spoken since that call from Mike. He had returned to the Leengate office in Lenton, Nottingham many times. Was Miss May tasked with watching what was going on? Who knows. The rumour spread that he couldn't keep away but eventually the visits stopped and Bill really was no more. There was no formal communication internally or externally. I was to learn that this was Mike's style. Whether coincidentally or not, Peter once said in another context that "for a senior executive, doing nothing is very powerful, it is a decision in its own right." It seemed very poignant at the time but as time passes, more so.

I am very worried. Our combined businesses based locally are headless. A list of group executives arrives. It is to do with a review of personnel benefits. I am not on it. Trying not to sound panicky, my call to Mike early next morning gets the call-back response that it is a mistake, not to be concerned, I have a future with the group, carry on as normal. Mmm, again.

My two boys are still young, I still have a big mortgage even after paying off more than the minimum over these last years. I am in a good top-hat pension scheme and have been paying advanced voluntary contributions (AVC's) to make the pot bigger and have good life insurance cover through the company but if I get the heave-ho, I will be in a mess. A big mess. It turns out the bets were laid on the wrong horse. The Jim with the engineering anvil motif on the cap has won. The Bill with the three bells motif on the shirt has lost. Step forward the Jim men, shudder the Bill ones. I know I am right. When will the hatchet fall? A study of the new CAI organisation chart confirms that when once I was number two in the biggest division, now I sit as a very lowly MD with some functional responsibility for various central services. Backed the wrong horse boy, cuillere de bois. And no-one ever said a word, it all just happened. Just like a game of chess against Garry Kasparov. Except I didn't even know I was playing chess, never mind who I was up against.

The Sword of Damocles seems appropriate except I'm no sycophant (am I?) and Mike no Dionysius in that surely a tyrant communicates. Isn't that the very essence of pressure? Yet there are no memos, no telephone calls, only silence. And I soon decide to stop calling him since the only detectable reaction, if any, is irritation. Cold sweats and that nauseating gripe in the pit of the stomach now occur on a frequent if unpredictable basis. Why do I keep thinking of the original John Smith and all he achieved? I genuinely had begun to see myself as the agent of atavism. Fool.

No-one to talk to either. Confidence oozing away. It is the waiting that is the problem. Waiting, wondering, not knowing. Then, at a meeting in Nottingham, Mike drawing deeply on his cigarette expresses a view that this rabbit-warren of an old Tannery building that we own and occupy at Leengate could be better utilised. That is, released for development. We, the Operations HQ people ought to have a modern building with up-to-date facilities. He hands me this as a project. I am taken aback. Was he genuine when saying I had a role in the new set-up? Maybe not so cant?

My endowed and delectable if of subdued charisma secretary Sue, now starts the desk-top search. It's the blind leading the blind but she sends me off walking the city looking at empty places with some parking, with no parking, with lifts, with no lifts, open plan, little boxed offices, ground floor, top floor, all floors. What a bloody job. Then I find the perfect place. Recently abandoned by a large insurance company, it has the right floor area on two levels only, huge car parking space and best of all faces the famous Forest park and playing field area of Nottingham with its open green views and best of all the promise each October of the world famous Goose Fair. The lease is negotiable with an ingoing rent-free holiday and there will be minimum in-going costs. Perfect and it hasn't taken me long.

My report is bullish, clear and precise and confident. At the next board meeting, Mike breaks off to view this proposal, walks smartly around the building and returns pronto to the meeting. He lights his next fag, leans back in his chair and throws the next pebble in the new corporate pond. Have we thought of the new Bell-Fruit Manufacturing R&D building sitting immediately behind us where the old labyrinth machine shops used to be? Building such a plush facility was another indulgence of the old management and now that Jim had reorganised the brand new manufacturing plant across the road, it was feasible to fit the software guys into a secured corner of it. The R&D block would need modifying but it was worth a thought. We could sell off the old Operations building, invest capital in the existing R&D block and release funds for CAI. John could now work to this plan having had a good look around the town.

Very logical and easy for an outsider to see. I was beginning to appreciate the brain behind the helm. Obviously motions had to be gone through first and Smith could be spared as the instrument leading to a pre-ordained case. I must admit, I liked it. But, I felt no safer, in fact the opposite. This heralded a much different HQ outfit.

This property lark is incestuous. Sales agents beget architects, beget quantity surveyors, beget structural engineers, beget consultant engineers, beget planners, etc, etc. It's enjoyable really, a bit like being leader of the orchestra. Wave up the big drum here, draw out the first violin there, encourage the little piccolo, stop dead the tuba. What you cannot do and what's frustrating is to tell the leading cellist to leave. He/she might be out of key and slow to respond and lack expertise but still that instrument is part of the orchestra now for better or worse.

Today it's called project management, then it wasn't called anything in particular except sell the old building, get a team together to plan, cost and implement the restructuring of the now ex-R&D block and, as would prove most difficult of all, construct a new car park. I would have though car parks were easy. Level the ground, throw in some tarmac and draw some white lines. Unfortunately, the river Leen runs underneath our site and this place really was a tannery. A bedrock of animal skins overlaying a river is, apparently, not ideal for any structural purpose as this complicated technical report from the experts who were brought in to drill the exploration holes is explaining.

Then there was Mr Zodeh. This small neatly dressed man has perhaps the most smiley, pleasant, beaming face of anyone I have ever met, even including my badminton playing colleague Lawrence from Singapore. Sue has ushered him in because his bid, remarkably and surprisingly, is by far the highest of those responding to our sale advert for the office complex we all still occupy. He wants to show me the detailed plans that his brother has drawn up following their earlier walk around. To me they are absolutely amazing. They can construct ninety-odd self contained flats all with their own private entrance. Look, here is the luxury one made out of this very office we are sitting in.

We discuss the terrible events in Beirut. Mr Zodeh and his brother are Lebanese. They have had to get out but will return to their beautiful homeland one day. They are serious. They have the money in cash. No problem there. Mr Zodeh will continue to smile through the whole tortuous process, no problem with this, no problem with that. One cannot but admire those that have a dream and make that dream a reality. In a foreign land and with a starting point of a high risk capital price far above the local firms (had the clique all got together?), my personal preference was never in doubt. Sold to the board with the reckless air of someone who believes it is his last job anyway, only Jim's little doubts about funds and sources of funds dent the excitement. Mike seems unconcerned.

But, smiley Mr Zodeh, you made me sweat. Funds in tranches. Funds via New York. Jim so nearly scored another bull's-eye, so nearly claimed another scalp. But he didn't. We all moved out, the Zodeh clan moved in and the flats got built and sold. My beaming friend even offered me the first apartment to be finished at a special discounted price. I thought about it and was tempted, but declined. A year later, I would regret this decision and sod the consequences. But then, none of us can see a year ahead, can we?

What about the pension?

I have decided to wage a war on the pensions front. Seems a bit silly in that I am still in the early years of what should be a twenty-nine year stint in the exceptionally good senior managers' tier of the fund with its final salary scheme benefits. Whilst I still enjoy the trappings of a senior manager, I am aware that in reality things are different. What Bill created is gradually being dismantled. Mike wishes to introduce a more modern contract of employment, one that will have a one-year rolling feature. One that will reduce any pay-off I might get eventually. Within my limited ability, some self-protection is called for.

Strengthening my pension position is feasible in two ways. First by opening a second fund by transfer from the deferred pension from Price Waterhouse (a delightfully termed Section 32, anyone who has ever tried to accomplish this whether successfully or not will almost certainly end up being sectioned) and secondly by undertaking the wonderfully evocative process of *additional voluntary contributions* or AVC's. In the event the Section 32 will take over eighteen months to unlock and the AVC's will take less time but keep me locked in until, if ever, I reach age 65.

Whilst deep into my pension purge, a missive comes from Mike covering substantial improvement in benefits under the existing scheme. It was unheralded and issued with no prior consultation. Much effort and one assumes some large professional fees must have gone into the groundwork for the changes and now that I am beginning to get a proper feel for this complicated field, the real improvements are that much more obvious. Since the opening paragraph of this six-page screed explains that the cost will be borne by CAI "and there will be no increase to your contributions", then obviously every single senior manager will be well pleased.

The most significant change is that pensionable earnings can be calculated as "basic earnings in the 12 months prior to retirement". It follows that the more senior one is so the higher are ones earnings, then the better the eventual pension. No-one will be too concerned about that, after all what is sauce for the goose is sauce for the gander, although of course the goose is a big fat one whilst the gander is small and lean. So, I can now look forward to a well rewarded retirement at age 62 rather than 65. Great. But 62 seems an awfully long way from here.

"I'm heading for your car John, its twelve-thirty, time for lunch." It was another of Gordon's coded messages that we need to talk. The first schooner of sherry hadn't quite gone down before, in typical Gordon style of shooting straight from the hip, came the assertion "think its time you came back to me." He could see clearly just how exposed I was, the last vestige of a crumbling division, a thorn in the side of the three-tier to two-tier organisational change pushed by London. Why make it easy for them? Time to tie up the horse, walk into the saloon and join the boys, clean your gun and next time the raiders come into town, we'll be waiting for them.

Gordon was in earnest, ordering his "one-and-a-half plaice – same as usual" from faithful Vera that always looked after him in his beloved Châteaux and attacking the first bottle of white with a venom intended for elsewhere. Need to put daylight between you and Reg Conway as well, what good is any business that in the end cannot deliver a product? The proposition is this (we are now on the double Bells), you come back into the Operations as my official deputy and I will push like hell for you to take over when I go. You bring the central services with you and we continue to buy up the club routes until the money dries up, you hammer any division that is not performing. "It's a good plan John, what do you think?"

At the next board meeting the plan is agreed in every detail, Gordon has Jim on side and, I have convinced myself, Mike does actually want me in the group, it was just a matter of finding the what and the how of it. Gordon has provided the answer. He who flippantly skips through the Daily Express whilst interviewing, he who survived the Italian campaign from South to North, he who emigrated to Canada and sent his new wife back to England whilst he single-handedly build their first timber house, he who qualified as a Canadian accountant, fathered five children (one who is in a senior position in the Foreign Office) but most of all he who is a man's man. Never swears, never smoked and who smashed the nose of an idiot chap who propositioned his Rene in a bar one fateful night.

Gordon, if sometimes this world will not move at your pace and in your straight lines and you let the booze get the upper hand, I forgive you. For now though, Mike is using an expression new to me. "Back boiler". Apparently it is what we should put my research company on. We have given it our best shot, spend over £250,000, and we can save all the software source codes and a sample of each piece of hardware until the time is right to think again and when the market has caught up with us. Well yes. I do not have the strength to swim against the tide, other things in my life have seen to that. Just another ex-Bill thing to hit the dust.

And yet today, tactile pre-priced key pads are everywhere, electronic controls are everywhere, remote data collection is commonplace. LPE could do these things twenty years ago. If I had had more about me, I would have said to that board, to hell with your consolation job (sorry Gordon), sod the fruit machine game, I will take little LPE off your hands. But, unlike television scripts for famous detectives, situations do not come at you singularly. I am an emotional wreck. But what good are excuses, probably wasn't man enough for it anyway. Just surviving is all I can handle.

Reg was as good as gold. LPE had not been our goldmine. All he wanted was his pay-off to go directly to his pension fund. It was hard for me to see him as near pensionable age, the energy level never let up. Still driving like a maniac, still riding his classic motorbike, still commuting at weekends back to his stricken wife, still loving his ladyfriend. One by one we talk to and dismiss the staff. We crate up the stock and equipment, clear the benches, sweep up and make tidy. Our dreams dissolve with the plastic. I learned much from Reg. About electrodes, resistors, capacitors, exhibitions, mark 1's and 2's and the rest and during nerve-racking demonstrations the diplomatic art of, what Gordon would call, bullshitting.

Amongst the failures and despairs had been some highlights. The mysterious world of the university research department and its unintelligible professor, the fronting of our latest product launch in London by the late and delightful Raymond Baxter (at his height with Tomorrow's World, but not this one Raymond) the waiting for the fleeting clip on the Central TV news of our electronic pub as interviewed by and presented by Anna, the daughter that David Soubry would have been so very proud of had he lived to see her media profile. But David has gone and LPE has gone and this is my last lunch with Reg at the Nottingham Knight and its ironic and maybe symbolic that as I thank him for trying his very best and, not least, for letting me use his little bungalow a few times, some bastard is busting my car boot lid and nicking my brief case and is about to run up some huge bills for electronic equipment fraudulently obtained on my credit card. A steal one might say.

Things have settled down. A crisis has passed. This is another Gordon lunch. We are tucked away in a corner in deep confabulation about current Operations issues and this time and unusually he leaves it until we reach coffee. He has been told officially by Mike that he will retire later this year on his 64th birthday. Immediately, he put me forward to replace him and effect a smooth transition. He stressed I had the confidence of all the regional directors, they would work for me, he had no doubt this would be so. It had gone to the main board. Mike was supportive and, somewhat surprisingly I thought in view of the Spanish affair, so was Peter. But I had been black-balled. Guess by whom? Of course, Gordon's biggest ally over the years, his HQ grapevine, his protector against Bill, old wily Jim. This was a vital objection. Jim was now firmly in charge of Bell-Fruit Manufacturing and the links were still very close. Jim's last retribution against Bill? Or perhaps he thought genuinely that I was not up to it. Anyway, an agreed route forward was to appoint headhunters. Gordon was sorry, he thought it a bad decision. He had been asked to advise me to go forward as an internal candidate and pit myself against whoever else the headhunters came up with. Well, all is not lost, we've rode some storms before. Let's have a drink, Vera, Vera. I'll go home afterwards, nothing spoiling at the shop.

There are three internal candidates for Gordon's job. We are to visit, on separate days, a firm with an odd sounding name located somewhere in the Victoria area of London. What is interesting is who the other two are. One is Tony Darling, who came in originally as new blood under Bill's succession plan to replace Gordon and who soon got sidelined, and the other is Barry Vail the director of the Eastern region who has constantly been at loggerheads with Gordon over matters of independence and who, until we bought it out, ran pretty much his own show under benevolent owners in remotest Norwich. Well, well. An ambitious dark horse? But we need not have bothered. Our several failures was not even communicated. Mike simply used his powerful ploy of silence that I was now quite familiar with. The only concession to how close I was supposed to have been to getting the top job came several weeks later with Mike popping his head into my office to say someone else had been preferred.

Paul Cox was his name. He would be good for us because he was ex-Whitbread, one of our larger customers, and had senior contacts not only within the brewing fraternity but also within our specialist business since he had been chairman of their own Operations company. At this time, the brewing industry was vertically integrated par excellence. They brewed the beer, owned the pubs selling it (or put tenants into the second tier sites), operated amusement machines within the sites (cleverly disguising this income stream from the core business flow), actually manufactured fruit machines and took joint venture stakes in a number of supply feeders to pubs (such as soft drinks). So Paul scored on two counts. Or, maybe, in the eyes of the headhunters three in that he had main board experience at a really senior level. He had, apparently, been the youngest person ever to reach main board level at Whitbread but had left by the time he was picked up by the headhunters.

It was always going to be difficult for us to get along. My feelings on being overlooked were strong and Paul would have received a full briefing on the background. He was younger than me and had had a far superior education and training in management. For the second time in under a year, the quick exit loomed. But Paul was not the part I expected. I had imagined someone slim, well dressed, fast talking, fast moving, professionally and personally disciplined, a bit superior, a bit browbeating.

In walks this red-faced, paunchy, jovial, bar-tender type chap. The sort it would be hard to fall out with whatever the background or circumstances. He was going to spend some time around the regions, getting to know the people, learning the business, but really he is no sergeant-major. He will be the new face of the business, the external presence, the strategic developer. And he is going to ask Gordon to stay on for a bit as chairman whilst he gets the feel and style of things right. But Gordon has had enough, he will take his special golden handshake and silver salver and move to the new bungalow he and Rene have found on the Sussex coast.

Paul wants me to take over about half of the country geographically (about three-quarters by profit) by having the regional directors report directly to me and re-affirm me as the official No2. As time passes he will want me to take positions in the trade association to increase my profile and he asks and will continue to ask over the next few years why I did not make more changes before. And I will talk of autocracy and in practice how difficult it is to influence a dominant chief executive when one is not financially independent. I will develop this theory over and over again in the future in the context of non-executives.

Motivation, motivation. Keep 'em on side. Keep them working for you. Their success is your success. But I have yet to witness democracy working at senior management level. Soundings, yes. Chris Collett back in PW flying his kites. But it is hard to rein in someone who is super confident bordering on arrogant, for a start he/she might just be right and for seconds I actually need this job right now, daddy is not going to step in and find another one for me. It is difficult for Paul to come to terms with all this. He believes in democracy. He will exercise democracy. He works through evolution not revolution. Mind you, he cannot do much good for Whitbread now he is no longer there. To be fecund one has surely to be in there.

Well anyway to hell with it and sod pride. Right now, of all times in my life, I need to be occupied. I need to work like stink. I will manage the Midlands, the North, the East, the club routes, I will manage anything I can get my hands on. And with a rod of iron, but democratically of course.

Gordon's farewell dinner more or less coincides with our move into the new offices in the now ex-R&D block. We can all get into the upper of the two floors and leave the ground floor vacant to grow one or more of our fledgling businesses (LPE might be on the back-burner but a few other things are warming up at the front) or we can take a tenant and get some nice miscellaneous income. As the R&D block, this huge floor was open-plan but now following the reconstruction it has offices around the perimeter and a central suite of four offices that, although not enjoying natural lighting, do benefit from air conditioning and delicate concealed lighting.

As if to prove the new egalitarian regime, Paul and I take the two larger of these central offices that sit side-by-side and have our secretaries in a cosy little open plan space opposite our respective doors. Or we did until beautiful Sue broke down in tears sitting opposite my desk. Yes she did have her outside interests, yes she was secretary of the Society of Advanced Secretaries and PA's, yes she had seen me through all the ups and downs and now it looked like a proper good period, yes she had married her ex-medical technician now qualified doctor man, but she was unhappy, not mentally satisfied. So we talked and I took time to think. We had started a little sideline borne of boxes housing coin mechanisms of which we were well familiar. Such boxes were adapted to create a market for visitors to petrol filling stations having to pay for air pressure currently free. The forecourt owner takes the cashbox, we take our rent, just like the fruit machine except with this we do not claim amusement. Does Sue want to take it on as MD and move into her own office down the corridor and if it should go well, maybe it could be a little buy-out for her? She does, and she did and it did work.

So Paul and I not only share more or less the same office space we decide to share Val too. Why set someone else on? Val is good, fast, discreet and Paul doesn't generate much work anyway, or so he says. Val earned her spurs with Gordon and if she could cover his tracks, she can certainly cope with us. Val knew when to lock Gordon's door and judging by the whisky bottles uncovered when his room was cleared, it was just as well. I liked Val. She was a great character and could get more work done in any morning than most secretaries in the entire day. This was just as well because she had this habit of downing two or three pints of lager in the working men's club just over the way each lunchtime and it was not unknown for her to have the odd *tinny* under her desk.

Before she ever came to the office, she worked a session with her husband in their newsagent shop and maybe that is where the tips came from since when we had a day out under Paul's new regime of hosting the customers, she backed the winner of every race at York. And regarding sessions with her husband, Gordon once needed her on an away night to take care of things and she told me the sessions lasted all the previous night so her jealous husband left her "with nothing left to give".

Paul came to see me one morning saying he was in an awkward position. Mike Peace, the new finance director, had made a complaint about Val's drinking habit. Being forced to do something, he had plucked up courage to call her to a meeting with just himself that afternoon. But he wasn't looking forward to it. Not one bit. Not being able to contain my curiosity and actually somewhat worried for Val's welfare in the face of this official complaint from the money-man, I chased up the outcome. Paul thought it had been a bit of a damp squib, "she was as sober as a judge and I was pissed."

Well time passes, things are going well. Paul is pretty remote, just as he promised, and the operations are balanced and swinging. Each month I visit my regional offices, review the results and we set our plans for the next period. I am left alone, it is clean, it is productive. The profits flow and the cash is generated. Paul gets put on the main board and wily old Jim appoints a young man Keith Healey from the London sales office to be MD of Bell-Fruit Manufacturing. Any semblance of an amusement machine division has now gone, maybe Paul's evolution process was actually learned from Mike. Certainly things change imperceptibly. One morning one discovers things are different. We are now Bell-Fruit Services Ltd, as devised by one of Paul's advisors, with our own distinctive logo and house style whilst they remain Bell-Fruit Manufacturing

Ltd. We have our own FD in Mike Peace and they have Jim's old faithful Keith Parsons as FD under the new MD. Apart from the small periphery companies, the two-tier job is done. Was there a master plan even this early?

If there was to be a master plan for the future, a plan for enrichment, for extracting dormant value, then the simpler the management and control structure, the better. Not that the group itself could be said to be simple and any outsider would, prima facia, have found it baffling. Yet there is a touch of irony that this simplification of structure is occurring under the stewardship of a man who will develop a reputation for extreme complexity, but successful complexity.

Louis had gone and Mike had come in on the coat tails of a takeover but one that preserved the market quote of CAI Ltd. It started with the gradual build up of shares in the market, extended to offers by tender and ended, at least for a time, with the corporately pressurising 29.9% that was just under but not quite necessitating a full-blown takeover. The master-mind was Michael Ashcroft, now Lord Ashcroft, through his own leisure vehicle called Hawley Leisure. Ashcroft's style was to stay non-executive, put in top managers to run a business and motivate the incumbents heavily to succeed. Not just senior managers either. It was well publicized that his original secretary had made a fortune from share options. Also that ego did not enter into his business world. He and a very small group of colleagues worked from modest offices in a modest location. His idea of a board meeting was one that took no longer than twenty minutes. His lack of favour in the City arose, seemingly, from two counts. First, he was an outsider and too clever by half and secondly he had a very astute tax advisor and his off-shore registrations left the UK tax man out of breath and out of pocket. Not that it was ever suggested that such arrangements were illegal, merely smart.

Senior managers in CAI were motivated by share

options in his set-up (cumulative preference shares) and encouraged to invest in ordinary stock on the open market. My attitude is this. I worked and grew, but at times really suffered, under the old regime. If this chap has done it before, he can do it again. On the one occasion we were brought together to meet him, he walked in briskly, tall, bespectacled and young and sat at a piano that just happened to be there and played a quick tune. You dance to my tune, I thought. He said little and was away.

I have just passed what I hope to God will be the nadir of my life. I am managing at a senior level now. I am on the up and up. I play Elton John's *I'm still standing* on the home jukebox over and over again. I will go for these shares, hook, line and sinker. For those brave enough, Michael Ashcroft will do us proud. Ok, it will take time. Ok there will be capital gains to pay (at this time spreadable over five years) but it will be the first time I have any spare funds, the first time money will be acquired other than through being a hired hand. It will start a habit of investing in equities, of trying to read the markets, of trading. A habit not to be lost. Of keeping me going in the private quiet hours. Ashcroft will go on to big things. Really big things. To me he is the bloke who showed how things can be done if one is clever enough, without pomp, without getting bogged down but by motivating those with a lower intellect to perform to their very best.

By the time the new Group Organisation and Control Manual is issued, a few other subtle changes have taken place. The financial controller is now reporting directly to the executive director of each of the groupings and as was clearly going to happen with Paul's elevation to the main board, Bell Fruit Services is such a grouping in its own right. The main board finance director has changed and, well, well, now Jim is listed as responsible on the main board for Bell-Fruit Manufacturing only, although two other engineering companies remain. Does this herald a wane? And finally, there is no controller of the leisure division since there is no leisure division. So Keith Parson's reign was fairly short lived and like our Mike Peace he is now simply a finance director reporting to one boss. Something is ripe for picking methinks.

Things are swinging

Ours is a people dominated service business and a lot of staff report directly through the structures to me. It's a microcosm of life itself. Life with its tragedies and highlights. Because I visit each region monthly and can get past the top man by sitting in on the management meeting, walk the workshops and talk to collectors, so I know many of the people. One who has been in this game man and boy is Brian Bedford the right-hand man to Barry Vail on the eastern flank. Like David Soubry before him, Brian is a smoker. A real smoker. Also like David, the disease grips in the autumn and by the time of the Christmas party, Barry takes me to talk to this man I now do not recognise. His face is like a balloon and he has no hair.

Brian Bedford died in early February the following year. Barry gave a most touching address in All Saints Church, Shotesham, Norfolk and five days later his widow June wrote me a letter crafted in impeccably tiny letters, the first paragraph was "It was kind of you to come to Brian's funeral. I am sure he would have wished me to write and thank you; he had a very high regard for you. He often said that, like him, he felt you were sympathetic to the needs and problems of the staff and that you had a "listening ear". He believed in teamwork and maybe what could appear trivial to management was, nevertheless, important in the eyes of the staff; if one had time for them, they would respond, and in turn reflect in the strength and efficiency of the

Company". I keep this letter because it says so much in so few words and it's about fags, about cancer, about the cruelty and inequity of life itself. Brian was 52 years old when he died.

But business can be enjoyable, very enjoyable. When work is busy and busy because you are in the momentum of things going well, success begets success and people are happy with their lot. The most crucial ingredient is the culture set from the top. If that is cerebral and the right people are in the right slots (I hear Goh Seng Kim again "digits John, digits"), then the days will swing and even a definition of work itself can become blurred.

What does a certain block of hours in the week matter? There are early mornings too, evenings, weekends if you want them. Paul set the scene and let us get on with it. As did Michael Ashcroft. These were good times. We made good money and milked it a little. At a memorable board meeting the vulpine-like Mike Peace raised the subject of annual holidays "to put us more in line with etc, etc," to which Paul replied "sure, sure, take as many as you want – who's counting?" Wonderful. Nearly on par with trying to admonish a lady with a drink habit when one is tiddly oneself. But that is Paul who I am getting to know quite well. We have a nice meal with him and his charming wife in their substantial home in Befordshire and chat in the huge split-level lounge with its fireplace in the very centre of the room. Not long afterwards he is in my office wanting a form signed that verified his income. It is as a guarantor of a mortgage application. An application from a lady who is about to take a house near Nottingham. A lady who used to be his secretary at a Whitbread base. She is his mistress and is pregnant and will I keep it quiet for the time being.

At Whitbread, Paul had evidently been used to hostings, entertaining customers, publicity drives and so on. It became clear that we were to get a taste of the same notwithstanding that our league was a peg or two down in scale. Somehow fitted into the work-week are parties at the Epsom Derby, The Grand National, Wimbledon, Queens Club, York races, Chepstow races, there is a shared box at Castle Donnington racetrack, a whole box at Nottingham Forest football ground, we are sponsoring an American Football team, we attend one of the first performances of Phantom of the Opera when Michael Crawford is the original star, and more. (Gordon – are you in wonderment? We thought your Chateaux canteen was a bit over the top). And Paul wants to be big in the trade association and achieves this once we two have attended the meetings and helped sponsor the National Ball and so on. He cultivates the editor of a magazine set up to rival the age-old traditionalist Coinslot. A bright bold glossy that rewards him with star-ranking publicity and often carries his thoughts on the future of the industry and on the next winning products.

One product that has more than an even chance to gain ground is a CD (compact disc) jukebox to secure inroads into the traditional vinyl jukebox estate. We have never been strong on the music equipment side that has been regarded as somewhat specialist. A northern based group dominates. It follows that if we could steal a march on them, whole swathes of territory could be won. The problem is our supplier is NSM in Germany who are proving to be arch conservative. They have a form of hybrid box but do not see a wholesome CD product as viable. Paul thinks we need to give them a nudge (a verb soon to make someone in the industry a fortune) so an elite group of Paul, me, Mike Peace and the main UK importer plus our respective partners, fly off to Frankfurt to be convinced by them that we are wrong.

NSM are the biggest vinyl jukebox manufacturers worldwide outside the USA. They are obviously prepared to throw money at not losing business to a new-fangled idea. This is only apparent after a most formal, not to say regimental and stuffy, tour of the factory during which each senior manager on being presented to us, feels the need to firmly click his heals together. An unendearing reminder of the past. But all this staidness is washed away on the boat trip on the Rhine from Bingen, at the regal pink sparkling wine reception up river on the far bank at St Goar (where we are informed the Queen Mother stops off) and especially at the dinner in Wiesbaden at which the place settings have seemingly more sizes of wine glasses than different wines that exist in the whole of Germany. We might as well fill our boots since there is this feeling that NSM is slipping slightly behind the eight-ball, so to speak.

Later we will return to Germany but based in Berlin. The excuse is to visit the NAAFI installations and review our machines in situ, the real reason is to see the divided city as exemplified by our coach trip to the Eastern sector. It is reminiscent of my foray into Bulgaria and Rumania in terms of the authoritarian stranglehold and the deadhand of hidden controllers and it did not take the stark comparison with West Berlin to appreciate it was infinitely worse. Nothing but decay, neglect and soul-less towerblocks of rotting concrete. The odd four-square black car or pick-up would trundle along otherwise empty streets. What have these armed guards in their caged towers got to protect? Nothing of course, the whole sorry pantomime is to stop the poor sods getting out, over or under this grotesque wall with its paradoxically fantastical graffiti that only a released mind could dream up. Not the mind of the old lady who is circling our coach with a mirror on a pole looking for propaganda or contraband hidden underneath and who without a by-your-leave confiscates my newspaper. Was it as a deliberate counterpoint that the notice on the door of the sauna in the hotel basement leisure complex instructs us "in the interest of hygiene, remove all your clothing before entering". Ok, relatively it's a minor matter but just like the other side of the wall, who knows what one might see.

Barn door to balance sheet

Back in blighty the trade events take on a momentum of their own and Paul wants me to join him at the monthly and secret meetings of the innocently sounding Coin Users Group. If anyone tells you that free-market competition precludes a get-together of the top boys to fix things, do not believe it. And national begets local and here I am presiding over the First Spring Banquet and Ball Extraordinaire at the Commodore International of the Nottingham and District Women's Licensed Trade Auxiliary. Do these things really exist? Back to my theory of sub-cultures and I will revise my estimate upwards, there must be at least a half million. All wanting sponsorships, all gagging for the presidential speech. A compensation is that Paul has struck up a deal with a limousine hiring firm and it makes sense on a number of counts to be chauffeur driven. Incidentally, fecund Paul has bought a Rolls Royce and is thinking of getting a second one. It all helps the image and I find myself thinking more and more of the three devastating weaknesses I learned to recognise as a consultant and now they have crept up right under my nose; freeloading, personal fiefdom and the vanity of status.

But then, I am branching out in other circles. Someone at head-office has put me forward as a trustee of the CAI pension fund on the premise that we have overwhelmingly more staff than any other group of companies and that these members ought to have their interests represented. This in turn gets me close to Goodwins who are the administrators and actuaries and now being very au fait with posh social events, it seems natural to be at Grosvenor House as their guest although winning the top prize in the raffle (a matching pair of men's and ladies' gold watches) was a surprise.

Downstairs in our new office, a tenant has been brought in. It is a PR firm and the boss man is out more and more at lunchtime with Paul. Often they do not return. This firm is organising more and more of these hosting events and we are paying a fat retainer for their services as well as an add-on organiser's percentage. Paul is getting even more remote and in the office less and less.

The end game

It is of-course well known that takeover bids and/or significant acquisition activity can be a distraction to management and that such a distraction can be played down or up depending on circumstances. What is possibly less well known is that managers can be conscientiously managing in blissful ignorance of planned or unplanned ownership changes. Maybe those managers could contribute to an ownership event, perhaps be alerted to a course of action being taken but for sure they ought not to be mere pawns in a game they know not the rules of. What actually has been going on here? We do know that after a good deal of brinkmanship, the entire share capital of CAI was purchased by new group and it will later become known that this was on behalf of an associated company. This is where the complexity comes in and explains the presence of Michael Ashcroft as non-executive chairman. Complicated enough for the troops to fathom but why then in the space of less than two years is CAI apparently up for sale again? Yet according to what Paul filters through to us, it is, and various groups have pitched and at one stage a clear favourite appears in the form of an Australian group because they are into packaging and engineering. If they win, what of us?

Of the parties expressing interest in buying CAI, one is a mysterious triumvirate that visited Nottingham as part of a grand tour and in relation to our business saw only Paul so the ability of anyone else to get any feel for these three individuals was nonexistent. Paul's impression is that they are acting in a private capacity and so how they can expect to compete with the likes of the big Australian group is baffling. But then, so is the need for the sale itself. Is this some sort of highly leveraged corporate carve-up? Was CAI somehow bought as a whole to be sold on in bits? Has there been a master plan all along: have we all been toiling away for a purpose far beyond mere numbers? Now, when we have owners that seem to want to play ping-pong with us, I form the view that the period when this was not so, was a wonderful time.

Let me just ponder on our particular business. It has been said that it is good to buy a business that idiots can run, because sooner or later one will. But what if the business cannot be run by idiots because difficult decisions have to be made quite frequently and capital has to be re-invested to handle market changes? To mark up and pass on as a cash cow is one thing but what if technology has changed and is continuing to change from clunk-click mechanics to unseen software that only the long-haired ones with rings in funny places can understand? Distract managers too much and court disaster?

And then, would you believe it, this little three-man team have put in the highest bid and won the group. This is confirmed by a meeting in London to which we top-notches are called by Mike Doherty and who announces with some emotion that "I am not for sale". So exits the big man. The man who restructured to get nearer to a two-tier organisation, the man to whom I reported directly for some time, who had the service contracts made more modern, who drastically improved the pension scheme for the top echelon and, thinking of which, on whose behalf there was a request for a quarter of a million sterling of his pay-off to come from the pension scheme surplus. We trustees, chaired by Peter, had to vote. The outcome was four to one in favour. This was many years before the respective roles of the independent trustees and the company executives became a hot issue. But I was thinking of the hundreds and hundreds of collectors and engineers and their families and to me it was just not right. I was the one vote against.

Who is replacing Mike? Who are the three? Well, two will assume a high profile and one will not and it is the latter that I will get to know best. Barely two months after CAI falls to the triumvirate, I am wading through a huge tome. With minimal preamble the report explains that the commission was to investigate the affairs of Bell-Fruit Manufacturing and the companies comprising Bell Fruit Services. The purpose was to provide information to prospective purchasers of the group. Well then nothing could be clearer, we were bought again to be sold again. Bloody great.

What I do know only too well is that we have the two up-front buddies. Rick Grogan is group chairman, David Hoare is group MD. The man in the background is Olivier Roux, the money man. To me this whole scene is very much a money driven deal. I am destined to have quite a lot to do with Olivier, on the telephone, in Nottingham and at a small tucked away office in London. The numbers being crunched clearly looked tasty, obviously too tasty for the sharpshooters not to turn a buck on. The language of the fast-talking, slim, fit and good looking American Rick still rubs off. At a meeting in Nottingham, he rides rodeo over the pained questioning of those under threat, under-told and under-positive. "Come on guys, we can all make out of this."

Paul has some startling news. The main CAI Board may consider allowing us to undertake a management buyout. This is fantastic. There is a real prospect that at last we can plough our own furrow, create our own future, stop being used as a cash cow by those above and get back to leading the consolidation of a still fragmented industry. Best of all, we can shake off Jim and the like. Paul has launched into a top-down re-budgeting and re-forecasting and injecting liberally the new compact disc juke-box that it is his dream to have designed by a certain two gentlemen who claim to have a clever patent and made by Bell Fruit Manufacturing on our doorstep. The Germans will rue the day they dragged their feet.

Mike Peace is cautioning against over-optimism and stressing that our results now are not actually as good as a year ago. Of course there are good reasons for this namely the distraction caused by the ownership changes. Still, it makes sense to put the best complexion on how good the business will be once we are set free. Independence will make a huge difference to staff morale and we the management will be highly motivated. After all, once we had been gobbled up, deflation set in. Our chance was gone. But now in no time at all they signal that we'll be off-loaded anyway. We can now pitch for the business. Whoopee.

Over time a pattern emerges, Paul, held back a bit by Mike Peace, works the internal numbers. Roux and I present the figures in a format required by potential financiers. Scenarios are new to me but make sense and I can see how cash is king and how Roux works to a pattern. And then the venture capitalists arrive in Nottingham. The day-time working sessions are highly volatile and the evening meals in the Mr Chang's restaurant even more so, the air and language sizzles more than the monk fish in black bean sauce. Perhaps we should all have stuck to the placid scallops.

This is an excellent business with a good mix of experienced managers and young blood. The industry is leading the electronic and technological charge with high potential for new products such as the new quiz machines and electronic dart boards and our CD jukebox. Ok, Ok but the seller is looking for £80m and given the level of senior debt and mezzanine debt we have to be sure. And the young chap from the mezzanine debt provider was the most irritating. He would not let the 20p play coin pass. How can we be sure that at the forthcoming triennial review by the Gaming Board the players will be allowed to upgrade from 10p to 20p as the play coin? Even should it be allowed, how can you be certain that the average machine take will increase by the amount in the financial assumptions? Well we can't but based on what happened last time such an upgrade in the play coin occurred, it is most likely. But that was ages ago and now with the super-fast play electronic machines, spend will occur much quicker and maybe the average punter will feel cheated? Bloody hell. Let's go home, fed up with all this.

Things get serious. A trade sale is on and we are in play along with others. The likely deal is that we, the Operations, purchase all of our Group for £80m and immediately sell on the factory to their management for £24m ish. Our team will be Paul, me and Mike Peace and we will put in £50k each of risk capital (that we can borrow) backed by a personal guarantee secured on our homes. There is a three-year highly geared exit strategy leading to a public float. If it works, we are rich. If it doesn't we lose our £50k. Our bid is on the table and there is every likelihood of acceptance. We are over the moon and the seller seems delighted.

At a time when we should all be pulling together in one direction, pooling our strengths, moving into top gear, I am being bugged, seriously bugged. What is getting at me most is Paul's absence from the business. He is finding lots of alternative things to do. We have pumped money into the CD jukebox project but the actual prototype sits on a bench in a backroom in Yorkshire with the inventors, I have been to see it. Ok, well everything has to start somewhere and certainly Keith Healey now running the factory is heavily committed too and allocating resources but something is just not right somehow. Why is the ownership structure so complicated? With a world-wide market so huge and the Germans and Americans with so much to lose, what are the odds of a really well engineered box hitting the market by surprise with technology different from that being developed by our little group? I have been chastened by the LPE experience, I know how easy it is to get carried away by an idea, by sheer enthusiasm. I want to talk about it. Then again there are the Paul absences as he pushes for power in the Trade Association (BACTA) and heads publicity in the trade press and at the trade exhibitions. I know it is good to have a charismatic front man because everyone says so and this is all solid ground work for when we own the business, and yet, and yet.

What really spurred me on was the acquisition programme. It had stopped. That is we had stopped the programme of buying owner-run smallish routes dominated by club machines, my original idea and my speciality. But we had not stopped buying. A leading light in BACTA was also chairman of a group whose main business was a direct but much smaller competitor of ours that specialised in jukeboxes and music systems generally. He and Paul got together and the result was our purchase of their Southern operation. This was a major event, far outweighing anything we had attempted before. Some 4,500 sited machines were involved and concentrated heavily in and around London. Depots were involved, off-site stock was involved and the whole gamut of operations plethora. The rationale was clear enough. They were not making money due to the heavy cost of operating in the South whilst we had an infrastructure and management in place to increase productivity and to house the expanded volumes. But did we? I kept thinking of the job for PW trying to marry the two national cake manufacturing operations and aside from all the physical aspects, the psychological battles likely to rage between two almost certainly conflicting business cultures. Why would this be any different? But I had supported it. It would be a big feather in Paul's personal cap and as such enhance the whole business in the eyes of the big customers and if implemented well would widen the tight margins of our own Southern flank.

My grouse once the deal was done was all about implementation. I wanted a working party to implement the integration into our Southern division and consisting of the present director for sure but also Paul, myself, a working accountant and at least one good operational practical man. Paul was insistent that Roger Channing wanted to do the job himself with solely his people. Paul would not budge and he had Roger reporting to him directly. Who knows whether my idea was best and whether the administrative problems that arose could have been avoided but we ended up writing off a considerable sum due to VAT accounting and *other* errors. The provision was so large, the external accountants' report had to highlight it. I was very unhappy with the whole of the Southern set-up. Could Roger actually cope?

The meeting between Paul and me took place three months after publication of the accountants' report and was worked in with the annual review. A bit like a top-flight interview. It is all very well knowing your subject and rehearsing answers to anticipated questions but one can be knocked off guard, completely thrown even by the response "so what do you want to do." Except that in understanding what has been going on, I do know what I want, namely a bigger role in managing the business and a bigger say in what is going on overall. Now we both know where we stand.

The personal letter from Paul a few days later confirms a salary increase of 5% and informs me that our new owners favour the use of exceptional performance related bonuses as a key element of the management reward package "with less emphasis on basic salary increases". Later will come precise targets for me to achieve in order to earn various levels of bonus over the next year. Then we get to it. He is making some "modest" organisational changes with immediate effect. He thanks me for agreeing to "manage" the Northern division directly whilst the current director is absent on secondment. He goes on to express his wish to "remove" the Midlands divisional director also on secondment. If he achieves this, he thanks me for agreeing to also manage directly that area too. As part of the process of directly managing these divisions, I am to identify an organisation structure which could cope with the permanent management of such an enlarged division. As recompense for the extra effort, I am to receive a supplementary payment of £5,000 in five equal instalments.

So once again we have the proof that no system, regulation or regime was ever put in place that could not be defeated. There will be less emphasis on basic salary increases but that does not preclude supplementary payments it seems. This "process" (Paul's favourite word) reminds me a bit of Bill being told to take direct charge of the factory and Jim's retort that he was now in the direct firing line. Jim's little joke.

Attached to the letter is a new organisation chart. It shows one other big move. Mike Peace is promoted to manage the Southern division and "gives up day to day control of the finance function but retains responsibility for financial policies." So now we have a new set-up slap bang in a period when we are up for sale again and pitching for the business ourselves. I am profit responsible for about 80% of the business, Mike Peace and Chris Gunther, who runs the NAAFI contract, have the rest. There are then five other direct reports to Paul, business development, purchasing, national accounts, financial control and acquisitions. It's like Paul wants to personally shed actual management to get on with bigger and more exciting things but simultaneously will not give up senior pushed-aside managers (except for Roger Channing who could not survive the Southern acquisition fiasco) in favour of functional roles that, as was proven under the original regime, ultimately have to be a line management responsibility. It is as if the latter days of Mike Doherty never existed. Reminds me of short-term politics when the country wants long term plans and stability. Would any of this have occurred were we not in this ownership pincer movement?

Then Paul makes his next move. Now that I have got one huge division, it would make sense for me to move out into my own office suite with my own senior people. He can then house his new direct reports right here in my existing office complex. Now we really do know where we stand, we stand apart.

Just before I move out one other big scalp is taken. Paul sacks Tony Darling who latterly has been running all the odds and sods businesses collectively titled Traderbell (that some unkind wag instantly re-named Tinkerbell). So the man who had the misfortune to have been brought in at the instigation of Bill to replace Gordon and who soon got sidelined, has finally left the field. Tony was no fool. He saw the writing on the wall and had already built up a small string of ladies hair-dressing salons and had a few other things on the go and most importantly was developing his idea for a brand new business concerned with holding temporary tenancy licences for the brewery site owners.

In retrospect it is interesting that Bill's other new blood to support Gordon namely Mike Peace has gone from strength to strength and followed me from finance to management. Like Keith Parsons, now firmly wedded to the manufacturing company, he represents that breed of industrial accountant that comes from the bottom via guile, protectionism and measured caution.

For the first time in the whole episode I am really fulfilled and happy. Corporate man has arrived. The lease on this sort of house on Derby Road near the centre of Nottingham City extends to three floors. I have recruited my old sparring partner in our second biggest brewery customer to be the marketing man and an ex employee to run the off-site stock. Kathy came through the interviews to be my secretary and she has her own assistant. This is our little HQ team. I have appointed the accountant at the old Midlands division to be finance director of my new big division and the account manager from Warrington to be the key account manager overall. I believe it will work well.

It is working well. I get in early each morning and stay till whenever. The whole top team meets monthly either at Derby Road or in one of the regional offices. We knock out considerable overhead and reduce stock dramatically. Paul leaves me alone. If only *the three* would abandon the sale and be content with what they have. Why don't they sell off the packaging side and what is left of engineering and retain the leisure interests? Makes sense to me and I say so to Rick Grogan but he thinks its funny and anyway he is off to see the boat race. It dawns on me that not only are the triumvirate hell bent on a trade sale, it is urgent, bordering on vital. No wonder Olivier Roux is so involved.

Is there some natural pre-ordained order that decrees that sweetness is short? That only ordinariness and humdrum and even distaste and pain are drawn out? Our reign has been only too short. Paul is telling me that Rick has informed him that they have agreed a sale. It is not to us. Our MBO has failed . We were short by £2m. The successful bidder was our Northern competitors from whom we bought the unprofitable southern flank. What! Apparently since they sold to us, things have gone from strength to strength. Their CD jukebox has gone well and so have diversifications into running leisure interests for local authorities and getting into France.

But Paul, they are only a fraction of our size and they do not know how to run a mixed estate such as ours, they are music specialists. I know. I know. But their share price is riding high and it's basically a paper deal through a new placement with institutions. The seller can offload the paper and so really it's as good as cash to them. Bloody hell. (Much later I will learn that the deal included a *sale* of the pension fund, contrary to what was offered in the accountants' report, or should we say they agreed to take it over. What was taken over was an independently valued pension surplus that was greater than the difference between our MBO price and theirs and so funding the extra consideration – good work you three, or maybe the guys up North).

If I was a bit off-the-rails with Paul before, I am really annoyed now. Since it became known that we have lost, he has gone completely walk-about or rather fly-about, mainly Greece and mainly with his PR mate and their partners. In a period from the new year to mid-May, he has been on holiday for six whole weeks (holidays Mike, who's counting – ha –ha). This leaves me really in charge and in particular handling both Rick on his now frequent visits to Nottingham and the buyer's due diligence process. Having waited for his latest return, we meet for lunch in my Chinese canteen opposite the office and rather stupidly called Ocean City since Nottingham is no Hong Kong.

I can't even stand football but I still ended up as sweeper for Bill's team and now I'm lumbered as King of entropy for you Paul. You always say there are one thousand reasons why not to do something, well the here and now is just one reason for you to be around. On the third or fourth (or more, I neither know nor care at this stage) bottle of white wine, Paul comes out with it. He has signed up to a loyalty payment. Rick is going to pay each of a few identified people £30k to co-operate fully with the transitional process, conditional only on completion actually taking place. Paul himself is on a separate sum that he has been sworn to secrecy not to mention. So why should he care? If we are merely in maintenance mode, then he knows I can handle it. If it falls through for any reason, then our MBO will be on again. I concede the point now knowing the score but why am I on the same deal as the others. My share of the pot is raised to £40k. We go our separate ways again. I know he will not welsh on this subsidiary deal, time for coffee.

Several years later, I bump into the still young and today very drunk Keith Healey of Bell-Fruit Manufacturing fame on St Pancras railway station. He immediately starts ranting about the old days and accuses me of not standing up to Paul and pushing the MBO through (at his request we had met for lunch at a crucial point and he asked me to side with him and go to Rick and cut out Paul. A proposition I declined on the basis that Paul was much better entrenched than I and was the only person they in London saw as able to deliver the deal they wanted). Since Paul alone was on the main board and did his deal privately (until our Chinese lunch), the logic of Keith's rant against history escapes me as does his aggression. Were it not for his sidekick Keith Parsons physically holding him back, I got the feeling he intended a side-kick, at me. As I walk away and up the platform he shouts after me "Paul got 250 thousand you know".

Years later still and sitting in the High Court in London waiting for my turn, the barrister representing the buyer is claiming that the loyalty fee was a bribe to induce us to dress up the profit, or at least that appears to be the pitch. Right, so we inflated the profit so the asking price goes up so we have to borrow more money to buy the business we wanted ourselves. I do not think so. It was to stop us all walking out and leaving their huge investment animal headless or to encourage us not to throw a corporate spanner in the works. Seems perfectly sensible to me. Rick and his mates were no mugs you know. If you take on the big boys you can expect a bloody nose now and again. I learned that at Newton school and I was not even ten years old.

Jesus only managed one. We had several: last supper

that is. The heads rolled in from Scotland, the North East and West the South East and West, the Midlands and even the Eastern flank. There was a reason for each. The real reason was to talk through and think about the sell-out affair. How had it all come about, what was going to happen? One of our managers had been employed by the buyers before and had left sharpish in disillusionment. Whatever, it is going through, this is probably the last time we will meet as the old firm. Only Paul, me and Mike Peace go to London for the final signing ceremony. Near the end, I notice the super fit and confident Rick go behind a staging and light a fag. This has been bloody important to them, much money has been made somehow – this little act of nervousness proves it.

I knew in advance who was going to run the new show. Not Paul (which would have been logical since his big friend at the trade forum and who had sold us the Southern pup, was chairman of the quoted acquirer) but someone called Clive. This information came from my main contact at our largest customer after they had been sounded out in advance of the deal. So one fine early autumn morning a gleaming jaguar pulled into the car park and Clive and his immediate boss walked in. An hour or so later Paul walked out leaving his Rolls Royce behind. That afternoon that jaguar pulled into my car park and I introduced the twosome around our little domain and we sat down to talk. As with Louis seemingly some two centuries before, I waited for the bullet that was not fired. Instead we went over how my patch was run and they were surprisingly interested in the computer systems and in fine detail. This was a harbinger, though I was not to know it. They knew I was going on holiday shortly and appeared peculiarly taken with the notion that I had intended to visit the big trade show in Las Vegas en-route elsewhere. It was fixed that we three would meet at 2pm on a particular day in September at their hotel on The Strip to discuss the future course of events. What a turn up. What a sunnyside-up curate's egg turn up.

And it is sunny, very sunny. And it is hot, very hot. And muggins here tries to walk, as is my wont, to that hotel from mine. This intense heat will not prevent the unconventionally located interview occurring but the absence of any concessions to pedestrians could well do so. Do Americans ever get out of their cars? Must be loos in these limousines and pick-ups and trucks that zoom from block to block as if their very life depended upon it. Actually it seems that it does since no-one intends to stop for even one nanosecond to allow for a split-second thought of getting across this highway. I might just as well have been born on this side. Though if that had been so, surely I would have mutated with special eyes, eyes that withstand last night's and every night's glaring red, yellow, blue, green, orange and you name the colour, flashing lights. And thinking of eyes, the wonder of that couple from Pittsburgh taking time out to visit the Hoover Dam on their *red-eye* trip. Why red-eye? Because we never sleep ya-know, out all day and pokkies all night, nothing like this out East, got to make the most of it ya-know. Right. Let's concentrate. How I am going to get to that hotel over there and out of this heat and into the heat?

Yet it's all pretty amicable really. Hadn't I demonstrated my commitment by deciding not to cancel this trip. Had I? And Paul has gone, he's out of the way, the decision was taken long before the deal was consummated. Was it? The plan is to merge the two businesses and then cut the country in half. I will take the midlands, east and north and their man will take the south. Bear in mind their heartland is in the north. Right. TSA, the NAAFI contract holder, will stay separate. We two big operators, Mr North and Mr South will plan our depot structure, no-doubt some closures, maybe some new locations, maybe some squeezing togethers and implement the changes.

Productivity will improve. Clive himself will concentrate on the computer and technical side. This is where their strength lies.

It has already been decided that their IT resources were superior to ours and that therefore their methodology would prevail. Not just in mainframe computer systems but also in areas such as data capture and the self-developed security monitoring of coin and token usage. Their operation has concentrated in these areas over the past years and that is why they have stolen a lead over Bell-Fruit and with the music products even nationally. Clive is extremely computer numerate and this asset is seen as key to making the acquisition work. The other chap is more your HQ man and his role is to ensure that the enhanced operation gels properly with the group philosophy. Oh and by the way one other person that you will get to know well is John Garvis because he is the group financial director reporting directly to the Chairman.

All that pension work. All the study of the subject, the jealously defended independence of being a trustee for the employees, the kick against the Mike take from the pot, the personal cajoling of senior colleagues to join, my own AVC's to get close to the dreamworld of retiring with still some spunk left on nearly two-thirds final averaged salary etc, etc, etc. What a farce. As my dad would have put it "what a bugger".

Here I am putting my name to this letter addressed to all our HQ staff. Not a document I have written, just one I am required to sign. It explains that "you can no longer remain as an active member of the CAI Group Pension Fund" simply because membership has ended and the new owners must assume responsibility. Basically this is an invitation to transfer the pension arrangements although there are two other choices. Option one is a right to a preserved pension in the old scheme "but you will then not be able to join the new ….. Scheme and your pension accrual will end". Or, you have the right to transfer the value of your benefits earned up to the effective date into a Personal Pension Plan , but future contributions would be at your own cost. Whereas, the transfer to them option WILL NOT AFFECT YOUR PENSION ENTITLEMENT BUILT UP TO DATE IN ANY WAY AND THE RIGHTS AND BENEFITS WILL REMAIN EXACTLY THE SAME. Right, so this is a really difficult decision then, or rather it would be if under the preserved pension option, one could join the scheme run by the new owners also, to hedge ones bets so to speak. Or, on creation of a Personal Pension Plan, the new owners were to contribute to it in the same way as the ex-owners had done until the moratorium. As it is, it is a non-decision and consequently the new owners take charge of a nice little pension fund surplus.

And what of the new trustees? They are to be all employees of the new owners. At this news I clash seriously with the group finance man John Garvis and tell him that they can be no more than "men of straw." He does not like it. I have made an instant and senior enemy in the new camp. I do not care. These are very emotional times again and the whole affair looks to me like daylight robbery.

Is it the same business with a few juke boxes tagged on? As I had learned times over with PW, any business is a bit more than a marketplace, a few products and a pricing structure. It is about leadership, about culture, about empowerment. Forget the management theory, it is about people willingly working for you. Not for the salary but for the sheer satisfaction of it. The pride of being part of the endeavour. Leave the bullshit in the field, it is about training and helping and encouraging, if in doubt, watch the ants take a prize back to their nest.

In my opinion, these people have no idea. They are small company men with small company outlooks and mentality. Look at it this way. Before, I arrive at my office at eight. By nine o'clock the post is cleared, the paperwork sorted, we can get on with the day. Now I cannot get through the inflow until eleven-thirty am at the earliest and I have two secretaries working flat out as well. Why for God's sake? Because I am copied on everything and it will be everything since the boss man apparently sees everything and if he sees it, we all have to see it just in case we get caught out. What a load of minutiae tripe. All those years learning to separate the wheat from the chaff (what we want is good wholesome bread, not bloody sawdust), of prioritising, of making time pay. Take these monthly meetings at the new HQ (and you are welcome to them), we are still on matters arising at three-thirty in the afternoon. Gordon had taken all his decisions by twelve-thirty, he had to, he wanted a drink and in the Italian campaign he had to get gone or be blown up. Those that were bogged down in mud and then paperwork and are now bogged down in e-mails, are bogged down.

Consider the then and the now. Sixteen years after the take-over, a story appears in the Times. Headed "Cosy Morrisons falls victim to culture clash with Safeway", it refers to Morrisons as the cosy northern family-style business which employs a conservative approach to its accounting whereas the much larger Safeway embodies a more mainstream corporate culture and is considered more upmarket, has typically been more aggressive. A fund manager was quoted as saying "The two supermarkets have very different cultures, with different customer bases and it is proving difficult for Morrisons to put it's stamp on the Safeway businesss". He was concerned about the difficulty of the supermarket's inexperienced management integrating two such different businesses. All of a sudden the family run business had become three or four times bigger and required different management skills. An analyst said the acquisition had made the business much more complicated and it needs to adapt.

We, ex our lot, had experienced management but we

could not employ it. We had no latitude at all. It was all detail piled on detail. Systems and procedures and right down to individual coin slots and coin tubes. It is not coin slots and tubes that matter mate, it's human slots and tubes. It is bad luck that that 20p coin as a play coin that so irritated me during the venture capital meetings had, in the event, not produced the extra revenue anticipated. On the contrary, it had put some punters off playing the machines, at least at first. So actually Mr Smartarse from London money pots, your caution was right and our MBO, had it gone ahead, would almost certainly be in trouble and with it my £50,000 of borrowed security.

If only we could get our culture back, what has happened to me could yet prove the best option, safer, and with no Paul, and a bigger challenge. And then, Clive has his big idea for improved productivity. The combined business will be split in two but not as now geographically but hiving off the cream managed house operation into a branded Newco company and leaving all the rest, and by far the greater volume, branded as the old Bell Fruit Services.

Newco will be highly tuned to the big brewery customers and highly automated. Bell Fruit Services will have more latitude to pitch for free trade work and bulk contract and tenancy work. From a marketing standpoint, it is sound. From a practical standpoint it is ludicrous. We have spent years devising the optimum size and shape or our regions and depots and routes and staffing to now face the prospect of actually splitting in two? Like actually building walls inside depots to segregate the cream from the also-rans? Stupid. Why not keep the infrastructure in tact and manage the streams? But this is another pre-ordained decision taken somewhere in the bowels of the new group. Clive says that I am to be appointed MD of the whole of Bell Fruit Services.

To consolidate my new status, I went on this grand tour of the UK and, as a deliberate act of sentimentality, did so by train. Starting from Doncaster on the East Coast line my hand-shaking and esprit de corps took in the North East, Scotland, the North West, Midlands, South West, South East and my two East Anglia depots. It was a conscious fusion of my direct report managers and the ones from the acquirer as now transferred in. Any semblance of the old *six direct reports only* theory had gone. This will be an empirically flat structure. They can each have their head and I will control it all from my information feeds. The group photograph taken at our first conference says it all. There are thirteen managers all grinning like Cheshire cats though this Cheshire is widely spread and we have the old spirit back. Four come from the acquirer and the rest are all my personal choice from Bell Fruit Services. This will be no cake men from one side and cake men from the other, no Singaporian TAS and STB. Now we will jointly sock it to the competition, just wait and see.

Time passes and my lean, mean fighting machine is firing on all cylinders. I budget and am making a quarter of a million profit per month. But the accursed pedantic dictatorial style continues to be imposed and far from being more efficient with the superior computery, the administration side is near collapse. Mr Garvis has seen off all the best accountants including my top man in Bilston but left an awfully risky vacuum and we face nothing short of a crisis in capturing historical data. The department at the new HQ just does not seem up to it. It has got too big and too complex for them.

The Bell Fruit Services top men go one by one. Our man in the South West, Barry in East Anglia, Mike Peace from the centre and only me and our man on NAAFI are left just two years from the take-over. I think it might be worth trying my old trick of seeing the top man and cutting out the lines in between. The private lunch I have with big chairman goes OK, well why shouldn't it, we got to know each other quite well at the trade forums that Paul pushed me into. All I am trying to get across is that Clive should adopt a different style, be less dictatorial, be more trusting, delegate and reduce the paperwork. This is a big business now, we need to adopt more corporate practices. Anyway and for the good of the whole perhaps he will think about it whilst I take a holiday in Spain. On returning, I am diverted to new HQ to see Clive. He says I am to see the external personnel people next week and not to return to Nottingham. I am sacked.

John G. Smith

CHAPTER TWELVE
Life shock

1984 -1988. Dear John. Fishing the Shannon. Dark days: analysis: recovery. Sufferers in common. Julia. Of Christmas dread. A new family. Divorce and marriage. Flight to Spain. Leaving the nest. Death. End of an era. The will.

Snooker, like its poor relation Pool, is unique. Whereas with other games the object ball is whacked by racquet or bat or toe-end or club to some end or other, in snooker it's cue-end hits ball *hits ball* to end up in a precise place and not just the second ball either. The first *object* ball, needs to finish off rolling at a particular spot too if the game is to be developed and the player have any hope of winning. This adds a second and infinitely more difficult dimension. Accuracy, patience, precision, stealth and nerve. Identifying these attributes is one thing. Implementation is entirely another. Even mastering, albeit temporarily, the first three will only encourage some sod of an opponent to better the fourth and pull-off a snooker by leaving a ball between your cue ball and the object ball. Failing this, the flush of success in stringing a few pots together will inevitably generate such an adrenalin rush as to cause the nerve to fail, the cue to waver and the all important black ball to miss the pocket.

But still, from that embryo cut-down pool table in John Smithsons parents' front room on Littlemoor Lane, Newton to wherever men gather in some hotel or Conservative Club, one has to keep trying. Which is what we (Craig, Chris and me) are doing at the Electricity Club in Mansfield this Saturday evening. Indeed, I have kept my membership going for this particular purpose plus allowing my old friend Derek Hooton to thrash us individually and collectively at table tennis. It has been a great night out. We have sweated from exertion at one table and from frustration at the other. We arrive back home in high spirits, noisy banter and still full of energy and it contrasts starkly with the house which is in darkness. No television on, no music playing and neither downstairs nor it seems upstairs, no June. Strange, didn't know she planned to go out. Then I find the note. It is a classic *Dear John* although it does not strike me as such at the time. She has gone and will not be coming back. She has to be alone. Do not try to find her because we will not be able to. She will make contact at some stage when she is calmer and settled.

It is just like when I was convinced Louis was going to sack me over the Spanish affair right here in the board room in London. Except this is not the board room but the kitchen at Sheepwalk Lane, our house, our home, everything we have worked for. A sickly cavern has opened up in the pit of my stomach, someone has hit me hard down there but I did not see who, I did not see it coming. I hear myself telling Chris and Craig that their mum has gone, has left. Gone where? What for? When is she coming back? I do not know, I do not know, I cannot think straight, I cannot think at all.

One bottle of Bells Scotch a week. I must not have more but I need that much. And it's only drunk late at night when the boys are in bed. But I cannot face that bed sober. Alone. We have always slept together. Twenty years together. And the adrenalin is pumping like crazy and I'm working like a demon except there is not enough to do at Leengate. Do not know if I even have a job now, what does Mike Doherty intend to do? He takes me to one side and says my position is "character building". It does not help. I would sooner not have a character than live in this nightmare. I am an instant useless bachelor. Domestic side. I am ignorant of it and ignorant at it. I meet John Smithson most evenings now, try to talk it through, try to sort it out, have another pint, smoke another fag. When he cannot come, I 'phone Derek. When he cannot come, I despair.

There is this Irish trip. It was borne of an after-dinner boozy discussion at some corporate group function. The idea of Tony Darling of tinker-bell fame and latched onto by myself and our man in the North-East, Alan Davis. It was to be an adventure with a difference and heaven-sent for our sons. We would drive to Liverpool and catch the night ferry to Dublin and drive north-westward to Carrick-on-Shannon to pick up our cruiser. We would cruise and drink and fish the Shannon as far as Athlone across what would seem the open sea of Loch Ree. We would catch whoppers just like the Germans do but we would not use their illegal technique of cutting off the fins of live fish to lure the biggest pike. We would do it properly.

I will have to drop out now, no heart for it, no stomach for it. But it has been planned for so long and Chris and Craig have been so looking forward to the trip and given what has happened, I cannot refuse them. It is different to Jerome K Jerome's comic Victorian novel. Three men in a boat, yes but not comic, merely a modern Elizabethan tragedy. I am morose and scribbling all day in my notebooks though I do not know why except it feels like a natural purge and one day not too far into the future I will play Elton John's *I'm Still Standing* and destroy these voluminous notes as a simultaneous act of atonement. But for now I keep on writing and baiting their hooks and running the legs off Tony and Alan back from the bar with a belly-full of Guinness. And as for these other two in the boat, Tony has adopted macho-man with his need to be the constant skipper at the helm, starting up the engine at seven-thirty each morning with can of lager in hand whilst Alan adopts a dual-time function. He is either in the loo or else he is cleaning.

Back home Chris has taken to cooking for us. No words were spoken, no requests were made, no offers given, it simply happened. It does not seem an issue of being impressed perhaps because we are in this thing together, it is more like being grateful. Well, I can't cook. Never had to. Chris gets out the books just as he has always done. He studies and learns and does. Ever since the first Sinclair computer and the more advanced Dragon, it had been dedicated, penetrating study. He wrote his own programs by the time he was ten years old and whether it is the weekly instalments of *How to fish* or *Chess, the great openings*, he is not going to leave this subject until it is understood and mastered.

Before he goes upstairs to work on his A-levels at the bureau I bought from Mrytle in the cost office at Ilkeston, the cook books are on the breakfast bar and the evening meal comes together. I have found a cleaning-lady but the housework nevertheless is ever-present, never-ending, a continuous circle of cloth and clothes – get washed, dried, aired, put away, take out, wear and put back in the dirty clothes basket, start again. A boring necessity of this empty new life and I have gone fastidious about keeping everything neat and tidy and clean and in its place. I take personal note that it takes until three pm on Saturday afternoon for me to get straight. Why, why? I do not know but just keep working, keep doing things, keep busy. I give the boys maximum rein. They must carry on as normal, the scouts, the youth club, the badminton and swimming and even our snooker. Much sooner they were home all the time but normal service must be maintained. Except what was high is now low, what was light in now dark.

    I only remember telling Craig to stay in bed, that I would do his Sunday morning paper round, whether I went to bed at all is crushed under the hammer blow of the night. Had it been possible to feel more sorry for someone other than myself, that person was June's mum. Ann Painter was a good woman. She had not deserved to be hit for a third time. Had the good gods of bingo and horse-racing turned on her again? First her husband Jack had dropped dead shortly after his sixtieth birthday and then her other daughter Margaret had left her husband and four children for another woman and now the responsible, dutiful, clever and successful by all accounts daughter June had run off. Why John, why? So Ann came with me to Nottingham and trawled around the banks and the building society to tell of the news to put stops on cheques, to change accounts, to stop the credit cards. Her own daughter, her own daughter at that.

I always believed I could find June. She had a close friend with a hair-dressing business who had a friend or relation who had a bed and breakfast place on the far side of Ravenshead down a long track. But June would be in purgatory. She had made a desperate choice. I was certain of it. To go seeking her out would be fraught with danger, for her, for me, for Chris, for Craig. I am dogged with foreboding but a little voice keeps telling me to let her have her distance. It will be the family diplomat, Craig, who will make the first move. But this is no foreign policy mission. It is a move from the heart. A fourteen-year old boy needs his mother very badly.

In mourning

Those early weeks are just snatches now. I awake in the early hours because she is calling my name outside. I rush downstairs in my pyjamas and open the back door to let her in. She is not there. I run around to the front door and still no-one. Strange. I go back to fetch a torch and walk all round the house and into the garden. Nothing. If I had any neighbours who were alive, which I haven't, and who happened to be looking out of their window, they really would think I was bonkers. Alone and bonkers.

Courtesy of the corporate perks at my still esteemed level of management, this is the point where the expert peers at the electro-cardiograph and says "your heart keeps missing a beat". Without even thinking I response as an automaton "not surprised." He moves on, no suggested treatment let alone a cure. What gets me is she used to say I was her very life, that the eyes on the photograph of me in the lounge followed her around the room as she worked. We went everywhere together, Singapore, Spain, Romania, all over the UK, fishing, crabbing with the boys, talking, cooking, think back to the Blue Kettle and the alcoholic pair, the Isle of Man with Gordon desperate to get to the pub at lunchtime for his first drink whilst Jeremy and I do the work and all that champagne afterwards, and then the Isle of Wight where Craig had his bad accident. Starting off at West Hallam and the first night losing our virginity and what is he doing to her now? Being flat broke, no proper honeymoon and borrowing money off Roy to get back home, the first bit of furniture on HP and much later June singing "I miss the hungry years". Learning to drive, the scooter, Blackpool and all that. I'm going mad, going under, I have this rope up the garden under the silver birch tree that has been dying ever since Chris dug this huge hole near its roots. Chris and my promise to him when he was born with the funny shaped head, Craig that I never had proper time for when it was needed, well it's needed now. Stop. Go back to the house, calm down.

Suppose I had better set the vegetable garden again, it is the perfect time and the weather is good but then again what is the point? At last engrossed in digging and sweating I look up and June is standing there all calm and dressed up and can she fetch some more things. I show her my finger with the nail half torn off having caught it on the hook lacing up my boots, she shows no interest. Take whatever you want except leave that large porcelain bowl full of the Singapore momento match box covers from the restaurants out there. It came from Great Aunt Pem's place and it reminds me of her.

June takes what she wants, mainly the Far East stuff. Later I notice the bowl has gone too. We did try a reconciliation, we even took a family holiday to Newton Stewart in Dumfries and Galloway but every five minutes she was away from the cabin calling him on the public telephone and when back was drooling over the wrist-chain or whatever it was he had given her. There is no feeling, it has gone, she has gone. I walk with her down the long straight drive of Sheepwalk since her car is parked on the lane outside. In the back window is a sticker advertising John Smith's beer and, laconically, I point it out but she looks blank and straight through me. It means nothing. John Smiths in general mean nothing.

Making sure that I am never alone does not work. For the first time in my life I am so terribly lonely. It's just a gaping emptiness. I cannot drag myself off the floor. All around the world, in restaurant after restaurant, on long moorland walks and on clifftops, prognosticating on a company's problems, digging and setting the vegetables, it has been just me. Never once have I felt isolated. My dad once said that he found me so independent it was frightening and he's telling me now, sitting in the best room of the George & Dragon in Newton this Sunday lunch, that he has read somewhere that for every man there is potentially a hundred suitable women. Oh dad, if you only understood that it is the one woman that matters, the one that had gone off with the man who "is no better than you

– more demanding though." It really, really hurts. I feel sick, let's go.

Everywhere I go, but everywhere; the acquisition meeting in Market Harborough, the conference room in Derby some bloody background or more likely foreground music system is playing Lionel Richie's *Hello*. I know it is their tune and I cannot escape it. I have to leave the room, they must all know something is wrong. Back at base Gordon has twigged. His answer is to ply me with drink, as if I need any more. But you see I am so terribly lost. Do you know that I stare into space a lot these days, that I cannot even read. If you would put down your Daily Express and learn some real words I will spell out emetic and egregious. No, I am not trying to be smart, merely to hurt. Hurt myself I suppose. Another pop song rabbits on about "Should've known better". No, that is not quite right. You mean *Should've seen it coming*. Craig says pop songs are no different now to what they have ever been, they are not getting at me, it is just that they suddenly concern me personally. Craig, I know you are right. But I do not want to know, do I? This man standing on St Pancras station is urgently trying to impress upon his bored friend how badly he has been done by. How he's been left to cope by himself when she went off with this bastard who must have been buzzing around her for ages. He is telling my story. How many more of us are there out there?

It's theatrical. You are sitting in the stalls as before. The stage is in the same place, so are the curtains, so is the lighting rig. But it is not the same, not at all. The leading players re-appear but look the scenery has altered. We are in a different place at a different time in different circumstances altogether. Things have changed.

Taking stock

Hurt, anger, self-pity starts to wane and the space left is filled by analytical pondering. The seedcorn was probably Singapore and she desperate to leave and me wanting to stay. My facile argument hanging on frequent returns to the UK, her long holidays with the boys in the UK and our new enhanced lifestyle in Kuala Lumpur almost certainly made matters worse, not better. The countdown days to leaving were being undermined. We would go back as agreed at the outset, she would see her mum and dad again on a permanent basis. And there lies the main trigger. It had not been permanent, a mere six and a half years and her dad dropped dead.

Think what a difference those lost eighteen months abroad would have made and there had been that warning in the letter from her mum that Jack had been in hospital briefly for a "small check-up, something to do with his chest." We knew he had the coal-face workers' endemic problem referred euphemistically as *the dust*. It did seem strange that on a Saturday afternoon when we called he was always lying asleep on the sofa, a big strong chap like him and who anyway only worked when he chose to these days. No male on his side of the family had lived to be sixty, so it was to be expected. Thirty years of *dripping* (pure animal fat with salt added) sandwiches in his snap-tin, so it was to be expected. Big heavy meals and a fulsome stomach, so it was to be expected. But it wasn't. When we rushed over and learned he was dead before the ambulance arrived, June stood toe to toe with me and thumped my chest over and over again, yelling, screaming. Never had I witnessed such an outpouring of emotion.

We buried him on Christmas Eve on a cold, dank, dark, drizzly day in Annesley Churchyard. Craig was just eleven years old and it hit him very hard. From being a toddler, Craig had been Jack's "best friend". It was to Craig that he passed the best cards under the table to cheat on Boxing Day. It was Craig that went with him "bod-nesting" down my dad's field to find the green finches' eggs that would be put on Jack's head under his cap to keep warm for the broody canary to hatch to cross-breed later to produce canary colours from the bright yellow through the greens to the sparrow-like grey-browns. And it was Craig who was now crying the most.

So that was the start of the big change. She went for this medical to check if she had inherited the family heart problem. Then it was the sporty episode, occasionally playing squash with me but more surprisingly taking up volley ball that was a very minority activity involving, so far as I could see from the places I took her to, mainly men. Concurrently there was the ladies' darts team events and after joining the Women's Institute many social gatherings in the neighbourhood. There was also more time and effort going into the job she had graduated to after doing the secretarial course at the same college that set me off in business studies all those years back. It developed only gradually but the free evenings at home got less and less and the time arriving back home got later and later. Sometimes I went looking for her and often she would be in a car after a meeting or game talking to a female friend.

During this transition she was on a diet, a successful diet and granted that her wonderful ginger-coloured hair was losing some sparkle, suddenly the style changed constantly, now short, now growing long again, now this colour, now that and including a most vivid red/bronze tint at one stage. But June is entitled to alter her image, if that is what it is. The boys are growing up and she has her own money now and independence, it's a fitting reward for the years of mothering and wifery. Anyway, I like the slim-down version, the new woman look, the bacardi and coke, cinzano and lemonade lady. Except our love-making isn't the same. Well it is in terms of frequency and spontaneity but for some reason the feeling isn't there. I don't know why, perhaps it's me, and most recently she turns her back on me a lot. And then this name crops up a lot, this maintenance bloke at the printing plant who's wife treats him abominably but who is a good dart-player and will I take her tonight to this pub where his team is playing, she wants to support them. Funny, I thought if I had to worry at all it was about that school teacher chap that she says is actively chatting her up at the volley-ball club. Yes, should've seen it coming all right, but I did not. They got it together in his car in the woods one night and afterwards he gave her something else. An ultimatum.

Recuperation

The reason I keep playing Elton John's "I'm still standing" on the jukebox is because I am getting better, pulling out of this tailspin. It pushes me on with these domestics, spurs me on towards three o'clock, to finish, to have a cup of tea outside on the sunny patio overlooking the garden with its profusion of flowers and wait. Pray and wait. Wait and hope that Julia will turn up. She will have been ironing my shirts and baking a cake, it's just a question of how she gets them here and when. It has reached this stage gradually, just out of the kindness of her heart really. I don't think I actually asked her to do any ironing but it was fairly obvious that the shirts in particular were getting badly neglected and Julia, being the person she is as I am beginning to realise, started taking them away and bringing them back all fresh and clean and beautifully pressed. And as for the cake, well she knows I like cake and there was always cake around when they came up to play bridge and like now as we sit and talk over the tea.

Julia had been the first person I had told and she poured out a whisky even at this early hour and tried to get out of me why June had gone. It was a mysterious blow to her and Alan grounded on friendship over several years now and founded on the Saturday evening bridge sessions alternating between our respective homes. I had suggested to Alan in the Nottingham PW office that we could teach him and his wife Julia to play bridge, a not altogether altruistic move once I had spotted the tall, dark-eyed Spanish beauty by his side at the cocktail party. I had increasingly flirted as time and bridge skills had moved on but it was no more than banter to go with the cans of Mansfield ale and Cinzano and gin and tonic and nibbles and my outrageous bids of six no trumps to contrast with Alan's super-cautious one spade openings.

Julia was a slow player and, as I increasingly became to appreciate, a good one. She thought deeply about the cards and only played when she understood them. Her decisions were calculated but when they came, they were right. This lack of impetuosity now made June's action virtually unfathomable to Julia. At least, I was reading it this way and aside from all else our evenings had suddenly stopped. Of the three of us left, Julia missed our bridge Saturdays the most, all we have now is our fleeting meeting for tea and a cake on these Saturday afternoons.

You can understand why people with a particular disorder, affliction, extraordinary problem, are drawn together. It often starts as a necessary congregation to receive expert help or be availed of specialist facilities. Whether the remote site in Devon for the autistic inmates of Cottage And Rural Enterprises with the heart-rendering generosity of spirit of the girl teacher in the soft-toy shop or the boy who ran the breeze-block manufacturing section or the head-man with his cows to feed and milk to sell at the market. You would cling to that isolated spot no matter if a famous cricketer or a common man if your son or daughter had that affliction. Just as a famous actor or the common man visits the local centre for the mentally impaired because their child was born that way.

Then the relationship grows into research of causal affects, treatments, consequences, philosophy. Bonds develop with others in the same position, associations are born, some transient, others stable. When life itself has changed, there is a new depth to understanding and in some cases a devotion will set in extending way beyond the individual event that triggered things off. To appreciate this facet of human behaviour is to realise why people are magnetized by your personal situation. At the superficial and flippant level there are the letters writ large on ones forehead that say something like *available* although the exact wording cannot be detected with certainty since you, the bearer, cannot see it. But then, it is not necessary to for it is beaming forth like a lighthouse beacon on a foggy night. They might be ladies at work, the quietly spoken woman who checks me in at the squash centre or complete strangers that pass on the street, it might even be a female in a neighbouring lodge as I suffer with the futile attempt at a holiday patch-up. At a deeper physiological level comes the common sufferer.

Because it has happened to you, so it is open season for confessions. I am told that this close member of my own family did it with a customer and because his wife found out, so she did it with an admirer. Then someone else says that this bird has done it with him and he has done it with someone else and her affair has been going on for ages but her husband, stupid sod, doesn't know and as for her, well, he's always on the pull and she doesn't care 'cause she hates him and wishes he would just bugger off permanently. Wow, and I never knew. But I know now don't I? They are not trying to hurt and they are not being much help either, it's just that my situation is not unique and they are placing me in the everyday camp. Admittedly being out of the blue and precipitately shoving off is a bit drastic mate, but there it goes, want another pint? Well, collectively, that's their sordid little lives. I want nothing to do with it.

This is the biggest surprise. A real heart-stopping jolt. Julia is telling me she is not happy. Having thought I was used to soaking up these personal stories, this is one I would never have expected. Not from Julia. Not of Julia. There is no feeling left, none at all. Alan is always working, even at weekends, up in his room. He does not notice her any more. How can anyone not notice Julia? My Spanish senora with the flashing dark eyes and legs to die for. She is dragged down by the confession. She looks so miserable. So beautiful. I move closer on the sofa and kiss her. Out of all this misery, we have found each other.

Brave new world

But Julia has to go away. This big family holiday with Alan and the children Stella and Neil has been planned for a long time. It's to California with a lot of driving, maybe two to three thousand miles apparently. I have this itinerary in order to spiritually track the progress after this low-spirited progress to Nottingham Midland Railway Station to where I have long since been commissioned to drive the family on the first leg of the great journey. Feeling an absolute heel is tempering my self-pitying depression at losing her so soon. She looks so gorgeous this bright morning as I wave them off as the train leaves on its journey to London St Pancras, that station that seems to store up more drama for me as the years pass. I stand a long time on that platform looking down the line that emptied of those accelerating carriages and a lot of me has left with them. This is the downline passing the Motive Power Depot of my first job at which I was with some duplicity advised both to be "careful" and "give it to" Betty. But then I thought I loved Betty, so it would have been alright either way, just as I was sure I loved June all those years. But perhaps I was wrong on both counts and have been wrong on so many things in between. What I feel now is so totally different, selfish, mean, a Judas, all these and more but it is so absolutely wonderful and beautiful that it just cannot be wrong. I know I am still emotionally a wreck but even so I do not see how I can have a future without Julia. But she has just left with a devoted long-standing husband and two very fine children and anyway she is far too classy for me. I am just a struggling worker bee whose career is looking increasingly in jeopardy. It is hopeless really and we have already told ourselves so. This is a very steep set of stairs up from the platform to the walkway to the carpark and I have stumbled twice already. I cannot focus properly, these eyes are full of water.

Many years later when turning out, three small papers come to light. They have a pre-printed heading Norfolk Education Committee and are stamped or written up for Burnham Market School as the Report of Attendance, Conduct and Progress of Julia Moorhouse for the three consecutive years when she was aged 9, 10 and 11. And I had thought Spanish. Just as good a pedigree though, North Norfolk from the Viking line? And here we have it, absolute proof. Position in Class – 1st, then again next year 1st and oh dear for year three dropping to 3rd, but that's ok it's only caused by Drawing and Handwork, five marks gained out of a possible twenty-five whilst Arithmetic and Mental both score fifty out of fifty. So what an incredible parallel with me except I had to escape to Tibshelf Secondary Modern from age 11 and had the dishonest guile to get one Raymond to do my Artwork for me and so disguise my equally large deficiency in that department. This is not the only coincidence either. Julia's dad made his living from about 38 acres of land, exactly as did mine, although his living proved to be far superior due to the quality of the land. Poor coal-ridden soil on hilly ground in down-market Derbyshire is no match for the rich and flat Norfolk fields in up-market Burnham Market that bred Lord Nelson next door. Sorry Mr Albert E Evans, head teacher but one cannot help notice that "Parents are earnestly requested to co-operate with the head teacher by carefully examining this report" contains two split infinitives.

The first card arrives and all the cleverer because the message is not in the words written on it (the bridge brain at work here). It is of Alcatraz as it (printed) "basks in the California sunshine in the middle of San Francisco Bay." A prison amongst the beauty. Just how I feel at this end. The card comes from the Smith Novelty Co. The next card, three days later, comes from Death Valley and the message ends "1 week gone – See you Sat." Gee, I hope so. You enjoy your "ice and whiskey" in your 90 degree heat, I will have a whisky and ginger, but later. Just a bit choked right now.

So we set off as we left off. And we have solved, partly solved, the problem of how to meet. Good old Reg Conway, my technical director, says I can use his little bungalow any time I like. We rendezvous in an intermediate and downbeat battered car park that matters not at all because we are riding this glorious high and see nothing of the surroundings. I wear my blazer because she wants me to as it is special to her and have my special way of looking at her that she has never known before and I bring the wine and she brings the towel and the lunch and I set this, to me, world record for the number of times in a daylight day. And it is awful when we part and often now Julia is getting home after the children are back from school which she is very guilt ridden about. In the morning as I drive down the lane she is at the bedroom window waving and looking and smiling and then waiting for my call from the office before the day starts. And sometimes we can meet at the Burnt Stump, Mansfield Brewery pub for a snatched lunch of prawn open sandwich in marie-rose sauce or at Woodthorpe park in Nottingham where we walk hand-in-hand as lost lovers. But today we do not leave the car because Julia has a stumbling speech to make that is oblique and deep and that permeates my brain only gradually. But at last I get it. We have to stop. It has to end. Her life, her security, the family, her children all demand it of her. She is going mad. It has to end and right now. John 'phones that evening and says we have to meet. Julia has called him at work and asked him to look after me, I am going to need help, extra special help.

It is a lot to do with expectations really. When I did the job at a police force I learned that most of the officers did not expect to be promoted. It was not part of the expectation package. Start as a constable and maybe years on after passing the exams and getting through the interview, be elevated to sergeant. Both jobs carry decent pay and pension prospects and are responsible positions. Nothing more is expected. Recognise that the university degree wallahs will come in as or be promoted rapidly to inspector level and above. Just accept it, after all it provides a lovely scorn target and everyone needs that.

The reverse is absolutely what is wrong with the professions. Just because you are deemed good or have had a stroke of luck, there is no reason to be promoted, just pay more, pay for worth. I never wanted to be elevated to manager and then senior manager at PW, I was content on the shop-floor actually doing consultancy jobs. And if there is a cultural expectation of promotion in so many years or whatever, it can breed nothing but disharmony. If one gets there, well that is standard but when one doesn't, there is natural disappointment, resentment and seeping anger. For what purpose? Why feed the expectation in the first place? We need long-standing experienced consultants just as we have with constables and sergeants. As a matter of fact, Jack Painter (June's dad) flatly refused the offers of promotion. Why should he even aspire to be an under-manager at the pit and then a manager? He wanted to keep doing what he was good at, working the coalface and being one of the lads. His insistence probably helped kill him. Anyway, the principle holds good.

That is what is hurting the most. I have been thinking a lot about it. The expectation had crept up on me. Julia and I would be together. In spite of the hurt we would cause, in spite of the impossibility of the contemplation and the enormity of the practical difficulties, we would be together. What would it do to the children? How would we manage them? Could they gel together? Aside from us, what about Alan? How could we consciously, deliberately set out to do to him what had been done to me? He is a good man, aside from coldness and some neglect, he has done nothing wrong. He even took me out for a drink to say that notwithstanding my situation, I should at all cost concentrate on my job, it was most important to keep working, keep the money coming in. Alan, I know you are sincere and I know you are right, but, but….

Even so, even so, in my heart I expected us to get together, sometime, somehow. I did not think my beautiful, desirable Julia who I know I have made happy, laugh, see excitement, subterfuge adventure, have passionate feelings, get wet through. I did not think we would come to a crashing full stop. But she is right.

Not everyone looks forward to Christmas. Frances Soubry whose David died on Christmas day, Ann Painter whose Jack was buried on Christmas Eve, all the bereaved at this time, all dreading it coming around again amongst the majority in excess; commerce at its most greedily grasping. All those who are ill, those that are dying and perhaps hated most of all by all those who are alone and those not alone but terribly lonely.

Julia has written me two notes both hidden under papers on the breakfast bar. The first a brief message "Darling, I hope I don't miss you as much as I think I will, if so it'll be an awful week. I love you so much, I just want to be with you all the time." The second more of a letter "My darling, I'm not very good at letter writing so this is brief. Think of me as I think of you, love me as I love you and pray for me over the next week – very hard. I need you so much, and I need your love and strength to get me through. As you said "nothing worthwhile is easy" how right you were. Don't ever stop loving me – I don't think I would survive it. I love you, Julia." Then the Christmas card "For John, Chris & Craig. With love from the Folks up the hill." They are staying at home so we will have to leave Ravenshead for the duration, it is the only way to get through this, duty and desire in direct conflict. My mum and dad will be pleased to have us and maybe Christmas day or Boxing day I will walk up to Tibshelf to see my sister and her family just for the family's sake. I haven't seen him since the confession. But really it will be so terribly hard, I would not have made an actor or a spy. My Christian upbringing was truly too straight for all this.

It had only lasted one week. Julia 'phoned to say she was so very low and unhappy and she had almost had an accident in the car after leaving me last week and had gone through lights on red, she just could not see straight or think straight and whatever the consequences we had to meet again. And I was thinking that I had been pulled from a whirlpool that some invisible hand had pushed me into with no hope of rescue and yet here I was on the bank panting and alive. Yes, that was it. Lifesaver. Julia has saved my life. I may have been a bad husband, a hustler, a pusher, a workaholic, a selfish one-sider but that would all change. I could change and I would change. Sod the job. Sod Bell Fruit Services and the lot of them, sod the whole stinking industry. Who cares what happens? I have been thrown this lifeline and I will always be in redemption. The only thing that matters now and from now on is Julia and the boys. I will be a good partner and father and this will be the number one priority. This is no passing feeling, it is permanent. No slipping back into old ways, a life saved is a life changed. I am so terrifically happy. I have never been happier before and I will never be happier again. My

Spanish senora has come back to me.

Julia is the practical one and she knows what we will have to have. There will be four children from ages eleven upwards in two yearly gaps. We will have to create two more bedrooms downstairs so the quiet small room will have to be converted and as the worst room with only the one north-facing window, we will take it. The games room can become Neil's bedroom with its large space and patio window facing the back garden but I will have to dispose of the equipment, maybe to the village youthclub? Well ok but not the jukebox, never the 1973 Wurlitzer that will now play Elton John's "I'm still standing" so that I can actually believe it. Can't I?

Stella will have my (ex mine and June's) big bedroom upstairs and so Chris and Craig can stay where they are, this will be most important if we are to have any chance of knitting the new family together, plus Chris is buried in books for his A levels and Craig has his own designer gear within his multi-coloured walls. It can work, we think, but two more beds are needed and Julia is so terribly nervous when we go to Mansfield Co-op furniture department. Will anyone she knows spot us together? What would she do?

One Saturday afternoon she tells me "1st February." That is the date she has decided upon. They are going away for a weekend to a favourite place in Yorkshire so that she can tell Alan properly and try to explain. I am wrong to think he might do something "silly." Alan is not like that. He will be shocked when he learns it is me though. Good long-standing friend and one-time office colleague John from up the road. How can I be so happy and be such a bastard at the same time?

Well, at least children are very adaptable (think how Chris and Craig got used to Singapore – far quicker than I did) and it's not as if they do not know me, after all we always picked up Neil when we went kicking the football into the nets on the playing field and we could hardly have got our little cricket team together on Burnt Stump Park without him, he being the best batsman. And Stella, well that is different of-course. Never had a daughter, this has been an all male household for a while now and how will they all get on under one roof and how will she get on with Chris and Craig. She is bound to develop a crush on Craig, all girls do. But there are always a thousand reasons why not and we have come too far by now.

John Smithson helps me to move the furniture around. This bed here, that wardrobe there, working to Julia's plan but there is no Julia, there never has been in an evening, that is her time for her family down the road and in my heart of hearts I still do not believe it will happen. We go for a pint. I am on the edge of a precipice again. He is very quiet. It is a strange surreal time. On this lovely bright clear day they are walking up the drive. Julia has Sheba the beautiful pedigree Samoyed on a lead and she and Stella and Neil are each carrying a case. The folks up the hill, less Alan, have joined the folks down the hill. True to her thoroughly thought through and considered word, Julia has done it. A full stone in weight lighter than the slim Julia I first ventured to kiss on the sofa, she is here in the kitchen with her family and is trembling and Sheba does not know what to make of my mongrel part-collie Bonnie or my ginger cat Asti. Actually, now it has happened, none of us know what to make of each other.

Alan dealt with their divorce very efficiently. They remained good friends, there was no animosity, merely sadness on both sides, it was all very civilised. Julia fetched the few personal things she wanted like the small furniture pieces made by her Uncle Albert the retired stonemason and now church lay-reader and who magnanimously was the first amongst equals at the Norfolk end in shaking my hand and saying "welcome to the family". A gesture never to be forgotten, an act of etiquette possibly but from an old Norfolk gentleman one of deep Christian significance. A change of partner to someone of his generation is hard to acquiesce but he had taken me to one side in his cosy little bungalow across from Burnham Westgate parish church and said he had never seen Julia looking so happy and bright. He poured me a sherry from the wall-mounted corner cupboard that some years later he would leave to Julia in his will.

We married in as low a key mode as we felt we could get away with. We took even less interest in the back-street ordinariness of Mansfield Registry Office than we had of the shabby car park of our early rendezvous. Ours was not a glamorous stage set. The whole thing was over in twenty minutes and almost less trouble in total than Julia had signing the certificate with a hand shaking from the events of the past eighteen months. We lunched at Perkins because it had been the romantic setting of our very first proper and clandestine date. Not that any of the other twelve diners in our party knew that or cared. The four children were too occupied playing at adults and Neil in particular too busy dashing hither and thither making sure he was on every single photograph. They had got on well with each other and did not judge or challenge but accepted the new order and welded us all together. There were no outsiders to be embarrassed by my choked-up attempt at a speech that was supposed to be about keeping the family together and making Julia stay happy. John and Marilyn had driven my mum and dad and then there was just Phil Holmes, my second trustee of the dark days, and Margaret his wife and Julia's best friend Brenda and husband Frank. And that was that. The biggest celebrity event of the year. There was no-one from Norfolk, no-one from Julia's family. Would her mum and dad have come? Julia did not think it was right to put them on the spot and at this time she was not close to her sister though that is destined to change in the years ahead. So she stood alone in the new set-up. Everything is on the line. All bets are on the one number. It has to work out, there is nowhere else to go.

The highly-charged drive from Perkins to our village hotel near the airport is the first time we have been without the children since the start and the wave-off has had an eerie resonance. Julia is clinging on to me like grim death and after the emotion and champagne, I am having to concentrate really hard to navigate back around Nottingham to find Castle Donnington. But now can we loosen this intensity, do we have any chance of being ourselves again? This bottle of champagne in our bedroom courtesy of my boardroom colleagues is sure to help as will the four-poster that might, but does not, take the strain.

The early morning flight and the long rainy drive north from Alicante will take us to Javea and Paul's villa up the hillside at Rafalette. This marvellous gesture is boosted by his meticulously written notes on the locality and its offerings including the nearest supermercado with its "mind-blowing array of booze". And on that theme, here is yet another bottle of champagne for us and he bought this hideaway during an alcoholic fuelled feverish hot Spanish afternoon session. Well cheers Paul, good decision man, good decision if only I could work this gas-bottle-fuelled energy supply or re-set the electricity after every lightning strike. But fortunately Charles across the road can fix things for me whilst his dear old plump wife imbibes Julia not with the alcohol that all seem to believe we need but with advice on how to relax about the left-behind children. They will be fine and she can and must unwind and enjoy this heaven-sent belated honeymoon. I reward Paul with our selection of a nice Spanish pot protected in the case by the undies and by showing him a photo of Julia standing on his balcony without undies but in her multi-coloured itsy-bitsy bikini taken by me standing in the garden below. He always had a ruddy- coloured face but right now I honestly think he might explode.

It is a test of management. Fairly advanced management

and not heavily dealt with in the text books. Welding two families into that which might approximately be regarded as one, takes managerial skill. If the free-wheeling laissez faire and often absent style of child rearing rubs up against the more disciplined rule-bound structure, it can be expected that at certain times things might be inclined towards the fractious. It may be that a certain young lady might storm up the stairs to her room because something has been said out of turn, or that the joint head of the household might walk into a certain young man's bedroom and encounter his dalliance with a first girlfriend or the other joint head feels the need to call a board meeting of all the occupants in a vain attempt to lay down rules aimed at cutting the executive telephone bill. However, that is what management is all about, managing a situation you find yourself in. Will we survive it? You bet we will.

The first to leave the nest is Chris. He has been accepted at his first choice university Bath, first because it has five professors of maths and that is what he will read both pure and applied. His conscientious studying paid off with two A's and one B at A level and so he is well in. And out, well or not. I am drawn to his small room like a magnet with its now deserted old writing bureau that I used to see him sitting at even at weekends when I was in the garden. A lot of his books and model ships are still here but he has gone and I have this feeling he will not come back. I feel very sad and I will try to shake it off and not come up tomorrow night, but I do. It must be like this for all parents and yet with the three of us living together after June went and Chris taking on the cooking and keeping me mentally alert, it really seems that it is worse for me. The little one I vowed always to look after has left of his own volition to start a new life many miles away in some dingy pokey hole of a student house. I want him back. But as the disciplinary parents, of which I was never one, say "I want doesn't get."

If time didn't heal we would all be cast permanently

onto the emotional rocks with no hope of getting back into the swim. As it is, we can breast-stroke the sea of potential acquisitions. Any on the South coast or in the South West can cause me to stop off in Bath for a drink and a meal in the great little French restaurant we have found just over the bridge, and anyway its an adventure to go up the steep hill and see the bustling concrete edifice at its university best with all sizes and races rubbing together in intellectual endeavour and then drinking together in the crowded town bars. It brings me back to my bell-ringing dreaming days in Nottingham amongst the students and wishing I could have been as them. Never mind, make the most of these precious hours and Chris telling me about his tutor professor who lives in this flat with no furniture or trappings at all. His mind is on higher things.

Later, when he has his year out working for British Gas at Cramlington north of Newcaste upon Tyne, I can visit my depot up there and he can walk from his digs at Hazlerigg (wonderful names as in the next village of Wide Open as taken from the rocks off the North Northumberland Heritage Coast amongst the Farne Islands), past the racecourse to my posh hotel in Gosforth. We use the leisure facility, with its barrel of iced water to plunge into after the sauna, and drink in the ship-shaped bar before I buy him a meal and pour him into a taxi. If only such days could last.

As time passes so the family will disentangle. Stella will move back to be with her father who still lives alone, Craig will go off to his university in Liverpool where he has cunningly arranged to be with his now long-standing girlfriend Newal, and eventually even Neil will leave school and head north to Newcastle for a masters in civil engineering. And so we will be alone and as Paul pronounces as he assesses against a list of qualitative headings the relative merits of his wife versus his mistress and turns his attention to our select group of directors "but

John and Julia are solid as a rock."

And it is a wonderful life. Throughout these first few years, that Julia would stay and settle and be happy amongst the work and chaos and mis-aligned upbringings was beyond my realm of hope. But somehow a form of compromised harmony predominated and maybe the fact that is just has to work and that we two have to be undivided and self-supportive, that there is no option because of what we did and the way we feel about each other, maybe all this makes life work. Actually it's the fear that she will not stay that has been the hardest to conquer. A scar from a bad event can be both deep and slow healing. When Julia goes shopping or "home" to Norfolk or out with her children, why should she come back? Will she come back? It is only when she does so consistently over a long period that it even begins to seem natural. Only very slowly does the anxiety start to seep away and only now have I virtually forgotten that it used to be the most powerful thing in my whole being. Mine was a modest and common wound; think of those lanced by a murder or rape or fatal accident or maiming or disappearance. How will that scar ever heal and especially, unlike me, if the grieving person cannot come to terms with even wanting it to?

So there are no demons and I'm thinking straight and clearly and in the best possible place for cogitation, my very green and now half-harvested vegetable patch. It is a lovely, sunny, warm August Saturday afternoon and Julia is knocking on the kitchen window to get my attention. My brother Alan's wife Lynn is on the 'phone saying my dad has been taken ill, they do not know what is wrong but have called an ambulance and will I come over straight away. As I walk across the farmyard my sister comes rushing up to say she thinks my dad is very ill, it all happened very suddenly, one minute he was ….., she is still talking rapidly when I get to the kitchen where it is very quiet and Lynn comes up and says with little emotion that my dad is dead.

The ambulance men got him out of the bath in a sling and have taken him into their ambulance and pronounced him dead. She is a carer and understands these things. All the children are standing around in silence, my mum is somewhere in the background saying nothing. The ambulance men want to know if I will follow the van to Chesterfield Royal hospital to "deal with the formalities."

All I could think of was that I had promised to go over last Wednesday evening because he did not feel so good last Saturday after initially recovering well from his operation. But I did not go, I was so busy at work. Bloody work again. Bloody work. I simply cannot understand how he could have died, he was as strong as any of the bulls we used to walk our heifers to and as before he never stopped doing things. True, he had stopped walking down the fields to the pit hills because he had difficulty getting back up the really steep bit before the stackyard but he was always walking around the farmyard, feeding and fetching and carrying. In fact he had apparently just collected the hen eggs before going for his bath in the downstairs bathroom from which Lynn heard a strong gurgling sound prompting her to go in and see him lying there in the water.

We were talking together in the farm garden last Saturday and he had one of his cackling laughs after telling me that the consultant thought he ought to know that they had injected him with some form of female hormone "but don't worry George, you wont turn into a woman." Well it was funny, after all he had been sorted out. Those varicose veins had been stripped out some years ago as each leg was done on separate occasions, those awful knotted legs that he attributed to years of hard physical labour on the farm and not least, in his view, those early years when he had to clean out and get the cows ready for milking before he even went into school and so earning the wrath of his teacher and which led to his lifelong hatred for that profession. "Call that a profession!" And the lifelong is over. It must emanate from the water trouble. It seems he had had trouble passing urine for some time before anyone knew, well he was secretive by nature (my mum saying "George gets the post and takes it to his desk in there and I never see it and I have no idea what's going on and he writes up his books for you on Sunday afternoon and I do not know how the farm is doing.") Poor mum, what will she do now?

He went in for some treatment though none of us knew quite what but it was an emergency in that he could not pee at all and in great pain. Whilst poking around they had also sorted out his hernia and again whether that was as a result of Julia's suggestion or it would have been done anyway, who knows. That's the thing with these hospitals, is it a case that they have a policy not to communicate because, say, they run the risk of being accountable for something spoken or for fear of letting some cat out of the bag or to consciously ameliorate undue foreboding from an ignorant public? And is that why there is never any obvious sign of management present in that if there were then we the concerned relatives might jump to a conclusion that such controllers might know some answers indeed might even proffer some chat about dad's condition, what they intend to do and hope to achieve. Mate, you live in what my uncle Harry would have called cloud cuckoo land. This 'ere NHS set up in poor old Derbyshire offers only mushroom management, that is, keep 'em in the dark and pour shit on 'em mate. A sad final state backed by nil points technology. Er, sorry mate, what did you say, pass computer files between you at the end of a shift to save the round-table twenty minute long hand-over chat with the eight of you in the private room off the ward, no way mate, always done it this way, safer this way and anyway someone might not be able to understand the other's notes ya see.

The hernia used to be a family mystery like the brown-paper envelopes that came through the post and the white Basildon Bond envelope in the bottom draw of the chest in their bedroom that had written on the outside in dad's hand "my will." When we went on the rare trip by bus to Mansfield for that specific purpose, I had to wait outside the shop with my mum whilst dad went inside the dreaded Surgical Appliances shop on Clumber Street. What had he gone in for? It took years of prying to find out that he had sustained a rupture as a very young man and he had to wear a special belt that literally held his guts in. And now the punic bastards had done him in. My wise counsellor, my best friend, the one who carried me on the crossbar of his bike, who bought me that first rickety bike from Chesterfield cattle market and rode it home, the one who cleaned my shoes every single night for work next day in the railway office in Nottingham, the one who taught me how to garden, how to treat authority with disdain. Sunday lunchtime will never ever be the same again, he turning to my mum "mother, is there anything in your purse?" And I didn't even say goodbye. I put stupid work first. I stop the car and cry uncontrollably. No-one knows, I do not want them to.

Julia says we must not stay too long and we can only look. And he looks perfectly alright. The deep furrows in his forehead and cheeks are there but they always have been and he still has his hair although it's completely grey but what I can't get over is his hands, they are still as massive as ever just lying there one on top of the other and they are still pitted black in all the creases. I thought to myself well they might have cleaned him up nicely but to take that away at the last would have been both a hygienic impossibility but more importantly a travesty. Those are the earning marks of years on the land with the crude implements and the animals and the garden soil and the muck-spreading and the frost and the sweat from the haymaking. I don't think he felt much at the end in his watery grave, I hope to God he didn't anyway. We mustn't stay any longer because aunt Ruth and cousin Nancy are waiting outside Wilkinson's

Chapel of Rest on this Old Blackwell Church Hill to pay their last respects too. I take one last look and Julia kisses him on the cheek and we leave.

On my dad's side of the family (he is still here watching over as far as I am concerned) Wilkinson's Funeral Directors have always dealt with things. Not that that made the old man immortal and his daughter is telling us that she took over but sub-contracts it all out to a really good reliable firm in Chesterfield and we will need two of their big cars and the pall-bearers are always smartly dressed out as I will know from the past. There will be a church service but he is to then go to Mansfield Crematorium. This is what he specifically wanted. He had lost his faith many years ago. That was one thing he had made no secret of. Even though we had gone year after year, Sunday evening after Sunday evening to that churchyard to take flowers to the grave of his young-dying mum and dad, even though Great Aunt Pem was there, even though uncle Edmund was there, he chose not to be.

End of an era

When a farmer dies and it is the end of the line, or as people keep on saying, the end of an era, a bit more than normal is involved in assembling the estate. There is most likely livestock and what the man from our chosen firm Bagshaws of Ashbourne is describing most unfortunately as "deadstock." Well, the latter can be left till later but whilst my brother Alan is looking after the animals for now this can only be temporary because he has a full-time job and will not be taking over the farm. So this is just about the most painful part of a too rushed episode, he and I are watching my dad's *young beasts* being sold at Derby cattle market. This place along with Chesterfield is where I have stood with him many times and watched frustrated as he let the best ones get successfully bid for whilst we ended up with what I thought were the cheap scrag-end and from which he nevertheless somehow produced a sellable fat young beast subsequently. And here they were going under the hammer for the last time.

Why wasn't Alan going to be the next farmer George? Because he did not have it in him. I used to puzzle over this phenomenon but now having, so called, risen to the job I do, I see clearly via the people below me. It is not a question of up and down, but of aptitude which is the same thing as saying the gene-set you are born with. I must come down from the original John Smith and Hedley Herbert Wilson, taking things on, taking people on, are not big issues for me. There are many in the ranks with far superior skills to mine, more dextrous, more arty, more learned, but what about the nerve side of things (passing exams that Tony failed for example), what about handling people, planting a seedcorn that turns into their idea, making them want to work? Years ago I thought Mick my brother-in-law ought to start his own building business and John my best friend ought to open a garage. Technically both were well equipped to succeed. But they did not, would not, could not. It is to do with risk aversion but more with responsibility, that is, not feeling they should carry it. Just as well really or else there would be no hands to hire.

So with Alan. He had been doing the bulk of the work since he was fifteen years old. Instead of throwing him into the big wide world, my dad kept him at the farm and he got a job. He would joke "how many blokes get their first pay packet at age fifty". How many blokes shelter a son that way? Alan knew the land, the animals and the neighbouring farmers and was an excellent tractor driver and was physically very strong. But …

As my dad got older, so there was less and less to be made out of a small acreage and Alan too got a job (or rather my dad got him a job where he worked at the cable repairing depot of the Coal Board at Hilcote) and so they ran the place together, part timers as it were. He owed his home to his dad too. Great Aunt Pem had left her bungalow to my dad but her house in Littlemoor Lane (that had been rented to my best friend John's parents) to Alan. Then my dad did a clever thing. He got the properties exchanged, installing Alan in the fine bungalow property, where uncle Edmund had developed a first-class garden, and he took the semi-detached house that he promptly sold. Smart bloke my dad. Alan was set up for life, no mortgage and little or no responsibility. The final piece in my dad's jigsaw was a few years later to suggest to Alan that he move with his family back to the farm and he and my mum take the bungalow as a nice retirement place close to the shops in the village and right opposite my mum's sister. Alan refused. That is how my mum and dad got stuck at the farm with my mum slowly going blind with closing cataracts and increasingly crippled by osteoarthritis. Once a paradise, now a prison.

What would happen to them and the farm used to worry me a lot trying with great difficulty, emotionally and practically, to raise it with him properly. The perfect chances came when we had our Sunday lunchtime pint at the Trust (Robin Hood) pub in Newton. But it never worked. Either I couldn't even start on the subject or when I did it was either too late to develop or he was too capable at fending me off. Sell up and move into Newton? "they'll take me away from the farm in a box." Leave it to me and I will pay off Alan and Margaret, make it a condition, that way it will stay in the family. If I cannot move there, still I'll make it work somehow. No response. Well, make a proper will anyway. "Arr, when I'm ready." That is how I know he knew. The proper will (what happened to the white envelope in the upstairs drawer?) is dated just two months before that terrible Saturday afternoon.

In his last year my dad must have given deep thought to his will. He had always been poor, but here we have my old friendly theory of revenue versus capital again. Impecuniousness is lack of what one can get ones hands on, by necessity or choice. Normally, at any rate at this time, capital is not readily available and if it consists of land, buildings and a living, not at all. However, he was very aware that on his death the low yielding farm would nevertheless command a good value to someone who didn't want it as a living but as the basis of a lifestyle.

So, founded on fairness whilst concurrently passing an inheritance through his children to the next generation, he devised a plan. A plan that contained initially a bad flaw, although it would be years before I knew of this. My mum, sitting with her feet on the footstool to aid circulation as she had been instructed, told me quite out of the blue "George told me what he intended to do and I said, but what about me?" Apart from the house contents, his proposed will excluded her altogether. He acquiesced immediately. How very odd, I cannot believe he wanted to hurt her, it must have been that his mind was wholly focused on how he could benefit everyone and this blotted out what, in under one year's time, would have been a partnership lasting a half century.

Yet it was and still is a puzzle, after all it would have been perfectly normal for him to have simply left everything to his wife "and let her sort it out" as he had said to me more than once. But he had very definitely decided sometime in those last months not to do this. Was this because he had a fear that his wife would cut out their daughter completely over all the trouble that had been caused over the years? Was it because he feared that pressure would be applied from that quarter to unduly influence an increasingly frail and disabled mother? Who knows, but it must have been that he wanted to make sure no matter what had gone on over the years that Margaret received her rightful share and so also her children, and just that.

Flesh and blood is hard to deny and more so when grandchildren come along. Margaret had always been a worry though she looks a sweety as a ten-year old on the wedding photograph of uncle Eric and aunt Betsy but looks can be deceptive and whether it started with a boy down the fields or whether it would all have happened anyway, I do not know. As she moved into the teenage years, her skirts were too tight, her blouses too low, her heels too high and her lipstick too red. She was pregnant by the sixteen-year old boy from the builder's yard and succeeded in having four children quickly, one after the other.

My mum and dad had no choice but to play a huge part in these grandchildren being fed, clothed and generally brought up and her loyal husband Mick worked his socks of all week, and all weekends too, bringing in the bread. Whenever she opened her mouth, it was trouble. I can see my dad now bent double walking the latest toddler round the kitchen or stackyard and pulling himself up straight with a groan holding his back as if he had just weeded a long row of peas in the garden or been singling turnips in the field. And whilst Mick laid bricks she brought her brood to the farm each Saturday morning to be fed by my mum before taking off with eggs, milk, vegetables and anything else going. Which was why she was there that Saturday. Alan would be mucking out the animals so, as usual, he would be mad. Happy families. But blood is thick as they say. Dad's chequebook shows the very last cheque was made out to Margaret for "teeth."

So here is the will. The epitome of egalitarianism. An equal five-way split. My mum, Margaret, me, Alan and the grandchildren in equal shares. But no special provisions for my mum. The only practical way to give effect to the five-way division was to sell the farmland and buildings and the farmhouse that went with it. So where is my mum going to live? Her share of the net proceeds, even though it will now include the two legacies passed to my dad only this year from the death of aunt Phyllis and consequentially the final winding up of uncle Edmund's estate, will be insufficient to buy her a home never mind leave money to live on. Dad, what where you thinking of? First she is not in the will at all and when she is, it is merely just one fifth and nowhere to live. I wonder if there may have been another motive, deep seated, maybe even subconscious. Was he afraid of money passing via my mum back to the Wilson side of the family? I will never know and well as I thought I knew my dad, I cannot understand. Agatha Christie, all is forgiven, send Miss Marple to see me before it is too late.

I have often wondered about the legitimacy of this will in relation to my mum's position. She was still alive, the surviving spouse. If the legal basis of the farm was as a joint tenancy, then my dad's share would have automatically passed to my mum. If the property was held as a tenancy in common, then it could only have been entirely my dads place to will away if the proportions had been, he 100% her nil. But for this to have been the case there should be proper documentary evidence for the transaction and a declaration should have been made to the Inland Revenue. I do not think either happened. If I am right, my mum was swindled. It has so bothered me that I have been back to the solicitor who drew up the will originally. He says it is kosher since my dad owned the farm in his own right and as there was no subsequent conveyance, my mum's share did not come into contention, so he could do with it as he wished. Yet, had they been divorced at any stage, almost certainly she would have been entitled to a half share. Something is not right.

One redeeming feature about Margaret was that she had a contact in the local council and through that put us onto a council bungalow for rent right on Newton Green in the heart of the village, perfect for mum to move into. Her energies did not however extend to getting the place in decorative order, buying furniture and carpets and generally moving in. That was left to Julia and Alan. But my mum had survived the loss of her beloved George who "knew everything", had seen the deadstock sold in the yard and the farm itself including the house sold at auction held in the upstairs room of the Trust pub. The same room in which my dad had had his sole New Years Eve binge years before and as a result suffered the rare wrath of his wife. The wife now alone, lonely, barely able to see or walk and shunned absolutely by her daughter. Why John, why? I do not know but Alan is a constant visitor and Julia and I are and, although you do not know it, I did shout at Margaret over the 'phone for not even bothering to visit dad in hospital. Or maybe it's just that the bountiful farm has gone and she and her children have had the money and as far as she is concerned it is all over. Perhaps it is me that is to blame, we two never got on, we are just such different people. Even so, how a daughter can walk past the bungalow of her mother on a regular basis and ignore her existence is beyond my comprehension.

The will had not finished. Whether my dad had paid heed to my desire for it to be kept in the family and yet at the same time knew that for most practical purposes only Alan could work it, again as with the treatment of my mum, I do not know. But it granted to Alan and then myself "successively in that order" the option to purchase the farm at the valuation set for Inheritance Tax purposes and if exercised the live and dead stock to be thrown in. This valuation was likely to be, and in the event was, lower than that achieved at auction. In other words the exerciser got a bargain especially as that party already owned a fifth through the will. One final twist. In the event of neither of us exercising the option to purchase, the farm could be offered to "any other adult beneficiaries under this will excluding my wife". This put Margaret into the frame as an advantaged purchaser and perhaps more importantly through her Mick or indeed any of the four children. And

Keith the eldest had always spent much time at the farm and was practically very able. So, in this time of great grief, what to do?

So my dad had thrown down his final gauntlet. If I wanted the farm, I could have it because he knew perfectly well that Alan would not rise to the challenge and even when I had offered to keep my share in and suggested that Chris and Craig as two of the eight grandchildren probably would too if I asked them, it was still a no. So Julia and I discussed it seriously. We had now been together three-and-a-half years and got over the settling in phase and I was at last going great guns at Bell Fruit Services with all the business that mattered under my control. Finance was not an issue, I could raise it easily. We could live there and then develop the farmhouse and buildings. Or, we could see if mum wanted to stay there with a companion and run the land through a contractor and maybe move down later or merely take on the land as a project.

We were both used to farming and understood it and in particular I wanted to take advice and grow something unusual and more valuable than grain and hay. Soft fruits, especially blackcurrants appealed as did asparagus and even, if the bottom field could be sufficiently sheltered, grapevines. Fanciful? Maybe. This was not the first time I had thought about the potential of the outbuildings for conversion. I once took Ellis Walker down during our frequent meetings over the development of Leengate but as he pointed out the big snag would be access with just the one single track road over the M1. The planners would view any expansion as an unacceptable addition to traffic volume. But now I was assessing the possibility of getting at the farm from the Huthwaite end via an existing lane leading to Tophams Farm. Could I negotiate joint usage and push the road through our fields, past the pit hills and on upwards to the stackyard? If so, could I then get permission to build a brand new farmhouse at the top of the knob facing East and looking over the valley? The same valley that my dad often said "will be completely built up one day but not in mylifetime." Well dad looks like not in mine either, it is still there as green as ever.

Practical schemes are as dreams when clouds hang dark and low. At the end of Red Barn Farm lane is Newton and two miles away is Tibshelf. Newton means Alan and Lynn and their children Mark and Simon and Tibshelf means Margaret and Mick and their four children. To all these the farm has been a second home for many years and in the case of Mark and Simon and Margaret's eldest child Keith, for all practical purposes, their first home.

Julia was with me all the way but what do I do, put up a new and large metal gate on the farm side of the motorway bridge and hang a great sign saying something like *under new management, all previous visitors excluded*? Better bow to the inevitable, the end of an era. If only he had lasted just one more year, he would have been so proud to have been in the huge marquee on the lawns of Bath University to see Chris walk up for his conferment of a degree in mathematics. He and I would both have known that this was only the second degree holder in the family on either side. He would have cried. But his ashes are now dust nestling in the hedge bottom far away in Mansfield as his genes pass on. Times have changed but the legacy of working hard and fending for a family and being your own man and laughing at life have not. Born into the wrong era. But a clever chap my dad.

CHAPTER THIRTEEN
A new beginning

1991-2002. The pay-off. Limbo-land. Pension pot to network marketing. The timeshare. A (failed) new business. Back to consultancy and the DTI. Derivatives. Investor in People. Document imaging. The High Court case. Selling businesses. Angus Macrae. Off to Riyadh, Tokyo and freezing New York, Columbus and Washington. A Canberra lecture. Move to Maxy to rise to fall. Back and re-train.

What will I do next? I am really sure about what I will not do. The fruit machine sector sucks, had a belly-full of it. But all the contacts I have, all the people I know, all the fun we have had, my reputation. As Gordon would have said "throw it in the trash can." Time for something completely new, let the buggers get on with it, I'll watch from a distance as it slides down the pan. Tell you something else, corporate man has gone too. This time I'll make money for me and Julia or go bust in the attempt, doing what though, don't know yet.

Top priority is to get my pay-off but the solicitor I have set on in Nottingham does not seem to be on my urgency wavelength. Of-course what is routine to him is unique to me except my daily and often aggressive calls to his office are probably edging this case upwards in his intray. They want to deduct tax at source, can they do that? And being a qualified accountant in my prime, I am likely to get a new position easily and if so that will stop the time clock for payment immediately. What has that got to do with breaking my contract for no good reason? Etc, etc.

It takes six weeks which to me is an eternity but to my solicitor is apparently a new world record – really! I thought that had been set by my sprinting time down from the vegetable patch to answer each 'phone call. Well, anyway we are here, Julia and I being kept waiting deliberately by this grubby firm of Leeds solicitors because the paperwork isn't quite finished. We have the cheque and head for Scotland, let's blow some of it and have a bloody good holiday.

This silence is a very odd thing. Setting up an office in Neil's old bedroom does not actually make anything happen, new 'phone line, new fax but nothing incoming. My 'phones never stopped ringing at Bell Fruit, sometimes two or three at a time, secretaries rushing hither and thither, meetings here and there, diary full to bursting. The old colleagues do not contact any more, why should they, they have their own work to do, their lives to lead. It's Julia I feel sorry for. She married a dynamic executive and now has a stay at home hubby with no money coming in. She is worried but it is about me and how I am feeling and what I will do, it is not about us or our future. I do not deserve Julia, she saved me before and she will do it again.

Within days of my being sacked a letter arrives from the family diplomat (Craig) currently lodging in Kremlin Drive, Tuebrook, Liverpool, a rather appropriate address considering that the internal bedroom doors are reinforced by metal bars and locking pins, that bicycle wheels have to be taken into the lecture rooms, and that when we visit the local curry house we have to knock on the locked door and pay for our meal before we enter. And when I leave the underground car park at six a.m. a complete stranger comes up to my car and kicks it, looks defiantly at me and shouts "bloody Mercedes".

A rough, tough town somewhat disguised by the clothes that the girls do not wear as they move noisily from late-night bar to club. Craig wishes to say that he is sorry about my "redundancy." He thinks it is very sad after the years I have put in and the things I have achieved for the company. My ex-colleagues he has spoken to greatly respect and admire me and he believes that I will be greatly missed. On the other hand, maybe it is a god send as I was not happy and not enjoying my work and if it gets to that stage he thinks it is best that I got out when I did. He hopes I will find something that I will enjoy and be successful at. Knowing me, he is sure that I will. Well thanks Craig, as usual you are ahead of me and I am sure that you are right. But just now it does not feel like it.

I may not be working exactly but having got my pay-off the next big push is going to be for my pension. I had told Mr John Garvis that I would not be a man of straw as a trustee. It followed that I was not approached to be a trustee of their fund once it had swallowed up ours. Because these trustees were both on the payroll and more importantly to me were, by their personalities, under the direct sycophantic control of the boss man, it was imperative that I got my money out and into a personal plan. If I have learned nothing else from my previous role, I am very aware that trustees of corporate pension funds are not to be trusted. If there are risks to be taken with my pot of gold – well hardly pot – then I will take them or I will choose the people that do. Is this a fighting spirit returning? Things might be quiet now but the prospect of doing my own thing appeals more as the days pass.

So the first missive is sent off from my actuary to theirs and reminding them that under the contractual agreement on leaving I am entitled to nine months extra credit pensionable service. I like this bit, it reminds one of a gestation period. Two things were amazing about the response. First, the contribution that I had actually made to the fund was only 18.9% of the transfer value offered. If I had really taken cognisance of this at the time, I might have been the first person in the country to have seen the gathering storm of the national pension crisis since the transfer value was a calculation derived from discounted future defined benefits.

Secondly, the total fund value of the additional voluntary contributions I had made was only just short of the main fund total contribution. This demonstrated the power of doing something extra and it reinforced the practice of, for example, paying more off a mortgage than the minimum. An added surprise in focus courtesy of the years rolling on was that these AVC'c were invested with Equitable Life, that stalwart of financial propriety aimed at the professional classes. And here was I pushing hard to get this fund out of their hands and into my own! We all need a spot of good fortune occasionally. And here is another surprising thing. Our side has put a value on the fund 26% greater than their side. A good old English compromise is agreed at a figure 15% more than the original valuation. And I thought actuarial work was very precise, it all depends on the basis of the calculations you see.

The false dawn

There is a subterranean species of worm so sensitive to the movement of busy executives that once the activity ceases it is picked up instantly. The caller, Peter Wood, and from whom I had been instrumental in buying a club machine route based in and around Birmingham, had heard about my leaving the corporate world. Although he and his "live-in lover" still had their successful manufacturing business, he had just had the most astonishing experience. Throughout the whole of his working life he had never before felt such a buzz. If I really did have some spare time and wanted to make "serious money" with my own business, why not come to one of the regular meetings in Solihull. Well, why not. Peter is a sensible business man, no Charlie-come-lately.

One thing has to be made clear at the outset, this has nothing to do with pyramid selling which is illegal. We are dealing here with Network Marketing one of the cleverest if not the cleverest systems of *smart* selling ever to come out of America. Is it not so that all these personal commendations being called for from individuals sitting in the audience and the involvement of named senior pillars of society, would not exist if this was not a proven successful formula built around a fantastic product?

Massive savings accrue from not spending on conventional advertisement and promotion and this is how your own network, or downstream, can afford to pay a percentage of their sales revenue to you just as you pay to your upstream consultant. The bigger the network you can build, so the more stock you will need to order and so the lower the net unit buying price. The examples being presented by the top guys on the stage prove this point and in fact the highest chap, sorry the one with the largest network, earns £10,000 a week. Wow. And the product is a world beater because it is founded on the one thing none of us can do without. Water. Yes, it is a water filter. A sealed unit plumbed under a sink with its own tap and through which the mains water flows upwards through these beds of highly technical filtration elements to arrive absolutely pure as the driven snow, actually purer than that as can be seen from this simple test that applies a chemical to our water and to your rubbish tap water. See the difference. Peter wants Julia and I to come to his place next weekend for a relaxing time and enjoy good food and wine and we can talk some more about how it all works and if I feel inclined I could sign up under him at the same time.

Peter's place is a revelation, it is in Worcestershire down a loop road leading nowhere off a pretty village. Quiet, dreamy, classy and beautiful. The large cottage host house is thatched and in its own grounds complete with tennis courts and a separate indoor sauna complex and two other discrete buildings. One is a smaller detached and again thatched cottage that used to be the local post office but is now ideal for guests such as ourselves and the other is a special brick build out-house. Special because it is occupied during the daytime by Henry who is so important that he is introduced to us first. Not so much introduced as imposed. Henry is a Great Dane. Actually he is the greatest dog in the world, sizewise, and has a big brown head on the scale of a milk bucket and as he comes lolloping up has a certain look in his eye that denotes a predilection for chomping your head as a tasty mid-term meal. Of-course he is harmless out here, he wouldn't be loose otherwise would he? And did you know that if Great Danes run for one hundred yards they end up exhausted? It is because their heart is too small for the huge frame. Really? Mind you there have been problems with the neighbouring dogs. It's when he is taken for walkies and let off the chain. Curiosity has not proven beneficial to certain other canines, they have been rather badly treated.

But it is all forgotten after the umpteenth pre-lunch gin and tonic and the most excellent white wine that accompanied the very special fish dish that live-in-lover Marilyn has spent all morning preparing with the fresh scallops et al that Peter went early to the wholesale market in Birmingham to purloin (not literally but really they are so cheap and the lobster, well ……). Business is so good and yes he did do well from the sale to us, but that has all been ploughed back into the manufacturing business. It seems that people cannot understand why they still bother, but Peter believes in manufacturing and one day its worth will be re-appreciated. Don't I agree?

And now this water filter business, he cannot believe his good fortune, such a buzz, such an opportunity, so easy to sell, what about a port with the coffee? Ok I will give it a go although I have never actually tried to sell anything before or at any rate it seems a good idea this afternoon. That was before I knew I had less than a day to live. Making assumptions can be bad for ones health. I assumed Henry lived in his detached brick house overnight and it was a surprise to be greeted by him at the foot of the stairs early the following morning. I had been on my way to the loo. Now there seems little point.

It is exciting actually and the first thing is to think of a name to call my new business. Well, our home is Heathlands so we will call it Heathlands Environmental Products – independent distributor. We need some letterhead and compliment slips and business cards and we are away. At last some proper use for my office. Peter signed me up didn't he so what is stopping me doing the same to others? True he caught me on the rebound, at a low point, without work so to speak and I actually do not know anyone in that position but still it's easy to make a list of past colleagues and some friends and even my two sons.

I can 'phone everyone on my list and tell them about the *opportunity* and invite them to a meeting and enthuse them, get them wowed. Sure. The ones that have been lucky enough to be introduced to the concept earlier are encouraged to stand up from the audience and tell their story. Here is a contract landscape gardener who derides his stupidity in the past in using his hard earned capital to buy equipment that merely depreciated rapidly and there is a ex double glazing salesman that at last has a product that is helpful to the environment and does not feature varying levels of quality undisclosed. But Peter does not stand up although he is asked to, he thinks some elements of his previous lives particularly bits involving armaments might be misunderstood.

We go to meetings, we buy our stock, we study the rules and learn the earn-off percentages and the declining wholesale prices if we order more stuff. I begin to notice that a key man at our most local rah-rah group is a plumber and I single him out and visit his home for a chat. The thing is you see, these devices have to be plumbed in, affixed in a certain way and holes have to be drilled in sink tops to fit the separate tap connection. Even the *puppy-dog* trial units that we are encouraged to fix in situ and leave for the miracle to be appreciated have to be fixed to the existing tap outlet and do I realise just how many different types of taps and mixers there are? Have I bought the bags of different fitments? No, oh well he can sell me some to get started.

But why is all this not brought out at the meetings and what am I going to do about the posh kitchen in Ravenshead where the kind accommodating lady has a tiny complaint about me scratching her chromium plated sink? I have spent so much time and effort and money on this opportunity now and got so many people involved that a big decision is called for. Is it really my bag to fix gadgets to domestic sinks and as regards the revolutionary new air filtration product, it has been a disaster, even Ellis wants it removed from his office.

I call a big *up-line* man in the network and debate the mundane issues. The conversation gets more and more argumentative. Admit it man, it's all one big selling fiddle isn't it? By this time, I know it is. One big lesson learned in the big bad hard world of non-corporate comfort zone. What I should have thought through at the outset is this, why would one ignore the age old proven patterns of marketing and sales? Why does, say, Proctor and Gamble or Du Pont or Unilever throw millions at promotion? Because it works that's why. So why do these people think they have found a better way. Because it would not stack up to transparency, that's why. Because it is a con, that's why. I am out of here, fool.

I am left pondering how one separates the morality of selling from the merits or otherwise of the product. A few years back Julia and I received through the post an invitation to attend a time-share presentation in Birmingham (Birmingham again). It promised the moon and stars and a few other worthy prizes just for attending. Well, why not. En-route I found myself taking an unaccustomedly stern stance with Julia along the lines of "do not be taken in on any account, we are only going for the experience and the prize, and certainly do not agree to any deal and *definitely do not sign anything.*" So, after we had left and I had bought a two-week time-share unseen on the Spanish Costa Del Sol, it was impossible not to marvel at the skill we had witnessed and at my gullibility. It is highly likely that leaders are born and not made. It is absolutely certain that salesmen are. And here is the rub. We still use our time-share and love it, we still have our water filter and love it. You work it out.

I have always had a soft spot for salesmen. It is probably due to antithesis. I made Derek Hepple the top earner in my Bell Friut Services team and sent him and his wife to Hawaii on holiday for reaching his target of flogging thousands of off-site fruit machines we had no use for. I saved my manufacturing salesman, late of our Bulgarian trip, from sacking by politicing bastards in Bill Pilkington's office one morning. I take the view that it is a wonderful gift to be able to sell, sell, sell anything you care to mention to punters who may or may not want anything. Caveat emptor, let the buyer take cover.

So, after the water filter debacle, I contacted Robin. He as in the one I had pulled from Bass plc to be my marketing man. He of the marketing degree and of the hard-man fast-talking presence. He of the somewhat larger than life character who on being shed sometime after myself, parked his, to be returned, company car "some streets from where I live, it led them a right ta-ta, took 'em hours to find it." My idea was to join forces and start a business. I would be the steady administrative and financial hand at the tiller whilst he would be the wild salesman/marketer getting the customers hooked in, but it would be 50/50 from the outset.

At first it went really well. We found some offices to rent off Gregory Boulevard in Nottingham, bought and installed telephone and other office equipment (or rather I did), threw around some ideas and started recruiting *commission only* salespeople. Robin's first idea was to sell a card full of advertising space called Homehelper. A business could buy a block of space and when the card was full it would be delivered to householders in specific upmarket locations. The card would be printed on a hard durable surface in multi-colours and kept by the householder next to his/her telephone as a memory jogger for a plumber, electrician, financial adviser, travel agent and so on.

The card would sell quickly, be distributed cheaply and make us a fortune. The trouble was, advertising space does still have to be sold and most small business people already have a full budget and in fact not much left after the ubiquitous Yellow Pages expense. Then again, commission only types are, well, certain types. They do not respond well to discipline, imposed or of the self-form and tend to be always short of ready money and come with oodles of personal baggage. It took a while to learn these things and during which the overdraft I had so painstakingly negotiated with the charming Bank of Scotland bank manager had been used up.

As this initial foray into our business union we called Business Development Associates or BDA for crisp shortness, started to wither so Robin found a franchise opportunity concerned with doing the books for a small business, running the payroll, doing the annual tax computation and such and generally acting as an outsourcer for the hard-pressed trader. It was called Prolapse or something of the sort but somewhere along the line the master franchisor went bust or went abroad or went berserk or whatever. Then we could earn from financial services by selling life policies as agents and the beauty of which was our income would stretch far into the future as drip feed commission arose.

The problem with me and Robin was not the ideas we generated. I genuinely believe some were good and some were to catch on albeit in a different guise. Much later, and for a time, my best shareholdings were with outsourcing businesses of which we could possibly have been one. No, the problem was one of deemed equality of partnership without really understanding whether this could be so. Robin, as it turned out, had no money so how was he ever to match my investment and when the bank wanted its loan back, who had the deepest pocket?

I was used to an executive life, eight o'clock a.m. till whenever. Robin now released from any corporate constriction really was the consummate marketing maverick. I had by now started earning consultancy fees outside our business venture, he increasingly left our office to the mercy of free-wheeling others. The moral is that here are two equal partners but they are not equal and one sees things one way and the other another. It could have worked but it isn't working and liabilities are piling up. I write a scathing letter to Robin from my hotel bedroom in London. The plug is pulled and I pay off all the debts and withdraw into my shell battle scarred and hurt. I should have listened to Julia, I will in future.

Back to square one

It was a pious hope. After two failed attempts to escape, I had better get back to the leisure industry. Ian Rock had been Allied Brewery's head of machine control and as such my largest customer in Bell Fruit Services. Now, following a series of executive and business manoeuvres, he had emerged as chief executive of a sizeable and quoted leisure group. This group owned and operated a large number of night clubs and dancing and drinking venues all over the UK. Nothing ventured, nothing gained, I went to see him. We chatted about old times and personalities and he thought I might like to take a look at the performance figures of some of the units and come back to him with my views.

So started a two-days-a-week consultancy stint that was invaluable in getting me back in the industry, analysing, travelling, reporting and gaining confidence but most of all in shedding the dross and the ill-founded dreams and earning proper money again. Unkindly, I thought, some close friends said I should have gone back into consultancy straight away after being sacked instead of messing around with duff business ideas.

Then, at his own request, I had lunch with a man with a most impressive name, Spencer Fox. It sounded like, and he looked a bit like, a film star. He had been to our BDA office for some reason that escaped me and wondered whether I might be interested in meeting an organisation that he worked for on a self-employed consultancy basis.

Phil Downing's office was his home, his home the firm's office, as it were. I was sitting in this sort of boardroom being sort of interviewed though in reality it was more of a what had I done, what they did and where would I fit in, sort of chat. They were a most friendly bunch and Spencer, my surprise sponsor, was obviously held in high esteem and I was definitely warming to what I was beginning to see as an unconventional set-up but one that worked.

The firm, if I understood things properly, had started

with Phil himself doing consultancy work for local Yorkshire firms in the area of manufacturing efficiency, factory layouts, time study, that sort of thing. Then Phil plugged into a rich seam of oil from a well drilled by the DTI (Department of Trade and Industry or as one leading newspaper insisted on calling it for many year Department of Trepidation and Ineptitude).

Small and medium sized businesses needed to be imbued with enterprise and so a government inspired initiative was called for. What it amounted to was this. If a business was prepared to meet one-third of the cost of a short sharp external consultancy assignment, then the DTI would fund the rest. The idea was to kick-start a mediocre dreamy business into life and so plant the seed corn for a vibrant UK enterprise economy. On the receiving end you got someone through your door who almost certainly would not have been encountered in the normal course of events. Then followed fifteen full days of being looked at, talked to and reported upon. On the giving end, Mr or Mrs expert walked into a business about which they knew nothing and were introduced to a unique set of circumstances.

Over time as the DTI's funds dissipated and the Tory government's appetite for enterprise was sated, the two-thirds contribution became one half, then one-third and eventually nil. But for now there are five schemes. Business Planning, Marketing, Quality, Design, and Information Technology. By a bit of judicious twisting and turning, Phil had managed to get his business listed on all five counts. A remarkable feat.

But then Phil was quite a remarkable man. Small of stature, fast talking, will-of-the-wispish and absolutely client driven. He believed in impression, status, expression of success. Before going to a client his huge four-wheel drive had to be cleaned and polished and he would have rehearsed his professional presentation. Phil took the stance

Barn door to balance sheet

I am successful and wealthy and if you are acceptable to me, I will consider taking you on as a new client. It was the antithesis of the approach *I do not make much out of this game, all the benefit accrues to you.* In many walks of life, in many different circumstances, his is the approach that wins out. So that is the man and to round him off, he gets up in the morning and walks his dogs over the steep hills at the back of his rambling beautiful home and for relaxation he restores classic cars and motorcycles and is an amateur stand-up comedian.

Having tapped the work, the firm's way to exploit it, its modus operandi, is exceedingly clever. It is unconventional and maverick. It works such that only the business itself can benefit ultimately and that is the same thing as saying Phil himself. The key concept is that no-one is actually employed. Each consultant accepted into the fold is a self-employed contractor who could not get the work independently because the inevitable bureaucracy dictates a registered firm via a registered specialist quasi-governmental organ.

It follows that if one wants to dip into this body of work then it must be through the auspices of an approved outfit such as this. Therefore you will get 35% of the client fee, maybe 37.5% if you get senior and successful with it. What! One other thing, fifteen days may be paid for under the scheme but as a consultant your share will be of fourteen days, the final day belongs to the firm as administration. When I analysed Phil's business accounts much later, I realised that although giving up one day's fees may not sound much, it is akin to the firm creaming 6.7% straight off the top.

There is general congratulations all round, I am in. There are always organisational/management/financial aspects to the Marketing assignments and also the Quality ones. Plus, after training and going on the job with Phil himself, I may graduate to actually taking on the highest paid work of all, that is, the Business Planning assignments and if so, Phil tells me confidentially, I could move up to take 40% of the fee. Actually I rather like the sound of all this, I want to be self-employed, I want to be free to do other things and most of all I want to try to help small businesses. I will learn much too, it may be all I have been searching for: thanks to some great controller somewhere, thanks to Spencer Fox. It is hard for my brain now to assimilate that after the full stop and the mistaken re-starts, the next ten years will bring the busiest times of all.

The diversity of businesses in this country, and I suppose by definition any other, is immense. The division of labour may one day end somewhere but it certainly has not yet. Backed by the marketing resources of the DTI and centred on major venues around the country, it is staggering to behold the variety of people that approach my Business Planning table at these Enterprise Initiative forums. And, bearing in mind that they must be motivated to come here in the first place and will get a generous subsidy for a finite outlay, the hit rate of signing up for the treatment is high. I find myself filling in Phil's developed 80-question questionnaire within the multifarious backdrops of pharmaceutical profiles, antiquarian bookshops, warranty administrators, bar fitters, marine shippers, plumbers, nursing homes, quantity surveyors, dyers, car bodyshops, acrylic manufacturers, English for foreigners, synthesiser repairers, music promoters and the rest.

Each with its unique business, each with a problem, each wanting to move on. But the rationale is the same as those early days in PW although here the motivation to take a sounding from an outsider is higher because this small business wants to get bigger or at any rate become unstuck whereas often before the entrée was forced by the auditor or some other statutory regulator.

Those that respond to questioning that lays facts bare and refuses to dally with opinions, probabilities, assumptions, pious hopes and the like and especially that highlight blanks in knowledge, see the answers for themselves. You only have to bring a little to get the party swinging and if one has grey hair and a world-weary face, well that helps too.

Phil's biggest contribution to a created business plan was the insistence that it must have a properly conceived marketing input and that is why Spencer was so valuable. Ask any small to medium sized businessman exactly what his niche market position is, who he is competing against both in product and in socio/economic strata/spending and what developments over the next year will impact on this position, and you have him thinking.

The cynic who talks of borrowing this man's watch to tell him the time is correct but look at it this way, we all need to be reminded of the time now and again and this time is only applicable for a fleeting second. The test is whether the man, the business, does change and whether the report pages stay open and he wants you to stick around for a while. Those that file and wave goodbye have wasted their money. What I would like to remind each businessman is of Heisenberg's uncertainty principle in that the more we know about the present position, the less we can know about its momentum. Too close to the trees my new friend. But of-course I shall not do any reminding, we do not want to be a smart arse do we?

The two years with Phil's firm were good. I learned a lot about the small business private sector and I hope gave a bit back too. There were drawbacks. The parties with Phil's gruesome stand-up routines, the nights away that I had learned to live without, the paternal culture and the favourites, the concentration around Yorkshire with its Yorkshire types "What the f.....g 'ell do you want, wot the 'ell 'ave yo got to bring tu party?" Nice one but just before I give you a robust Derbyshire strong-in-arm uppercut, a few questions for you my man. Of-course I would really like to engage in a little excoriation, but for the sake of the firm and the profession, I had better not.

The main thing about Phil's business model was its flaws. Not that he wasn't aware of them. The overwhelming proportion of the fees came from the Quality Standard initiative and this work was repetitive and boring and when the manual was done, that was it. The second big flaw was that the funding would dry up and then where would the business be? So Phil wanted his people to "stick in" a business but only he and I via the business plans seemed able to do this and as the financial support from the DTI lessened, so staff did start to drift away to do their own thing. As they were not actually employed, he could do little to stop this.

What Phil did do was look around for businesses to buy so he could put his best people in to run them. For this he needed more capital and his tame ex-bank manager drew up plans to re-finance his lovely home-cum-office to provide that capital in the teeth of the sages at Huddersfield Council sharpening their claws to stop him using it as a work base. He persuaded four of us to become *The Category B Partners* and put £10,000 each into the business to help the re-constitution. But the storm clouds were gathering.

Of derivatives and derivatives

John Sheild attended the London roadshow. He was not your ordinary punter. Drifting into middle age he was, age-wise, a good match for myself. In most other respects, much superior. The ruddy face and slightly protruding stomach were clothed in an immaculately-cut, narrow pin-striped, Savile Row bankers uniform suit of high quality. With his full head of well-groomed longish grey hair he was the sort of man who, as would be pointed out to me later, could approach the check-in at Heathrow as a common-or-garden average passenger because the company policy dictated economy travel only to be upgraded instantly to club class or similar. "It is his bearing you see".

After the usual opening gambit of his motivation for attending and what did he hope to get out of it etc, we get to the bit about what the business actually did. It would be true to say that I had not the faintest idea what he was talking about. But anyway it matters not since I have learned by now that there is no such thing as a unique business. The rules of engagement are the same, the trusty questionnaire will bring it all out.

So he signs up. It's all over pretty quickly really. Oh, just a few things from him to me. He does not know of our firm and neither does he want to because his condition is that I personally will do the business plan and by the way he does not own the business being just a small shareholder and his side is the marketing so he will be my leadman on the project. I will need to liaise with him carefully to fix dates since John Wisbey spends much time out of the country and it is essential that he be there for the start. Who is John Wisbey? Oh, didn't I say, he is the founder and owner, an ex-dealer with Kleinwort Benson. Nice chap, you will like him. Goodbye.

The dictionary is not much help. It starts with "derived" and then moves on to "based on other sources; not original" – well, let's face it, not much is – even more perplexing it goes on to say that in maths it is also called "differential coefficient" (probably a bit more involved that Dynamic Dave's differential cost centre recovery rate). I wonder if I should be getting worried if that is the extent of my pre-visit product research into what they say they are into. Rolls off the tongue nicely but what on earth is a derivative? Another puzzle is this place that the A to Z has led me to. No 741 The Strand or is it actually Fleet Street? Seems to be between the two and right opposite the Royal Courts of Justice. With such an address and location it would be reasonable to assume something posh but that doesn't square with these pokey stairs leading to cramped poky rooms. Yes, I really should be worried.

But John Wisbey soon puts me at ease. He is a much younger version of Shield and taller and wearing, I estimate, an even more expensive suit, shiny black shoes (again the banker's uniform and compulsory attire) and a complicated tie but his hair has all the appearance of having just got itself out of bed. He has a strong handshake and a wonderful smile, a bit reticent and shyish but there nevertheless. He talks fast and looks a brainbox, I think we will get on well.

You see every business has to start somewhere and he had become frustrated at Kleinworts with the lack of pace and had spotted a need in the market for much better software to handle the increasingly sophisticated financial instruments that were being called for. For simplicity let's just call them Swaps and Options. He left, set up his own business and worked night and day from his own flat in Victoria to get out a first working system. Shield was his first employee, pulled from the ranks of commercial banking in the City, to handle the front end. They had worked together before and he needed an elder statesman to open the market. Now there were twelve staff and already this office was bursting at the seams and John Shield was on the look out for a bigger place but it must all form part of a structured plan and that is where I came in.

There is no doubt that selling jobs under the firms's banner is getting more difficult and almost certainly directly proportional to the reducing finance from the DTI but Phil himself is a good salesman and so is his prodigy one Haley the beautiful young lady that sits by his side at HQ. Are they having an affair, is she developing a drink problem, why after each party does she start crying and talk of her husband "always shouting at me"? The rumours in the ranks resonate but I genuinely could not care less. I am about to enter the busiest year of my entire working life. The demand for business plans holds as does the follow up work. I am billing heavily, but there are other fish to fry too.

In order to legitimise the ever growing ranks of civil servants and re-swirl them under topical names to give the illusion of newness and freshness, the latest Government campaign is under way to bring all the many and varied bodies set up to help business do business, under one banner. The not-very-hard-working and much holidayed and much sickened final-pensionable-salary-defined-benefits brigade are to come together as a one-stop-shop which of-course is a great place for the little things of life that one has forgotten when doing the real shopping. The objective is to improve the efficiency with which officials can get at small to medium sized businesses to instil a greater degree of entrepreneurial zeal. Which due to the non-inferential nature of things is a contradiction in terms sated only by the fact that these re-branded boys and girls will not actually get involved directly themselves. They need signed-up registration-fee-paying experts such as myself. Yipee.

Having invested my time on the mandatory training days and paid the compulsory registration fees, I am now authorised to run this new programme that has the marvellous title of Investor in People. You could think of it as the full circle from, or the antithesis of, the old trade union days. Whereas in the bad old past employees invested their hours, days, indeed life in an employer whose power could only be kept in check by collective force, here we will have the employer actually taking positive action to give force to ("empower" is the buzz word) their staff. Get it?

Using confidential questionnaires, each employee is asked if he/she knows where the business is heading, how he fits into the whole picture, what he thinks his skills are and whether they have been matched to those required of the job he actually does, whether he is aware of the business's operating policies and about a million other things. The answers are then collated and presented to the management as an indication of whether the deemed investment in the workforce represents value for money or has miscued. All this will inevitably lead to a more malleable approach from the top, better communications, a more appropriately trained workforce and consequently boost efficiency and productivity. Everyone a winner.

There is possibly another whether. Whether the whole process opens some sort of Pandora's box in which resentment and frustration are amongst the jewels and whether encouragement is given to pay lip service to something that switched on management and employees of any real value would be in to as a natural outcome of working together in this little economic unit. Actually, I am personally resentful of all the time and money that has gone into paying for all these multi-coloured packs of questionnaires and *indicators* printed on expensive glossy paper when I struggled to get finance for a very modest version of marketing in my BDA venture. But the organs of Government are one thing and the small to medium size business sector is another. You would think in a well developed capitalist system that market forces would prevail and that good businesses with good management and good practices would float to the top without too much need to tick indicator boxes.

Anyway I go in with my packs of impressive forms, give the introductory talk, hand out the papers and fix a date to return to analyse them and report on the answers that will self-fulfillingly identify the need for skills updating and the like, that is to say implementation towards the magical award of the meritorious mark of becoming an Investor in People. Meantime I can get on with my real work for the Yorkshire firm and the increasing band of private clients I am building up during this hectic year, plus what I have started to think of as my specials.

Out of the blue John Wisbey 'phones to say he has heard of a business with a brand new pioneering technology that he thinks has a bright future and have I got time to look at it to see if it is worth buying. The location is Walton-on-Thames and the technology is imaging that I discover is about creating an electronic representation of a document so that from a point of initial capture, the paper itself is superfluous. The image passes from computer to computer and is capable of being changed, added to, deleted from and conjoined with others. The future would lie with the paperless office, the super efficient *back office*, the application of human-less *workflow* and generally substitute people with software.

I conclude that the technology is at a too early stage without disproportionate resources being thrown at it, that the order book is too dependent on one major contract for a Middle Eastern customer coming good and in summary that the business is being over-hyped for what it is. I advise against buying.

In another out of the blue occurrence, a letter arrives from one of the large London based legal practices. They have been engaged by Rick Grogan to defend an action being brought by the northern leisure outfit who intend to sue for a few million to recover the sum they claim they were misled into overpaying for the Bell Fruit group companies. As the most senior person they can practically locate, involved both before and after the sale, will I help? You bet I will.

What I didn't realise at the time was the amount of work those four little words could lead to. Nor what a contra-interpretation can be placed on seemingly the same set of facts. Basically they were saying they were duped, sold a pup, deluded into paying for things that were not there and generally taken for a ride. Fortunately I had kept a lot of my personal papers relating to the events catalogued in the massive affidavits from the principal protagonists and fortunately I have a good memory and fortunately I have hate on my side.

My lasting memories of the whole episode were of our heavily pregnant lead solicitor having to lug around her huge box files of evidential papers, of the honourable gentleman leading counsel being far too small for his huge paper-filled office in Lincoln Inn chambers and chain-smoking his way through my briefing and finally of Rick's evidence from the witness box at the pre-trial hearing. Perhaps it was the Judge's intervention that caused me not to have to go into the box myself and eventuated the scurrying in the corridor that itself precipitated the settlement "Is the prosecution telling the Court that their client was taken in by a fast-talking American?"

Thinking back to the businesses I had been instrumental in buying for Bell Fruit Services and of the failed MBO and of the exhaustive report done by the accountants in presenting that business for sale and of the many times I had examined an organisation's financial health, it occurred to me that I could take on a niche speciality of selling a business. It would involve some preparatory work such as compiling a business plan and also cooperating with due diligence until the legal process was concluded. I reckoned that Julia could handle the administrative work and between us we would make a real professional job of placing a business. And miraculously the chance came.

I had previously prepared a short-form business plan for a stationery business in London and during a follow up the owner John Payn asked if I could do precisely that, i.e. find a buyer. He had been unwell, wanted to get his children out of London and had an aspiration to live in Bournemouth. So the venture was born. We advertised in the Financial Times, despatched our confidentiality agreements, drip-fed information to respondents and negotiated. In the end we had our buyer, our price and our legal agreement and we learned something really new. We learned that "India is booming Mr Smith, booming." Since the fee was performance and not time based, the job from start to finish was highly risky, it could have resulted in nothing from a considerable outlay. That is why risk deserves reward. Later we were to taste sweet success again but also time-wasting debilitating failure. Still, given my time over again, Julia and I would build a business devoted solely to buying and selling others.

There was one other off-the-wall thing I wanted to achieve. Ever since the earliest East Midlands Electricity Board studies, I had always felt at home with one-off type assignments, the situations where there is an identified problem but no obvious solution that the insider seems capable or willing to find. If it leads to other such jobs, well that's fine and if you want me to stay on and make the changes happen, equally that's fine but I will remain an outsider and one day, maybe sooner rather than later, I will be off. Just like Wyatt Earp riding into the sunset, I am gone. Still, the chance to forge some sort of long-lasting relationship whilst having no intention to re-enter the corporate world came when, quite unexpectedly, Angus wanted me to keep coming back to advise on implementing the business plan prepared earlier.

More importantly though, what Angus Macrae wanted/needed was a sounding board for a whole range of things both business and private. Someone to talk to who had been around the block, someone he could trust and feel comfortable with. There is no doubt that most small businesses have this largely unclassified, maybe unclassifiable, need. So I started to go back and it developed as one full day each week, a day at the end of which I felt like the unfortunate chap who has done ten rounds with Mike Tyson at his peak. Angus was mentally and intellectually very draining. That, plus the fact that our backgrounds and experiences were so very different, was why we got on so well.

Angus had been the son of a very senior medical man and after a private education and having taken a good degree went on to start a business framing pictures. That led to having an art/craft gallery and later an industrial unit as well. The pictures begat the sourcing and supply of what was euphemistically known as Bric-a-Brac that in turn had spawned furniture. The important thing to me and perhaps why I was able to bring something to the party outwith business advice was that the marketplace was pubs and clubs and other leisure outlets. I was familiar with this scene and kept abreast of the ever-changing ownership cycle of the leisure groups and indeed was still running the ruler over the leisure sites being run by my old brewery customer. There was another attraction for me. Angus had made work what I had failed at. He had brought on a maverick salesman/marketing type and made him a forty-percent partner. He had achieved what I couldn't make happen with Robin. The mix I recognised as similar. One who could control and run the business and be financially aware and the other the laissez-faire extrovert business getter who abhors procedures and systems and stuff but just wants to get on with it. The perfect recipe if they can work together as opposites. Angus and his partner could work together.

In the midst of this myriad acitivity came a defining 'phone call. John Wisbey wanted me to come down to London and have lunch with himself and Shield. Despite my earlier report and the passage of time, they did intend to buy the imaging company since the manager-type chap who had kicked things off originally had returned with a story of the two, largely absent, owners being now desperate for funds, the Saudi Arabian contract having been won and this cherry being ripe for picking. Of-course such an event would also serve to perpetuate the employment of the message-man but that was recognised and probably held out more positives than negatives.

My role would be as their eyes and ears down at Walton whilst the legals were done, help with the schedule preparations and in particular superintend the people side of things. In short, oversee the transfer from there to here as a project. The business itself wouldn't cost much in terms of goodwill, it was more a case of taking on the debt and the ongoing running costs. In fact when John Wisbey had gone down to talk to the staff they were apparently particularly taken with his analogy of a well prepared field sown with the best seed corn that only needed "a sprinkling of rain" to effect a fine crop. Needless to say, if some wages and expenses have not been paid for a while, the territory can feel somewhat arid. The prospect of the two founders exiting and a city-based white knight riding in, was a genuine fillip to morale.

From my perspective they were a strange bunch. God knows what I was from theirs, but the blooding into the world of software was a hot one, literally. It had turned into a scorching summer and they had the misfortune to be housed on the mezzanine floor of a tin hut industrial unit. A very flashy designer high-rent tin hut but a cauldron nevertheless. There were not many of them really and yet as an external presentation, the company appeared large and successfully cutting-edge.

The message-man told me that this was deliberate, a sort of smokes and mirrors thing. They had needed a big fish to bite. Apart from my inculcator message-man there was Big Eric the master software writer and brains behind the whole project but who didn't have the money to go it alone and whose eyesight was very poor, and his number two Murray, the Scotsman, another competent software writer whose eyesight was not poor - as time would tell. The third man was Phil who was not deemed at their level but good at using the Visual Basic programing language, a slow walker but fast music-man (his real love) and who, due to his insight into internet technology and newer Java software, was destined to outstay them all and get some equity in the company when it was eventually floated.

But a stock market quote was a long way into the future and the transition would prove interesting. In support was Michael the sort of contractual customer liaison man, Deborah the secretary whose allegiance would soon switch to me, two junior programmers and the overpoweringly gorgeous Becky. She of the tall body atop long slim legs, beautiful face and imperious manner. Becky was the presenter of the system to the lucky potential customers.

So there we have it, the mixed bunch facing the perspiring double-whammy. Can they survive this scorching summer in their tin hut and will they survive the financial starvation of the owners now that the first phase of the Saudi bank contract had been signed. Sweat, sweat. The proposition was that John Wisbey would bankrole the development and via the complex clauses in the contract of purchase would claw back his sprinkling of rain from the otherwise purchase price.

The strategic point is this. Not merely will this imaging product be a winner in its own right, it will cross-sell to the existing risk-management banking customers of John's main business. Breadth and depth. Of-course software is software and development (don't I know it) is development and if you manage by measurable input to measurable output and keeping a constant watch on progress, then, my friend, being responsible for a software solution is not for you. Software producers tap and tap all day but do not ask to see the result, just do not ask.

A whole new floor has been taken for us in the building on New Fetter Lane, London. A small fortune has been spent on kitting it out not least because of the absolute requirement for *bridging networks* (really?) and bomb-proof windows now that the IRA have left their hinterland and moved to the City. The corner office is particularly scrumptious with its vertical Venetian blinds which, if one chooses to open, reveal a breathtaking view of the Thames and upstream the Houses of Parliament. Very nice. The two other Johns (Wisbey and Shield) take me to lunch in Shield's favourite basement wine bar round the corner where he, as always, confidently leaves his credit card behind the counter with his named barman. They want me to join them full-time and be MD of the new business.

Re-birth of corporate man

I discuss the whole thing with Julia. What to do? I had not expected it. I had got used to the jobbing game and perhaps against the odds and certainly to my surprise I had built up, with the very considerable help of Julia, what to my mind at any rate I now regarded as my own business. Did I really want to be a hired hand again? And I would let at least two people down. I would have to stop going up to Yorkshire and pull out of that firm altogether. Ok, there were the personal things but actually I did empathise with Phil and saw the energy behind and the business sense in what he was trying to do, and I had my investment in it. Then there was Angus who I was not only seeing each week but actually liked as a man and wanted to help and it was an easy journey. I could live with dropping the other things off.

Actually travelling is no small factor, Walton-on-Thames had been a sod to get to and central London is easier but this job will mean daily commuting from Nottingham. Long days and much unproductive time. John Wisbey had agreed to pay expenses for six months but what after that? Neither Julia or I want to live in or even close to London. We are both country bumpkins at heart and Julia has a lot of history from her early nursing days at Charing Cross Hospital. History she is not keen to repeat. Better sleep on it.

What, what? Yorkshire lot, Yorkshire lot. It's about four-thirty in the morning and I have woken Julia up talking aloud. What about Yorkshire lot? I will stay with them. Ok, fine. Go back to sleep. Over breakfast it feels all different. What am I thinking about, a proper full-time job in the City running a business at the forefront of technology, a good salary amongst high-class people and a real chance to build a second career. I have to take it. It will be hard telling Phil and even harder talking to Angus. But there it is.

And here it is in Riyadh, half way between The Red Sea and The Gulf, half way between red-eye and gulp. It started shortly after we boarded the plane and John Wisbey being told politely by the steward that the champagne was "expensive" to which John told him, equally politely, not to worry. It developed in the disembarkation hall when we stood in line for hours awaiting the most tortuous bureaucratic process imaginable and expensive too for the Saudi authorities taking as it did a whole stamp machine and pad to clear each weary unbelieving traveller to this magic land. It continued with the two Johns being cleared before me and taking the awaiting (long awaiting) car to the hotel and leaving me to find my own way there. It ended, temporarily, with the call to prayer made with the use of a loud-speaking hailer from an enormous pick-up truck and aimed directly at us as we walked peaceably outside to take coffee.

My off-beat moments abroad were being well augmented by this most un-musical of places. When one is good at getting orientated quickly, it is a shock to be completed lost and at the absolute mercy of the taxi driver. How does he know where to go when there are no road signs, no obvious indicator markers, no advertisements for places and worst of all this huge flatness bereft of higher-ground pointers? And when we are in the building of this large and respected bank, it is odd to be told that all the female staff could be pulled out at a moment's notice should the fundamentalists come calling. Never before have I been in a society where normal structure can be countermanded by a non-business, non-working, down-the-road group who act on instructions that seemingly no-one here has authority to address.

They appear to have a downer on females generally although judging by the number of children around, there must be compatibility as some stage. They have no faces and no legs and sit with their offspring behind a screen in each eating place, leaving by a separate exit from the exulted men. They cannot drive cars and, in theory, at least with some exceptions in such hybrid-owned international banks, cannot work. I was asking our link-man Arabian banker (who had spent four weeks in London going through the software and briefing us on what to expect) how on earth the youngsters actually meet, never mind the intricacies of what we quaintly might call a courtship. It seems they use a go-between and pass notes of interest leading eventually to liaisons "in the desert". The same vastness that might at times swallow up the illegal swallowers. But do not take an interest in this pursuit. Alcohol is forbidden and on such a delicate cross-culture mission such as this, definitely off the radar.

So on our last night, leader John treats us to non-alcoholic Champagne and non-alcoholic Chablis. It would be nice to admit that it was virtually no different to the real thing. But that would be a lie. It is certainly no comfort to poor old Big Eric. He cannot quite get things working, particularly the printing programs, he has to stay behind and we have been here two full weeks, way beyond the budget. In fact Big Eric, poor man, will be drying out for a further six weeks and his wife will keep on ringing up and complaining on behalf of the little children who miss their daddy. I feel like the heal that kept the Scotsmen in Cochin but this is our only contract and it has to work.

We all feel sorry for Big Eric, he is the only one that

really matters, it is his baby and he is a scout master and looks after more than babies. If Big Eric cannot get this phase signed off, then we are doomed. It makes it worse that he is poorly sighted. The image stays of him poured over the keyboard tap tapping long into the night until his head finally drops. But his impediment does prove the point of sharpening the remaining senses. How does he know it is me approaching his desk "because of the coins jangling in your pocket."

In the hotel in Riyadh eating beef steak my farmyard curiosity leads me to ponder aloud where the meat would have come from in this arid land to which Big Eric responds "a cow". Good old Big Eric. Poor old Big Eric. He has no respect for me at all. Who can blame him? If it was hard to get into the Kingdom then these officials have taken a lead from the ex-Iron Curtain countries and made it hard to leave too and so it is no little relief to actually be airborne and heading north. Relief tempered by the instant announcement that alcohol cannot be served until we leave Saudi airspace but then the sort of escape valve that otherwise only funeral wakes seem to provide. The male air host brings around the drinks and I tentatively ask whether it is possible to have two rather than the proffered single small bottle of whisky to which came the no-doubt well-used reply "possible sir, it is compulsory." Thank god for British Airways and for heading back home.

As time passes and the business grows, at least in terms of resources, so I get more senior. More salesmen come in, two via my own contacts, more programmers and a few more contracts most notably through the work musical Phil is doing, proving to local authorities that they can let the public access planning paperwork on the internet. We sign up Wandsworth Borough Council and the fees start to role. It is just as well since the strategy of broadening the base to encapsulate existing risk management customers is not working, they seem to have too many issues with the comprehensiveness of the risk software to want more experiments. It could be that the local government route is the one to tread. I keep thinking of the LPE days. Are we too early for a paperless back office for the big investment banks? If so, let us get what we can get and be patient, if the money will hold out.

But John Wisbey does want to force the pace and who can blame him with so much personal cash and kudos at stake? We will sock it to them over there, which first means Japan. The business is rightly proud of what has been built in Japan, it amounts to a fair slug of regular rental income and I am off with the head of customer care for the main business who has to deal with a few things anyway. The briefing on business etiquette includes the essentiality of handing over one's business card holding the bottom corners with each hand to avoid insult, by slight of hand, so to speak, and the bow forward from the mid-rift as an act of respect that will rankle with me as still harbouring an unsatisfied hatred of this race from the Singapore days. They are small, quiet and smiley behind those eyes and, as in the video machine days of Bell Fruit Services, do their strange business in packs (how can this land be so productive when it takes six to do the talking of one?).

My impression of this land is tainted by being boarded in a tatty hotel that is not in the main swim of Tokyo life and we never come across food that I can eat, it being sort of nibbles and things wrapped in green leaves. Added to the excruciating cost of everything, this is not my favourite trip of all time and I am minded of the backlash to the disciplinarian regime of Singapore when, after the workday here, groups come to drink and the noise is horrendous as if the blue touch paper has been ignited. It is a more over-the-top release than in New York. But with this difference. Here the boss-man of the group is very obvious. This is not Chinese but it is kowtow and furthermore no-one but no-one leaves until he does, even apparently to the extent of missing the last train. There is always those funny little box things to spend the night in and watch the porno shows.

And here's another thing about these strange people. When they travel on the underground, they read comics with illustrations of sexually explicit acts. We are talking about morning rush-hour not late night after-bar. There is a pop song about turning Japanesey. Not in my case. And as they all sleep on this thirteen-hour flight back, I watch for hour after hour as Siberia rolls slowly beneath with its gaunt fissures breaking up the massed plains. This world is an odd mixture of contrasts. Here lies the vast emptiness hiding huge natural resources that one day may well hold the West to ransom and back there was the huge mass of squashed up humanity hiding nothing and due to their past hubris and insular cultural barriers will never again hold anyone to ransom. In fairness, I should return to Japan one day and view it in an independent more wholesome light. But there are plenty of other places I would rather go.

The business is strong in New York too and Shield is destined to run the office there for a while after they have fallen out with the sparky lady now running it. In fact both John's are regular visitors and just about as familiar with that City as London. So it is logical that I go there too and promote our new imaging software and darling Becky is to come and do the actual demonstrating. Software, yes, but also the beautiful English rose with especially long stems. We are looked after by the sparky lady and her boyfriend and eat well, not least the house lobster below Grand Central Station, as frequented by James Bond apparently, and the lunch-time salads in the outspoken Irish/American bars.

The office has a fantastic setting high above Fifth Avenue and from where one can see the traffic rushing towards and underneath the building. It needs to rush since if stationary it would freeze solid. Never have I experienced such cold. To cross a street is to have a strong man grab the face and squeeze in the cheeks and press hard on the chest. Becky has a nose-bleed and has to see a doctor and I have a credibility bleed cogitating on how to sell new technology software in such a vast place in such hostile conditions. Henry Miller described the cold of a New York winter made more poignant by being penniless and hungry. We only had the first to deal with, but it was enough.

But we are not just doing New York, a round trip has been fixed. We are off to talk to refreshingly casual senior bankers in jeans and sneakers in Chicago, Columbus and Washington. My sons made a friend "American Steve" in Spain and I look expectantly down at his home town in Indiana, the evocatively named Fort Wayne, but there is no town, just vast flat whiteness. Funny isn't it. Siberia and the Mid-West look similar, except the old USSR is more beautiful in its winter coat. And beautiful Becky keeps up her pecker throughout, crossing her long legs and draining every last drop from the system demonstration. And yet nothing is as it appears, nothing is perfect. Becky is the sole breadwinner. Fact is her husband developed an odd sort of illness that prevents him from working and his solace is the golf course that he plays to a handicap of four. It does not take an Einstein to work out that he, sooner rather than later, might have another handicap.

Here is another highlight. After playing squash on a Friday evening, my best friend John (so many of them – what an imaginative race our parents were) and I debate the Falkland Island conflict and the disaster of HMS Sheffield and what would happen if the converted troop ship Canberra was hit? Well, on the top deck of this huge old ship, we have been hit. Not by an Argentine-fired exocet missile but an English Channel fired storm. It is early morning and from what I can make out we never did cruise around the Channel Islands but went straight over to a French port and now because we have to dock back in Southampton, the captain has decided to run to that port whilst the drunks sleep it off. The seas are tremendous and the wind noise truly astonishing and the few of us left might as well be on deck witnessing it as in a lounge being thrown from side-to-side. It had been Shield's idea and sold to Wisbey. Go on this special weekend trip selling software to the City bankers. He as a seller pays the mammoth fee to the organisers but I as a lecturer go free. Two for the price of one, so to speak. And speak I do on what is, in reality, one megalithic piss-up. Stowed to stoned.

Once again the circus, early morning to late night to being away to being dead tired; if there is no way out, I will be dead for sure. So Julia and I have a think and the answer is move to somewhere near Peterborough. That way I can swap the badly-in-need-of-upgrade so-called Midland Mainline (on which the train times from Nottingham to St Pancras have not lessened since my steam days in the Motive Power Department) for the swish, fast track East Coast Main Line to Kings Cross. In theory, this would cut the on-board time from two hours to forty-five minutes.

Julia rustles up her sister Geraldine and they find a vicarage to rent, in a village that time has forgot, called Maxey. This gorgeous retreat could have been plucked from the Cotswolds except it is superior. The stone houses have merely evolved from the rich soil and the thatched roofs of the oldest cottages reach almost to the pavement. It is a heaven-sent spot in a part of England we never even knew existed. OK, the terrain is flat, but the compensation is that each village has been surrounded by trees as if to isolate the quiet residents from the cruel outside world. Across the road we can walk around a series of lakes that will be home to nesting swans. Our favourite pair will beget eight signets that we will watch emotionally as they trail their parents from bank to bank. Eight, that as late spring drifts into high summer will dwindle down to four. My neighbour says they are taken by pike. Cruel world for them too it seems.

Julia and I are hooked and there is one pub too, the

Bluebell, but we like to eat at the Red Lion in neighbouring West Deeping. The host village of Market Deeping is seeped in history and has "the best fish and chip shop in England" to bring it down to earth. This day the pubs and shops and offices suffer from clogging traffic but one day the by-pass will sort that out and, as with Maxey, restore a medieval splendour. We both loved the area and even today when flashing past by train I cannot resist peering across the flat landscape in search of the comforting square tower of Maxey church.

Due to the increasing prospects for the imaging system and my commitment to the business through extensive travel both throughout the UK and Southern Ireland and overseas plus our home move to make the commuting more practical, I am getting more senior in John Wisbey's empire. I am now on the main board and have played a major role in acquiring a further technical business based in Suffolk and bringing that into the City offices. I have had a large salary increase and have taken over the whole of the main firm's programming floor of some seventy software people to give some oomph to the deadlines that are being consistently missed. John says he has plans to make me a sort of MD of the group and having spoken to his banking friends, maybe a title of Chief Operating Officer will be best suited to the role he has in mind.

Maybe it started with his note in late November setting out certain "Strategic issues" and was compounded by my studious, long, and part constructive but part critical, response at the end of December to finish off the year. I have been handed a letter following the discussion and that, "with much regret", requests my immediate resignation as MD of my business and as a director of the others. It is now early February and as I have just said to John Wisbey, "I need this like a hole in the head." Julia and I are nowhere near the end of our committed lease term on the vicarage, we have tenants in Sheepwalk Lane and aside from these practical things, it had come like a bolt from the blue. All the indications were that I was on the up and up. I have worked my rocks off for the past eighteen months and genuinely tried to bring some democracy into an otherwise fairly autocratic set-up, tried to add some formal structure to a main business that has grown very quickly and not least tried to introduce the idea of marketing as an over-arching discipline to the Shield-led all out sales push.

The justifications in the letter are the accumulated loss over eighteen months exceeding the current annual turnover and the failure to hit the latest risk management software deadline. I could contest both vigorously, but I shall not. When the knife is in, that is it. It is not the first time. But it will be the last. John's letter ends by saying that he thought it might still be appropriate for me to concentrate on running my business (as distinct from the other work I had been asked to take on) but that after detailed discussion with the other shareholders (he still held, as far as I knew, 98% of the equity), he believed it would be a mistake. As I walked into the main office the following Saturday morning to sign the papers and pick up my cheque, I overhear John Shield in John Wisbey's office. He was at first just talking but now he is laughing.

As I go back to Peterborough on the much slower and different-peopled Saturday train, I feel surprisingly elated when logically I should be down. I will be with Julia again on a full-time basis and, especially coming as a shock, that has a good ambience. I have the cheque and as John Wisbey so kindly pointed out "it is equivalent to five months after-tax pay".

First I will get myself fit again, maybe buy one of those cycle things that one peddles on furiously without actually getting anywhere, and did I get anywhere? Well, the weight has piled on, even my mum has told me so, and that would have stunned me into action anyway. It is to do with the wine at lunchtime and the excellent filled rolls and the beers after work and the sitting on trains and generally the lack of self-discipline, that now I see as so easy to slip into in this sort of lifestyle. A lifestyle, that now I think about it, there will be no regrets about giving up. It is also the deception. Everyone seems driven to put on a face, why is that? As if the whole work thing in the City is an act. Is that why the noisy release is so palpable as the London Pride ale goes down? Not that it is an exclusively London thing, far from it. New York and Tokyo are the same. Shout and shout and get all that pent up stuff out man and when you are really yourself on that inter-city express, sod the word and excel files.

> *In this world of high finance*
> *I'm quite a whizzy star*
> *Whisked from Leeds to Kings Cross*
> *Courtesy, GNER*
>
> *Observed from just two seats away*
> *it's a shame I'm worked so hard*
> *the mobile shrills, the laptop's hot*
> *the software plays a card!*

I must have done some good surely? They must have had a lot of confidence in me at some stage, I have not deceived anyone, I have been myself. John Wisbey had pointed out that, as he headed for his dream result of floating the business, I would be too old and certainly as, say, group finance director, would not present the right image or have had the right background for the city. Appearance is important. I was told about my brown shoes. Polished black is the banker's uniform. Why do I keep thinking of Kenneth Clark when he was Chancellor?

Start all over again

Angus thinks it will be hard for me to adjust to the mezzanine floor with only artificial light when I have been used to the view out of the plate glass window overlooking the winding Thames. But he hasn't "replaced" me and he would be happy to pick up where we left off, one day a week will be fine, let's agree a figure and start next week. I push the pedals on my static bike and sweat and think things out. Julia and I walk the fields and lanes and lakes of Maxey and talk and go out in the evening, if we want to. We are happy. I have probably lost out on £'s millions but then the failed MBO at Bell Fruit Services probably saved my shirt. As the VAT man is about to say, "Lets call it a one-all draw."

The clients will creep back, although the likelihood is more and more on the old patch, since I have hit the local mafia wall at this Peterborough end. It is a shame, because we could buy this vicarage and stay put and work on modernising it. After all, Julia and I have already worked a miracle on the large garden, and she has made some good friends of the neighbours, as a refreshing change from the half-dead lot at Ravenshead. Ah well, better kick our tenants out and go back home. Goodbye Maxey, you did us proud, we will not forget you.

There will be no let up now until I retire that in reality is a euphemism for drawing down the pension fund. That is correct. I shall not be selling it to an insurance company. I will keep the capital, thanks for asking anyway. Over these years I have learned a little about the role of capital.

It seems that I can go through the Association of Chartered Certified Accountants' training courses and get a certificate allowing me to actually practise for the first time as a public accountant (though not on a quoted company) and do tax computations. I can prepare the year-end financial accounts wrapped in all their meaningless gobbledegook that is no help to the business and whose short-form version filed with Companies House is no help to the public. But regulations are regulations and we all want to get fat again, don't we?

In my sojourn back in the world of small business I try to point the way for a signage business, hip-hop back in London for a music promoter, re-write the stationer's story, live out the buy-to-rent game, note the growing pains of a new-technology message-taking service, regret the publishing shyster, attempt to distribute the film man, and then there was David Croft.

How did it all come about? I had tried to get involved with an accountancy practice in Nottingham to develop with them a consultancy service but, as in the old days of PW, had run up against the *audit-man keepeth unto himself* the long established cherished client syndrome. But the boss man referred me to his Newark branch office and the beautiful Monica that ran it had a client wanting business advice. He was David Croft and the business was based (I do not believe it) in London.

So started the long entanglement. Difficult, rewarding, worrying, engaging entanglement. Daniel was a questioner in Angus's league. What, when, why and how, until my head screamed out for release. Coming down from Birmingham as a young man he was, as many before and after, an aspiring musician who either through lack of talent or opportunity or both did not quite make it. But he did make the maintenance man for a band that, against all odds, had a No1 hit called *Don't you want me baby?* and he toured the world with them banging it out. If you can keep the instruments going in five continents, you can certainly keep them going in London. So reasoned David and he set up his own repair workshop to prove it. The key musical driver is our old friend technology and, in this scene, electronics and soon to be our second old friend software. David is a wizard at electronics and not bad at programming either. So, technically, a round peg in a round hole. Even if not the preferred hole. But, as with so many others, these qualities do not make a business manager and due to a positively pernicious rent hike in his unit in Chalk Farm, his problems were mounting.

I will help David all I can because I like him. He is genuine, straightforward, gritty and a worker. He needs help because he cannot see the wood for the trees; corny but true. He cannot delegate or train or recruit successfully and has, and will always have, staff problems as a result. He can always dive in and sort it out himself and so he does, he works from early morning through into the late evening and most weekends. He represents a major management consultancy challenge and when things really get him down, he has a vicious migraine attack that literally takes him to ground.

We went to Los Angeles together and sitting on the stand he is obviously in the frustrated artiste's paradise of the biggest music exhibition in the world.

David is not a high-flying go-getter and the contrast between him and some others is vast. I met his mother before she died and carried synthesisers and organs to the new building with his father. They are a genuine salt-of-the-earth Brummie family whose lad made good in the big smoke. As someone pointed out to me, you would not put him into a sartorial competition. But you could with confidence enter him for the better human being event. He would get my vote every time.

Who else would take my long-rested ex-Bell Fruit Services 1973 utilitarian electro-mechanical Wurlitzer jukebox into his workshop and fix it and for free? So I will try and fix his business and take his grinding questions in the Mexican restaurant on Streatham High Street at ten-thirty at night when I am knackered. And help him buy out his competitor who has assiduously whipped away a customer base from under his nose. In my book it is because if anyone deserves to succeed, then David Croft does. I admire and empathise with the small man. He battles with everything and everyone just to be himself, just like my dad did.

CHAPTER FOURTEEN
Philosophy of a retiring mind

Pondering on the end game. Simple made complex. Time pressure and rants. Children no more. A Donald Rumsfeld thing. Death of a good one. The tragic marriage. An actuary crowned. Old boss nostalgia. A South African jaunt. Of home.

Retirement is a strange concept. I cannot get my head around it. Have I always been at work? Will I always stay working? Have I always been retired? It is all to do with definitions. And wrapped up in all this is something else I cannot fathom. Why did it have to follow that juxtapositioned with the massive increase in efficiency and therefore productivity over the years (I think of the time and effort in the railway office and in the electricity office adding up figures, making them balance and then the two minutes I would take now using an excel spreadsheet, Mr Bill Gates – you thoroughly deserve to be the richest man in the world – you brought riches to the world) came mind-boggling complications?

Is it, as in nature, that a vacuum has to be filled? Does the time saved have to be absorbed in unravelling consequential complications? Why should they be consequential? And why now that we are all so much richer, are we so much poorer? Technology has not bought time to savour non-money things and monetary affluence has not led to spare financial capacity to, say, breed more children merely for the enjoyment of having them around.

Just think of this. My mother was one of thirteen children that lived, one did not. Starting in 1903 and ending in 1927, the little lady produced successively Edwin, Jack, Arthur, Frank, Annie, Fred, George, Ernest, Mary, Madge, Harold, Edna and Eric. Aside from the social considerations, there is arguably not an ordinary family man in the Western world today who could financially contemplate such an issuance. But in the inefficient and poverty stricken early part of the last century, Hedley Herbert Wilson master butcher, could. I wonder if he set out consciously to out-do the Smiths who, according to the ancient history of that distinguished surname, have since the 13th and 14th centuries proliferated births over deaths annually by an increase of between 35% and 40% compared to the rest of the population's rate of 5% to 10%. It is a strange fact, not entirely due to changing economic circumstances, that the offspring of the great creator Wilson hardly bred at all.

We have the modern tools and we are better educated and communications are superb. Yet, here is an extract from an e-mail sent to Craig, my younger son, and others in England from American Steve who has moved from peaceful Fort Wayne to the hurly-burly of California. "Amy had a tough year splitting time between two schools. Imagine spending half your day at one office and the other half at another. To compound that, imagine spending one hour each at four different desks in the second office, having to cart around with you all of your files. In regards to my work, I'm in the spotlight working at the corporate HQ. There's never time to do everything and therefore balancing the need to be here to succeed and the need to be home in the evening is difficult. So whereas you normally are supposed to rely on your partner to get through tough times, we opted to go the more destructive route of beating the crap out of each other on a daily basis." This was sent a few days before Christmas. I forwarded it to Chris, my elder son. Here is his reply "I think we should all go back and live in caves, things were much simpler. When did we all decide we had to do everything? Blokes trying to do the woman's job, women trying to do the bloke's job, both failing and neither wanting to talk about it due to a combination of fear, vanity, pride or not wanting to be sexist. Basically my generation is spending all its time working so that it can pay for somebody else to do the stuff we can't do because we are all working and then in what little spare time we have we feel guilty about not doing the stuff we actually want to do. This does not create an environment that is easy to thrive in! I hope Steve manages to sort himself out and that the next generation don't inherit our stupidity."

And this from two bright, well travelled modern men. What chance have I got? Have you tried to buy any decorating paint lately? When you say white, do you mean rose white, apple white or any one of the other fifteen adjectival whites. Sorry just white! What is that? We do not actually stock a colour cream sir, care to try buttermilk? I have always hated milk of any sort and I hate you and as for whisper green, what the bloody hell is that? I want plain green man and am shouting about it. The answer sir is mix-your-own using our fancy new gadget, but if I wanted to invent my own colour I wouldn't be hear in the first place. Pratt.

Another thing. Soap. The thing you wash yourself with used to be sold in handy little bars, handy to hold and handy to massage into a nice lather. There was still a vast choice from simple square cheap carbolic to my mum's choice, when things started to look up, the wonderfully shaped and beautifully perfumed and coloured *Pears*. Where have all the soap bars gone? Who said we didn't want them anymore? What on earth is the use of a plastic bottle with a press down top to extract a tiny squeezy bit of insipid glue. How do I rub that around my goolies? And it is not just an English thing. I searched high and low in a local Spanish supermarket for a humble bar of soap, the triumphalism of finding which evaporated the second I returned when Julia threw it into the bin. It was something to do with the grooming of those fine Spanish stallions apparently.

And as for eating out, I have absolutely given up trying to fathom what is being described. Is it the dish, an ingredient, the method of preparation, the mode of cooking? What does that mean? Will it be as unpalatable as the patent bullshit it is? But I do keep trying to appreciate the progression of it all, the development from when Hedley Herbert Wilson fed his flock on his home-cured meat. A flock that all lived and continue to live to a ripe old age. My dad's grandmother used to pick maggots out of the meat and cheese as she ate it and loved to drink the left over sour milk. She lived to be ninety-four. Progression, progression.

Remember the days when you received a telephone bill that told you how may calls had been made at what unit cost and total cost. Have you unpicked your latest bill? Really! Liar. It is intellectually and mathematically impossible.

Another thing I was thinking about is the movement from things being satisfactory anyway, through wonderful innovation to, well let's face it, back where we started. Or are we not supposed to notice? Do you remember the era from Brownie to flashy Pentax camera when one's roll of film was taken to Boots the Chemist for developing and then the sheer thrill of collecting the package courtesy of Kodak to see "how have they turned out?" Now that is old hat. The digital era has dawned so that we can view the shot instantly on the camera screen, still a thrill but without the anticipation, without the build-up, somehow not the same. So you want a permanent representation? In a little while we will have the technology of a docking station to download the chip to your desktop computer and not only see but manipulate the *image* on the monitor. That is right, you can actually change what actually existed. A bit further down the line you will be able to print it off and eventually, with such high resolution on such good quality paper, it will be almost as good as the analogue print. Better still, there is now, believe it or not, a machine in your local Boots the Chemist store that will take your chip and print off your shots so you can come away with the thrill of holding a package of high quality prints of your photographs. Whirligig.

My friend Ellis and his wife Sheila made special arrangements as part of their planned train journey to Germany to be met on the platforms and for their cases to be taken to the awaiting taxi or coach. It was just a little extra to add to the ease of things. When I started work on the railway, porters swarmed onto the platforms at St Pancras to take the heavy cases and hat boxes forward. I think that is what a porter is employed to do. In this vein, I often think of Bernard. He used to come to the farm to take the weekly order. The following week it would be delivered in a cardboard box. Now, Tesco do more or less the same thing except you input whereas he used to write it down. The lady in front checking out at the much posher supermarket explains that she is buying the fancy box of twelve quails' eggs because they are "reduced". Compared to even my bantam eggs, they certainly are.

And consider this. The patients that waited their turn to see Dr Graham in his Tibshelf surgery might well have been referred to the local cottage hospital. It would be a quick and easy matter since he knew personally the matron who ran it with a rod of iron. Maybe the family just wanted some temporary respite from the troubled one, maybe it would act as a holding bay pending a bigger decision, maybe it was convalescence, maybe even a last resting place. Both Julia's mum and her uncle Albert spent a comfortable and peaceful transition in the cottage hospital at Wells-next-the-sea. Things move a little slower in Norfolk and so that dear little place has only just been closed.

Now read this for pleasure. Avoid the pain of thinking about it. "A property investment company is raising £110m to set up new village hospitals in a bid to take advantage of Government initiatives to devolve more healthcare provisions to local centres. Medical Property Investment Fund, one of the largest funds which specialises in buying sites used by GP's, is issuing 65 million new shares at £1.70 per share. MPIF, which already owns 82 sites which it rents out to doctors, plans to upgrade some of its existing premises and will also buy new sites for the larger practices, which have been dubbed "village hospitals" or "super surgeries"…….. MPIF shares fell 8 to 178."

It could be that potential investors have memories and wonder why the previous resource was wasted and when the tide will turn again, and not just at Wells-next-the-sea either. But as I learned in my consultancy days, changing resources or in this hapless case reverting to that which used to be, is one thing. Changing the culture is another. In a report published by the Centre for Policy Studies a recently qualified staff nurse explained that she had spent the majority of her training on sociological and gender issues. The practical aspects of nursing, doing for the sick what they cannot do for themselves, has been downgraded. She said "You can go through the whole three years without anyone asking you about bed sores". The report goes on, but it is too depressing to quote further.

Nevertheless it is easy to fall into the trap of over-simplification. Some things are complex and one simple mind cannot possibly hope to comprehend the multitudinous nuances. I was reading in the paper about a man called Richard Abbott who it seems labours under the title of Executive Director for the Procurement

Workstream in the Office of Government Procurement. Wow. If, as is reported, he concluded that some departments pay up to fifty percent more for the same goods and employ the same consultants to give them the same advice, then we can only conclude that he must be a buyer. But there must be more to his job than that. You see, it must be so easy to be great at execution but terrible at choosing what to do, that is to say good at getting unimportant things done. Busy, busy but at what? Be a fine technician, never be a spectator, but for goodness sake try not to think about it, you do not need to know you are a busy fool.

Fledged and gone

An adventurous young lady tries to fly with the condors in a paraglider or similar but unlike the expert birds, comes down to earth with a bump. She damages her body but also her pride. There is nothing quite like catching up with ones offspring to come down to earth with a bump. How to balance the philosophy of free-flight with wanting and trying to help but still not intending to constrain, interfere, make them feel beholden, be a drag from the past?

Craig is in Fort Wayne and after the blank period post-university and no job, he sounds happy to wallow in the excellent facilities that have flown from American Steve's finding of a temporary job. The summer weather is beautiful, there is swimming and tennis after work and a "pretty, intelligent and sporty" real American girl called Kara. He is sad that our cat Asti has died and he hopes the gardening project I gave him in the blank period "has produced the goods". In answer to my main question, he is "living within my means". It did not seem so bad when he was at university, Liverpool was easy to get to. I had a terrible time seeing him disappear through the departure gate at Gatwick, all my theories about independence left with him. My little boy "best singer in class", "we have put him on the slow table, he is so far behind", has gone.

The letters from No 2, Annie Street, Ramsbottom, Bury, Lancashire are all about "means" and contain "the elusive statements as requested". Times had improved for although Craig had to return once his green card expired, the American work experience had done the interview trick and he now got job offers. The temporary one had turned permanent and he was a project manager on the Little Hulton Project that was transforming the council housing in Salford, Manchester. I paid the deposit and he took the plunge and bought the end terrace house on this quaint stone built street overlooked by the impressive Peel Monument. We walked the high moors over Rammy and listened for the steam train as it made its way up the valley and he talked of his new friends, the local pie shop and his visits to watch Bury Town play football on wintery days, a far cry from the 85 degrees of a Fort Wayne summer. He asked my advice on a moral issue concerning a lady who was unhappily married and sometimes visited No 2. Craig and his new life.

Craig came to see Julia and me at Maxey. He was in trouble. Money trouble. He was not asking for money. He wanted me to help him re-schedule his debts, sort of take over his finances, he was being overwhelmed and could not see a way out. What debts? We sat down in the office and went through it all. It all started at University, the main purpose of which appears to be to learn how to socialise, and of-course he went up with Newall, his then long-term girlfriend who was very beautiful and needed much looking after. So much so that she had to take a decision, and it split them. Craig is not stupid and naïve with money. It is just that he has a generous nature and such people can be taken advantage of plus his mother's new husband is ill, very ill and causing Craig to make many expensive trips back to

Kirkby to help out. It all adds up. Adds up to what exactly?

There is only one answer. We all know it. I shall liquidate. Out go the privatisation issues. Goodbye Rolls Royce, so long British Airways, off you go Baillie Gifford. One day I will start again to play the market, but for now there are more pressing things to do.

For now, I will only know what it has been decided is needed to be known. Sometime later another debt will arise. It will not be via a bank or a finance house or a student loan and so there would be no obvious path to knowledge. Later still as I am drenched in sweat culling the roadside boundary of rampant holly, two full size trees, nettles and general undergrowth (clearing the jungle to let the light in – so to speak), Craig walks down the drive to fill me in on the combined debts of himself and his new wife that have, I learn, been partly re-financed by drawing down a mortgage on their otherwise unencumbered house. His new wife had insisted he told me. She felt it was only right, given the history, that I became aware of how they had jointly worked things out financially. Had I been as smart as a US defence secretary I could have put all this in context. Made sense of it you might say. But I wasn't and did not. So the immortal words of Donald Rumsfeld explaining to journalists the consequential aftermath of the invasion of Iraq struck home "There are known knowns; there are things we know we know. We also know there are known unknowns; that is to say we know there are some things we do not know. But there are also unknown unknowns – the ones we don't know we don't know". Quite.

But life moves on, or rather does not. Further down Sheepwalk Lane and on the other side lived the Bolt family. Mum, dad and three sons although rumour had it that dad was not biological but step. It mattered not, they were a close-knit hard working family and both parents were senior school teachers. That said, it always seemed a bit odd that come the long summer holidays, off went mum and dad in the campervan to tour France leaving the sons behind in the care of grandmother, who lived further down the road. Perhaps for this reason, added to both parents working full-time, the youngest boy Neil was extraordinarily precocious in terms of self-reliance. From a very young age he could cook his own meals, wash and iron his clothes and generally fend for himself. We knew all this since he was a classmate of Chris and a good friend and because in those long summer holidays he practically lived at our home. He was a sort of third son. Whether we went swimming, playing football, cricket or snooker or most likely fishing, always Bolty went too. He was part of the family set-up. He was good looking, blonde, had a broad captivating smile and an extrovert personality. This natural combination begat one further appealing attribute. He always pulled the best looking bird and she almost always tagged along too. One could always rely on Bolty to bring along the ravishing girl.

At a very young age he married one of these beauties and restored a terrace house in Kirkby-in-Ashfield as a love nest. He then set up his own joinery business, no doubt as second best to becoming a snooker professional. Precocious to start and to remain. But the marriage went wrong (although he would not talk about it) and Chris having gone away, he was now a close friend to Craig. So Craig looked after Bolty during his bad time and soon he bounced back with another good-looker on his arm. This time it was Lisa with the bubbly smile and bright red lipstick but who had a mind of her own. Whilst she finished off her degree in English at Worcester she was not overly keen on Bolty's season ticket at Nottingham Forest football club on the Saturdays when he could otherwise have come to see her, or his continuing nights out with the lads with whom he stilled played weekend football. She was divulging the gist of this as I painted my new garage door that Bolty's firm had made and I proffered a view that they did not appear overly compatible. "Oh – he has his uses".

So the relationship was dynamic and off more than once and it was a surprise when we learned they were to marry. True to form he got hold of a house in Mansfield that was structurally very sound but old fashioned and set about using his weekends to modernise it. Right up to the Friday before the wedding on Sunday he had been decorating in the morning and had picked up his wedding suit in the afternoon. In the evening they were with his parents making last minute arrangements and I was playing squash with John as usual. It may have been late June but it was cold and raining heavily. At 12.30 a.m. whilst driving Lisa home, his Rover car rounded the bend leaving Ravenshead and was hit head on by a car on the wrong side of the road coming the other way. They kept him alive until Sunday evening but he was dead, very dead. Neil James Bolt, age 30.

Lisa was damaged too but remarkably, considering she was in the passenger seat, only superficially. At any rate physically. But here was a beautiful young girl with an hourglass figure and a singing voice of an angel stripped of her first true love on the eve of her wedding with no forewarning and no apology following. Is that wholly survivable? Just a little earlier whilst on a visit to "Rammy" and after a night out with Craig, I had stumbled into his spare bedroom only to find Bolty and Lisa fast asleep in the bed. I can still see them there.

The memory of the whole football team lining the rear of the crematorium wearing their red and white playing shirts and of the voice of Lisa from a recording singing a folk song, is still vivid. But time drifts on and in successive stages we latch on to the fact that things are happening. It began innocently enough. Lisa started to telephone Craig and then went up to Rammy to see him. Consolation. But then Craig has applied for a new job with Broxtowe District Council in Nottingham and has got it. It happens to be based right alongside Trent Bridge in the usual splendid offices of the type that only local authorities can afford. He can, as part of the removal package, get six months rent-free accommodation and then removal expenses and his patch is the upmarket area south of the river. Perfect, except that instead he has opted to move into Lisa's spare room so that he is better placed to help her through the mourning. When I visit, the spare room looks to me more like an office.

Then Craig and Lisa come to see Julia and me. She is back to her ebullient self, bright red lipstick, talkative, excited. They have fallen in love and are going to get married. Oh. They have looked at various places but want something special. Special to them is the English Lake District and will we come to vet this hotel in Troutbeck. Craig appreciates that Trevor, the owner, is a bit OTT but as he predicted after his sales spiel, "when you have seen the rest, you will be back." They do not really believe that his wife is "one of the finest hairdressers this country had ever produced" but even if she is quite good it will at least solve one of the logistic problems, at a price.

Everything about it will be at a price, Trevor's price, although with regard to the room rate, the happy couple will subsidise the tariff. Getting there will be a problem, his grandma is getting old and at the other extreme Chris, who will be his bestman, and Heather are expecting their baby just a few weeks before the chosen date. Still, the dependable Sam (Lisa's step-dad) has volunteered to drive a mini-bus to take the family, so that is OK. Afterwards, and after the fireworks (only £500 extra) they will be whisked away by a friend to a hotel near Manchester airport for the early morning flight to Cancun, Mexico. All fixed then, just the special waistcoat to order and fetch from London and the rings to have made from that specialist place they have found in Southwell.

We lads will stick together. We always have done and we

always will do. Chris gave his speech/stand-up comedy routine punctuated with his one-liners to bring the house down whilst little Colette slept in her basket at his feet. I read my poem that I really, really hoped they would take some notice of.

Near the end of the evening and to great surprise and delight, Lisa took the microphone from the singer in the band and sang to Craig one of the latest pop songs. It was something to do with having found eternal love and of always being true.

Less than a year later Julia and I were returning from the Isle of Wight on the car ferry and to pass the time I got Craig on the mobile 'phone. I was trying to pin him down for arrangements at Christmas. He was more distant than 200 miles would justify and non-committal. That was my proof and I told Julia so, it was not clever, merely tragic. A few weeks earlier, Craig had come to see me in the garden, a rare event. He wanted me to know that he and Lisa had hit a bad patch. He could not understand what was going on, she had continued to talk about her life with Bolty – that was no change and he understood it – but now she went out "with friends" a lot and often he did not know where she was and in fact one evening when she was at her mother's house, she was not.

A deep ache started in the pit of my stomach. Poor Craig, it was so sad. Worse than that, it sounded so dreadfully familiar. Soon after our holiday, Craig came down the garden again. He and Lisa had decided to split, he was crying. I handed him over to Julia. There was no-one else, they just couldn't get along any more. Then came the real shock. The marriage had never been consummated "properly". She just did not want him to do it to her. Not even in Cancun, on your honeymoon? No. Christ. Just a few days earlier, I had called at their home unexpectedly to fetch back some of my garden tools now that the landscaping had finished. Lisa came tripping down the stairs in a very short skirt talking loudly on her mobile; she appeared very happy.

The neighbour to whom I had been chatting over the fence on those hot days of labour, creating a garden out of rubble, had told me about the Saab car that was often parked on the side road next to his house and about the owner who then walked around to Craig's place. Craig, I thought but did not say, you may not know it or you may and now do not care and Lisa may well be in denial, but she is definitely having an affair. The house that Bolty bought and prudently insured against his death in favour of Lisa, even though they were not yet married, was being sold. Lisa wanted her equity out. The best price quoted of £94,000 would leave about £15,000 each. Yet, it started debt free, Sam had done all the driveway and windows and ceilings for free, Bolty's parents had polished the floors and fireplace for free and I had done the garden for free. So where had the debt difference gone? Just living, just living.

Craig will come back home to live until a life starts again. I asked Genya, Lisa's mum, what had gone wrong "Lisa still loves Craig but she is not *in love* with Craig." I asked Sam what had gone wrong "How was Craig ever going to compete with a ghost?" We had just finished a day on one of the hardest stretches of the South West Coastal Path and were drinking and listening to an excellent rock band in the pub in the village of Paradise (sic). Craig went very white and very quiet. They were knocking out a certain song. He was still hurting. Very much so.

It is a very proud moment for a father when his son walks up to receive his fellowship of the Institute of Actuaries. At that time hardly anyone, even amongst the educated, had even heard of an actuary. Now, thanks to our Chancellor of the Exchequer who, arguably, pulled the plug from under the best pension schemes in the world and then compounded this by sheer inaction, everyone knows what an actuary is. Even the man on the Clapham omnibus, since his newly privatised owner has just scrapped his defined benefit scheme.

Chris could not have known that an actuary would become such a key ingredient in not just financial services but in the heart of the business decision, especially with acquisitions and mergers. He could not have known that the active actuary in the corporate sector can just about write his own salary cheque. But then, after seven hard years of study and exams, it seems only right and proper. You get what you pay for. You earn what you work for. This is a gloriously sunny spring day in the splendid grounds of Staple Inn and Julia and I are about to go into the presentation ceremony in the great Hall and afterwards attend the reception in the Council Chamber. Not bad for the little mite with the funny shaped head and the dad that cannot speak for being choked up.

It had been a long hard road full of flops and surges and always the mock exams to do before the day is finished. After I was sacked from Bell Fruit Services, meeting Chris became more difficult. He was well entrenched in the South West and now unlikely to move, save possibly to London, whilst I was scratching a living in the East Midlands. Julia played a key role in his getting the first job after university. She 'phoned a lady in HR at Sun Life after they had balked at the quality of his degree. It reminded me of her call to John Smithson when she called off our affair. A remarkable lady is Julia. It was in the summer of our first long-distance walk when he dragged a leg (literally) along the whole of the North Norfolk Coastpath from Holme to Cromer that I realised that Chris would stick at the very difficult actuarial syllabus, and see it through. Hard long walks and life itself are not poles apart.

It had been a bit of an endurance test in the love stakes too. Chris did have a girlfriend at university called Nicky, who we all liked, but that ended acrimoniously and then he spotted Heather in the study room of Sun Life "pouring over a simultaneous equation or differential calculus" or something of the sort as he said in his wedding speech. This would be no easy conquest. Heather had a live-in boyfriend who would have to be side-tracked, prised out and then bought out. And when the flat had to be sold after the wedding, a legalistic discovery was made. The original conversion into seven flats did not have ground leaseholder approval and our man now in Portugal had long since sold his interest to one of those firms who make their money out of such occurrences. So the blood money had to be paid, and by each flat owner, nasty.

I miss Chris a lot. He is my mental punchbag and my kindred spirit. I sent a cheque and a card for his birthday and it must have had a note inside because it stings him into a rare letter. He is upset that I said that we do not meet anymore and he feels our telephone calls are "formal." Although this is late August, two dates he proposes we might meet are in mid and late October. Such is life. Such is sadness. He wishes me luck with my new job. I am about to start with Wisbey.

He took over the investment club at work and pulled it around and that gets us thinking. We collaborated at first on the preferential offering in Sun Life's French parent company and then moved on to work together and combine our shares portfolios. He does the clever stuff, I do the donkey-work, and so far it has proved a winner, partly because we have made money but mainly because we have to keep in touch on a regular basis. My contact with Chris is my shot in the arm. Nothing stronger is needed.

A penchant for shares and investing in paper generally is just as well, it compensates for bricks and mortar. Well I would think that wouldn't I? It had all started with the death rattle of Bell Fruit Services when the MBO was not going to happen and I was fed up to the back teeth. Ellis Walker and I were meeting more often and we decided to go into property development. It made sense because his firm had all the technical skills and supplier contacts and he personally had the professional connections in town. We travelled extensively to find the right opportunity and at last it came up right on my old doorstep.

We bid successfully for a vacant piece of land in the village of South Normanton, Derbyshire, the same mining village that mum and dad and me and Margaret would walk to some Sunday evenings over the field with the large multi-stepped stile and up the steep hill past the church. Stile and steep hill sounds familiar; will become familiar. Constitutionally it was an overkill, constructually it was easy, time-wise for the housing market, it was a disaster.

The company we set up, Heathland Estates Limited, was 50% owned by myself but the other half was held by a partnership that itself was owned 40% by Ellis and 30% each by the two fellow partners of his main firm. Add to that a most elaborate shareholder agreement draw up by a leading firm of solicitors in the Ropewalk in Nottingham and you get a recipe for stagnancy under pressure.

At the start, all went well. It was an exciting time and Ellis and I were on the brink of a profitable joint venture that heralded my get-out from the leisure industry and his easement from his firm. We paid £38,000 for the land and budgeted £53,000 for the building of three small houses. With all the other costs taken into account and at a modest selling price of £42,500 for each property we stood to make 25% clear profit in a short timeframe. We would be launched.

We had to borrow £90,000 from the bank, but it was a friendly bank, new to the town and I had built up a good rapport with the manager. But this was 1989 and the market had collapsed. The properties would not sell. Never mind we can go into the rental business. But the rental game attracts costs and more importantly in this location with this sort of property only attracts a certain type of tenant. A tenant who might be female, a single parent and most crucially *on the social*. Or it might be a most dubious family with a hatred of cleaning and a love of dogs that are flea-ridden. Julia, who does most of the work trying to keep the wretched places in order, and Ellis and I are just not used to this strata of society. It requires a certain knowledge of the underclass and how it functions, a conversance we do not have or want.

As time passes we cannot even meet the interest payments on the bank loan and have to top-up. My contribution is of-course 50% of what is needed. And then the bank gets tough, my friendly bank manager in the politest possible terms and wrapped up in a long complicated letter, wants a substantial capital repayment so that the consequential reduction in interest has a chance of resulting in our meagre monthly income repaying some of the principal off the loan. It is all very reasonable except that Ellis's two partners refuse to cough up.

The bank cannot see its way to agreeing to my suggestion of a waiver of their interest and/or some loan write-off in favour of a future capital gain when the market picks up. So the bank took over and arranged a fire sale. Not literally, but it might well have been. The bank had to write off £36k when, given a relaxation of its rules, it could have had a share of an embryo little property business or sacrificed a bit of interest. Still, that is my perspective and I am sore. Eight years from when we started, it is over and I have blown the whole of my dad's inheritance. Sorry dad. Looking back I should have played it differently, or is that a line from a musical?

The end game

In these latter years I have thought about my old bosses quite a lot. The aristocratic boss of PW Nottingham with his analysis of the non-audit fees as "ten-per-cent of fuck all" and his puffing on his fags between courses at the Victoria Club showing off his dirty nails from last night's weeding in his mansion garden. Then the down-to-earth and very bright Henry who took me under his ample wing and reticently told me I lacked polish but put me into all the best jobs anyway and taught me how to drink Indian gin and whisky at the Malibar in Cochin notwithstanding my ulcer and whose name has now gone from the Christmas card from Babs. Sorry but he passed away this year, no he wasn't very old, sixty seven, yes that is right just six and a bit years of retirement at the wonderful old barn in beautiful Warwickshire. He went very quickly. I can still see his big smiling face now.

The following year I get the sorry letter from Rene too. Gordon died last July. He had two major operations but then caught the MRSA bug that led to a lung infection. "He was in intensive care for nine weeks but they could not cure the infection." I am so desperately sad, he was utterly indestructible, running the Operation with an iron hand until he retired aged sixty-four to live the quiet life in Seaford, Sussex. Gordon who really did push me on. He who told Bill Pilkington that I must be the next group FD and who wanted me as his successor and not some outsider. Gordon who never had an intray, the antithesis of the professional man who makes you wait your turn. He did not wait for your thing to get to the top of his pile, he dealt with it now. He had to, it's lunch at twelve-thirty and in the evening he will march his lads from restaurant to snooker club just as he marched through Italy during the war. I cannot believe he is dead at seventy-six. Well it is longer than Henry lasted but then Gordon's father lived independently until he was ninety-four. Then again perhaps his dad did not knock off a full bottle of scotch before he went home. Rene put up with that. She will be very lonely now. Do not stand at my grave and cry, I am not there, I did not die. I did obey the last order, albeit unwittingly, but

I would have cried and now these widows tell me that you both did die. All that life and experience gone for ever.

We did pick up a life, well two actually. On a brand new day of this brand new year we are flying to South Africa. Julia's nephew is marrying his girlfriend whom he met on the MBA course in Cape Town. Though it will be Durban first for the posh ceremony in the Country Club, we shall journey down the garden route and visit Ray and Roy enroute. It is twenty years since Roy left the UK to make his fortune in grinding wheels and some of those have been grinding years. It has not been a bed of roses as Roy has been explaining. They have been poor, very poor and they have struggled with the workforce and the culture and with the ever-overhanging Aids epidemic.

On the other hand, the fishing and the wildlife and the wine have been paradisiacal and Jonathan, the younger son, has taken to the life such that he is a recognised expert on scorpions. He has written a book, appears on TV as an expert and is now a fine strapping chap who would like to have met you again. Mark, the elder son, is here in the retirement place of Port Alfred with his lady and inherited daughter. But in this world of contrasts, he is not too bright (Ray thinks she dropped him as a child, physically that is – not maternally, she will always be his mother but where did she go wrong?). Mark actually is with us all in this room but is playing games on the computer, he has nothing to say about the missing twenty years.

But we have lots to say and they take to Julia as if she had been June, whose heart nearly broke when Ray left, and Roy has taken us to the pub/bar and now is doing his "barby" with enough South African wine to sink a battleship. I recall our wine-making out of my dad's bullaces. Nothing really changes and yet everything has changed. We are in the floating restaurant lunching before we drive on and Ray is telling me that if anything happens to Roy she will "come back home". Julia has to say the goodbyes as I creep out and wave from the bankside. It is a very hard parting. As is leaving the Jackass Penguins of Boulders Bay with their staccato gait seeping into ones subconscious.

Goodbye South Africa and more importantly, good luck. Will one day you be a Singapore with your races all intermingling, all pulling one way, colour irrelevant, townships now in town? The scale is on a different planet, size is important and size can be too big, so I somehow doubt it. But good luck anyway as we bump our long way back over the equator heading ever more north.

I am still wondering about Ray and Roy. Will they die happy in South Africa? You always have to put the best complexion on large decisions taken personally and so everything, a creeping everything, can be clouded in pretence. Ray did drop a hint with her "go back home" remark. There was something to be learned from the long-term expats of Singapore through the cocktail hours getting drunk slowly, and sentimental rapidly, about "the old country." Trying to persuade my mum and dad to retire and move to Ravenshead got the instinctive response from mum "it would be too far." If, like me, you need to ask "far from where?" then that is precisely a failure to understand.

OTHER BOOKS BY JOHN G. SMITH

Derbyshire boy: Rural middle England as it was

The year is 1942, the British are stoical but fearful, the war could go either way. A boy is born in middle England on a small tenanted farm that might be lost to the Germans. He knows nothing of this nightmare since the early years are idyllic.

Hating school and failing the crucial exam, the omens are not good. But he is bright and works hard and against the odds gets an office job aged 15 and is plunged headlong into an adult world. A world of steam trains and post-war characters. It will take a big push to penetrate the realms of accounting and finance, yet it can be done. A time long gone. An endeavour as relevant as ever. Wallow in 1940's and 1950's England, it will be worth it
ISBN: 979-8756142280

John G Smith's Credit Crunch Diary 2008-2010: The economic fallout

When on 15 September 2008 the news broke that Lehman Brothers had filed for the largest Chapter 11 bankruptcy in US history I knew that financial war had been declared. Although I had no idea what the full consequences might be I had a greedy need to learn and a gut feeling that only by recording the most salient events to come would this need be assuaged.

For a full year from October 2008, I assiduously logged events until QE, T1 ratio, monetary and fiscal stimulus and those funny packaged debts mingled with the cornflakes for breakfast. John G Smith's Credit Crunch Diary tells the story of how this crisis year unfolded. It objectively and in plain English shows how we were all taken for a ride by a load of greedy people whose legacy to our grandchildren will be no less destructive than the events of 1939 and the

Other books by John G. Smith

years that followed
ISBN: 979-8796378670

John G Smith's Corporate Survival Guide: A primer for accountancy students and management trainees

The content of this book is drawn from experience. It starts by giving tips to the young executive on how to survive and flourish in the corporate world. To those aspiring students of accountancy it explains in plain English how to read and interpret a balance sheet and a profit & loss account before stressing the importance of the cash-flow statement.

As a part-serious, part humorous interlude it decodes much of the terminology that infests the business and financial world. The book includes a history of the UK stock market and sets out the fundamentals of investing, the structure of the market, share value terminology, how to choose an investment strategy and some consequences of such a choice. This section is intended for those interested in private investment and is a taster for those elite few who will enter the lucrative world of investment banking.

The author was for many years a management consultant and he gives some guidance for those considering this as a career.

Finally, for the small to medium size business, comes some fatherly advice on dealing with debtors and creditors and on understanding this lifestyle choice.

ISBN: 979-8402757967

The Whitby Trilogy Part 1 - Eugene

Eugene returns to Britain in 1949 after a harrowing tour of duty as an RAF conscript in war-ravaged Burma. Unexpectedly excluded from the family firm, he sets out to climb the business ladder, embracing and exploiting the innovations and opportunities that present themselves out of the privations of post-war Britain.

Other books by John G. Smith

Yet, for all his rapid advancement in both work and play, Eugene is forever mourning the loss of his first love, a beautiful Burmese nurse named Chit. Will he ever see his first love again?

The Whitby butchery business is set in a small-town community located on the Nottinghamshire/Derbyshire border and enjoys considerable success, fattened by black market trading.

Eugene is driven to succeed with a strong sense of purpose but a shadowy figure taunts and haunts his life.

ISBN: 979-8773582007

The Whitby Trilogy Part 2 - Pearl

When Eugene Whitby died, he left two legacies. One was of wealth but the more important was being accused of murder.

After deep soul-searching, Pearl sets about disproving the defamation. Once again she seeks help from Kyaw, a Burmese student, and from her new friend Naing. Their journey of enquiry includes a return visit to Burma.

Concurrently, the soul of a policeman who worked on the original missing persons' case, can only rest once Eugene's guilt is proved. The two conflicting enquiries clash in a devastating denouement.

With no bodies and no DNA, the task seems impossible but, given the will and human ingenuity spliced with old skills and new technology, there is hope. The story of Pearl is haunted by a shadowy figure.

ISBN: 979-8405569697

The Whitby Trilogy Part 3 - Luke

Luke Brown is a fourth generation Whitby with a single burning ambition: to make his fortune in as short a time as possible. Nothing will stand in his way.

From two fortuitous early events:- first, a business idea springing from a university thesis paper and secondly the

Other books by John G. Smith

inheritance from a great uncle, he establishes a financial service enterprise based on sophisticated computer software. Choosing technically competent staff, the computer applications have global reach beyond the UK. Gradually, Australia, China, Singapore and Europe come on board.

But this success serves merely as a launch pad: he invents a method of moving money between countries quickly and cheaply and exploits Artificial Intelligence to build robots for a specific medical application.

No fortune is garnered honestly is a theme permeating this third book of the Whitby trilogy. Luke uses people, often shamelessly. Old adversaries are circling: the net closes in. Can he stay one step ahead?

ISBN: 979-8408906543

The Whitby Trilogy: The complete works (E-Book only)

This series of three novels recites the vicissitudes of the leading members of a huge middleclass English family of slaughtermen and butchers. Out of nineteenth century coalminers, smallholders and stockbreeders and via meat purveyors and shopkeepers, the twenty-first century produces a fifth-generation globe-trotting computer software expert possessing the resolute intent of his forbears.

The first main character, Eugene Whitby, sees himself as a post-war successful businessman. But is he merely seeking atonement for a lost love? Spurred on by an older brother and resented by another, his revelations to a family outsider leads to criminal examination. The reader will question the Whitby clan's place in modern English history

ASIN: B0933GVSH2

Other books by John G. Smith

For children

The adventures of Eugene

Eugene was a butcher boy. When he was only twelve years old he could make sausages and pies and cut up joints of meat. But, when he was eighteen, he was sent to Burma to drop rice from an aeroplane to villagers starving in the jungle. The Japanese soldiers were running scared.

Eugene fell in love with a beautiful Burmese girl named Chit, but when he returned to England, she was not allowed to come with him. They were both very sad.

Years later he married Dorothy and they opened only the second supermarket in England.

Things started to go wrong. There was an explosion down a coalmine, a terrible car crash and then Dorothy died: but how? Worse was to come. Two brothers disappeared without trace and then a farmer's dog sniffed out a man's arm buried in a field. The police came to see Eugene. Had he killed his brothers after a family argument?

As an old man, Eugene made friends with a lady named Pearl. She listened to his life story, drew his family tree (inside this book) and went to Burma to find Chit. She returned with wonderful news but a big shock awaited her. Had Eugene murdered his two brothers after all?

What do you think?

ISBN: 979-8408938643

Printed in Great Britain
by Amazon